To read.

Introduction — The Religious wars &
        the Peace of Westphalia.

Chaps. 1, 2, 3, 4,
        9, 10, 11, 15

A TEXT BOOK OF MODERN
EUROPEAN HISTORY
1643-1848

A TEXT BOOK OF MODERN
EUROPEAN HISTORY
1643-1848

BY

GEORGE W. SOUTHGATE, B.A.

Illustrated with 36 maps

J. M. DENT AND SONS LTD
BEDFORD ST LONDON W.C.2

PREFACE

IN response to a number of requests from teachers and lecturers who are making use of *A Text Book of Modern European History*, 1789–1930, two other volumes have been prepared, to cover, respectively, the periods 1453–1661 and 1643–1848.

This volume, therefore, is one of a series which presents a general account of the history of Europe from the close of the Middle Ages to the present day. An effort has been made to avoid the inclusion of such an amount of detail as would obscure the broad view of European affairs; at the same time it is hoped that the narrative will be found sufficiently full to be interesting and intelligible.

The general plan of the work is similar to that followed in other works by the same author. The sketch-maps are simple, and are relevant only to that part of the text with which they are associated; when the book is used for the purpose of examination preparation they will be found suitable for memorising. Genealogical tables and lists of rulers have been included for reference. Summaries have been appended for the use of candidates for examination.

G. W. S.

PREFACE TO THE REVISED
EDITION, 1947

ADVANTAGE has been taken of the opportunity afforded by a
reprint of this book to make a few typographical and other
corrections. The three volumes of the series are now arranged
to cover, respectively, the periods 1453–1661, 1643–1848, and
1789–1945.

G. W. S.

PREFACE TO THE REVISED
EDITION, 1953

SOME further corrections have been made in the latter part of
this book to correspond with those made recently in the first
few chapters of *A Text Book of Modern European History*, 1789–
1945. The overlapping parts of the two books are in full accord
with each other.

G. W. S.

CONTENTS

CONTENTS

MAPS

CONTINENTAL RULERS

HOLY ROMAN EMPIRE

EMPERORS:

Hapsburg:

Ferdinand III	1637–1657
Leopold I	1658–1705
Joseph I	1705–1711
Charles VI	1711–1740

Wittelsbach:

Charles VII	1742–1745

Hapsburg-Lorraine:

Francis I	1745–1765
Joseph II	1765–1790
Leopold II	1790–1792
Francis II	1792–1806

AUSTRIA

EMPERORS:

Hapsburg:

Francis I	1804–1835
Ferdinand I	1835–1848
Francis Joseph	1848–1916

BRANDENBURG-PRUSSIA

ELECTORS OF BRANDENBURG:

Hohenzollern:

Frederick William	1640–1688
Frederick III	1688–1713

KINGS OF PRUSSIA:

Hohenzollern:

Frederick I	1700–1713
Frederick William I	1713–1740
Frederick II	1740–1786
Frederick William II	1786–1797
Frederick William III	1797–1840
Frederick William IV	1840–1861

CONTINENTAL RULERS

FRANCE

KINGS:

  Bourbon:

    Louis XIV 1643–1715

    Louis XV 1715–1774

    Louis XVI 1774–1792

FIRST REPUBLIC 1792–1804

CONSULATE:

  First Consul:

    Bonaparte 1799–1804

FIRST EMPIRE:

  Emperor:

    Napoleon I 1804–1814
                           and March–June 1815

KINGS:

  Bourbon:

    Louis XVIII 1814–1824
                     except March–June, 1815

    Charles X 1824–1830

  Orleanist:

    Louis Philippe 1830–1848

SECOND REPUBLIC:

  President:

    Louis Napoleon Bonaparte 1848–1852

SPAIN

KINGS:

  Hapsburg:

    Philip IV 1621–1665

    Charles II 1665–1700

  Bourbon:

    Philip V 1700–1746

    except Luis 1724–1725

    Ferdinand VI 1746–1759

    Charles III 1759–1788

    Charles IV 1788–1808

  Bonaparte:

    Joseph 1808–1814

  Bourbon:

    Ferdinand VII 1814–1833

    Isabella II 1833–1868

PORTUGAL

KINGS:

Braganza:

John IV	1640–1656
Alfonso VI	1656–1667
Pedro II	1667–1706
John V	1706–1750
Joseph	1750–1777
Pedro III	1777–1786
Maria I	1777–1816
John VI	1816–1826
Pedro IV	1826
Maria II	1826–1828
Miguel	1828–1834
Maria II (restored)	1834–1853

THE NETHERLANDS

STADTHOLDERS:

Orange:

William II	1647–1650
William III	1673–1702
William IV	1748–1751
William V	1751–1795

(Batavian Republic, 1795–1806)

KINGS:

Bonaparte:

Louis	1806–1810

(Annexed to France, 1810–1814)

Orange:

William I	1814–1840
William II	1840–1849

POLAND

KINGS:

Ladislas IV (Vasa)	1632–1648
John Casimir (John II) (Vasa)	1648–1668
Michael (Wisniowiecki)	1669–1673
John III (Sobieski)	1674–1696
Augustus II (Wettin)	1697–1704
Stanislaus I (Leszczynski)	1704–1709
Augustus II (Wettin)	1709–1733
Augustus III (Wettin)	1733–1763
Stanislaus II (Poniatowski)	1764–1795

SAVOY-SARDINIA

DUKES:

Savoy:

Charles Emmanuel II	. . . .	. 1638–1675
Victor Amadeus II .	. . .	. 1675–1730

(King of Sicily, 1713–1720)

KINGS:

Savoy:

Victor Amadeus II .	. . . .	. 1720–1730
Charles Emmanuel III	. . . .	. 1730–1773
Victor Amadeus III .	. . . .	. 1773–1796
Charles Emmanuel IV	. . . .	. 1796–1802
Victor Emmanuel I .	. . . .	. 1802–1821
Charles Felix .	. . . .	. 1821–1831
Charles Albert .	. . . .	. 1831–1849

THE TWO SICILIES

KINGS:

Bourbon:

Charles III	. . . .	. 1735–1759
Ferdinand IV (Ferdinand I after 1815)	.	. 1759–1825
Francis I	. . . .	. 1825–1830
Ferdinand II	. . . .	. 1830–1859

NAPLES ONLY

KINGS:

Joseph Bonaparte	. . . .	. 1806–1808
Joachim Murat .	. . . .	. 1808–1814

DENMARK

KINGS:

Christian IV .	. . . .	. 1588–1648
Frederick III .	. . . .	. 1648–1670
Christian V .	. . . .	. 1670–1699
Frederick IV .	. . . .	. 1699–1730
Christian VI .	. . . .	. 1730–1746
Frederick V .	. . . .	. 1746–1766
Christian VII .	. . . .	. 1766–1808
Frederick VI .	. . . .	. 1808–1839
Christian VIII .	. . . .	. 1839–1848
Frederick VII .	. . . .	. 1848–1863

BELGIUM

KING:

Saxe-Coburg:

Leopold I 1831–1865

SWEDEN

KINGS:

Vasa:

Christina .	1632–1654
Charles X	1654–1660
Charles XI	1660–1697
Charles XII	1697–1718
Ulrica	1718–1720
Frederick I	1720–1751
Adolphus Frederick	1751–1771
Gustavus III	1771–1792
Gustavus IV	1792–1809
Charles XIII	1809–1818

Bernadotte:

Charles XIV	1818–1844
Oscar I	1844–1859

RUSSIA

TSARS:

Romanoff:

Michael	1613–1645
Alexius	1645–1676
Theodore	1676–1682
Ivan V	1682–1689
Peter I	1682–1725
Catherine I	1725–1727
Peter II	1727–1730
Anne	1730–1740
Ivan VI	1740–1741
Elizabeth	1741–1762
Peter III	1762
Catherine II	1762–1796
Paul	1796–1801
Alexander I	1801–1825
Nicholas I	1825–1855

TURKEY

SULTANS:

Ibrahim	1640–1648
Mohammed IV	1648–1687
Suleiman II	1687–1691
Ahmed II.	1691–1695
Mustafa II	1695–1703
Ahmed III	1703–1730
Mahmoud I	1730–1754
Osman III	1754–1757
Mustafa III	1757–1774
Abdul-Hamid I	1774–1789
Selim III.	1789–1807
Mustafa IV	1807–1808
Mahmoud II	1808–1839
Abdul Medjid I	1839–1861

POPES

Urban VIII (Barberini)	1623–1644
Innocent X (Pamfili) .	1644–1655
Alexander VII (Chigi)	1655–1667
Clement IX (Rospigliosi)	1667–1669
Clement X (Altieri) .	1670–1676
Innocent XI (Odescalchi) .	1676–1689
Alexander VIII (Ottobuoni)	1689–1691
Innocent XII (Pignatelli) .	1691–1700
Clement XI (Albano)	1700–1721
Innocent XIII (Conti)	1721–1724
Benedict XIII (Orsini)	1724–1730
Clement XII (Corsini)	1730–1740
Benedict XIV (Lambertini)	1740–1758
Clement XIII (Rezzonico) .	1758–1769
Clement XIV (Ganganelli)	1769–1774
Pius VI (Braschi)	1775–1799
Pius VII (Chiaramonte)	1800–1823
Leo XII (Genga)	1823–1829
Pius VIII (Castiglione)	1829–1830
Gregory XVI (Cappellari) .	1831–1846
Pius IX (Mastai-Ferretti) .	1846–1878

INTRODUCTION: THE RELIGIOUS WARS & THE PEACE OF WESTPHALIA

IN order that the reader may understand the period of European history with which this volume deals it is necessary to make some reference to the state of Europe in the sixteenth century and the first half of the seventeenth.

European history in the sixteenth century is concerned in the main, though by no means entirely, with religious movements — with the Reformation and the Catholic reaction, which is often referred to as the Counter-Reformation. Ecclesiastical controversy gave rise to a series of religious wars which continued with little intermission till the middle of the seventeenth century; their object was, on the Catholic side, to restore the formal unity of western Christendom under the papacy, and, on the Protestant side, to win the right of survival. In all these wars the religious was not the only motive for conflict. The Anglo-Spanish War of Elizabeth's reign was occasioned by the determination of English adventurers to contest the Spanish monopoly of overseas possessions and trade, as well as to maintain the independence of the national Church from Rome. The desire for national independence as well as for religious freedom inspired the Dutch in their struggle against Spain. The religious wars in France were a disintegrating force; the nobles, Catholic and Calvinist alike, aimed at securing for themselves a measure of independence of the crown of France. The contest in France was settled by the victory of the Crown and the issue of the Edict of Nantes by Henry IV.

The last and the most bitterly contested of the religious wars was the Thirty Years' War in the Holy Roman Empire. Most of the nations of Europe were involved in some part or other of the struggle, and all of them were profoundly affected by it. Like the other religious wars, the Thirty Years' War had a political as well as a religious aspect. On the religious side it was a great and final effort by the Catholic powers to overcome Protestantism and bring the rebellion against the Church to an end. Politically, it may be viewed as the last attempt of the Emperor to make the Imperial power a reality and to reduce the princes to some sort of subjection.

Four periods may be distinguished in the history of the war. The Bohemian phase lasted from the outbreak of the war in Bohemia to the transference of the electoral dignity from Frederick, Elector Palatine, to Maximilian of Bavaria in 1623. The second period, from 1624 to 1629, witnessed the intervention of Christian IV of Denmark; the third, from 1630 to 1635, that of the Swedes, whose King, Gustavus Adolphus, was killed in 1632. The final period, from 1635 until the final settlement in 1648, was that of the intervention of France.

In the latter part of his reign Henry IV of France had begun the work of destroying the political power of the nobles, which was carried on in the reign of his son by Richelieu. Henry's foreign policy was directed towards freeing France from the stranglehold of encirclement by Hapsburg powers. This aspect of his work, also, was continued by the Cardinal, and it was on account of his hostility towards the Emperor and Spain that Richelieu threw the forces of France into the Thirty Years' War on the Protestant side.

At first the war went badly for the French, but in 1638 Breisach was captured, and within a few months the whole of Alsace was occupied. Condé's victory over the Spanish at Rocroy in 1643 dealt a heavy blow at the power and prestige of Spain. Further victories were won by Condé and Turenne, and at length negotiations for peace were opened and were brought to a successful issue.

The terms of the Peace of Westphalia, 1648, may be considered under three headings—religious, territorial, and constitutional. The religious question in the Empire was solved by the retention of the principle *cuius regio eius religio*, laid down nearly a century earlier in the Peace of Augsburg, and its extension to include the Calvinists, who thus for the first time received legal recognition. In the trial by the Imperial Chamber of cases in which the parties were of different faiths the judges were to be drawn from both religions. The question of ecclesiastical lands was settled by taking 1624 as the test year. All that was in Protestant hands in that year remained Protestant.

The territorial arrangements were, in the main, what might be expected from the course of the war. Maximilian of

Bavaria retained the electorate, which had already been conferred on him for life, as a hereditary dignity, and the Upper Palatinate was added to Bavaria. The Lower Palatinate was restored to Charles Lewis, the son of Frederick V, and a new electorate was created for him. Sweden, recognised as a member of the Empire and entitled to representation in the

THE EMPIRE IN 1648

Diet, retained Western Pomerania and the bishoprics of Bremen and Verden; she thus controlled the mouths of the Oder, the Elbe, and the Weser. Brandenburg was confirmed in the possession of Eastern Pomerania and received, in addition, the bishoprics of Halberstadt, Camin, Minden, and the reversion of most of the archbishopric of Magdeburg, besides Ravensburg, and, in the Rhineland, Cleves and Mark. Saxony received the rest of Magdeburg, with the province of Lusatia. France retained Alsace (not including Strassburg), with the fortresses of Breisach and Philippsburg, and her right to

Metz, Toul, and Verdun in Lorraine was recognised. In Italy she retained Pinerolo. The treaty gave formal recognition to the independence of the United Provinces and of Switzerland.

The effect of the Peace on the Imperial constitution lay in the practical recognition of princely independence. The forms of the old constitution remained; there were still an Emperor and a body of Electors, a Diet and an Imperial Chamber. But after the Peace of Westphalia each German prince possessed all the essential attributes of independent sovereignty. He could declare war or make peace, send and receive ambassadors, conclude treaties (so long as they were not directed against the Emperor or the Empire, a restriction of little avail in practice), make laws, and coin money. The authority of the Emperor was reduced to insignificance, and his sovereignty was henceforth a mere formality. The Empire thus assumed its final form, and the princely tendency, which had been in evidence for centuries, to cast off the shackles of Imperial control was carried to its logical issue.

The Peace is a landmark in the history of Europe. Old questions were settled, and the attention of the powers was directed to other matters in years to come. The German religious controversy was ended by the permanent recognition of Lutheranism and Calvinism as being on legal equality with one another and with Catholicism. There was in the Peace no proclamation of religious toleration, and though no prince was bound to exercise toleration within his dominions the rarity of persecution in after years was an indication that the age of gross intolerance was passing away.

The Hapsburgs did not sink into insignificance. The Emperor was still a power to be reckoned with, on account, however, of his hereditary possessions and not of the Imperial dignity. Hapsburg policy ceased to be concerned mainly with Germany, and the opportunity of securing a firm hold on the Rhineland and the privilege of defending Germany from French aggression was left to Brandenburg; this led to Prussian aggrandisement in the nineteenth century. Austrian statesmen in the future turned their faces to the south-east and the south-west, with the intention of dominating two of the Mediterranean peninsulas, Italy and the Balkan peninsula, and of establishing Austria as a great Mediterranean power. The effort to strengthen and extend the Austrian position on the

Danube led to competition (and not co-operation) with Russia in the expulsion of the Turks and the occupation of the Balkans —a competition which went far towards preventing the Turks being expelled at all. The Austrian effort to maintain a hold on Italy was continued until the second half of the nineteenth century.

The effect of the peace on some of the other countries of Europe must be noticed. Sweden reached the zenith of her power. With extensive territories in north Germany and with membership of the Imperial Diet, she had prevented Hapsburg predominance in the Baltic and had secured it for herself, thus overcoming the menace to her independence and her religion. But Swedish greatness was transitory. Her population and her resources were small and her territories were scattered; those to the south of the Baltic were exposed to the attacks of powerful states in the hinterland; and she failed to make good her claim to recognition as a great European power. France also emerged from the struggle with enhanced prestige and an extension of territory. Definite advance had been made towards the realisation of the Bourbon dream of Rhine frontiers, and the stage was set for the great wars of the reign of Louis XIV. Spain was in a state of utter exhaustion. Since the outbreak of the Revolt of the Netherlands she had hardly at any time been free from war, and sometimes she had been engaged in two or three wars at once. No power on earth could have met such a drain on her resources without disastrous results. Yet Spain was not included in the Peace. The struggle between her and France was continued. Had it not been for the interlude of the Fronde the end must have come quickly. The Fronde gave to Spain the opportunity for a temporary rally, but the end was inevitable. French victory was registered in the Peace of the Pyrenees, 1659, and Spanish decline continued until, when another generation had passed, the powers were ready to fight over the division of her possessions.

The weakness of the Empire was extreme. Apart from the exhaustion of its resources, the territorial acquisitions of foreign powers entitled them to representation in the Imperial Diet. The Kings of France, Sweden, and Denmark were German princes by virtue of their possession, respectively, of Alsace, Pomerania, and Holstein, and to them was added in the eighteenth century the King of Great Britain as Elector of Hanover. In so far as the Diet exercised any influence on German affairs these might henceforth be determined by the interests of neighbouring countries rather than of Germany.

Germany had suffered terribly from the war. Its ruthless character, and especially the practice of maintaining armies by the plunder of occupied lands, had resulted in the utter devastation of large tracts. To the horrors of ravaging succeeded those of famine, and it is believed that two-thirds of the population of Germany perished between 1618 and 1648. Some regions reverted to wilderness. The economic collapse of the country was so complete that not until the nineteenth century were the traces of the Thirty Years' War obliterated.

CHAPTER I

MAZARIN

VIEWED in true perspective, the career of Mazarin appears to have been little more than a postscript to that of Richelieu. Mazarin was in every way inferior to his great predecessor. There was nothing original about him. No new policy was evolved by him. He merely carried to completion, though by different means, the work begun by Richelieu. A man of personal charm, he was a master of intrigue; in contrast to Richelieu, who struck ruthlessly and inspired terror, he preferred to gain his ends by persuasion and bribery.

Only two topics of any importance demand attention in an account of Mazarin's ministry—the Fronde and the war with Spain. The Fronde, in its later stages at least, stands out clearly as the final incident in that conflict between central authority and noble privilege which had been waged since the beginning of the seventeenth century, and in which Richelieu had taken so strong a line. The Spanish war was the completion of the struggle which had been begun under Richelieu for the satisfactory determination of the frontiers of France and the humiliation of the House of Hapsburg.

Mazarin had served for some years under Richelieu, who before his death recommended the Italian, already a cardinal, to Louis XIII as chief minister. When, within a few months, Louis followed Richelieu to the grave, he was succeeded by his son, Louis XIV, a boy five years of age. The dying King had nominated a Council of State to control affairs during his son's minority, but Anne of Austria, the child's mother, boldly demanded of the Parlement of Paris recognition as Regent. The Parlement, as in 1610, was gratified at the appeal. It appointed Anne to the regency and refused to recognise the Council of State.

Mazarin was now secure in the possession of power. He was bound by ties of close friendship with Anne; it has been asserted that, although he was a cardinal, he was secretly

1

married to her, and there seems to be some ground for believing the story. While she remained Regent he had nothing to fear. But Anne was the only person in love with him; by everybody else he appears to have been detested. He was handsome and graceful, polished and scholarly, diplomatic and deferential. These qualities failed to make him acceptable to the people of France, who remembered that he was a foreigner, that he was of low birth, that he was cruel and selfish, and that he was avaricious.

For a short time at the beginning of the regency, nobles and others who had been exiled in the time of Richelieu expected to recover their influence at court. They were mistaken; a plot to assassinate Mazarin was used as the pretext for the imprisonment of the Duke of Beaufort, while the exile of other nobles was confirmed.

The movement known as the Fronde lasted for nearly five years—from January, 1648, to October, 1652—and it had several aspects. It appeared at one time to be a constitutional struggle against absolutism; at another time, a genuine uprising of the people of Paris against intolerable oppression; and at another, a sinister disturbance fomented by selfish and ambitious agitators; in the end it was revealed as a struggle of factious nobles, irritated at the advancement of men of the middle class and even of foreigners, for the recovery of power and privileges lost to them in the past half-century. The common element in all these phases of the movement was hatred of Mazarin, and the completeness of his ultimate triumph is the measure of the failure of the Fronde.

In the early days of the regency the Parlement of Paris appeared to be of greater importance than at any previous time in its history. Since the institution of the *paulette* its members had been secure in their positions. Twice within living memory the Parlement had been appealed to, as a kind of supreme court, to settle the government of France. It was now disposed to claim some voice in determining the principles upon which the government of the state should be carried on. In England, the Parliament was meeting with some success in its efforts to enforce a claim of similar character, and though there was little in common beyond the name between the Parliament and the Parlement the latter was inclined to pose as the champion of constitutional government.

In January, 1648, an edict was issued by the court, imposing an octroi duty on goods entering Paris. The exaction was unpopular, and the Parlement refused to register the edict. Registration was achieved by a visit of the young King to the Parlement to hold a *lit de justice*, but the Parlement declared this to be invalid, and controversy continued. The Parlement appointed a committee, known as the Chamber of St. Louis, to consider the question of constitutional reform, and in due course the Chamber formulated twenty-seven demands, the most important of which were the abolition of the office of Intendant, a reduction of the *taille*, the right of arrested persons to be charged and brought to trial within a reasonable time, and the control of taxation by the Parlement.

The first two of these four demands were not of vital importance, but the others represented important constitutional principles whose adoption would have struck a serious blow at despotic government. The principle, so long accepted in England, that "the King should live of his own," and that if he required for the work of government any part of the wealth of his people he should obtain the consent of those who were to be taxed, had never been accepted in France. The right of arbitrary imprisonment, also, was a natural concomitant of absolutism. The weakness of the constitutional movement lay not in the nature of the demands, but in the character of the Parlement. It was a close corporation which in no way represented the people of France, and, if it had succeeded, the common folk would have been no nearer to the acquisition of true constitutional liberty than before. It is, indeed, possible that victory over the court might in time have been followed by "Parliamentary Reform"—but this is purely conjectural.

For the moment, the court yielded to the extent of abolishing some of the Intendancies, reducing the *taille*, and inquiring into some financial abuses. When, however, news reached Paris of a great victory won by Condé over the Spanish at Lens, it was resolved to celebrate it by the singing of a solemn Te Deum in Notre Dame, at which the King and the Queen Regent were to be present. Mazarin thought that the opportunity had arrived to take strong action against the Parlement, expecting that the popular enthusiasm over military success would outweigh his unpopularity. He ordered the arrest of Broussel, a counsellor of the Parlement who had been prominent in the constitutional agitation. The mob burst into an uproar; barricades were raised in the streets, and Mazarin was compelled to yield and release Broussel. For a time the court retired to Rueil, on the assumption that the armies shortly to be released from war service by the conclusion of the Peace of Westphalia would be at its service to intimidate Paris. But Condé could not be relied upon, and in October, 1648, the court returned to the capital. The demands of the Chamber of St. Louis were accepted, and the first phase of the Fronde was at an end. (It may be remarked that the victory of the Parlement was by no means to the advantage of the state; the abolition of the Intendancies threw provincial administration into disorder, and the reduction of the *taille* threatened the state with bankruptcy.)

The Fronde in its later stages was inspired less by principles than by ambitions. The Paris mob continued restless, under the sinister influence of the able and unscrupulous Paul de Gondi, the Coadjutor-Archbishop of Paris, who was aspiring to a cardinal's hat. (He was afterwards known as the Cardinal de Retz.) Some of the nobles joined the movement; they were at least as contemptuous of the Parlement as of the mob, and they hoped only for the recovery of the privileges of their order. For the moment, however, in their hatred of Mazarin, they were willing to make common cause with Paris against the court.

Early in 1649 the court withdrew to St. Germain. Condé was now prepared to support it and was placed in command of troops to be used against the capital. A blockade of Paris was established, but neither party was quite prepared to plunge France into civil war, and in April, 1649, the Peace of Rueil was arranged. It was a peace in no more than name, for agitation continued, and Condé intrigued with the opponents of the court.

In January, 1650, Mazarin again attempted to take strong action. Condé and some other nobles of royal descent were arrested. This was the signal for an outbreak in Paris and the provinces. But the provincial revolts had no unity of aim, and were easily suppressed. It became clear that the disaffected had no common bond other than dislike of Mazarin, no aim in common beyond his removal. A year later, in February, 1651, Mazarin retired to Brühl, in the electorate of Cologne. It was assumed that he had fallen from power for ever. The capital was overjoyed, and received the princes, upon their release, with acclamation.

Condé remained turbulent and overbearing, and soon quarrelled with Gondi. He left Paris, and Gondi allied with the Queen, obtaining at this juncture his cardinalate. Condé raised a rebellion in the south of France. Mazarin returned from his exile, and the command of the royal forces was entrusted to Turenne. Condé was defeated and took refuge in Paris itself. The Parisians were no longer disposed to support him, and only the continuance of Mazarin in power hindered them from returning to their allegiance. Mazarin retired to Sedan in 1652, and Paris admitted the King. Condé, left without support, fled to Spain, and for some years he commanded Spanish forces in the war against France.

Louis XIV entered his capital in October, 1652, and the Fronde was at an end. Its leaders were punished, and the Parlement was forbidden to concern itself with affairs of state, of administration, and of finance. Henceforth its functions were limited to the registration of royal edicts and the administration of justice. The nobles, also, lost all political power and were compelled to accept subordination to the Crown. One result of the Fronde was its effect upon the character and future policy of Louis XIV. He was deeply moved by the humiliations and insults heaped on the court at the height of the trouble, and throughout his life he was determined to crush any symptom of democracy and to make himself absolute. Yet the Fronde was not really dangerous to the monarchy. The aims of the Frondeurs were too varied; they were by no means in accord with one another. The leaders of the movement were not patriot-martyrs, but selfish and ambitious intriguers, and their failure was inevitable.

In 1653 Mazarin returned from Sedan and resumed office, which he held until his death in 1661. De Retz was for a time imprisoned. He escaped, and retired to Rome. He was afterwards permitted to return to France, where, however, he ceased to exercise any political influence.

The war with Spain was not terminated by the Peace of Westphalia. In the early years of Mazarin's ministry Turenne, Condé, and the Duke of Orleans gained important victories for France. Mardyck and Dunkirk were captured, Roussillon and Cerdagne were occupied, and at one time the province of Catalonia was in French hands. The Spanish fleet was defeated off the Tuscan coast, and a serious revolt broke out against Spanish rule in Naples. A more vigorous policy on

Mazarin's part in support of the movement might have resulted in the expulsion of the Spanish from that kingdom. In 1648 Condé, by winning the Battle of Lens, dealt a shattering blow at Spanish power in Flanders. Spain was in a desperate plight, and would probably have been compelled to accept humiliating terms of peace had the attention of France not been distracted for some years by the Fronde.

The breathing space thus afforded to Spain enabled her to recover some of the ground she had lost. Catalonia was re-conquered, and the French were compelled to abandon Mardyck and Dunkirk. The defection of Condé placed at the disposal of Spain a first-class general, but his efforts were foiled by the determination and capacity of Turenne. In and after 1653 the course of the war moved in favour of France, and conquests were made. Negotiations for peace were begun in 1656, but were not successful, and the war continued. Mazarin had for some time been seeking an alliance with Cromwell, and a preliminary agreement between them was reached in 1655. An alliance, offensive as well as defensive, was concluded in 1657, by which Cromwell promised English assistance in the operations in Flanders. The Spanish were defeated at the Battle of the Dunes in 1658 by Turenne, who had the support of a brigade of 6,000 men of the New Model Army. Dunkirk and Mardyck were captured and handed over to the English, and some other places were occupied by the French.

Peace was made in 1659 by the Treaty of the Pyrenees. France surrendered part of her conquests in the north-east; she retained the province of Artois, beside Gravelines, Landrecies, Avesnes, and some other towns. In Luxemburg she acquired Thionville. Spain recognised the right of France to Alsace. France abandoned the few Catalonian forts she still held but retained Roussillon. Condé was pardoned for his treason and his estates were restored to him. The treaty provided for the marriage of Louis XIV to Maria Theresa, the daughter of Philip IV. Maria Theresa renounced, for herself and her descendants, all claim to the Spanish crown, and the payment of a dowry of 500,000 crowns was stipulated. (The non-payment of the dowry was afterwards made the pretext for putting forward a French claim to the Spanish throne.)

The Treaty of the Pyrenees was the completion of the Peace of Westphalia. To a very large extent France had obtained those defensible frontiers the acquisition of which was a feature of Bourbon foreign policy. In the south-west the Pyrenees, to the south-east and east the Alps and the Vosges, marked her limits; she was strong not only for defence but for offence, since she held passes by which her armies could pour into the territories of her neighbours. To the north-east the position was not so satisfactory. The acquisition of Artois removed the frontier a few more miles from Paris, but it remained for Louis XIV to strive to carry his dominions as far as the Scheldt and the Rhine. Spain emerged from the war exhausted and decadent. She had been a great power in Europe, but she had exhausted her resources in war, her administrative system was corrupt and inefficient, and she was tottering to her fall.

Mazarin had little of the greatness of Richelieu. Though he was a collector of rare books and manuscripts he did nothing for literature and art in France. His administration was corrupt; he aimed at acquiring wealth, and he did nothing to improve the condition of the people of France. Yet when he died in 1661 he left to the young King a realm in which his authority was unquestioned, and which had attained a commanding position in Europe.

CHAPTER II

LOUIS XIV

LOUIS XIV succeeded his father as King of France in 1643, when he was only five years old. He assumed personal control of public affairs at the death of Mazarin, in 1661, and he retained it until his death in 1715. His effective reign thus extended over a period which included the reigns of four English sovereigns.

Louis was the supreme representative of the type of kingship, absolute monarchy, which in the latter part of the seventeenth century was regarded as ideal. The court of Versailles was a pattern of elegance, culture, dignity, and splendour which other monarchs tried to reproduce.

The work of kings and statesmen of the earlier part of the Bourbon period was carried to completion under Louis XIV. The forces which had attempted to compete with the power of the Crown were no longer active. French nobles ceased to strive for semi-independent authority in the provinces. Their ambition was to live at court in the presence of the King and in the enjoyment of his favour; a formal direction from the King to a noble to retire to his estates was a sentence dreaded hardly less than imprisonment in the Bastille. No meetings of the States-General occurred in the reign of Louis XIV, and the Parlements were submissive to his will.

The absolutism which was built up by the Cardinals was perfected by Louis. He aimed not merely at securing complete obedience and submission but at being the centre round which every aspect of French life should revolve, the source from which every movement should draw its strength and inspiration. Such an ideal might be, and was, magnificent, but it was not without its weakness. In the France of Louis XIV there was no place for independence of thought and action, and no man of his reign could be greater than the King. And as the King, for all his magnificence, was not a man of first-rate ability, those whom he gathered round him were courtiers rather than

8

statesmen, clerks rather than financiers, subalterns rather than marshals, agents rather than diplomats. There were, indeed, men of genius in the reign; Condé and Turenne led Louis's armies, Colbert organised his finances, Louvois strengthened his forces, Bossuet defended his ecclesiastical position. But these were men who had grown up and entered public life in the time of his predecessors; when they died there was nobody of equal calibre to replace them. The latter part of the reign was singularly barren of great men, and the fact that he was without rival in his own country helps to explain the prominence of Louis on the European stage in the early years of the eighteenth century.

Louis was absolute, not merely in the sense that there was in France no person, no influence, no group, which dared to oppose his will, but as the head of every aspect of French life. He was the *Roi Soleil*; it was his will that from him should spring the strength and inspiration of art and letters, of music and poetry, of science and philosophy. Whatever enjoyed the royal favour should flourish; whatever was deprived of the beneficent influence which emanated from the throne must wither. The elegance, the taste, the culture, which characterised his court should be a pattern for the whole of France, and, indeed, of Europe. That the reality should fall short of this ideal was inevitable; nevertheless, it did not fall so far short as to leave any doubt of his right to be described as *Le Grand Monarque*.

Yet Louis was no genius. Holding a lofty conception of his position, he was dignified and gracious, refined and chivalrous, and, despite the sycophancy of his courtiers, he was a shrewd judge of character. He gave close personal attention to the business of government, and, though he left to Colbert the management of details of internal administration, he retained in his own hands the conduct of foreign affairs. He was a master of the art of diplomacy. His representatives abroad, ranging from spies to ambassadors, were men of his own selection. He conducted negotiations through them, and at no time in his reign did he resign the direction of foreign affairs to other hands. His foreign ministers were little more than superior clerks. He made mistakes, but, in view of the length of time during which he was the outstanding figure in European diplomacy and of the complexity of the affairs which demanded his attention, it is remarkable that they were not more numerous

and more serious. The king who could have improved on
Louis's record in diplomacy for a period of more than half a
century would have been a superman.

In the earlier part of the reign of Louis XIV the internal
administration was directed by Colbert, one of the few men of
financial genius ever produced by France. Colbert rose to
power at the fall of Fouquet, Surintendant of Finance in the
time of Mazarin. Fouquet was extravagant and corrupt, and
he left the treasury in a condition which suggested that France
was not far from ruin. The fault was not entirely his, for
little attention had been paid to the proper organisation of
national finance by Richelieu, while Mazarin had been careful
to enrich himself at the expense of the state. Fouquet added
to the disorder instead of diminishing it; he accumulated a
large fortune, and in his accounts the revenues of the state were
mixed up with his private wealth.

When Colbert took control the usual abuses were in evidence
—a huge debt (much of it raised at exorbitant rates of interest),
the farming of taxes (of the proceeds of which only a small part
reached the treasury), arrears in collection, the sale of official
appointments, and the absence of efficient book-keeping.
Colbert took drastic steps to restore financial order. Some
loans were repudiated on account of the dishonesty which had
characterised their issue, and the interest on others was reduced to a reasonable figure. Punishment was meted out to
dishonest tax-farmers, and they were compelled to refund
moneys illegally collected, to the extent of seventy millions of
francs. A new assessment of the *taille* was ordered, and claims
for exemption were scrutinised, and, where possible, disallowed.
Strict accounts were kept, and the whole system of revenue
collection was placed under the supervision of the Intendants,
who were again appointed and who remained a permanent
feature of the French administrative system until the Revolution of 1789. Public expenditure was reduced wherever
possible, though Colbert was unable to deal with the extravagance of the court. By these measures Colbert, without increasing a single tax (some were even reduced), eliminated the
annual deficit and secured a surplus in the treasury.

This was not his only, nor even his principal achievement.
He aimed, by the development of industry, trade, and agriculture, at making France economically self-sufficient and her
people prosperous. The principles upon which his policy was

based were essentially the same as those which gained wide acceptance in England and which have been known to later generations as Mercantilism.   The aim of Colbertism in France as of Mercantilism in England was national power and inde- pendence; the nation viewed its neighbours as actual or potential enemies, and it could not feel strong if it was compelled to rely upon them for the supply of food or of any other essential commodity.   Economic activity of all kinds was subject to state control, and, though the interests of some people might suffer, the special interests of no individual, no region, no class, could be permitted to weigh against the supreme importance of guaranteeing the safety and indepen- dence of the state.

In order to facilitate the marketing of the products of in- dustry and agriculture, Colbert abolished the greater part, though not all, of the provincial customs duties and the octrois. Until this time duties were payable on goods which passed from one province to another, so that the transmission of merchandise for long distances involved the payment of duties again and again.   Octrois were duties upon country produce which was brought into a town for sale.   Colbert was not able to sweep away all these hindrances to internal trade.   Local interests were sometimes too strong for him, but he did much towards the realisation of the ideal of internal free trade for France.

Colbert protected the foreign trade of France by a system of tariffs devised to promote the export of the products of French industry and to hinder the import of articles which might compete with home manufactures.   Export duties were sub- stantially reduced or entirely discontinued, and heavy duties were imposed on certain commodities.

Colonisation was encouraged by Colbert, as providing sources of supply of the raw materials, and markets for the products, of French industry.   The formation in 1664 of an East India Company and a Company of the West indicated the importance which he attached to expansion overseas.   The Company of the West lasted no more than ten years; its privileges and possessions were then taken over by the Crown.   Other companies formed or reorganised under the patronage of Colbert, for trade or settlement, included the Northern Com- pany (for Baltic trade), the Levant Company, and the French African Company.   In this as in other matters Colbert made the mistake of attempting too much control. The state held a large proportion of the shares in these and other chartered companies, and their operations were hindered by excessive regulation; their record is one of failure and even of bankruptcy.

One feature of Colbert's policy with regard to foreign trade was not well thought out. He prohibited the export of corn. By retaining within the country all the corn produced in France he hoped to ensure an abundance of food at all times. The effect of the prohibition was the reverse of this. In times of good harvests the market for French corn was insufficient, and prices dropped, with the result that some land went out of cultivation. Then, when conditions were less favourable and the crops were less plentiful, scarcity and even famine were experienced. If Colbert had permitted the export of corn the French peasant might have found a market and a fair price for his grain even in times of abundance; land would have remained under cultivation, and it would have been sufficient (and probably unnecessary even then) to prohibit export in time of war or deficient harvest.

New manufacturing industries were established, and existing industries were strengthened and expanded. Metal work, the manufacture of stockings, the production of glass ware, and the weaving of silk flourished during this period. The King set the fashion, readily followed by the aristocracy, of using articles of French manufacture in preference to those of foreign origin, and over a hundred industrial establishments were privileged to use the word 'Royal' in their official style. The immigration of skilled foreign artisans was encouraged, in order that the standard of French production might be improved; French workmen were forbidden to depart, lest their skill should be placed at the service of other countries. In industry, as in commerce, Colbert is to be criticised in that he attempted to exercise control to an excessive degree. The regulation of industry was entrusted to the gilds, themselves acting under the direction of the state. Prices were fixed by the state, and a system of rigorous inspection was set up to ensure the maintenance of a satisfactory standard of quality. Such measures were inconsistent with that degree of freedom which was necessary for the full development of industrial enterprise.

Communications were improved. The roads were put in order; Colbert has been described as the greatest road-maker in France since the time of the Romans. Some canal construction was undertaken; the Languedoc canal, one hundred and sixty miles long, connected the Bay of Biscay with the Mediterranean.

Colbert was active in the increase of French military and naval strength. He devoted attention to the navy throughout his ministry, though he held the office of Secretary of State for the Navy only after 1669. In 1661 the French navy was small; ten years later there were two hundred ships of war. Naval arsenals and docks existed on the Atlantic and Mediterranean coasts, and France henceforth rivalled England and Holland as a naval power. A fleet of galleys was maintained in the Mediterranean. The vessels were manned by criminals, prisoners of war, vagrants, and even Indians captured in North America. The treatment accorded to galley-slaves was brutal in the extreme, and it has been asserted that even the few who survived to complete their sentences failed to secure release. Colbert was not so directly responsible for the strengthening of the army, though in this sphere also his influence is to be observed, since as Controller-General of Finance he provided the funds which were needed. Army reorganisation was undertaken by Louvois, Minister for War. The army was enlarged and brought more directly under royal control. Regimental allegiance was owed to the King, and no longer, as in earlier times, to great nobles, who, if they held commands, now did so by virtue of the King's commission. The status of the infantry, hitherto looked upon as an inferior branch of the service, was raised, and during the reign the bayonet was introduced as an infantry weapon. The Hôtel des Invalides was established for the benefit of disabled soldiers.

Colbert within a few years greatly increased the prosperity of France. The burden of taxation was lessened, financial administration was purified, debt was reduced, trade increased, and the fighting forces were augmented. The expenditure of the court was not diminished (this was beyond Colbert's power to touch), but the royal treasury was well filled. Yet it may be doubted whether Colbert's protective system tended to the permanent enrichment of France. The establishment of order in the administration, especially in the finances, was unquestionably advantageous to the country, though, even in this, the benefit was limited by the continued existence of exemptions which Colbert was unable to cancel. The effect of the prohibition of the export of corn has already been noticed. His policy of encouraging exports and limiting or even prohibiting imports could not meet with ultimate and permanent success. In the long run exports and imports must pay for each other; there must be some sort of balance between them. Under conditions prevalent in the seventeenth century, if there should be a regular and substantial surplus of exports over imports, the balance would be rectified by an influx of gold and silver, which would ultimately have the effect of raising the general level of prices throughout the land. And if the prices of French products advanced the flow of exports would be checked. Moreover, it may be doubted whether it was desirable or possible for any country to be absolutely independent of others. If all countries attempted to enforce a like policy, international trade would be diminished, to the general detriment. Protective tariff would be met by protective tariff, and tariff wars might easily develop into wars. This, indeed, happened; there was a definitely commercial aspect to most of the wars in which France was involved in the eighteenth century.

Colbert, as did most of his contemporaries, failed to realise that international trade was beneficial to all countries concerned in it. He thought that the prosperity of one country was contingent upon the poverty of another, and that France could be enriched only through the impoverishment of England and the United Provinces. He never realised his mistake; his attachment to this idea led him to bestow approval on the Dutch War of 1672-8, the expense of which nullified the beneficial effects of his reforms.

The reign of Louis XIV was an age of literary activity, and some of the greatest names in French literature belong to this time. Corneille, Racine, and Molière are unrivalled in the history of the French drama. Much of Corneille's work was produced before the period of Louis's personal rule, and Molière was already well known, though the comedies upon which his reputation is based were written within this period. The tragedies of Racine, in the classical style, belong wholly to this time. Boileau enjoyed a great reputation in his own time, but posterity has not endorsed contemporary opinion of his merits. La Fontaine is best remembered for his Fables.

Bossuet, Bishop of Meaux, was the greatest contributor to the theological and philosophical literature of the reign. He was a great orator and a great debater, and he was a warm defender of Gallicanism against the Ultramontanists. He evolved and published a system of political theory which found strong Scriptural justification for the principle of the Divine Right of Kings—not, as in Stuart England, the Divine Right of legitimate as against usurping monarchy, but the Divine Right of any firmly established form of government, a right derived directly from God and not mediately through the Pope. Fénelon, the tutor of Louis's grandson, the Duke of Burgundy, and the author of *Télémaque*, a man of letters who was associated to some extent with a religious movement known as Quietism, contributed to the philosophical literature of the period. Pascal belonged to the preceding age, but some of his work was not issued until this time.

Louis recognised the importance of art and literature as contributing to the glory of his court. He continued the Academy established by Richelieu, and he set up several other Academies, including those of Science and Music. The King's interest in literature did much to make it fashionable, and he deserved to be remembered as a patron of letters.

The court of Louis XIV was thronged with nobles who desired to be associated with the most brilliant society in Christendom. The atmosphere of flattery prevailed everywhere, and etiquette was strict, extending to the most minute details of daily life. That the court was licentious cannot be denied; yet at least the formalities of religion were not neglected. Courtiers were witty, and there was a marked improvement in manners and refinement as compared with what prevailed in earlier times. In this respect the French aristocracy set an example which was followed in other countries. It may be asserted that the improvement was permanent and that it formed a definite contribution to the advancement of civilisation.

In the earlier part of his reign the private life of Louis XIV was disfigured by his neglect of the Queen and his association with a succession of mistresses. In 1673 Madame de Maintenon was appointed governess to his illegitimate children. She was a deeply religious woman, and Louis, although at first repelled, in course of time was much attracted by her character and personality. Maria Theresa died in 1683, and in the following year the King married Madame de Maintenon. It is probable that he would have recognised her as Queen, but, if the offer was made, she declined the rank; nevertheless, the fact of the marriage was not concealed, and her position at court differed from that of a queen only in points of formal etiquette. Louis, despite the irregularities of his private life, had never been entirely irreligious, and from the time of his friendship with Madame de Maintenon he became profoundly devout, paying the closest and most regular attention to the observances of religion. The extent of Madame de Maintenon's influence over his religious policy has been variously estimated. It must be recognised that his action towards the papacy, the Huguenots, and the Jansenists was consistent with the character of his whole reign, and it seems probable that he would have followed the same general course even if Madame de Maintenon had not been connected with his court.

The Church in France, even after the Concordat of Bologna in 1516, maintained a considerable degree of independence of papal authority. The Crown could not fail to be interested in any attempt of the papacy to augment its influence in France, and was prepared to support the national church in resenting foreign dominion, if only the more certainly to subject it to a form of royal supremacy. Jesuits had been admitted to France only on conditions; only those decrees of the Council of Trent which did not conflict with the rights of the Crown or the Gallican Church were accepted in France; the Cardinals who ruled France had followed a line of policy which did not commend itself to the court of Rome. The question of the relative extent of papal and royal authority over the French Church came to a head in the reign of Louis XIV. In a large part of France the Crown had long enjoyed a right known as the *régale*; by this the revenues of bishoprics reverted to the Crown during vacancy. In some of the provinces in the south of France this right had never been recognised, and in 1673 Louis, with his passion for uniformity, proclaimed its extension to every part of France. The Bishops of Alet and Pamiers protested against the edict and appealed to Pope Innocent XI, who, after some hesitation and delay, pronounced in their favour. Crown and papacy thus became involved in a dispute of the gravest character. For Louis to recede from his position would be an admission of the existence of limits to his power; for the Pope to give way would be an acknowledgment of Gallican independence. Opinion in France strongly supported the King. The Church, the Parlement, and the theologians were prepared to champion the royal claims; the Pope even hinted at excommunication. The controversy continued for some years, and in October, 1681, an Assembly

of the clergy was held at St. Germain at which the right of the
King to the *régale* in every part of France was asserted. The
Assembly proceeded, in March, 1682, under the guidance of
Bossuet, to formulate four resolutions asserting the liberties
of the Gallican Church. By the first, it was declared that
papal authority was limited to spiritual matters and that royal
authority was in no way dependent on the papacy, with the
corollary that kings could not be deposed nor subjects absolved from their allegiance by the Pope. The second asserted,
as had been claimed by the Council of Constance though never
admitted by the papacy, the superiority of a General Council
over the Pope. The third resolution specifically denied the
right of the Pope to override the customs and constitutions of
the Gallican Church. The fourth resolution admitted the
jurisdiction of the Pope in matters of faith, subject to the
important reservation that his decisions were not irrevocable
and finally binding until they had received the general assent
of the Church.

It could not be expected that the Pope would accept these
decisions. He condemned them, and he refused to sanction
the elevation to bishoprics of priests who had accepted them.
In the next few years a considerable number of sees became
vacant and remained so, their revenues passing into the royal
treasury. The French clergy as a whole supported the King,
and it seemed possible that the outcome of the quarrel would be
the separation of the Gallican Church from Rome and the formal proclamation of royal supremacy, as in Tudor England.
This did not happen. Neither side was anxious to push
matters to extremes. Louis was not excommunicated; for his
part, he refrained from any act which should make ultimate
reconciliation impossible. For some years the struggle continued almost in silence. In 1691 Innocent XII became Pope;
he was inclined to compromise, and in 1693 Louis quietly
withdrew the four resolutions, while the Pope accepted Louis's
nominees to the vacant sees in France. In form, it was a
papal victory; in fact, the royal authority over the French
church was very considerably strengthened.

The desire for uniformity, which had been one of the
motives inspiring Louis in his dispute with the papacy, was
equally potent in urging him to take a strong line against the
Huguenots and the Jansenists. Since the Peace of Alais, 1629,
the Huguenots had ceased to be a political factor in France.

Quiet, orderly, and skilful, by their energy in industry and commerce they contributed substantially to the prosperity of France. Foreign trade and internal manufacturing industry were largely in their hands, and if they added little to the literature of France they contributed a good deal to the treasury.

The good sense of following a policy of toleration would thus seem to have been evident. Louis was less concerned with its wisdom than with the indication it afforded of a divergence from that uniformity in every aspect of French life which was his ideal. From the early years of his personal rule edicts were issued which made the position of the Huguenots more difficult. An Edict of 1666 professed to maintain the principles of the Edict of Nantes, but it promulgated a number of rules which limited the full freedom of the Huguenots in the exercise of their religion. The meeting of their General Synods was forbidden, and newly - acquired territories were declared to be outside the scope of the Edict of Nantes. Some of the clauses of the Edict of 1666 were withdrawn in 1669, and there was little direct persecution before 1680. But facilities were offered for conversion to the Catholic faith, and penalties were imposed on converts to Protestantism. A Treasury for Conversions was opened in 1677, and money became available for bribing Huguenots to change their faith. Bishops competed with one another in the work; the production of a lengthy list of conversions became a passport to royal favour and ecclesiastical promotion.

With the development of his quarrel with the papacy Louis was anxious that no suspicion of compromise with heresy should be attached to his name. Year by year he became more rigid in the observances of the Catholic religion, and his measures against the Huguenots more severe. To what extent he was influenced by Madame de Maintenon it is impossible to say; it is probable that he needed little urging. But it is certain that the powerful influence of Bossuet was exerted in favour of strong action against the Protestants.

In 1681 Huguenots were excluded from official or professional careers. The children of Huguenot parents were, at the age of seven, permitted to declare themselves Catholic, and money and other inducements were offered to them to do so. From the Treasury of Conversions proceeded a stream of bribes, in the form of offers of pensions or official posts, to assist the wavering in reaching a decision. Many Huguenot churches and schools were closed, and Huguenot ministers were forbidden to preach. The natural result of these measures was seen in the flight of thousands of Huguenots from France to England, the Empire (especially to Brandenburg), and to the United Provinces (whence some of them migrated to South Africa). Emigration from France was forbidden by an edict issued in 1682, and the attempt was made punishable by the galleys; nevertheless, many thousands made good their escape. A rising, or, rather, a peaceful demonstration, was organised in the Cévennes in 1683; it was made the excuse for the Dragonnades. Troops were sent into the district and quartered on the inhabitants. The licence permitted to ill-disciplined men on defenceless women and children was the most odious feature of the whole movement for the suppression of Protestantism in France. It is probable that the King was imperfectly acquainted with what was going on, but it was the natural outcome of the policy upon which he had embarked, and he cannot be absolved from responsibility for it. To avoid the licentiousness and cruelty of the soldiers many of the remaining Protestants submitted to "conversion." It was at last reported to Louis that the work was complete. The toleration extended to Protestants by the Edict of Nantes appeared to be no longer required, and in October, 1685, the Edict was revoked. Protestant worship was forbidden, and the remaining Protestant churches were closed. Protestant ministers were to be exiled, though their children over the age of seven were to remain in France. The penalties for the emigration of Huguenots other than ministers remained in force.

The number of Huguenots who held to their faith in spite of persecution was much greater than Louis had been informed. The recalcitrant, not only in the Cévennes but in other parts of France also, continued to be subject to the Dragonnades, and the most ferocious edicts could not prevent attempts at escape over the frontiers. Many, no doubt, were caught, and ended their days miserably as galley-slaves. But many more crossed the frontiers; it is impossible to estimate their numbers with any pretence to accuracy, but the extent of the whole emigration has been put as high as a quarter of a million. From an economic standpoint these people were the pick of the French nation. With their settlement in other countries much industrial activity was transferred from France to her competitors. Some of the *émigrés* were soldiers and sailors who willingly fought against their oppressor; brigades of Huguenots, men of Puritan type, comparable with Cromwell's veterans, fought against France in the Wars of the League of Augsburg and the Spanish Succession. The whole sorry business resulted in the weakening, military and economic, of France, and it did not even achieve its purpose of securing religious uniformity. Protestantism was not stamped out, and the discontent aroused in the region of the Cévennes made it necessary for Louis to maintain an army there even in the darkest days of the Spanish Succession War.

The principles which guided Louis XIV in his dealings with the papacy and the Huguenots were responsible also for the determination of his attitude towards Jansenism. The Jansenists, who have been described as the Puritans of the Roman Catholic Church, both on account of their doctrinal beliefs and on account of their inclination to attach greater importance to spiritual life than to ecclesiastical ceremonial, were opposed to the ultramontanism of the Jesuits, who were very powerful at the court of France. They were the followers of Cornelius Jansen, a professor of divinity at Louvain, who wrote a book on the theology of St. Augustine. This work was not published until 1640, after Jansen's death. It asserted the inadequacy of the externals of religion as means of salvation, and emphasised the importance of conversion. But conversion could be brought about by God alone; it was beyond the power of the individual sinner to convert himself. And, since God converted some people and not others, the logical corollary to this line of thought was the doctrine of pre-destination.

Such views, if not absolutely heretical, were not likely to be acceptable to the authorities of either Church or state. The Church had always insisted that salvation was to be attained by belief in its teaching and obedience to its directions; it could not be expected to admit either that the official way of salvation was in any respect open to question or that any other way was possible. The state, as personified in Louis XIV, was certain to frown upon any independence of religious thought or any deviation from strict orthodoxy.

The leaders of the Jansenists in France in the time of Louis XIV were the Arnaulds, brother and sister. Antoine Arnauld was a member of the Sorbonne, the theological faculty of the University of Paris. Angélique Arnauld was Abbess of Port

Royal, a convent near Versailles; she died in 1661, but her
influence survived to make Port Royal the headquarters of the
Jansenist movement.

Antoine Arnauld wrote and preached in support of the views
of Jansen, and in 1649 the Sorbonne selected five propositions
from the *Augustinus* and declared them to be heretical. Most
of the French bishops agreed, and in 1653 the Pope, Innocent X,
approved the action of the Sorbonne. The Jansenists were
thus faced with the choice between surrender of their opinions
and excommunication as heretics. They evaded the issue by,
as loyal Catholics, accepting the papal decision, but they contended that Jansen did not hold the propositions in the sense in
which they were denounced. They implied, in fact, that the
ecclesiastical authorities had misunderstood the work which
they had condemned. In 1656 Pope Alexander VII carried
the controversy a stage farther by declaring that Innocent X
had condemned the propositions in the sense intended by
Jansen. Arnauld, who by this time had been expelled from
the Sorbonne, and who had no reason for exercising restraint,
attacked this decision on the ground that, although the Church
was infallible in its interpretation of dogma, it was not so in
its knowledge of the intentions of Jansen. (It may be observed
that Arnauld's argument, though logically irrefutable, was
relevant to the issue only if accompanied by an admission that
Jansen had failed to make his meaning clear.)

The official position, if not the official argument, was over-
whelmingly strong, and a statement accepting the condemnation
of the *Augustinus* was required of all suspected Jansenists, and,
in course of time, of all priests, monks, and nuns throughout
France. Some protest was evoked, but the dissidents at length
made a qualified submission which satisfied the Pope (Clement
IX), and for the time being the controversy died down.

The Duchess of Longueville, who was inclined to support
Jansenist views and who had some influence over the King, died
in 1679. As Louis grew more bigoted in the years that followed, he determined on strict measures against the Jansenists;
nevertheless, they were not subject to any persecution comparable to that of the Huguenots. Arnauld fled from France
and died in exile; his place as leader of the movement was
assumed by Quesnel, whose work, *Moral Reflections on the New
Testament*, was widely read. It received the official approval
of Noailles, Archbishop of Paris.

Some of the Jansenists advocated the practice of receiving the condemnation of the *Augustinus* in "respectful silence." This implied a mental reservation which was inconsistent with the obedience which the Church required of all good Catholics, and in 1705 the Pope issued a Bull condemning "respectful silence."

Louis in his old age did not weaken in his determination to extirpate heresy. For many years the convent of Port Royal had been forbidden to receive novices, and in 1711 the few aged nuns who remained were expelled, and the convent was destroyed.

The final measure against Jansenism was the issue of the Bull *Unigenitus* in 1713, an utter condemnation of everything even remotely connected with the movement. The King was determined to secure its acceptance in every part of France, but a number of bishops, including Noailles, held out against it, and in the midst of the controversy Louis died.

CHAPTER III

I. To the Peace of Ryswick

WHEN, upon the death of Mazarin, Louis XIV took the direction of affairs into his own hands, France was already pre-eminent in Europe. The supremacy of the Crown had been firmly established in every part of France, and no other state in Europe was the equal of France in strength. Spain was utterly exhausted as the result of a long series of wars and of a ruinous economic policy; the Empire was the loosest of loose confederations, and none of its members, except the Emperor, could be ranked as a great European power; the Emperor, with the Turk at his gates, was in no position to contest the primacy of France; the England of Charles II was far from being the equal of France in population and resources, while Charles, tricky and unreliable as he might be, was usually more eager for alliance than for war with his cousin; the United Provinces, though still powerful, were not so strong as France, and, as the events of Louis's reign were to show, were unequal to the strain of keeping in the first rank of European powers. Conditions, therefore, were ideal for a monarch who wished to make himself supreme in Europe.

Such a monarch was Louis XIV. He was the inheritor of the Bourbon policy of natural boundaries for France, and he desired to push forward the frontiers of France in any quarter in which they were not already easily defensible. In particular, he wanted his dominions to extend to the Rhine, and, since the Rhine flowed through the Empire and the United Provinces, this involved the acquisition of certain Imperial and Dutch territories in addition to the whole of the Spanish Netherlands. With Louis holding to such a policy, wars with the Emperor, Spain, and the Dutch were inevitable. But this was not all. Louis, by virtue of a claim through his wife, Maria Theresa, aspired to the acquisition, for himself or his grandson, not only of the Spanish Netherlands but of the whole of the dominions of the Crown of Spain. Charles II, King of Spain, reigned from 1665 to 1700; his health was poor, and his death at any time during this period would have occasioned no surprise. The possibility of the Spanish Succession question coming to the front was always present in the minds of the diplomats of Europe.

Louis's plans included the substitution of French for Spanish influence in Italy—the revival, in fact, of the ambitions of the Valois kings, Charles VIII, Louis XII, and Francis I. This was intimately connected with his aspiration to the Spanish throne, since Milan in the north and Naples in the south of Italy were appanages of the Spanish monarchy.

By his diplomacy and his subsidies Louis schemed to reduce the later Stuarts in England to the position of vassal allies. The extent to which Charles II of England was his tool is a matter on which opinions vary. That astute monarch, by far the ablest of the Stuarts, followed a general policy of alliance with France; he accepted Louis's money but was careless of the obligations into which he entered. By skilfully playing off Louis, the English Parliament, and the Dutch, one against another, he secured his own ends, and used the King of France for his own purposes quite as much as Louis used him. James II, while faithful to the French alliance, followed a more independent line than his brother, and Louis's influence over English policy diminished. On the whole, it may be doubted whether Louis obtained value for his money and his pains in his dealings with England.

For a time Louis seems to have entertained aspirations to the Imperial Crown. His position would enable him to over-awe the Rhenish electors, and he was not without hope of securing the Bavarian vote. This ambition explains his activity in the affairs of certain Rhenish states, especially Cologne and the Palatinate.

The complete realisation of these schemes would have made Louis XIV all-powerful in every part of western and central Europe—King of France and Holy Roman Emperor, with vassal rulers in Spain, Italy, and England, and with the United Provinces his humble dependants. He would have been as absolute in the Europe of the seventeenth century as Charlemagne in that of the ninth. But it is doubtful whether Louis ever seriously expected to realise the whole of this grandiose ambition. He never made any formal statement of his aims, which are to be inferred from the course of his actions and the trend of his diplomacy. Nor should it be assumed that this scheme of aggrandisement existed, fully developed, in the mind of the Louis of 1661. Some of his aims, no doubt, were present from the first. The extension of his frontiers and the reversion of some part of Spanish territory in Europe could not have been absent from his mind at the beginning. But his wider ambition developed with the passage of time.

Some incidents in the early years of Louis's personal rule afforded him opportunities of demonstrating to the world at large his sense of his own greatness. A scuffle in the streets of London between the suites of the French and Spanish ambassadors was made the occasion for a sharp rebuff to Spain and for the issue of instructions to French envoys that they were to yield precedence only to the ambassador of the Emperor. A somewhat similar incident in Rome was settled only by the humiliation of the Pope, from whom a formal apology was extracted. These were trifles, but they served to indicate to Europe what manner of king sat upon the throne of France.

In pursuance of an engagement with the Dutch, entered into in 1662, Louis in 1664 with great reluctance declared war upon England. No serious fighting took place, and peace was restored at the conclusion of the Anglo-Dutch War in 1667. The first real war in which Louis was engaged was the War of Devolution. This was a war of aggression, designed to secure for Louis the Spanish Netherlands, and undertaken upon the flimsiest of pretexts. In the province of Brabant there was a custom by which the rules of succession to landed property which prevailed generally in western Europe were subject to some variation. The common usage was that sons succeeded in preference to daughters; in Brabant, if a landowner had been married twice, daughters by the first marriage succeeded before sons by the second. It must be emphasised that this practice was applicable to the succession to private estates and not to the government of the province; also, that it prevailed in Brabant, and not throughout the Spanish Netherlands. Louis made this custom the basis of a claim to the possession of the whole region. Philip IV, King of Spain, died in 1665. He had been married twice; by his first wife he had a daughter, Maria Theresa, now the wife of Louis XIV, and by his second wife a son, who succeeded him as Charles II, King of Spain. If Philip IV had been a country gentleman in Brabant the application of the Law of Devolution would have provided Louis with a claim, through his wife, to his father-in-law's estate. He applied the principle to the sovereignty of the Spanish Netherlands as a whole. (It may be noticed that thus early in his reign Louis was prepared to disregard the renunciation which was incorporated in the arrangements made at his marriage.) It is hardly necessary to point out that, if Louis's claim had been submitted to an impartial tribunal for consideration, it would have been laughed out of court.

Louis thus embarked upon an aggressive war upon utterly inadequate grounds, but at a very opportune time. England and Holland were at war, and the activity of the Turks was sufficient to tie the hands of the Emperor. Spain was in no condition to offer effective resistance, and other states had not yet had sufficient evidence of Louis's ambitions to view his every move with alarm, as they did in later years. In the campaign against the Spanish Netherlands some resistance was encountered, but the French were everywhere successful, and the greater part of the country fell into their hands. Louis next turned to Franche Comté, the conquest of which proved an even easier task.

The extent and ease of French victories caused some alarm in other countries. Throughout the seventeenth century it had been a cardinal feature of Dutch policy to maintain the Spanish Netherlands as a buffer state against French advance, and Louis's success was viewed with dismay. Peace was concluded between the United Provinces and Great Britain in 1667, and this was followed, early in 1668, by the formation of the Triple Alliance of England, Holland, and Sweden to resist French aggression. The alliance was remarkable in that each of these powers had within the past century fought against Spain as the representative of Catholicism in Europe; they were now banded together in her defence. Louis was wise enough to know when to stop, and in April, 1668, he agreed to the Treaty of Aix-la-Chapelle. He restored Franche Comté and a considerable part of his conquests in the Netherlands to Spain, but he retained a number of border fortresses and part of the province of Flanders. He thus gained what he really wanted, since the French boundary was extended to the northeast and the frontier was strengthened. The captured cities were fortified by Vauban, the greatest engineer of the age.

From this time Louis was possessed of great animosity

towards the Dutch. This was to be expected, since France and the United Provinces were rivals in naval strength and commercial activity. Louis disliked the existence of republican institutions in a powerful country so close to France, and he was enraged at the arrogant attitude of the leading burghers, and especially at the suggestion of the Dutch Government that it should mediate between France and Spain in the War of Devolution. Most of all, he was angered at the formation of the Triple Alliance. He assumed that the Dutch were the promoters of the alliance, and he determined to punish the republic for its temerity in thwarting his plans.

Before attacking the United Provinces Louis took care to break up the Triple Alliance. He sent the Duchess of Orleans, sister of Charles II, to England on a mission to her brother. She secured the assent of Charles II to the Treaty of Dover, 1670, by which England was to abandon the Triple Alliance and co-operate with Louis in an attack upon the Dutch. Sweden also was bought over, and promised to assist France in the coming war. Louis also made treaties of alliance with several German princes of the Rhineland; if they gave him no assistance, at least their territories were available for the movements of his armies.

The Dutch were left isolated, and they were at the moment in no condition to defend their country. De Witt feared the revival of the power of the House of Orange quite as much as French invasion. William III, at this time entrusted with the command of the Dutch forces, found that even the garrisons of important strongholds were reduced much below their proper strength in consequence of the enmity of de Witt to a Prince of Orange.

The campaign began in 1672, under Louis's personal direction. Three armies, under the real command of Turenne, Condé, and Luxemburg respectively, marched down the banks of the Rhine and invaded the United Provinces. There was little resistance; many places fell, and if Louis had pushed on he might have captured Amsterdam at once and brought the war to an end.

The position was desperate for the Dutch. As related elsewhere, De Witt suffered for his mistaken policy, and William of Orange was appointed Stadtholder. The Estates offered Louis terms of peace which included the cession of certain territories and fortresses; the King of France demanded much greater territorial satisfaction, the toleration of Roman Catholicism in the Provinces, the abrogation of tariffs hostile to French commerce, a war indemnity of twenty-four million livres, and an annual public acknowledgment of the dependence of the United Provinces upon France. Such terms were hopeless, and the Dutch determined to fight to the end. Amsterdam was saved by the cutting of the dykes and the flooding of the land, and William held on anxiously till the winter. He felt confident that before the French campaign could be resumed in the spring of 1673 a European alliance could be formed against France.

His confidence was not misplaced. Frederick William, the Great Elector, was alarmed at the attack on Protestant Holland by Catholic France, and, with Louis in an aggressive mood, uneasy for the safety of his Rhenish duchies; he prepared to take up arms on behalf of the United Provinces. Spain, exhausted as she was, could not view the encirclement of the Spanish Netherlands by the French without making an effort to retain them. The Emperor, too, was alarmed, and in 1673 an alliance of the Emperor, Spain, Brandenburg, and the United Provinces was formed to resist the aggressions of France. Other states joined the league, and Louis now found himself isolated except for such assistance as he might receive from England and Sweden. Charles II of England made a separate peace with the Dutch in 1674; Sweden remained faithful to the French alliance till the end of the war.

The immediate effect of the formation of this coalition was the relaxation of pressure on the Dutch. Louis had to meet enemies on several fronts and had to act, in the main, on the defensive. In 1674 the French forestalled attack through Franche Comté by overrunning the province and capturing Besançon. Dutch and Spanish marched through the Spanish Netherlands for an invasion of France from the north-east, and, though Condé held up their advance, William inflicted a severe check upon him at Le Fay. Another attempt at invasion, planned to take place through Alsace, was foiled by Turenne. A third attack, by Spain in the south-west, met with little success.

France thus succeeded in holding back the enemy at several points at the same time, and continued to do so in the following years. Turenne was killed in Alsace in 1675, and Condé retired from active service. A Swedish force was defeated by

the Great Elector in 1675 at Fehrbellin, but the Swedish operations had at least the effect of relieving France from direct
Brandenburg attack at this time.   In the later years of the war
the fighting was concentrated on the north-east border of
France, where Louis's forces captured Valenciennes, Cambray,
and St. Omer.   But the end was drawing near.   William of
Orange married the Princess Mary of York in 1677, and this
was generally regarded as the prelude to English participation
in the war on the side of the Dutch.   Charles II had no wish
to take up arms against Louis, but it was doubtful whether he
could long withstand the pressure of public opinion, and he
was certainly not prepared to risk the loss of his crown in his
cousin's cause.

Louis by this time was in serious financial difficulty.   What
had been planned as a short triumphal march into Holland, to
be followed by a dictated peace, had developed into a bloody,
expensive, defensive conflict from which little could be hoped.
He realised the necessity for peace, and in 1678 the Treaty of
Nijmegen was drawn up.   France gained Franche Comté on
the east, and, on the north-east, a number of places which
Vauban turned into fortresses.   The chief loser was Spain;
Holland, the original object of attack, emerged from the war
without loss of territory.   In the peace with the Empire
Philippsburg was yielded by Louis to the Emperor.

It is usual to regard the Peace of Nijmegen as marking the
zenith of Louis's power.   It is at least arguable that the treaty
indicated the beginning of his decline.   It is true that by it he
gained territory while by later treaties he ceded it.   He had
repelled attacks, and French forces enjoyed immense prestige.
But he had failed in his primary purpose of inflicting condign
punishment upon the Dutch.   Further, the course of the war
had shown that his ambitions were unrealisable.   His policy
of aggression had alarmed Europe, and whenever and wherever
he launched an attack the powers of Europe would combine in
an effort to check him.   Unless he could overcome the rest of
Europe single-handed he could not succeed.

Louis was not engaged in any great war during the next ten
years; yet it was in this period that his aggressions appeared
most pronounced.   France had been assigned territorial gains
in various treaties, notably those of Westphalia, the Pyrenees,
Aix-la-Chapelle, and Nijmegen.   In 1679 Louis set up in
several frontier provinces *Chambres de Réunion* to investigate

the terms of these treaties and to determine to what extent, if at all, they had not been carried out. If this duty had been assigned to arbitration courts of an independent and inter-national character no possible objection could have been raised. But the *Chambres de Réunion* were French courts, subject to the will of the King of France, and their decisions were not in doubt. Louis was suitor and judge in his own cause. Large dis-tricts were assigned to France by the Chambers, and Louis sent troops to occupy them. Without even the pretext of "Re-union," he took pos-session of Luxemburg and Casale, and on the judgment of a Chamber he seized Strassburg.

Great indignation was felt at these pro-ceedings, but Louis had chosen his time with judgment. The Emperor, with the Turk advancing up the Danube towards Vienna, dared not embark on a war with France. Spain did so, but was beaten, and in 1684, by the Truce of Regensburg, Louis was confirmed for twenty years in the possession of his recent gains.

French aggression in the Rhineland could not be dissociated

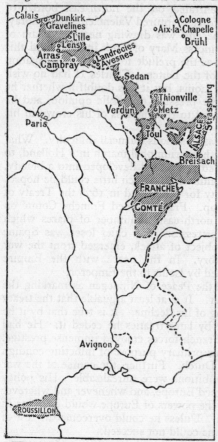

THE ACQUISITIONS OF FRANCE, 1648–1688

from Louis's Imperial ambition. To what extent he seriously aspired to the Imperial Crown we cannot determine, but it is evident that he was in a position to overawe the Rhenish electors, and his intervention in the affairs of the Palatinate and Cologne was full of significance. (Louis's failure to become Emperor is explained by the simple fact that no vacancy occurred till the death of Leopold in 1705, by which time Louis was growing old and was engaged in the War of the Spanish Succession.)

Circumstances began to turn against Louis. The defeat of the Turks at Vienna was followed by their expulsion from Hungary, and the Emperor was free to turn his attention to affairs in the west. The Revocation of the Edict of Nantes strengthened Louis's potential enemies by inspiring them to resist him and by adding to their resources. In 1686 William of Orange was able to establish the League of Augsburg, consisting of the Emperor and the rulers of Sweden, Spain, Bavaria, and other German states, and with the support of the Pope, the United Provinces, and Savoy. (The actual League was an association of princes of the Empire only; other powers were adherents, but not members. The Kings of Spain and Sweden were, of course, princes of the Empire.) The Elector of Brandenburg did not join the League, but he made a treaty of alliance with the Emperor. Louis was thus left without an ally except England. In England James II was pursuing a line of conduct of which the issue was his exile and the enthronement of William of Orange.

Events in two Rhenish electorates contributed to bring about war between France and the League. The Duchess of Orleans, the second wife of Louis's brother Philip, was the sister of Charles, Elector Palatine, who died in 1685, and Louis put forward on her behalf a claim to the greater part of the electorate. The new Elector, Philip William of Neuburg, appealed to the Emperor for protection, and the points in the dispute, which were complicated, were by agreement referred to the arbitrament of the Pope.

In 1688 occurred the death of Maximilian, the Archbishop-Elector of Cologne, and the choice of his successor involved Louis and the Emperor in another dispute. Louis favoured the claim of Cardinal William von Fürstenberg, who, with the support of the Elector Maximilian, had already been chosen Coadjutor-Archbishop, while the Emperor put forward Joseph

Clement of Bavaria, a youth in his teens who was not yet a priest. Neither candidate obtained the necessary majority of votes in the election by the Cathedral Chapter, and the matter was referred to the Pope, who declared for Joseph Clement. Louis refused to recognise this as a settlement of the question.

Louis's negotiations with the Emperor in 1688, immediately prior to the outbreak of war, exhibited him in an aggressive and unreasonable temper. He complained of the delay in according her rights to the Duchess of Orleans, regardless of the fact that if there had been undue delay it was attributable to the Pope, to whom the Palatinate problem had been referred. He complained that the Emperor had deprived Cardinal von Fürstenberg of the Cologne electorate; this, again, was the work of the Pope, and it was Louis's own policy which had driven the Pope into an attitude of hostility, so that he deliberately advanced the candidate who was backed by Louis's opponents. He complained that the Emperor was hastening on peace with the Turks in order that he might turn his arms against France; surely a most extraordinary contention, that if the Emperor succeeded in getting free from embarrassment in the south-east in order to be able to defend his position in the west France was thereby aggrieved! Louis further demanded of Leopold that the Truce of Regensburg should be converted into a definitive peace—in substance, that the gains which had already been ceded to him for twenty years should be yielded to him in perpetuity.

Meanwhile, events in England reached the point at which leading men of both parties sent an invitation to William of Orange to invade the country and free it from the rule of James II. William was not desirous of obtaining the English crown for its own sake, but he was very much interested in the possibility of securing English support for the League of Augsburg, and for that reason he was prepared to accept the invitation. Louis was well served by his spies. He knew what was going on, and he warned the Dutch Estates-General that an attack on England would be treated as a declaration of war against France. He warned James of his peril, and offered him advice and assistance. James treated the offer as an affront; he publicly disavowed any alliance with France. "A King of England," he stated, "needeth not, like an Archbishop of Cologne, the patronage of any sovereign." Louis thereupon resolved to let events take their course. While his plans were uncertain it was out of the question that the Estates-General of the United Provinces should consent to the departure of a large fleet and army to England, on an adventure the issue of which could not be predicted. Louis therefore withdrew his fleet from the Channel into port, and he began the Augsburg war by an attack upon the Palatinate. The Dutch were relieved of their immediate apprehensions, and permitted William to sail. It is certain that Louis neither desired nor expected the victory of William in England. He probably thought that the expedition would involve both William and James in serious difficulties, and that the King of England, in alarm, would seek the support he had so far declined. The assistance of a brigade of French troops would enable James to defeat William, and Louis would have the satisfaction of inflicting a serious, perhaps a final, blow upon his principal opponent and at the same time of bringing a too independent ally to heel.

It is well known that Louis misjudged the affair. William's progress from Torbay to London was unhindered, and James, deserted by his subjects, fled to France, where Louis received him graciously and assigned him a residence and an income. But the position of affairs in Europe was definitely changed, and for Louis it was a change for the worse. When England joined the coalition of his enemies he was left friendless. The War of the League of Augsburg was of little interest. Louis began hostilities in September, 1688, by the siege of Philippsburg, and before the end of the year he declared war on the United Provinces. Philippsburg was captured, and part of the Palatinate was occupied. It was not retained, however. Louis found it necessary to withdraw his forces, and, in order to hinder the allies from making it a base of attack upon France, he ordered it to be laid waste. Towns, villages, and crops were destroyed by the retiring troops. The devastation of the Palatinate was one of the worst incidents of its kind in the seventeenth century, being exceeded in ruthlessness only by the great sack of Magdeburg by the Imperialists in the Thirty Years' War.

The most important military events of 1689-91 occurred in Ireland. Louis supported James in an attempt to recover that kingdom and to make it a base of operations against England. James landed at Kinsale and was well received by the Roman Catholic Irish. Violent measures against the lives and property of the Protestants resulted in their retreat into Ulster, where, at Londonderry and Enniskillen, they held out bravely and successfully against James. At the Battle of the Boyne, 1690, William defeated James, who fled to France. The struggle continued for another year, during which time the French general St. Ruth vainly attempted to check the progress of Ginkel and Churchill. With the fall of Limerick in the autumn of 1691 the Irish campaign ended. It had not been well planned. If it had been successful the conquest of England would have been no nearer. Moreover, agreement between James and the Irish was only superficial. He wished to overcome William as his rival for the throne of England; they, and especially the Earl of Tyrconell, their leader, aspired to separation from England. If James had been victorious he would soon have found his Irish subjects in revolt against him. Louis would have been better advised to plan a direct invasion of England.

An opportunity for invasion actually occurred in July, 1690, when English and Dutch fleets were defeated off Beachy Head by the French under Tourville. A small force landed and destroyed the village of Teignmouth, but no serious invasion was attempted, and the chance was allowed to pass. On the border of the Netherlands Luxemburg gained a victory over the allies at Fleurus, but this, also, was not followed up. In the south-east, however, Marshal Catinat gained an important success over the Duke of Savoy at Staffarda, and occupied most of the duchy. In the following year the French took Nice.

In 1691 Mons, and in the following year Namur, were captured by the French. William, being unable to relieve Namur, attempted to avenge its loss by an attack upon Luxemburg at Steinkirk. He was defeated and driven back, but he withdrew his forces in good order, and the French losses in the battle were nearly as great as his own. Meanwhile, the long-deferred invasion of England was being prepared, but, before it could take place, the command of the Channel had to be reasserted. In the Battle of La Hogue Tourville was defeated with severe losses by Russell, and no invasion could take place.

In the Netherlands in 1693 Louis was unable to take Liége, and a severe battle took place at Landen, in which William's forces, greatly outnumbered, inflicted heavy losses upon the French under Luxemburg before being compelled to retire.

As after Steinkirk, William's troops were not disorganised, and his army still existed as a fighting force. The only gain to the French from their victory was the fortress of Charleroi.

Both sides were suffering from the strain of the war. The beneficial efforts of Colbert's reforms were no longer felt in France, and the old financial abuses reappeared. Money was raised by the sale of offices, by farming taxes, and by debasing the coinage. In England, on the other hand, national credit was organised by the establishment of the National Debt and the Bank of England.

In its later years the war languished, and notable events were few. In 1695, however, William attacked and captured Namur, which was thought to be well-nigh impregnable. The recovery of Namur was William's greatest military achievement. It had no profound effect upon the position and strength of the two sides, but the loss of the fortress was a blow to French prestige and an encouragement to the allies.

Negotiations for peace reached a successful issue in the Treaty of Ryswick, 1697. Terms of peace with Savoy had already been settled and were incorporated in the treaty; the independence of the Duke of Savoy was recognised, and he recovered Pinerolo, Casale, and Nice. The French conquests in the south-west and the north-east at the expense of Spain were all to be surrendered. Only in the east did Louis hold his own; he refused to give up Alsace and Strassburg. The territorial arrangements may be summarised in the statement that France surrendered every acquisition since the Peace of Nijmegen, with the solitary exception of Strassburg. William III was recognised as King of Great Britain, and Louis promised to give no further assistance to the Stuarts. The Dutch were permitted to place garrisons in certain fortresses on the border of the Spanish Netherlands. Joseph Clement remained in possession of the electorate of Cologne, and the claims of the Duchess of Orleans were compounded for a money payment.

If the war was uninteresting this epithet can hardly be applied to the peace. Its terms were such that it must be treated as registering Louis's defeat. The surrender of the gains of twenty years, including everything (except Strassburg) won by the *Chambres de Réunion*, was a humiliation for the Great King. The recognition of his rival as King of England must have been bitter to him. Yet it would be wrong to consider the Treaty of Ryswick as a dictated peace. Louis was not crushed; he had been checked, but his armies were intact and his resources were still vast. France was still powerful for offence as well as defence. A few years of peace and reorganisation would suffice to prepare her for another great war. That war was approaching. A settlement of the Spanish Succession question, which had been in the minds of European statesmen for a generation, could not be postponed much longer. The reign of Charles II of Spain was drawing to a close. Louis did not intend to be caught unprepared. He made sacrifices for an immediate peace at Ryswick in order that France might be in a commanding position when Charles should die.

CHAPTER IV

THE FOREIGN POLICY OF LOUIS XIV

II. THE SPANISH SUCCESSION

ONE of the most remarkable facts in the history of the latter part of the seventeenth century is the decline of the power of Spain. This great monarchy had been exhausted by nearly ninety years of almost continuous warfare (1572–1659), and between 1659 and 1697 she was involved in four wars with Louis XIV—the War of Devolution, 1667-8; the Dutch War, 1673–8; the short war of 1683–4, which ended with the Truce of Regensburg; and the Augsburg War, 1689–97. She was uniformly unsuccessful, and every treaty (except Ryswick) into which she entered in the seventeenth century involved loss of territory. The fact that she drew apparently inexhaustible supplies of treasure from the New World distracted the attention of the people from the development of Spanish internal resources, and her industries and commerce were insignificant by comparison with those of other countries of western Europe. Not only were the New World possessions of Spain not a source of real strength to her, but they were a positive handicap, in that her retention of a monopoly which she could neither exploit nor defend excited the jealousy and antagonism of the maritime powers.

Spain was still medieval in character. Nobles and clergy enjoyed excessive privileges, including a large measure of exemption from taxation, and the peasantry was down-trodden. The activity of the Inquisition had succeeded in exterminating all traces of Protestantism, and had crushed all independence of thought. The wealth of the Church was enormous, and priests and monks swarmed in all parts of the land. The population of the country declined during the seventeenth century; exact information on this point is not to be obtained, but it is believed that the population of Spain at the end of the seventeenth century was less than half that of the time of Charles V. The finances of the country were in a chaotic

37

condition; revenues were anticipated for several years, offices were sold, taxes were farmed, loans were raised at exorbitant rates of interest, and no satisfactory accounts were kept.

An energetic and far-seeing king might have revived his country, restored her finances, developed her trade and industry, and cut down ecclesiastical and feudal privileges. But Charles II, King of Spain from 1665 to 1700, was a weakling

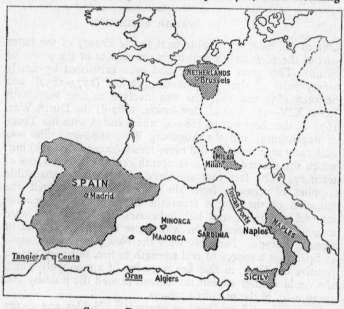

SPANISH DOMINIONS IN EUROPE, 1700

in body and mind. He has been described as an imbecile. If he had been more definitely insane he might have been replaced by a Regent, to the great advantage of the country. His case may more truly be described as one of "arrested development." He had the mind of a child, and was incapable of even understanding the problems of public business. He was twice married—on the first occasion to Louise of Orleans and on the second to Marie of Neuburg—but he had no children, and the question of succession to his throne remained uncertain. For many years the kings and statesmen of Europe had known that at his death the question would call for settlement, and as time went on and his health, never good, declined the problem became more acute. It was probably this fact, rather than any consciousness of defeat, that led Louis XIV to agree to the Peace of Ryswick in 1697.

In spite of the fact that it had fallen on evil days the Spanish monarchy was still a prize worth winning, and under an able king it might recover much of its former greatness. Its possessions were more extensive than those of any other country in the world. In the Old World, besides Spain itself, the Netherlands, the kingdom of Naples, the duchy of Milan, certain places, known as the Tuscan ports, on the west coast of Italy, the islands of Sicily and Sardinia and the Balearic Islands, and some places on the north coast of Africa belonged to it, so that the western Mediterranean was almost a Spanish lake. Altogether, the Spanish King had four capital cities in Europe—Madrid, Naples, Milan, and Brussels. In the New World Mexico, Central America, and most of the West Indies and South America were included in the Spanish Empire, while the Philippine Islands off the south-east coast of Asia also belonged to it.

Charles II had no children and no brothers, but he had two sisters, of whom the elder, Maria Theresa, had married Louis XIV, and the younger, Margaret Theresa, had married the Emperor Leopold I. The Dauphin, therefore, would seem to have had a good claim to succeed Charles II, and if he did so the Spanish monarchy with all its possessions would be added to the kingdom of France, already too powerful. But when Maria Theresa married Louis XIV she renounced, for herself and her descendants, all claim to the Spanish throne. This would have disposed of the Dauphin's claim had not the Treaty of the Pyrenees, which included the renunciation, also provided for the payment of a dowry of 500,000 crowns, which in fact had not been received. If, as was argued by the French lawyers, the renunciation was conditional upon the payment of the dowry, it would not hold good. It was contended, in addition, that succession to the throne of Spain was by "indefeasible hereditary right," which meant that no renunciation could hold good and that no person in the direct line of succession could forfeit his right by any such document. In order to diminish the opposition which other powers would offer to a French succession in Spain, the Dauphin passed his claim on to his second son, Philip, Duke of Anjou (since his eldest son, Louis, Duke of Burgundy, was in the direct line of succession to the throne of France). From the point of view of strict hereditary right the French claim was clearly the best.

Charles II's younger sister, Margaret Theresa, who married the Emperor Leopold I, had a daughter Maria Antonia, who married Maximilian Emanuel, Elector of Bavaria; she had a son, Joseph Ferdinand, the Electoral Prince, whose claim was put forward in opposition to that of Anjou. But Maria Antonia had upon her marriage renounced her claim to the Spanish throne, and this would have been fatal to her son's prospects had it not been contended that in making the renunciation she had acted under compulsion from her father, the Emperor.

If both renunciations were treated as valid, it would be necessary to go a generation farther back in the Spanish royal family in order to find a king for Spain. Philip IV had two sisters, and, singularly enough, the elder of these married a French king and the younger an Emperor. Anne of Austria married Louis XIII and became the mother of Louis XIV, who, therefore, was personally entitled to claim the Spanish crown through her. But Anne of Austria renounced her claim upon marriage, while her sister Maria, who married the Emperor Ferdinand III, made no such renunciation. Her son, the Emperor Leopold I, therefore claimed through her. He passed his claim on to his second son, the Archduke Charles.

The settlement of this question could not be determined solely by genealogical considerations. It was thought that if Anjou became King of Spain he would act under the influence and control of his grandfather, whose power would be overwhelming. Such a succession would seriously disturb the Balance of Power—the principle that no European state ought to become so powerful as to be a danger to the rest of Europe. A similar objection would apply, though not to the same extent, to the selection of the Archduke Charles, whose elevation to the Spanish throne would strengthen the Austrian power. To the succession of the Electoral Prince, Joseph Ferdinand, no such objection could be urged, for Bavaria, to which he was heir, was not a great European power. To summarise the conflicting claims and arguments, it may be stated that the strongest claim, genealogically, was that of Anjou; legally, that of Charles: politically, that of Joseph

Ferdinand.   The fact that Joseph Ferdinand was a child, while the other two were men, added to the force of his claim.   If either Anjou or the Archduke became King of Spain, that country would receive a foreign king.   But Joseph Ferdinand might be brought up in Spain as a Spaniard.

Some other factors had to be taken into consideration in settling the question.   Reference has already been made to the question of trade with Spanish possessions in the New World. The maritime powers had long been dissatisfied with their exclusion from the ports of Spanish America, and no settlement was likely to win their approval which did not provide for their participation in South American trade.   Trade in another direction, with the Levant, was carried on at considerable peril from Corsairs, and, as the western Mediterranean was dominated by Spain, Levantine trade could not be carried on at all but by the permission of Spain—a state of affairs in which the maritime powers could hardly acquiesce permanently without loss of dignity.   Great Britain, at least, looked forward to the acquisition in the Mediterranean of a base to serve the needs of her fleet.   Nor could a settlement of the Spanish Succession question be regarded as satisfactory to Austria unless it took account of her aspirations in Italy.   Since the Peace of Westphalia had registered the virtual extinction of Imperial authority in the Empire, Austria had turned to the south.   She hoped in time to become a Mediterranean power by dominating both the Balkan and the Italian peninsulas, and from the Spanish settlement she expected to secure at least a foothold in northern Italy.

As far back as the War of Devolution Louis XIV had recognised the possibility that Charles II might die without direct heirs.   In 1668 he had concluded with the Emperor Leopold I a secret Partition Treaty by which Leopold was to have the crown of Spain, with Milan and the colonies, while Louis was to receive the Netherlands, Franche Comté, Navarre, and Naples and Sicily.   This arrangement was no longer adequate.   Louis was now in possession of Franche Comté, and his frontier had been pushed forward in the direction of the Spanish Netherlands.   The England of Charles II was on friendly terms with France; that of William III was her resolute opponent.   The acquisition by Louis of the whole of the Spanish Netherlands would be strenuously opposed by both England and the United Provinces, and, as indicated above, these powers would not readily acquiesce in their permanent exclusion from American and Levantine trade.

After the Peace of Ryswick an attempt was made to settle the question by agreement between Louis XIV and William III, neither of whom was eager to embark upon a struggle of which the result could not be predicted. Negotiations were opened by Louis in 1698. William was at first unwilling to treat, but he at length consented to do so. Diplomatic exchanges were prolonged, but it appeared that the aims of the two kings were not irreconcilable. Louis was more anxious to prevent an Austrian succession than to secure the Spanish crown for his grandson; William would not sanction a French succession. It was possible for them to agree upon a Bavarian succession.

A Partition Treaty was drawn up in 1698, by which Joseph Ferdinand was to become King of Spain (with the Spanish Netherlands and the New World possessions), while the Archduke was to receive Milan and Luxemburg, and Anjou was to have Naples, Sicily, the Tuscan ports, and Guipuscoa. The Spanish Netherlands would thus form a buffer state between Holland and France; Milan in Austrian possession would prevent French expansion in Italy and would give Austria the foothold she coveted; Guipuscoa would offer to the French a gateway into Spain in the event of future war. Neither the Emperor nor the King of Spain was a party to this treaty. But the Kings of England and France believed that, while the Emperor might threaten, he would not by himself fight for his son's claim—or that, if he did, the war would be serious or lengthy. The Spanish people, however, were indignant at the idea of foreign kings partitioning their empire, and Charles II made a will in which he named Joseph Ferdinand as heir to the whole of his dominions. Neither the treaty nor the will became effective, since Joseph Ferdinand died early in 1699. It was officially stated that the cause of his death was smallpox, though there were rumours that he had been poisoned.

The work of negotiation had to begin again. It was a more difficult matter to reach agreement this time. There was no third candidate of any importance, and the accession of either the Archduke or the Duke of Anjou would affect the Balance of Power. But William would not consent to the enthrone-ment of Anjou, and Louis at length agreed to the crown of Spain passing to Charles. But at different times in the negotia-tions he claimed Luxemburg, Navarre, and Milan, in addition to Naples, for his grandson. William agreed to the addition of Milan to Anjou's share only on condition that it should be exchanged for Lorraine, and the second Partition Treaty was concluded on this basis in 1700.

At first sight it might appear that Louis had been out-manœuvred in the negotiations, and that France stood to gain little by the treaty. Closer consideration indicates that the gains of the House of Hapsburg were showy, while those of France were substantial. The close connection of Spain with Austria, which would be the outcome of the Archduke's accession, would not really increase the strength of either; only such change in the political and economic structure of both countries as would amount to revolution would suffice to revive them and enable them to dominate the European stage. France, on the other hand, would under the treaty establish for herself a very strong position in Italy. The acquisition of Milan would enable her to sever communication between Austria and Spain, and though Milan was to pass to the Duke of Lorraine he could be relied on to support French policy. Moreover, as mentioned above, the acquisition of Guipuscoa was of strategic value to France.

The treaty met with a mixed reception. The dislike of William in England prejudiced the people against a treaty of which he was the author, and the republican party in Holland disapproved of it for a similar reason. Elsewhere it was accepted, except by the Emperor, the Duke of Savoy, and the King of Spain. Although by the treaty the greater part of the inheritance was to pass to the Archduke Charles, the Emperor would be satisfied with nothing less than the whole, and he withheld his sanction from the agreement. The Duke of Savoy played a waiting game, being ready to cast his alliance on one side or the other as circumstances might suggest. In Spain the news of the conclusion of a second Treaty of Partition was received with the greatest indignation. By this time Charles II was dying, and efforts were made to secure a will from him; it was uncertain, however, in whose interest the will would be made. The Queen, Marie of Neuburg, was the sister of Eleanor of Neuburg, Leopold's wife, who was the mother of the Archduke Charles. Marie was working in the interest of her nephew, but a few days before the Spanish King's death the Archbishop of Toledo, Cardinal Porto Carrero, took control of the palace and excluded the Queen from the King's bedroom.

C 1643–1848

He succeeded in obtaining the dying man's signature to a will which named Philip, Duke of Anjou, as heir to the whole of the Spanish dominions. If Anjou refused the offer of the Spanish crown the whole inheritance was to pass to the Archduke Charles.

Charles II died, and in due course an ambassador reached Paris with the formal offer of the Spanish crown to the Duke of Anjou. The real decision rested, of course, with Louis XIV. He had negotiated the Partition Treaty, and every consideration of honour pointed to his keeping it. But if he had refrained from negotiating with William he would have had the whole prize without any effort. And he might still have it if he allowed his grandson to accept the offer now made to him. Further, if he adhered to the treaty he might lose everything, since the offer to Anjou would be withdrawn and would pass to Charles, who could accept without hesitation, since the Emperor had not been a party to the Partition Treaty. Louis realised, moreover, that enforcement of the treaty would be difficult while acceptance of the will would be easy. Since the Emperor claimed the whole inheritance for his son the danger of war was no greater from following the one course than the other. French and Spanish opinion was strongly in favour of the will; Louis would be enthusiastically supported by his subjects and by the people of Spain in an attempt to place his grandson on the throne of Spain, while a war with the Emperor for the purpose of giving the bulk of the prize to the Archduke was nearly inconceivable. There remained the maritime powers, but Louis could count with some confidence upon the unwillingness of the English to fight in a quarrel which they regarded as no concern of theirs, and upon the hostility of the Dutch republicans to their Stadtholder. In the end Louis accepted the will, and recognised his grandson as King of Spain with the title of Philip V. Until his departure for Spain Philip was treated at the French court with the etiquette which was followed when it was visited by a foreign king.

During the next few months Louis acted with less than his usual acumen. He should not have forgotten that his disregard of a treaty formally concluded was patent to all Europe, and he would have been well advised to abstain from any action which might appear to be aggressive. A conciliatory attitude on his part would have minimised the danger of war. William, indeed, was ready to fight, but neither English nor Dutch were prepared to support him, and the turn of events must have brought him to the verge of despair.

Louis did not follow a conciliatory policy. He sent French troops to occupy certain frontier towns in the Netherlands which were garrisoned by the Dutch under the terms of the Treaty of Ryswick. The Dutch garrisons were captured, and were released only when the United Provinces consented to recognise Philip V. He refused to permit any barrier of fortresses to the Dutch, and he declined to consider the grant of any territorial compensation, in Italy or elsewhere, to the Emperor. Edicts were issued—from the French and not the Spanish court—which gave to French ships certain commercial privileges in Spanish colonial ports. These measures aroused apprehension, and English opinion became increasingly hostile to France and Spain. In the summer of 1701 negotiations were set on foot for the formation of an alliance against France. In the autumn of 1701 Louis made a fatal mistake. James II of England died at St. Germain, and Louis recognised his son, a boy of thirteen, as King of Great Britain and Ireland. This gross violation of the Treaty of Ryswick roused the English people as William by himself could never have done. Louis endeavoured to represent his action as formal only, comparable with the practice of English kings since the time of Edward III in styling themselves Kings of France. This explanation was far from satisfying the English people, and Louis was to learn that he was mistaken in thinking that he could place a king on the English throne as easily as on that of Spain. Whigs and Tories alike were eager for war. Army and navy were increased, and an Act of Attainder was passed against the young "king"—the Pretender, as he was commonly called.

The Grand Alliance was formed in September, 1701; it originally included only the Emperor and the maritime powers. It provided for concerted action with a view to obtaining—by peaceful means if possible; if not, by war—the Netherlands and the Italian provinces for the Emperor, and colonial possessions and trading privileges for the maritime powers. It left the question of the Spanish throne open, so that the Emperor might at any time lay formal claim to it. The alliance was strengthened during the winter by the adhesion of five of the Electors (Brandenburg, Hanover, the Palatine, Trier, Mainz), together with some other German princes. Louis could rely

upon the support of only two of the Electors, the brothers
Maximilian Emanuel of Bavaria and Joseph Clement of
Cologne. Savoy and Portugal also were inclined to side with
Louis; within a year or two both of them had gone over to the
Grand Alliance.

Louis XIV entered upon the war with high hopes. He had
at his disposal a band of experienced marshals, including
Tallard, Vendôme, Catinat, Villars, and the Duke of Berwick.
His armies were large, well-trained, and undefeated. He had
a strategic advantage over his enemies in the possession of
interior lines of communication. Fighting took place on
several fronts, and troops could be moved from one area to
another in accordance with the varying requirements of the
situation. He possessed, also, the enormous advantage of
undivided control, while his enemies experienced the usual
disadvantages of an alliance—jealousies, half-hearted efforts,
divided purpose, and the like.

The forces at the disposal of the Grand Alliance were fully
equal to those of France, though only time could show to what
extent the adherents of the alliance would be faithful to their
undertakings; in the case of the great military electorates,
Brandenburg and Hanover, the struggle was maintained with
vigour, and treaty obligations were not only fulfilled but
exceeded. At sea the fleets of England and the United
Provinces were more than a match for those of the Bourbon
powers. The greatest advantage of the allies, however, lay in
the genius of their generals. The Duke of Marlborough,
Captain-General of the English and Dutch armies, was the
greatest strategist of his age, and he was at the same time an
able tactician; as a politician and a diplomatist he was almost as
skilful as in the field. Eugene, who directed the Emperor's
forces, was a military commander of outstanding capacity, who,
had he not been the contemporary of Marlborough, would have
been recognised as the foremost captain of his day.

The fighting took place in several theatres of war at the same
time—in the Netherlands and Central Europe, in Italy, and
in Spain, and there was a certain amount of fighting at sea. It
will be convenient to trace separately the course of events in
each field of conflict.

The war in the Netherlands began in 1702. The French
occupied the Spanish Netherlands, which they might at any
time use as a base for a march into the United Provinces.

Marlborough, in command of English and Dutch forces, realised that the critical point in Europe was not Amsterdam but Vienna, which lay dangerously open to attack. Yet he was not free to move to the assistance of the Emperor, since the Dutch Estates-General, which controlled his actions, feared invasion. In 1702 he gained some successes against Boufflers and established himself on the lower Meuse and Rhine.

In the following year Marlborough advanced up the Rhine as far as Bonn, which he captured. Bonn was the capital of the electorate of Cologne, and the Elector was compelled to withdraw from the war. Meanwhile, a direct attack on Vienna was being planned by French and Bavarians. French armies under Tallard and Villars moved towards Bavaria; had the Elector acted with decision Vienna might have fallen, but he turned aside to crush Eugene first. The defection of Savoy from the French cause alarmed the Elector, who retreated, and the opportunity passed.

In 1704 a determined effort was made to put the French plan in operation. Marsin replaced Villars, and the combined armies of Marsin, Tallard, and Maximilian Emanuel prepared to march upon Vienna, while another French army under Villeroi was dispatched to the Netherlands to hold Marlborough in check. Opposition to the French advance could be offered only by the Austrian army under Eugene. Marlborough saw the danger; on the pretext of undertaking operations on the Moselle he left the Dutch frontier and marched up the Rhine. He was joined by a Brandenburg contingent at Mainz and continued his march to join Eugene. He thus placed his forces between the French and Vienna. At the Battle of Blenheim Marlborough and Eugene inflicted a crushing defeat on the French and Bavarians, Marshal Tallard being taken prisoner. The Elector of Bavaria was forced to withdraw from the war; the Emperor was saved; Louis XIV's forces for the first time suffered defeat; the English army gained in reputation, and it was realised that in Marlborough the allies possessed one of the greatest generals of all time.

The interest of the war reverted to the Netherlands in 1705. Marlborough hoped to force his way into France by way of the Moselle, but the death of Leopold I and the withdrawal of Imperial forces from the Rhine caused him to abandon the plan. He drove Villeroi back to the Netherlands, and if he had been adequately supported by the Dutch he might have crushed him.

In 1706 the opportunity came. At the Battle of Ramillies Marlborough defeated Villeroi and drove the French back to their frontiers. Almost the whole of the Spanish Netherlands fell into his hands. Some of this territory was recovered by

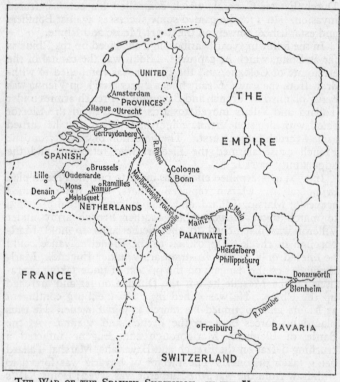

THE WAR OF THE SPANISH SUCCESSION—IN THE NETHERLANDS AND
CENTRAL EUROPE

the French in 1707 and 1708, but in the latter year they sustained a third great defeat when Vendôme was overthrown by Marlborough at Oudenarde. The battle was followed by the siege and capture of Lille, and only the fortresses of Mons and Namur remained to hinder the advance of the allies upon Paris. Negotiations for peace, referred to below, were unavailing, and Louis made an appeal to the French nation to make one further effort on behalf of their country. Money poured in, another army was raised and equipped, and in 1709 Villars was ready to oppose Marlborough and Eugene. For some weeks he remained behind entrenchments, but a threat of attack upon Mons by Marlborough forced him to advance and give battle. At Malplaquet occurred the bloodiest and most fiercely contested battle of the war. In the end the allies were victorious, and Mons fell into their hands.

Villars in 1710 contented himself with the formation of fortified lines by which he hoped to prevent the advance of Marlborough into France. But the heart had gone out of the war. Though Marlborough captured Douai and some other places he could obtain no help from his allies, and with the fall of the Whigs and the establishment of a Tory ministry his own position as Captain-General became precarious. In 1711 Marlborough, by a brilliant tactical move, pierced Villars' fortifications, but before he could take advantage of his success the blow fell. He was dismissed from his command, and his successor, the Duke of Ormond, was instructed to remain inactive.

Eugene, deprived of Marlborough's support, continued the war. In 1712 his depleted forces were defeated by Villars at Denain, and before the end of the year the French gained some further successes. The conclusion of peace between France and the maritime powers forced Eugene to transfer his forces to the Rhine, where in 1713 further fighting occurred between him and Villars. Ill-luck dogged him; his forces were hopelessly inferior to those of the French, and it was not until Freiburg was captured that the Emperor authorised him to negotiate for peace.

Some fighting occurred in Italy in 1701. Marshal Catinat occupied Milan and advanced eastward to meet Eugene. The Austrian general outmanœuvred him, and he was forced to retreat. Villeroi, who was sent to supersede Catinat, was defeated by Eugene at Chiari, and a few months later he was surprised and captured at Cremona. Eugene maintained his position throughout the year 1702, although the Emperor was prevented by the critical position of affairs in south Germany from sending him reinforcements. In 1703 the Austrian general was pressed back to the Tyrol by superior French forces under the command of Vendôme, but a change of sides by the Duke of Savoy relieved the Emperor of the fear of immediate attack from the side of Italy and imperilled the communications of Vendôme with France. The Duke was isolated and hard pressed in 1704, but in 1705 Eugene was able to advance to his assistance.

The year 1706 was decisive in Italy. In the spring Vendôme attacked the Austrians, Eugene being absent, and drove them back to the Tyrol. Eugene returned from Vienna with

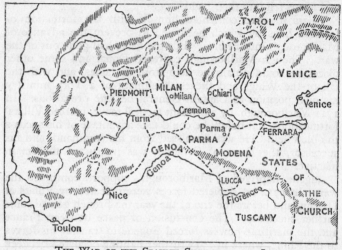

THE WAR OF THE SPANISH SUCCESSION—IN ITALY

reinforcements drawn from several allied German states, and marched through north Italy and joined the Duke of Savoy. At Turin he completely defeated Marshal Marsin, and the French army retired from Piedmont into France. A few isolated garrisons held out for a few months, but by the end of the year the whole of the Milanese, including the city of Milan itself, was in the possession of Eugene. Early in 1707 the French abandoned northern Italy.

During this year Eugene planned an attack upon Toulon. Unfortunately, at this time Austrian forces in Italy were divided. A brigade was detached for the reduction of Naples, which was easily accomplished, since the Neapolitans detested Bourbon rule and the Spanish garrison was weak. Eugene with weakened forces was unable to reduce Toulon, and he withdrew into Italy.

No attempt was made to establish the Archduke Charles in Spain before the year 1704. Some naval operations had been undertaken by an English fleet under Sir George Rooke in 1702, and the Plate fleet had been captured at Vigo. Portugal joined the Grand Alliance in 1703, so that a useful base was obtained for land operations against Spain. Charles landed at Lisbon in 1704, supported by English and Dutch troops, but little was achieved. In August of that year, however, Rooke attacked and captured Gibraltar and defeated a strong French fleet which sailed to its recovery.

In 1705 an English army under the Earl of Peterborough arrived in the Peninsula to support the Archduke, who was taken on Sir Cloudesley Shovell's fleet round to Barcelona, which Peterborough captured. The whole of Catalonia and Valencia adopted the cause of Charles, and the English army in Portugal, now commanded by the Earl of Galway, advanced into Spain. A French attempt to recover Barcelona failed, and Galway marched to Madrid and proclaimed Charles as King of Spain. (For a short time in 1706 all the four Spanish capitals in Europe were in the hands of the allies.) But the Spanish people, except the Catalans, were solid for Philip, and it was found impossible to hold the capital in the face of national opposition. Galway retired towards Aragon, where he joined Peterborough, who, however, soon afterwards sailed for Italy.

In 1707 Galway determined to renew his attempt on Madrid, and he advanced from Valencia towards the capital. At Almanza he gave battle to the Duke of Berwick (a Jacobite in the service of Louis), and was completely defeated. Aragon and Valencia were lost, and only the Catalans remained faithful to the cause of the Archduke.

Galway returned from Catalonia to Portugal in 1708; desultory fighting occurred in this and the following year. In 1708 an important operation was undertaken by Stanhope, resulting in the capture of Minorca; the possession of Port Mahon, on the island, made possible the permanent maintenance of a British fleet in the Mediterranean.

In 1710 allied troops under Starhemberg advanced from Catalonia into Aragon and defeated the Spanish at Almenara and Saragossa. He was able to enter Madrid, but, as in 1706, the determined hostility of the Spanish people rendered the position untenable. The allied forces withdrew in two divisions; one, under Stanhope, was forced to surrender at Brihuega, while the other, commanded by Starhemberg, was defeated at Villa Viciosa. The war in Spain was at an end. The Archduke retained only a foothold in Spain at Barcelona.

On several occasions during the war attempts were made to negotiate peace. For some years all such efforts were unsuccessful, on account of the attitude of the Whig party in

THE WAR OF THE SPANISH SUCCESSION—IN SPAIN

England. In their eagerness to make the Protestant succession absolutely secure the Whigs wished to bring about the complete defeat of Louis XIV, and the only terms they would consider were the abdication of Philip V and the recognition of the Archduke as King of Spain. "No peace without Spain," was the Whig slogan.

In 1706, after the Battle of Ramillies and the occupation of Madrid, Louis offered to recognise Charles as King of Spain, provided that the right of Philip to Milan, Naples, and Sicily was conceded. He offered also a number of fortresses in the Netherlands to be garrisoned by the Dutch as a barrier against French aggression. These terms were substantially what was contained in the Second Partition Treaty. They were quite unacceptable to England, and Louis was made to understand that terms agreed upon in 1700, before the war, could not be considered in 1706, after important victories had been gained.

In the winter of 1707-8 further tentative suggestions, including some commercial concessions, were made by the French to the Dutch. These also were foiled by Great Britain, and a resolution was adopted by the House of Lords declaring that no peace could be satisfactory which permitted the retention of any part of the Spanish dominions by a Bourbon prince.

Early in 1709 negotiations were opened at The Hague. Louis at first proposed that Philip should retain Naples and Sicily, but subsequently he conceded the withdrawal of his grandson from the entire Spanish monarchy; he offered, also, to recognise the Protestant succession in Great Britain and to cede Newfoundland. The allies demanded, in addition, barrier fortresses for the Dutch, the surrender of Alsace and Franche Comté, the dismantling of Dunkirk, and the expulsion of the Pretender from France. This was not all. Philip was in actual possession of Spain, and there was no certainty nor even likelihood that he would peacefully surrender his kingdom at the bidding of his grandfather. The allies required an assurance from Louis that, in the event of Philip refusing to give up his crown, he should join the Grand Alliance against Spain. This was more than could be expected of the King of France, even in his desperate plight. He replied that if he must fight he would fight for, and not against, the King of Spain. Negotiations fell through, and the war was resumed. The blame for their failure has often been assigned to Marlborough; it is now known that he regarded the terms offered to Louis as unreasonable and dishonourable. Responsibility for the breakdown of this effort to make peace should be attributed to the obstinacy of the Emperor and the Dutch, and, on the British side, of Townshend.

Negotiations were resumed after Malplaquet, and representatives of the warring powers met at Gertruydenberg early in 1710. The Hague terms were treated as a basis for discussion, but the attitude of the allies was not quite so extreme as in 1709. It was suggested that Philip should retain Sicily, though the idea was opposed by the Emperor and the Duke of Savoy. Louis, who would have been glad to hear of Philip's resignation of the Spanish crown, still declined to fight against his grandson, but he offered to pay a subsidy to the allies for their campaigns in Spain. This was rejected by the Dutch, and once more the war was resumed.

The extremists had overreached themselves, and within a short time the whole position was changed by events in Great Britain and the Empire, so that things were working out for Louis better than he knew. The power of the Whigs in Great Britain had for some time been declining, and in 1710 the Whig ministry of Godolphin and Marlborough was replaced by a Tory administration, of which the chief members were Harley and St. John, who were ready to treat for peace on less extreme terms. In the Empire, Joseph I, who had succeeded his father, Leopold I, in 1705, died in 1711. He left no son, and was succeeded by his brother, the Archduke Charles, who became Emperor as Charles VI. The elevation of Charles to the Imperial throne altered the whole aspect of the Spanish Succession question. It might be contended that by his acquisition of the Spanish monarchy the Balance of Power would be endangered to a greater extent than by the recognition of Philip. Charles VI might become as powerful as Charles V.

In face of these new circumstances the combatants, with the exception of the Emperor, opened negotiations at Utrecht in 1712. Eugene, on the Emperor's behalf, continued the war against Villars, as narrated above, and discussions between them were not begun until November, 1713. Separate treaties were drawn up between France and her several opponents. Some of these were signed at Utrecht in 1713; that between France and the Emperor was concluded at Rastadt in 1714; terms of peace between France and the Empire were settled at Baden in 1714. Terms between Great Britain and Spain were separately arranged, and the agreement by which the Dutch barrier was settled was contained in yet other instruments. It is unnecessary to distinguish the contents of these treaties separately; they may be considered collectively as the Peace of Utrecht.

It was agreed that Philip V should be recognised as King of Spain, but that he should renounce all right of succession to the throne of France and that the crowns of France and Spain should never be united. The Emperor was to be compensated for his failure to obtain the Spanish crown by receiving the kingdom of Naples, with Milan, Sardinia, and the Tuscan ports. (In this way was established that Austrian predominance in Italy which was to last until the middle of the nineteenth century, except during the Napoleonic period.) Charles VI was also to be given the Spanish Netherlands, known hence-forth as the Austrian Netherlands, but was not to be put in actual possession of these provinces until he had agreed to yield to the Dutch a line of eight barrier fortresses. Three-fifths of the cost of the Dutch garrisons of these fortresses was to be born by the Emperor. The safety of Holland was further guaranteed by a British pledge of assistance in the event of attack.

The Duke of Savoy received the island of Sicily, with the title of King, and the peace confirmed the recognition of the Elector of Brandenburg as King of Prussia.

Great Britain retained her conquests of Gibraltar and Minorca, and her claims to Newfoundland, Nova Scotia, the territory of the Hudson's Bay Company, and the island of St. Christopher's were admitted by the French. Louis XIV recognised Anne as Queen of Great Britain and undertook to recognise any person who ascended the British throne under the Act of Settlement. The Pretender was to be expelled from France. The fortifications of Dunkirk were to be dismantled.

Certain trading concessions by Spain to Great Britain formed an important feature of the peace. The Spanish monopoly of South American trade was broken into by the conclusion of an agreement, known as the Asiento, by which Great Britain was granted the right to supply negro slaves to Spanish colonies for a period of thirty years. The number of negroes specified in the Asiento was 4,800 per annum, but this was not to be re-garded as a maximum, and might be exceeded. A further concession to Great Britain provided that Porto Bello, in Central America, might be visited by one ship of six hundred tons every year for the purpose of general trade.

It is to be observed that the peace was incomplete, in that the Emperor declined to accord recognition to Philip as King of Spain, while the latter gave no formal consent to the partition of the Spanish monarchy.

Treaties of peace which mark the conclusion of long and devastating wars have usually been subject to criticism by historians, and the Peace of Utrecht conforms to this rule. Some of the criticisms of the peace will be noticed here, but it should be remembered that it is very much easier for the arm-chair critic to state what should have been done than for diplomats, faced with many difficulties and compelled to take heed of many factors, to achieve the ideal settlement.

To the criticism that the allies had fought great battles and won victories for Charles and that in the end they had conceded recognition to Philip, it may be pointed out that the whole position was changed after the accession of Charles to the Imperial dignity. In so far as the allies were fighting for the preservation of the Balance of Power, this principle was better served by the acceptance of Philip than by the enthronement of the Emperor in Spain. This settlement, moreover, had the advantage of giving to the Spanish people the king of their choice, a consideration which probably weighed very little with the diplomats at Utrecht.

A further comment on the peace, from the British point of view, is that the war was waged by the Whigs but that the peace was concluded by the Tories, who, in their eagerness to bring the war to an end for their own purposes, were accused of the sacrifice of national interests. It is true that the Tories, some of whom were prepared to scheme for the succession of the Pretender to Queen Anne, wished to bring the war to an end before the question of the succession should arise. But it is difficult to maintain that British interests were inadequately considered when terms of peace were agreed upon.

A more serious criticism of the treaty remains to be considered. The province of Catalonia had supported Charles throughout the war, and it now passed under the rule of Philip. The treaty stipulated that Philip should not exact vengeance upon the Catalans, but it provided no guarantee of fair treatment. As a matter of fact Philip invaded the province and captured Barcelona, whose inhabitants suffered cruelly at his hands, many of them being sold into slavery. Their neglect to secure the safety of the Catalan people stands to the lasting discredit of the allies.

The settlement reached at Utrecht was the basis upon which the peace of Europe was maintained, except for minor wars, for nearly thirty years. It did not really endanger the Balance of Power; the security of other states was not threatened, as had been feared, by a close alliance of the Bourbon powers, and for some years after the death of Louis XIV a marked feature of the European situation was the antagonism of France and Spain. The fact that neither Philip nor Charles was satisfied with the settlement, and that both of them, in the years to come, tried to overthrow it, is some indication that the scales were held fairly evenly between them. Spain received the

king she preferred, and the territorial arrangements were made
on the basis of existing facts. The lands assigned to Charles
were already in his possession or in that of his allies. Philip
was in possession of Spain. The British gains were already
in British hands. No extensive movements of troops were
necessary to put the treaty into force.

The terms of peace corresponded closely with the aims which
had inspired Great Britain to take part in the war. The
Protestant succession was recognised, and the right of Great
Britain to choose her king and to settle the terms of his
occupancy of the throne was triumphantly vindicated. The
coveted naval bases were secured in the Mediterranean, and
the mercantile interest obtained a footing in the trade of
South America.

The Peace of Utrecht marks the true end of the seventeenth
century, and the beginning of the eighteenth, in the history of
Europe. Wars of religion came to an end, and wars for trade
and colonial empire took their place. (The War of the Spanish
Succession displayed the characteristics of both types; if it was
a war for trade and colonial possessions it was also a war of
religion, since Great Britain was fighting to maintain the
Protestant succession and to exclude a Roman Catholic king.)
The peace also marks the final failure of the plans of Louis XIV.
He had ruled for a long time, and for many years he had been
the outstanding figure in European affairs. His pride was now
humbled, and the power of France was shattered. There
is something tragic in the figure of the old King in his last
days, defeated and bereaved, about to pass to the grave with
the consciousness that the work of his life had failed.

CHAPTER V

THE UNITED PROVINCES

An Act of Survival, passed in 1631, made the stadtholderate of the United Provinces practically hereditary in the House of Orange, so that in 1647 William II automatically succeeded his father in that office. He had been married to Mary, daughter of Charles I of England, while they were both no more than children. The new Stadtholder abandoned the cautious attitude of his predecessors, and determined, by means of a *coup d'état*, to convert his office into a monarchy. With a body of loyal troops he marched in 1650 against Amsterdam, intending to seize it by surprise. The effort failed, and the city closed its gates to him. He hesitated to attack it, and a few weeks later he died of fever.

The power of the House of Orange collapsed. It was for the time being without a head. The son of William II was not born until after the Stadtholder's death, and it was out of the question to appoint an infant to the headship of the state. The republican party seized its opportunity. A constitutional assembly, representative of all the provinces, resolved to leave the stadtholderate vacant; its functions were to be carried out by the provincial Estates.

For the next twenty years the government of the republic devolved upon John de Witt, Grand Pensionary of Holland, a man of great ability and integrity. He believed firmly in the necessity of maintaining republican principles, and he viewed the ambition of the House of Orange as a danger to the well-being of his country second only, if at all, to the menace of foreign conquest. He aimed, therefore, at strengthening the supremacy of the Estates of Holland, and he was prepared to oppose the succession of the young Prince of Orange to the stadtholderate and the command of the army and navy when he should reach man's estate.

The danger of a renewal of Orange ascendancy could not, in the nature of things, become great for many years. In the meantime de Witt had to face perils of another kind. The establishment in the British Isles of a Puritan Commonwealth, in religion and constitution not unlike the Dutch Republic, was followed by a period of antagonism between the two countries. Similarity of religious views was outweighed by commercial and maritime enmity. The Dutch had for many years been keen rivals of the English in the Far East, and the massacre of Amboyna, in 1623, when English merchants were murdered by the Dutch, had never been avenged. More immediate causes of friction appeared at this time. A Commonwealth envoy to The Hague, Dorislaus, was murdered there by Scottish royalists, and this was made the occasion for demands for the exclusion of Charles II and his followers from the United Provinces and for the formation of an alliance on terms which would have been equivalent to the union of Dutch and English republics under English rule, demands which could not be conceded. The Dutch were further angered by the passing of the English Navigation Act of 1651, which was intended as a blow to their carrying trade, and was followed by war. The fighting was limited to the narrow seas; Blake proved more than a match for Tromp and Opdam, and in 1654 de Witt was glad to make peace with Cromwell, who was now Lord Protector. By the Treaty of Westminster, 1654, the Dutch agreed to recognise the Navigation Act, to salute the English flag in the narrow seas, to pay compensation for English property destroyed or confiscated at Amboyna, to expel the Stuarts from the United Provinces, and to the perpetual exclusion of the House of Orange, which had intermarried with the Stuarts, from the stadtholderate. To this last clause de Witt found no difficulty in agreeing, and an Act of Exclusion was passed in the same year.

After 1660 the position of de Witt and the republican party was not so strong. The accession of Louis XIV to power upon the death of Mazarin in 1661 brought to the front of European affairs one who viewed any government of burghers with disfavour. The restoration of Charles II to the English throne in 1660 encouraged the adherents of the House of Orange to press for the repeal of the Act of Exclusion, and this was conceded by the Estates. Nor had the causes of Anglo-Dutch rivalry been removed by the terms of the peace of 1654. Ill-feeling remained, and in 1664 fighting occurred. The Dutch settlements in North America, known as New Holland, were seized, and became the English colonies of New York, New Jersey, and Delaware. The formal declaration of war in 1665 was followed by a renewal of naval fighting in the North Sea. An English victory at Lowestoft forced the Dutch to take refuge in their harbours. Shortage of supplies retarded repairs to the English fleet, and a part of it was laid up. In 1667 Dutch ships under Ruyter and Cornelius de Witt sailed up the Thames and the Medway to Chatham and burned three or four ships of war. Nevertheless, by the Treaty of Breda, 1667, the advantage lay with the English. The North American colonies remained in English hands, although some relaxation of the Navigation Act was conceded in favour of the Dutch.

The Prince of Orange was growing up. De Witt realised that the magic of the name of Orange counted for a good deal. It was associated with victory, whereas the period of republican ascendancy had twice witnessed the defeat of the Dutch by the English. It was necessary to take action if the ascendancy of the republican party was not to be overthrown, and in 1668 de Witt secured the assent of the Estates to the Perpetual Edict. The stadtholderate and the supreme command were to be kept perpetually separate, and William of Orange was to receive the appointment of Captain-General and Admiral-General when he reached the age of twenty-two. By implication he could never become Stadtholder, and de Witt thought he had secured the safety of the republic from monarchism.

The Dutch government had for many years realised the importance of the Spanish Netherlands as a buffer state against French aggression. In spite of the memories of the struggle against Spain for Dutch independence, it was no longer Spain, but France, which was to be feared. If the French should overrun the Spanish Netherlands and secure Antwerp and the Scheldt, the trade of Amsterdam would be threatened and the territorial integrity of the republic would be endangered. Louis XIV desired to secure the Spanish Netherlands, or at least the fortresses on their southern frontier. His activity in the War of Devolution, his unconcealed contempt for the Dutch, and the commercial measures of Colbert, all indicated that the prosperity and the integrity of the United Provinces were being threatened.

De Witt was alive to the importance of a good understanding with England, and in 1668 the Triple Alliance of England, Sweden, and the United Provinces was concluded. The allies bound themselves to compel Louis XIV to accept peace with Spain on the terms of the surrender to him of either Franche Comté or a few border towns in the Spanish Netherlands. Louis was too good a diplomatist not to accept the inevitable, and the Treaty of Aix-la-Chapelle brought the War of Devolution to an end.

The King of France was determined to punish the Dutch for their temerity in thwarting him. At the moment a direct French attack on the republic would be followed by the formation of a European coalition in its defence. The ground, therefore, had to be prepared by diplomacy. By the Treaty of Dover, 1670, the terms of which were not fully made known at the time, Charles II of England was won over to the support of France. The Emperor and several German princes promised neutrality, and in 1672 Sweden abandoned the Dutch and made an alliance with France.

De Witt failed to appreciate the significance of these events. He was unaware of the full terms of the Treaty of Dover, and he believed that in the event of attack Europe would not stand by and permit France to trample on the liberty of the republic. He thought that Louis would not dare to make war, and in his fear of the popularity of the Prince of Orange he would not even augment the forces of the state.

The invasion of the United Provinces by the French in 1672 led to an outburst of popular fury against de Witt. The nation as one man turned to William of Orange, who was chosen Stadtholder and Captain- and Admiral-General, and the supremacy of the republican party was at an end. The great services of de Witt for more than twenty years did not avail to prevent his murder and that of his brother at the hands of the mob, a crime which William made no attempt to prevent.

In the war of 1672–8 the United Provinces found themselves, with inadequate means of defence, exposed to the attack of a French army of overwhelming strength, while English and French fleets were ready to give battle to Ruyter. Louis marched to within striking distance of Amsterdam almost without meeting resistance, and if he had pressed on at once the city must have fallen. His hesitation enabled the Dutch to use their supreme weapon, the sea, and by the cutting of the dykes Amsterdam was saved. A breathing space was thus gained, and it was all that was needed. Louis might have snatched a speedy victory, but he was less likely to win in a lengthy campaign. The Dutch were confident that a European coalition could be formed in the winter of 1672-3. If the powers of Europe had no great reason to love the Dutch they had every reason to fear the ambition of Louis. The Dutch were not disappointed. By October, 1672, the Emperor and the Elector of Brandenburg were at war with France. In the following year Spain, and in 1674 Denmark and the Elector Palatine, joined the allies. England withdrew from the war, and only Sweden remained faithful to the French alliance.

The pressure on the Dutch was thus relaxed, and the war was fought on the Rhine and the border of the Spanish Nether-lands. Its course is indicated in another chapter. The terri-torial adjustments agreed to in the Treaty of Nijmegen, 1678, did not affect the Dutch, who were not required to surrender an acre of territory, while they secured a modification of French commercial regulations which had been framed against them.

In Dutch eyes the hero of the struggle was William of Orange, who, frail of body, and not of outstanding capacity as a military commander, fought patiently and pitilessly in defence of his country. William's aim, during this war and until the end of his life, was to overthrow the power of Louis XIV. His diplomacy for the next few years was directed to this end. In 1677 he married Mary, daughter of the Duke of York and next to her father in succession to the English throne. In the natural course of events he might expect his wife to become Queen of England. Actually, at the Revolution of 1688-9, he and his wife became joint King and Queen. But he was not desirous of the crown of England for its own sake; he valued it merely as a means of bringing the maritime powers into permanent alliance against France.

The continued aggressions of Louis XIV on the Rhineland and elsewhere enabled William to form the League of Augsburg to resist French aggrandisement. The League included, as members or supporters, all the more important states of Europe, except England, even Sweden deserting her old ally. And although James II of England would have nothing to do with the League, he was less concerned with supporting Louis than with the reconversion of England to the Roman Catholic faith. Louis should have struck at the League while it was weak and ill-organised. He failed to do so. The course of events in England led to the flight of James II at the end of 1688 and to the enthronement of William and Mary early in 1689.

Louis might have prevented William's expedition to England, but, for reasons explained elsewhere, he did not take action until too late. He could not possibly view the deposition of his ally and the triumph of his chief opponent with equanimity, and he determined to wage war in order to reverse this turn of fortune. In the War of the League of Augsburg William's qualities as a general were shown to advantage. He was defeated again and again, but on every occasion he was able to withdraw his troops in good order, and to yield very little ground. The French gains of three or four years were counterbalanced in 1695 by William's recovery of the fortress of Namur, the most brilliant military exploit of his life. The Treaty of Ryswick, which ended the war, marked a further stage in the decline of Louis's power. He returned to the allies most of his gains for nearly twenty years, and he recognised William as King of Great Britain.

The possibility of a peaceful solution of the question of the succession to the dominions of the King of Spain was explored by William and Louis between 1698 and 1700, and two Partition Treaties were drawn up. The interest of the United Provinces in the matter was the maintenance of the Spanish Netherlands as a buffer state against French aggression, and unless this could be secured the continuance of negotiations would have been futile. By the First Partition Treaty, 1698, the Spanish Netherlands were to pass to the Electoral Prince of Bavaria. His death in 1699 necessitated the making of another arrangement, and in the Second Partition Treaty it was agreed that the crown of Spain, with the Spanish Netherlands and some other territories, should be assigned to the Archduke Charles, the younger son of the Emperor. With the Netherlands in the hands of a Hapsburg prince the Dutch might at last feel safe.

Before his death Charles II made a will by which he bequeathed the whole of his dominions to the Duke of Anjou, grandson of Louis XIV. After some hesitation the King of France sanctioned the acceptance of the Spanish crown by the Duke, who assumed the title of Philip V, King of Spain. William's patient work in negotiating the Partition Treaties was thus overthrown, and he saw with dismay the Spanish Netherlands pass under the rule of a king who might be regarded merely as a viceroy of his grandfather. For all practical purposes the French were encamped on the very frontiers of the United Provinces.

The outlook was indeed dark for William. His lifelong
enemy was triumphant, and the very independence of his
country was threatened. England was in no mood for war.
Even in Holland, where the republican party was still to be
reckoned with, the consequences of this latest move were not
recognised at first. But Louis made a fatal blunder in 1701,
when on the death of James II he recognised James III as King
of Great Britain, in violation of the Treaty of Ryswick. England was roused to war, and within a few weeks William was
able to form the Grand Alliance of England, the Emperor, the
United Provinces, Brandenburg, Hanover, and some other
states against France. William was not to live to see the result
of his labours, but when he died, in March, 1702, the prospect
was more hopeful than at any previous time in his life.

In the Spanish Succession War Marlborough was Captain-
General of the Dutch as well as of the English army. In a
series of brilliant victories he expelled the French from the
Spanish Netherlands, which, when peace was made, passed
under the rule of the Emperor Charles VI. To the Dutch
was assigned the right of maintaining garrisons in eight
fortresses on the southern border of what was henceforth the
Austrian Netherlands, which, as a buffer state, served for the
defence of the United Provinces throughout the eighteenth
century until the European states system was thrown into the
melting-pot of revolution.

The United Provinces did not play so great a part in European affairs in the eighteenth century as in the seventeenth; they
had passed the zenith of their power. For this it is not difficult
to account. From William the Silent to William III (and not
forgetting de Witt) they had had the advantage of being guided
by men of outstanding capacity. After William III's death in
1702 the stadtholderate was in abeyance for many years, and
the republic was controlled by lesser men. Further, common
hostility towards France in the last few years of the seventeenth
century and the early years of the eighteenth had drawn the
United Provinces into alliance with England, and England
proved to be the predominant partner in the connection. The
Dutch lost something of their importance in Europe as their
political dependence on England, which continued until the
eighteenth century was well advanced, became patent to all.
Their resources were not exhausted, but they must have been
affected by the recurrence of lengthy and desperate wars. (In

the forty years preceding the Peace of Utrecht the Provinces were engaged for twenty-five years in war.) Their navy declined in importance by comparison with the British fleet in the eighteenth century. Their trade remained considerable, but it ceased to expand, while that of France and England grew year by year. (Towards the close of the eighteenth century the Dutch East India Company became bankrupt, while the English Company almost monopolised European trade with the East.) The Dutch were too few in numbers, their territory too small, their resources insufficient, for the United Provinces permanently to rank as one of the great powers of Europe.

CHAPTER VI

BRANDENBURG-PRUSSIA, 1640–1740

THE character of Frederick William, known to history as the Great Elector, who ruled in Brandenburg from 1640 to 1688, was unattractive. He was mean and unscrupulous—yet of outstanding ability, military, diplomatic, and administrative. His life was devoted to the aggrandisement of the electorate and to the formulation of those lines of policy which were to lead, long after his death, to the establishment in central Europe of a great military monarchy which became the leader of a united Germany, or, rather, in which the rest of Germany became absorbed. His ideal—for himself and his successors—was a strong centralised government free from constitutional checks and resting on military force, and characterised by constant territorial aggression with a view to the extension and consolidation of his dominions. The history of his reign may conveniently be divided into three parts. Until 1653 he was engaged in disentangling his dominions from the Thirty Years' War and in securing freedom from Swedish occupation; between 1653 and 1660 his attention was directed towards securing the freedom of East Prussia from either Swedish or Polish control; after 1660 he was concerned mainly, though not exclusively, in promoting the economic development and the administrative organisation of his dominions.

The territories to which Frederick William succeeded in 1640 were extensive, but they were disconnected, and to a considerable extent they were in the occupation of other powers. He succeeded, in fact, to claims rather than to territories. These lands consisted of three main blocks—Brandenburg with Pomerania, East Prussia, and the Rhenish duchies. Cleves, Mark, and Ravensburg were actually in Dutch possession; East Prussia lay under Polish suzerainty; Brandenburg itself was not free from Swedish troops, while the Swedes were firmly established in Pomerania and were not disposed to recognise the Elector's right to the province. Evidently the young Elector's initial task was to gain possession of his territories and to free them from external control.

His first achievement was the conclusion of a treaty with the Swedes in 1641, by which Brandenburg was freed from the incubus of invading armies. During the next five years Frederick William strengthened his army and reorganised the finances of the electorate, with the result that when negotiations for the termination of the Thirty Years' War were being carried on he was in a far stronger position to assert his claims than might have been expected from a review of the state of his dominions at his accession. By the terms of peace his claim to the eastern part of Pomerania was recognised, and as compensation for the loss of Western Pomerania he received the ecclesiastical territories of Minden, Halberstadt, and Camin, and he was promised the succession to the archbishopric of Magdeburg at the death of the existing administrator (which occurred in 1680). His right to the duchies of Cleves, Mark, and Ravensburg, which had been assigned to the Elector John Sigismund by the Treaty of Xanten, 1614, was also recognised, and Dutch troops were withdrawn. The Swedes were reluctant to give up Eastern Pomerania, and it was not until 1653 that Frederick William obtained full possession of the duchy. The territories of the Great Elector in 1653 were still scattered and disconnected, but a beginning had been made of the process of linking them up, and the electorate might henceforth be considered the strongest power in north Germany.

The second period of his reign was mainly concerned with his relations with Sweden and Poland, and it illustrates to the full the faithlessness which was a feature of his character when the interests of the state were in question. War broke out between Sweden and Poland in 1655, and Frederick William, who was inferior in strength to either combatant, sought opportunity to gain advantage from the quarrel. Charles Gustavus of Sweden demanded and obtained permission to land troops in Eastern Pomerania and use it as a base of operations against Poland. The Swedish King defeated John Casimir of Poland and then turned to besiege Danzig. Frederick William, assuming that Charles Gustavus was fully occupied with the siege, negotiated for a triple alliance of Denmark, Poland, and Brandenburg against Sweden. But Charles Gustavus was informed of the course of events; he withdrew from the siege of Danzig, invaded East Prussia, and, by the Treaty of Königsberg,

1656, forced the Great Elector to acknowledge the suzerainty of Sweden over East Prussia and to ally with Sweden against Poland.

In 1656, therefore, a force of Brandenburgers accompanied Charles Gustavus in a new invasion of Poland and helped the Swedes to win the Battle of Warsaw. In the meantime a Danish invasion of Sweden was being planned, and Charles

BRANDENBURG DOMINIONS

Gustavus was forced to withdraw from Poland to defend his own country. A Russian attack on East Prussia offered a plausible pretext for Frederick William to demand the assistance of his suzerain in the defence of the province. By the Treaty of Labiau, November, 1656, Charles Gustavus renounced his suzerainty of East Prussia, and sailed for Denmark.

No sooner had the King of Sweden departed than Frederick William negotiated with John Casimir of Poland, offering his alliance against Sweden in return for the Polish renunciation of sovereignty over East Prussia. The bargain was struck in the Treaty of Wehlau, 1657. Charles Gustavus was naturally angry at the conduct of the Great Elector, but for the time his hands were tied by the Danish War. Before he was free to invade East Prussia pressure was applied by England and the United Provinces upon the combatants to stop the war. Charles Gustavus died early in 1660, and soon after his death the Treaty of Oliva was entered into by Sweden, Poland, and

Brandenburg. The authority of the Great Elector in East Prussia, free from all suzerainty, was fully recognised by all the northern powers.

During the remainder of his reign the Great Elector was engaged in strengthening his authority and making it absolute, and in using that authority for the economic advancement of the territories under his control. At the beginning of his rule a Diet existed in each of the principal provinces of his dominions, and the constitutional rights of these assemblies were limitations upon electoral absolutism. He experienced little trouble with the Diet of Brandenburg, which he overcame by the simple method of refraining from summoning it to meet. The Diet of Cleves was able for a time to resist him, but at length he overawed it by the presence in the duchy of Brandenburg troops. The Diet of East Prussia gave him more trouble, since it was strong enough to assert its constitutional rights. Fortunately for Frederick William, party spirit was strong in the Diet, and he was able to play off the nobles, led by Kalkstein, against the burgher party under Rhode. Rhode was arrested in 1662, and the burghers henceforth gave little trouble. In 1663 Frederick William issued a Charter which recognised the right of the Diet to meet once in six years and to be consulted before new taxation was imposed. This was accepted by the Diet, but the Elector interpreted the document in the narrowest possible way—that rights not specified in the Charter were lost to the Diet, and that the Elector's power extended to everything not definitely prohibited in the Charter. Power was thus transferred from the assembly to the ruler, and within a few years Frederick William felt strong enough to take action against the nobles. Kalkstein was directed to withdraw to his estates, and, being accused of treason, he fled into Poland. The King of Poland refused to surrender the fugitive, and Frederick William violated Polish territory in order to arrest him. The incident might have been, but was not, followed by a Polish declaration of war, for which Frederick William was ready. Kalkstein was beheaded, and the Elector's power in East Prussia was henceforth unquestioned.

A certain amount of administrative reorganisation was undertaken by the Great Elector. He extended the jurisdiction of the Brandenburg Council of State to cover all lands subject to him. He separated military from civil finance (revenue as well as expenditure), and placed the former under the control of a minister who was directly and solely responsible to him. There existed in his dominions many local authorities with some degree of independence in the conduct of local affairs. Frederick William gathered into his own hands the right of making appointments, so that his own nominees existed to carry out his will. The system thus brought into being was the forerunner of the modern Prussian bureaucracy.

The diminution of the political power of the nobility was not accompanied by any decline in their social importance. Their authority over the peasantry remained, and the continued existence of serfdom was recognised by the Elector.

In no respect is Frederick William's claim to greatness more evident than in his religious policy. Many sovereigns have been, rightly, censured for the persecution of those opposed to them in belief, regardless of the fact that persecution was inspired by sincerity of religious conviction; others have been applauded for a toleration which was no more than the result of indifference. Frederick William presents the less common spectacle of a ruler of genuine religious feeling who followed a policy of toleration broad enough to include not only different Protestant communions but also Roman Catholics, Jews, Arians, and Socinians.

Frederick William was conscious of the necessity of developing the natural resources of his dominions. It is hardly an exaggeration to say of Berlin, after the ravaging of the electorate in the Thirty Years' War, that it was "the centre of a desert." Population had been very much reduced, and large tracts of the countryside had reverted to wilderness. Frederick William encouraged the settlement in his dominions of refugees— especially religious refugees—from other countries. Grants of land were assigned to them, and they were for a period exempted from taxation. Dutch, Flemish, and French immigrants were welcomed in large numbers, so that in after years a substantial element in the population of the electorate was of alien descent. The Revocation of the Edict of Nantes by Louis XIV in October, 1685, was answered by the issue, in the following month, of the Edict of Potsdam, which offered the Huguenots an asylum in Brandenburg. These immigrants were, as is pointed out elsewhere, skilful and industrious, and their presence in the electorate strengthened it in many ways. Agriculture was revived and horticulture was introduced; the woollen manufacture was developed; science and art were encouraged. The population was increased in numbers, and the new-comers helped to swell the ranks of the electoral army.

It was during the reign of Frederick William that Brandenburg became of importance as a military power. In his later years he maintained an army of about 30,000 men; upon this as a foundation was built the great Prussian army which was used by Frederick the Great in the wars of the eighteenth century. The Great Elector also built ships for a Prussian navy.

Frederick William was anxious to develop the overseas trade of his dominions, and he followed the example of other countries in granting trading monopolies to privileged trading companies. The Brandenburg African Trading Company was founded in 1682, with its headquarters at Königsberg, in East Prussia. Settlements were founded on the Guinea coast, but these brought the Company into conflict with the Dutch, whose hostility was fatal to the enterprise.

The foreign policy of Frederick William in the later years of his reign calls for attention. In 1667 he allied with Louis XIV, and he held aloof from the Triple Alliance of the following year. But he was alarmed at the increasingly aggressive character of Louis's policy, and he engaged in the war of 1672–8 as an ally of the Dutch. He was at first beaten by Turenne, but in 1675 he gained a great victory over Louis's allies, the Swedes, in the Battle of Fehrbellin. The battle was followed by his occupation of Western (Swedish) Pomerania, almost without resistance, and before the end of the war the Swedes had been entirely expelled. Frederick William was not permitted to retain his conquest, since Louis stood by his friends and, in the Treaty of St. Germain-en-Laye, 1679, insisted upon the restoration of Western Pomerania to Sweden, the Elector receiving an indemnity of 300,000 crowns as compensation for its loss. The importance of the campaign lay in the evidence it afforded of the decline of Swedish military power and the growth of that of Brandenburg-Prussia.

Frederick William considered that this, to him, inglorious ending of the war was due to the indifference and inertness of his allies, and especially of the Emperor. For a time he reverted to friendly terms with France, and the coolness between Emperor and Elector was so considerable that Leopold declined an offer of assistance from Brandenburg against the Turks who were threatening Vienna. But this phase in

Frederick William's policy was inevitably only temporary. The French policy of aggression, which had alienated him before, was certain to do so again. After the Truce of Regensburg, in 1684, by which Louis was confirmed in the possession of his gains through the *Chambres de Réunion*, Frederick William drew away from France. The action of the King of France against the Huguenots further estranged him. In 1685 he allied with the Dutch, and in the following year he came to an understanding with the Emperor. The way was now clear for the formation of the League of Augsburg, and when, a year or two later, William of Orange made his bid for the English crown, it was understood that the United Provinces could rely upon the protection of Brandenburg in the event of French attack. Frederick William died in 1688, before these great events had come to pass, but he had lived long enough to fix the policy to be followed by Brandenburg in the troubles which spread over Europe in the reign of his successor.

The ambition of Frederick III, who succeeded his father in 1688, was to obtain the royal title for himself and his line. This aspiration need not be regarded as either surprising or censurable. For centuries the Electors of the Holy Roman Empire had, in dignity, power, and importance, ranked far above other German princes, and they considered themselves to be not much, if at all, inferior to the kings of other countries. While this state of affairs continued, they had no reason to aspire to a title which would add little or nothing to their rank. But in 1648 the sacred circle of seven Electors was enlarged by the addition of an eighth (Bavaria), and in 1692 of a ninth (Hanover). Moreover, before the end of the century there was some prospect of these upstart electorates being associated with monarchies. Only the death of Joseph Ferdinand, Electoral Prince of Bavaria, in 1699 prevented his succession to the throne of Spain, and only the slender thread of the life of the Duke of Gloucester hindered the Elector of Hanover from being placed in the line of succession to the English crown. Of the older electorates, Bohemia (now in the possession of the Emperor) had from the first been a kingdom, and Saxony after 1697 was associated with the Polish crown. It could hardly be regarded as unreasonable for the Margrave-Elector of Brandenburg to aspire to monarchical dignity.

Frederick III supported the allies in the War of the League of Augsburg, but was disappointed at his failure to secure recognition as a king in the Treaty of Ryswick. When, a year or two later, the Emperor was desirous of his assistance in the War of the Spanish Succession he determined to secure his reward beforehand, and he demanded recognition as a king. The Emperor Leopold was reluctant to confer upon the powerful north German electorate the status of a monarchy, but he realised that if he wanted the Elector's army to fight for him he must pay the Elector's price. As a concession to appearances, however, he stipulated that the royal title should be associated with Hohenzollern territories beyond the boundary of the Empire. Frederick agreed to this, and became Frederick I, King of Prussia. His title was admitted at once by the allies, and the recognition was extended and became general by the Peace of Utrecht. He was crowned with elaborate ceremonial in 1701, at Königsberg.

In his treaty with the Emperor, Frederick promised to send a body of 8,000 men to support the Imperial cause in the Spanish Succession War. In the course of the war the Brandenburg contingent attained a strength of 40,000, and it served with distinction in the great battles in the Netherlands. Frederick was also involved in the war between Charles XII of Sweden and Peter the Great; in this he met with little success.

Frederick tried to model his court on that of Versailles; there was a considerable advance in dignity, in splendour and ostentation, and in the development of etiquette, in the course of his reign. He was interested in learning; he founded the University of Halle in 1694, and in later years he established the Berlin Academies of Arts and of Sciences, in imitation of existing French institutions.

Almost the last trace of Imperial control over the dominions of the King-Elector was removed by the discontinuance of appeals from the electoral courts to the Imperial Chamber. A Supreme Court of Appeal was set up in Berlin to hear cases remitted from courts in any part of the Hohenzollern dominions.

The reign of Frederick I witnessed a continuance of the economic progress which had been begun in the time of his father. Frederick maintained the Great Elector's policy of religious toleration. The immigration of refugees from France and elsewhere was still encouraged, and the population of Brandenburg increased, while industry and trade made steady progress.

Frederick William I succeeded his father as King of Prussia and Elector of Brandenburg in 1713. Under him the re-organisation of the Prussian administrative system was carried further. The Council of State which had replaced the Brandenburg Diet in the time of the Great Elector continued to exist, but much of the detailed work of administration was entrusted to an inner council which consisted of the Ministers of Finance, Foreign Affairs, and War and Justice. Local officials were appointed by the Crown, so that the King's authority was respected in every part of his dominions.

The reign of Frederick William I is remembered for the expansion of the Prussian army. It attained a strength of 80,000, which was larger, in proportion to the population of the state, than that of any other country of Europe. It was recruited by conscription, rigorously enforced upon nobles and peasantry alike, the former being compelled to serve as officers and the latter in the ranks. Discipline was enforced with brutal severity.

The cost of the army, to which everything else was subor-dinated, was a heavy burden upon the finances of the kingdom. The splendour and extravagance which characterised the court of Frederick I disappeared. Rigid economy was practised at court and in all departments of state other than the War Office, and the weight of taxation was heavy. The control of the finances and the command of the army were retained by the King.

Frederick William continued the policy of his line in en-couraging immigration. People from other German states and from other countries were attracted to settle in East Prussia by promises of exemption, for a period of years, from taxation and military service. They were granted leases of lands on the royal domain; the efficient management of domain lands added substantially to the royal revenue in the later years of the reign. Manufactures, especially clothweaving, were developed, and a system of government control was established for the purpose of raising the standard of production. A good deal of the cloth manufactured in Brandenburg was exported to Russia.

The control of a large army made Frederick William a person of importance in the diplomatic activity of the time, and his friendship was sought on all sides. Nevertheless, he took little or no part in the wars of the period, and contemporary sovereigns may have been a little contemptuous of a king who devoted so much of his revenue to the maintenance of an army which he would never risk in war. But the power which he was building up and which he declined to dissipate was passed on to his son Frederick the Great, who was able to use it for the establishment of Prussia as one of the great powers of Europe.

CHAPTER VII

THE EARLIER PART OF LOUIS XV'S REIGN

LOUIS XIV was succeeded by his great-grandson, Louis XV, a child five years of age. The person marked out by his rank to be Regent was Philip, Duke of Orleans, nephew of the old King and next to Louis XV in succession to the throne. Louis XIV disliked his nephew, and though in his will he nominated Orleans to the Regency he imposed restrictions upon his power and associated with him a Council of Regency to which real authority was to be assigned. The two previous Bourbon reigns had begun with regencies; in each case the preceding king had made arrangements which had been disregarded at his death. Orleans resolved to follow the precedents established by Marie de Medici in 1610 and Anne of Austria in 1643, and the Parlement of Paris, upon being appealed to, annulled Louis XIV's will and recognised the Duke as Regent with full powers.

The death of Louis XIV marks the close of an epoch in both the foreign policy and the domestic government of France. Louis's foreign policy was reversed, and in the internal administration of France the Regency abandoned the principles which had prevailed during the reign of *Le Grand Monarque*. Louis XIV was devout and austere, Philip was profligate; Louis was orthodox and intolerant, Philip a freethinker who was inclined to suppress the Jesuits and patronise Jansenists and Huguenots; Louis employed as his ministers men not of noble birth, Philip selected aristocrats for the chief posts in the administration. The Regent was a man of ability and intelligence, but his character was marred by indulgence in the grossest vices.

A new administrative system was evolved by the Regent. In the time of Louis XIV each department of government was in charge of a minister who reported directly to the King and received instructions from him. Orleans placed at the head of each department a Council instead of a single minister. Each Council consisted of about ten members, who, for the most part, were great nobles. The function of the Councils was to advise the Regent, with whom, in any important question, final decision rested; it is obvious that, with an easy-going and indolent head of the state, their real power was considerable. The Councils were seven in number; they controlled, respectively, Foreign Affairs, Finance, War, Navy, Commerce, Home Affairs, and Religion. The new system did not work well. The nobles possessed little aptitude for public business, and much of their time was occupied in the consideration of points of etiquette. In 1718 the Councils were abolished, and the Regent reverted to Louis's system of a single minister responsible for each department.

The failure of the nobles to co-operate satisfactorily in the work of government was not the only difficulty which beset Orleans. The religious controversies of the late reign were not extinct, and the attitude of the Parlement of Paris to these questions brought it into conflict with the Regent. After the wars of Louis XIV the finances were in the utmost disorder and demanded the most careful attention. Further, the changed circumstances of the time demanded a new orientation of French foreign policy; in this respect, the Regent for a time was able to carry with him neither the people of France nor his leading advisers.

Louis XIV did not live long enough after the issue of the Bull *Unigenitus* to effect a final suppression of the Jansenists, and his successor reversed his policy. The Jesuits fell into disfavour, and Father Le Tellier, Louis's confessor and close adviser, was exiled. Cardinal Noailles, Archbishop of Paris, whose inclination towards Jansenism was well known, became head of the Council of Religion, and many Jansenists were released from prison. Controversy continued, however, and a compromise was at length reached between the Pope and Noailles. The Cardinal agreed to a modified interpretation of the *Unigenitus*, and ordered its acceptance. This was agreed to by the Parlement of Paris, but a number of bishops and clergy held out. Dubois, who exercised great influence over the Regent, wished to conciliate the Jesuits and the papacy, as he was aspiring to the cardinalate, and the dissident ecclesiastics were ejected or imprisoned.

This was not the end of the struggle. Jansenism still lingered on, and many religious people were convinced that the condemnation of the *Moral Reflections* and the *Augustinus* in the

Bull *Unigenitus* was without justification. Others supported the movement through antagonism towards the Jesuits, and without understanding the theological points at issue. The Sorbonne was orthodox, and supported the Jesuits; the Parlement, in its hatred of the Order, continued to champion Jansenism. A revival of controversy led to the King holding a *lit de justice* in 1730 and ordering the registration of all papal Bulls against Jansenism. The movement lingered on in a debased and even squalid form; miracles were reported as having happened through the agency of reputed Jansenists, and religious fervour degenerated into gross superstition. The reaction from this state of affairs did not lead men back to orthodoxy; rather, it contributed to the agnosticism which was so widespread in the France of the eighteenth century.

The finances of France in the time of the Regency were, as stated above, in a serious condition. The public debt was colossal, and revenue failed to balance expenditure. Orleans was unwilling to go to the length of formal repudiation of the debt, but a tribunal was established to investigate the conduct of the financiers, many of whom were ordered to refund large sums of money. Some loans were cancelled, and the interest on others was reduced, but the state gained little from such measures, since their effect was to lower the public credit. Some attempt was made to reduce public expenditure, but that of the court was untouched, and no material improvement was effected in the financial position.

John Law, a Scot, laid certain proposals before the Regent at this time. He was a man of considerable ability, who had had an adventurous career, in the course of which he had lived in several countries and had paid much attention to the principles of public finance. He had observed the success of the Bank of Amsterdam and the Bank of England; he believed that the prosperity of the United Provinces and of Great Britain depended upon the proper organisation of the credit of these countries.

He put forward a two-fold plan. He wished to establish a national Bank of France which might issue paper money in large quantities. He realised that this currency would not maintain its value unless confidence was maintained, and that this would involve the holding of securities in reserve. But he thought that property of any kind would serve equally well with bullion and specie as security for the issue of paper currency. His second, and greater, project was the foundation of a company which, controlled by the state, should monopolise the commerce of France. All private ventures would be extinguished or would be merged in the company. From its profits the state would be able to pay off its debt, meet its expenses, and reduce and ultimately discontinue taxation.

In 1716 Law was permitted to establish a private bank. Its issue of notes was not excessive; they circulated readily, and in course of time the Regent ordered that they should be accepted in payment of taxes. The bank thus prospered, and two years after its foundation it was transformed into a State Bank.

Meanwhile, in 1717, the Company of the West was founded, with a capital of one hundred million livres. Law's ultimate aim was to secure for it a monopoly of all the foreign trade of France. It was granted the exclusive right to trade with Louisiana, which was granted exemption from taxation for twenty-five years. Within a few months the Company acquired the tobacco monopoly, from which tremendous profits were anticipated, and in the course of a year or so it absorbed the Senegal Company, the East India Company, and the China Company.

The great success which attended the early stages of these ventures encouraged Law to embark upon new measures. The Company acquired the control of the mint; it secured from the Government the monopoly of farming indirect taxation; it lent the Government the sum of 1,500 million livres at three per cent to pay off the National Debt, itself thus becoming the sole creditor of the state.

In February, 1720, the Bank and the Company were amalgamated under Law's management. Hitherto, as a Protestant, he had been ineligible for any public appointment. This technical disqualification was removed by his formal conversion to Roman Catholicism, and he was appointed Controller-General of the Finances. In order to meet the expenses which faced the Company the Bank made large new issues of paper money, and the Company issued fresh shares which were eagerly sought. A speculative frenzy set in, and the price of the shares rose to many times their nominal value. This was a feature of the movement which Law had not foreseen, and he tried to check it without damaging the credit of the Company. But when the price of shares began to decline the fall was as rapid as the rise had been, and though many speculators made fortunes by selling at the right time many thousands of people were ruined. Within a short time the shares of the Company were unsaleable, and there was a run on the Bank to secure payment of its notes. The Bank was unable to meet the demands on its resources, and the disaster was complete. In December, 1720, Law left the country. The Government reassumed responsibility for its debt, but at a reduced rate of interest. The Bank was abolished, though the Company survived as a private trading concern. The finances of France were in as bad condition as before the bubble, and France produced no Walpole to set them in order.

The foreign policy of France during the Regency was to a great extent under the control of Dubois, a man not of noble birth, who was naturally disliked by the nobles of the court. He had been tutor of Orleans, and for many years he acted as secretary to his former pupil. His private life was profligate, but his political influence over the Regent was exercised wisely, and in the interests of the country. His tenure of office as foreign minister was marked by a diplomatic revolution of great importance.

The young king, Louis XV, was not expected to survive for many years, and the question of succession to the throne of France occupied the attention of statesmen of the time. The nearest relative to Louis XV was his uncle, Philip V, King of Spain, who had been compelled to renounce all right of succession to the crown of France when peace was concluded at Utrecht. Next in the line of succession to Philip V stood the Regent. It was clearly to the interest of Orleans to maintain the Utrecht settlement intact; of Philip V, to overthrow it. For this reason it was inevitable that France and Spain should find themselves in opposition to one another. In Great Britain, also, the throne of George I was by no means secure, though the lack of success attendant upon the 1715 revolt showed that the number of people who were willing to replace George by the Pretender James was not great. Nevertheless, the position and the interests of George I and the Regent were sufficiently similar to suggest the possibility of an alliance. This was the project which Dubois fostered, so that the alliance of France and Spain against Great Britain in the last fifteen years of Louis XIV's reign was followed by an alliance of France and Great Britain against Spain in the first fifteen years of that of his successor.

Some difficulty was experienced in bringing the negotiations to a successful issue, since George was suspicious of the Regent's attitude towards the Pretender. Dubois had a personal interview with Lord Stanhope at The Hague, and another with the King himself in Hanover. At length difficulties were overcome, and the Triple Alliance of Great Britain, Holland, and France was formed in 1717. (Holland, rapidly declining to the rank of a second-rate power, followed Great Britain.) Philip undertook to demolish the fortifications at Mardyck, near Dunkirk, to secure the expulsion of the Pretender from Avignon (whither he had withdrawn after the Peace of Utrecht), and not to permit him to return to France. Great Britain promised to assist in the maintenance of the Peace of Utrecht in whatever concerned the crown of France, and France promised to maintain the Protestant succession in Great Britain.

The new turn of events was to be commended. It brought to an end the diplomatic isolation of France, and provided her with powerful allies. Although some fighting occurred within the next year or two, in the main the Alliance was a guarantee of European peace, which remained unbroken by a major war for the next sixteen years—the longest spell of peace enjoyed by Europe during the eighteenth century. Nevertheless, the Triple Alliance was unpopular in France, where public opinion in general regarded the King of Spain as heir to the French throne, and only the firm support of the Regent averted Dubois's fall from power. The Alliance was opposed by the Council for Foreign Affairs, a circumstance which, no doubt, contributed to influence the Regent in his decision to abolish the Council system. Dubois was appointed Minister for Foreign Affairs.

The Emperor was at first indignant at the conclusion of the Triple Alliance. Far from approving the Utrecht settlement, he also wished to overthrow it, though not for the reason which appealed to the King of Spain. But the activity of Spain caused him to realise that his interest lay with the maritime powers and France, and in 1718 he joined the Triple Alliance, making it Quadruple.

Alberoni, the chief minister at the court of Spain, was unwilling to embark upon a European war at this time, but his hands were forced. The arrest of a Spanish Inquisitor-General in Milan by the Emperor's orders was treated as an insult to Spain not to be tolerated. In 1717 a naval expedition was successful against Sardinia, which was conquered, and in the following year a Spanish army landed in Sicily and overran the island. By the Treaty of Utrecht Sicily had been assigned to the Duke of Savoy, and its conquest was undertaken in order to anticipate its threatened occupation by the Emperor. Although Great Britain and Spain were not at war, a British fleet in the Mediterranean, under Admiral Byng, destroyed the Spanish fleet at the Battle of Cape Passaro, and the army in Sicily was isolated from Spain.

Meanwhile, Alberoni prepared to support the cause of the Pretender against George I, and he induced Charles XII of Sweden to prepare for an attack upon the British coast. The death of Charles in 1718 put an end to any possibility of danger to Great Britain from this source. At the end of 1718 Great Britain, and early in 1719 France, declared war against Spain. The French invaded Spain, and the British fleet attacked Spanish ports and shipping. Spain was in no condition to resist. As a preliminary to negotiations for peace Alberoni was dismissed from office and exiled from Spain. By the Treaty of London, 1720, Philip agreed to join the Quadruple Alliance, thus by implication announcing his adhesion to the general arrangements agreed upon in the Peace of Utrecht.

Dubois received his cardinalate in 1721, and in 1722 he was granted the title of First Minister of France, which had been in abeyance for many years. With every year that passed the question of the succession became less pressing, since the anticipated death of Louis XV did not occur, and Dubois began to consider the possibility of reviving Franco-Spanish friendship. To this end the King was betrothed to a Spanish Infanta, Maria (then five years old), in 1721, and the princess was sent to be brought up in France. Louis was declared to be of age in February, 1723, when he reached the age of thirteen years. The Regency thus came to an end. Dubois retained the title of First Minister until his death in August of the same year. Orleans then occupied the post, but he died in December.

Fleury, Bishop of Fréjus, and tutor to the young King, exercised great influence over him. He might have become First Minister, but he declined the position and recommended the nomination of the Duke of Bourbon to the vacant dignity, which, in view of the King's tender years, was practically a regency. Bourbon disliked the Duke of Orleans, son of the late Regent, who, while Louis XV was unmarried and childless, was heir to the French throne. There was no possibility of Louis being married to the Infanta Maria for several years, and Bourbon was anxious for an immediate marriage. He therefore cancelled the betrothal, sent the Infanta back to Spain, and arranged a marriage between Louis and Maria Leszczynska, daughter of Stanislaus Leszczynski, an ex-King of Poland. The marriage was celebrated in 1725. The affront thus offered to Spain hindered that revival of Franco-Spanish friendship which had been meditated in the last few months of Dubois's life, and the Anglo-French alliance continued for some years longer.

During the ministry of Bourbon an attempt was made to levy a *cinquantième*, an income-tax of two per cent on all revenues, irrespective of privilege. The protests of nobles and clergy were so vigorous that the tax was withdrawn in 1727. The importance of the incident lies in the evidence it affords of the inability of the Government to compel the privileged classes to contribute to the national revenue. Another proposal, to strengthen the national forces by systematic conscription, was abandoned.

Bourbon was jealous of the influence of Fleury over the King, who was accustomed to consult the Bishop on matters of state. He made two attempts to secure Fleury's exile from court. He was unsuccessful. On the second occasion Fleury withdrew from the court, and the King requested him to return. Fleury did so, on condition of the dismissal of Bourbon. Fleury, seventy-three years old, became First Minister and held that position until his death in 1743, in his ninetieth year.

Fleury's aim was to maintain peace and to promote the prosperity of France. In this respect he was comparable with his contemporary, Walpole, in Great Britain, and so long as these two ministers held office there was little likelihood of the understanding between France and Great Britain coming to an end. During his tenure of office there was a great expansion of French trade. He made an attempt similar to, but less successful than, that of Walpole in Great Britain to strengthen the finances of France. Like all other pre-Revolution statesmen in France, he was unable to touch the roots of the evil—

the expenses of the court and the privileges of the nobles and clergy. In other directions he endeavoured to promote strict economy, and he is open to the charge of having neglected the army and navy.

In the latter part of his ministry his influence at court was not unchallenged, and his foreign policy was criticised by a war party which wished for a reversion to the traditional Bourbon hostility to the Hapsburgs. This party, led by Villars, was not interested in the maintenance of the Anglo-French *entente*, and preferred a policy of Franco-Spanish co-operation, with Turkish assistance, against the Emperor. Fleury, by himself, might have preferred an understanding with the Emperor, anticipating the policy afterwards associated with the name of Kaunitz, but the war party was too strong for him, and his hand was forced.

Fleury has been criticised for not foreseeing the Franco-British struggle in India and for his inability to realise the inherent antagonism of the colonial aims of Great Britain and France. Had he done so he might have appreciated the desirability of closer connection with Spain against Great Britain. But it is at least arguable that the colonial aspirations of France and Great Britain were not as irreconcilable as is commonly assumed and that the unsettled regions of the world were extensive enough to satisfy the legitimate claims of both powers. It is not suggested that this was Fleury's view, but it might have received more attention had his successors tried to keep the Anglo-French *entente* in existence. If it be true that Fleury did not grasp the importance of overseas enterprise, it is equally true that when his political opponents succeeded him in office they also failed to appreciate it. They also limited their attention to affairs in Europe; it was left to British statesmen to take the wider view.

CHAPTER VIII

PHILIP V AND ELIZABETH FARNESE

THE first part of the reign of Philip V was occupied with the War of the Spanish Succession. He did not obtain general recognition as King of Spain until the Peace of Utrecht was concluded, and even then it was withheld by the Emperor, his rival. Philip's first wife, Maria Louisa of Savoy, died in 1714, having borne him two sons, Don Luis and Don Ferdinand. Before the end of the same year he married Elizabeth Farnese, niece and step-daughter of Francesco Farnese, Duke of Parma, and by her also he was the father of two sons, Don Carlos and Don Philip. The history of Spain, and, indeed, that of Europe, during the latter part of Philip's rule, is concerned with the political and dynastic ambitions of the Spanish King and Queen.

Philip regarded the terms of the Peace of Utrecht with great dissatisfaction, and for many years he schemed to secure their revision. The renunciation of his rights of succession to the throne of France sat lightly upon him, and his determination to make a bid for the French crown in the event of the early decease of Louis XV involved Spain and France in antagonism and even in open hostility which did not disappear until after the marriage of Louis and the birth of a Dauphin. Philip desired to recover the lost possessions of Spain in Europe, and this kept him in a state of hostility towards the Emperor, who for many years maintained his own claim to the throne of Spain, and towards the maritime powers, which were resolved to uphold the Utrecht settlement. The turmoil into which Europe was plunged by these conflicting aims was complicated by the aspirations of the Queen, Elizabeth, on behalf of her two sons. Succession to the throne of Spain would naturally fall to Don Luis, and, after his death in 1725, to Don Ferdinand. Elizabeth was determined to secure for her two sons principalities in Italy. Neither of her two uncles, Francesco Farnese, Duke of Parma, and his brother Antonio Farnese, had a son, and she hoped to obtain that duchy for one of the boys. By virtue of her descent from the Medici she hoped to secure for him also the reversion of Tuscany. In course of time she schemed to obtain, in addition, the kingdom of Naples, now in the Emperor's possession. It cannot be asserted that her plans were evolved as a complete scheme at any one time, but she took advantage of every circumstance to further her aims, and her influence must be regarded as for many years a factor inimical to the maintenance of peace in Europe.

Alberoni, an Italian and a Cardinal, was chief minister of Spain for only five years—from 1715 to 1720—but during that time he initiated many valuable reforms. He was given general charge of all departments of the administration. His financial reforms resulted in an increase of revenue and a diminution of expenditure; agriculture, commerce, and industry were revived; a real effort was made to develop the internal resources of Spain, so long neglected; the army was re-organised and the navy was strengthened; ships were built and arsenals established; communications were improved. He was in general sympathy with the aims of the King and Queen, and he regarded the regeneration of Spain as a necessary pre-liminary to any attempt to carry them out. For the full development of his internal reforms Alberoni hoped for a period of ten years, or at least of five, of peace. This was denied him. The impatience of Philip and Elizabeth in the pursuit of their schemes abroad hindered the revival which might otherwise have taken place. Yet his work was not without effect, and it may be noted that the Italian aims of the King and Queen, with which Alberoni was especially in sympathy, were ultimately carried into effect.

Alberoni, dependent upon the King and Queen for con-tinuance in office, was unable to follow the foreign policy of his choice. He was not disposed to encourage Philip's hopes of succession to the throne of France; he preferred to support the anti-Hapsburg aims of Elizabeth in Italy. For a time he seemed to be seeking an understanding with Great Britain, but the interests of the maritime powers required that Philip should be held in check, and the conclusion of the Triple Alliance, followed by the Quadruple Alliance, left Spain almost isolated, her only ally being Sweden.

The Triple Alliance was a diplomatic defeat for Alberoni. Nevertheless, he continued his policy of internal reform in

Spain, hoping that hostilities might be avoided as long as possible. This was not to be. In May, 1717, the action of the Emperor in ordering the arrest of Cardinal Molines, Spanish Inquisitor-General, who happened to be travelling in Lombardy, provoked an outbreak of war which Alberoni was powerless to prevent. A Spanish fleet was dispatched to Sardinia, which was conquered within a few weeks. The Duke of Savoy, who since the Peace of Utrecht had been King of Sicily, was at this time negotiating with the Emperor for an exchange of islands, and in 1718 the Spanish fleet sailed for Sicily also, and troops occupied the island.

These events were generally regarded as indications of an aggressive Spanish policy. It should be observed, however, that the original provocation to war came from the Emperor, who, moreover, was hoping to arrange for the exchange of Sicily and Sardinia. This would be a breach of the Utrecht settlement; the Emperor's possession of Sicily would weaken the position of Spain in the Mediterranean, so that the movements of the Spanish fleet might be regarded as legitimate acts of war of a nature essentially defensive. It may be noticed, also, that both Sardinia and Sicily had been connected with the Crown of Aragon since the fifteenth century; the people were Spanish in sentiment, and Spanish rule was more popular than Austrian or Savoyard. Nevertheless, the attack on Sicily was a mistake, in that it bore an appearance of aggression which was certain to arouse the hostility of the maritime powers. Negotiations were opened with Sweden for the purpose of bringing about a diversion in the north of Europe; it was suggested that Charles XII should launch an attack upon Bremen and Verden, Swedish duchies in the Empire which had been occupied by Hanoverian troops, and that a descent upon the British coast in the interests of the Pretender should be arranged. A strong British fleet in the Baltic prevented the execution of these plans, and another British fleet in the Mediterranean, under Admiral Byng, attacked and destroyed the Spanish fleet off Cape Passaro. War had not yet been declared, but last-minute efforts to reach a settlement failed; at the end of 1718 Great Britain, and in January, 1719, France, declared war on Spain.

The Spanish coast was harried by the British fleet, and a French army entered Spain. Austrian troops invaded Sicily and conquered the island. But the war was not unduly prolonged. As a preliminary to the discussion of terms of peace the allies insisted upon the dismissal and exile of Alberoni. By the Treaty of London Philip was forced to accept the aims of the Quadruple Alliance in maintaining the general terms of the Utrecht settlement. It was agreed that Sicily should remain in the Emperor's hands in exchange for Sardinia, which was to pass to the Duke of Savoy, henceforth King of Sardinia. Other questions at issue between Spain and the Emperor were postponed for settlement at a Congress to be held at Cambray. The treaty was followed by an arrangement that the King of France should marry an Infanta of Spain, and for a year or two there appeared to be some prospect of a revival of Franco-Spanish friendship.

This hope was premature. Dubois wished to restore amity between France and Spain without sacrificing the Anglo-French understanding, and the Duke of Bourbon, who followed him, at first carried on a similar policy. This could not be maintained, however. Bourbon was eager to bring about the immediate marriage of Louis XV to Maria Leszczynska in order to destroy any prospect of an Orleanist succession to the French throne, and he broke off the Spanish marriage project, sending the Infanta back to Spain. On the other hand, Elizabeth Farnese was impatient at the slow progress of her plans towards maturity, and she was contemplating an Austrian alliance. It was inevitable that Franco-Spanish hostility should remain and that the alliance of Great Britain and France should continue.

Elizabeth was ready to entertain the idea of an alliance with the Emperor. The approach of France in 1721 had produced no result; France was unlikely to assist either in the recovery of Gibraltar or the establishment of Don Carlos in Parma. Charles VI, also, was prepared to consider the advantages of an alliance with Spain. He had no male heir, and he had prepared a document, the Pragmatic Sanction, which asserted the right of his daughter, Maria Theresa, to the succession to the whole of the Hapsburg dominions. He hoped to obtain for the Pragmatic Sanction the guarantee of every European power; a Spanish alliance would secure for his plan the support of Spain. Moreover, in order to develop the trade of the Austrian Netherlands he had established an East India Company with its headquarters at Ostend, a proceeding viewed with disfavour by the maritime powers; through an understanding with Spain important trading privileges might be granted to the venture.

Negotiations were carried on at Vienna by Ripperda, a man of Dutch extraction, who for a short time exercised great influence at the court of Spain.   In 1725 a treaty, since known as the First Treaty of Vienna, was concluded, by which the Emperor renounced his claim to the throne of Spain and recognised Philip V, recognised the right of Don Carlos to the succession in Parma and Piacenza, and promised to use his good offices for the recovery of Gibraltar by Spain.   Philip undertook to guarantee the Pragmatic Sanction and granted certain trading rights to the Ostend East India Company.   By secret articles agreed to afterwards marriages were arranged between the two sons of Philip and Elizabeth and the two daughters of the Emperor.

The result of this singular alliance between two ancient enemies was a renewal of the league of powers hostile to Spain. By the Treaty of Hanover, Great Britain, France, and Prussia agreed to oppose the aims of the Vienna alliance and, especially, to prevent the aggrandisement of the Ostend East India Company; this group of powers was soon strengthened by the adhesion of the United Provinces, Denmark, and Sweden. Other powers joined one or other of the alliances, and the stage was set for a European war in which, in addition to the questions immediately involved, other matters might call for settlement— matters such as the expulsion of the Turks from Europe, the restoration of the Stuarts in Great Britain, and the extension of Catholicism.

Yet no general European war occurred at this time.   Prussia soon changed sides; in 1726 the King reached an understanding with the Emperor and gave his adhesion to the Pragmatic Sanction.   Spain was in no condition to wage war effectively, though the reforms initiated by Alberoni were being continued by Ripperda, who, however, fell from power in 1726.   (The inability or unwillingness of Philip and Elizabeth to give consistent and prolonged support to statesmen of ability was a factor detrimental to the recovery by Spain of her former status in Europe.)   On the other side, neither France nor Great Britain was eager for war.   A British fleet blockaded Porto Bello, and the Spanish attacked Gibraltar.   But the Emperor gave no assistance to his ally, and coolness sprang up between them.   The fall of Bourbon in France and of Ripperda in

Spain paved the way for a reconciliation between the Bourbon powers which Fleury was genuinely anxious to bring about without sacrificing the British alliance. His influence was thus on the side of peace, which was concluded by preliminaries signed in 1727 and confirmed in 1728. Gibraltar remained in British possession, and the privileges of the Ostend East India Company were suspended.

The Austro-Spanish alliance was thus shown to be of little value as a means of furthering the aims of Elizabeth Farnese. The birth of the Dauphin in 1729 virtually extinguished the dynastic difficulties which lay in the way of a Franco-Spanish alliance, and the Spanish Queen sought and obtained an alliance with France and Great Britain which was registered in the Treaty of Seville. The Spanish claim to Gibraltar and Minorca was tacitly dropped, the privileges granted to the Ostend Company by the Vienna treaty were discontinued, and the powers agreed to support the claim of Don Carlos to the Parmesan succession.

It was not at first certain that this new grouping of the powers would endure. There was a strong body of opinion in Great Britain which held that British interests demanded an alliance with the Emperor, who had no colonial ambitions to conflict with those of Great Britain, rather than with the Bourbon powers. In 1731 matters were brought to a head by the death of the Duke of Parma. Charles sent his troops into the duchies, and war appeared to be inevitable. Though Fleury was unable to move, war was averted by Walpole, who offered to guarantee the Pragmatic Sanction in return for the Emperor's recognition of the succession of Don Carlos. The bait was too tempting for Charles to resist, and in the Second Treaty of Vienna, 1731, he recognised Don Carlos as Duke of Parma and withdrew his support from the Ostend East India Company; in return, Great Britain and Holland guaranteed the Pragmatic Sanction. Before the end of the year Don Carlos was in possession of the duchies.

For the moment the condition of Europe appeared to be more tranquil than at almost any time since the conclusion of the Peace of Utrecht. Philip V's ambition to secure the crown of France was necessarily a thing of the past, and France and Spain were in a condition of friendship, with no important questions at issue between them. Elizabeth had realised her aim with regard to Don Carlos, and Spain had acquired a foot-

hold in Italy, where the Emperor's position had been weakened.
Spain had recovered some of her strength and much of her
prestige, and she was again a power to be reckoned with in
Europe. The apprehension of the maritime powers with

ITALY IN THE EIGHTEENTH CENTURY

regard to the danger to their trade from the Ostend East India
Company had been allayed.

The tranquillity of Europe at this time was only superficial.
The rivalry of Spain and the Emperor for predominance in
Italy had not only not been allayed but had become intensified
by Spanish success in the Parmesan question. In both France
and Spain there were strong parties aiming at the establishment

of a close connection between the two countries, and this, if it should come into existence, could not fail to be to the detriment of British trade. The friction between Spain and Great Britain arising out of the abuses connected with South American trade was growing more acute year by year. Any trivial cause might be sufficient to bring about a European war. It was supplied by the death of Augustus II, King of Poland, in February, 1733.

Louis XV was resolved to secure the election of his father-in-law, Stanislaus Leszczynski, to the vacant throne; the candidate favoured by the Emperor was the son of the late King, Augustus, Elector of Saxony. Alliances were formed on both sides. The Saxon Elector was supported by Russia as well as Austria, while Stanislaus was backed by France, Spain, and Sardinia. Walpole refused to be drawn into the conflict. French efforts to bring Turkey into the war against the eastern powers met with little success; by the time the long-drawn-out negotiations were approaching a favourable issue the war was over.

Stanislaus was elected King of Poland in September, 1733. The problem which faced France was not to secure his election but to maintain him on the throne when chosen. It would not be easy to send a French force to Poland either by land or sea, and the only practicable aid which the French could give to their nominee would be in the form of an attack upon the Emperor's possessions elsewhere. This did not prevent the invasion of Poland by Russian and Saxon armies and the enthronement of Augustus III. Stanislaus retired to Danzig, where he was besieged for some months. A French brigade landed and helped to prolong the resistance of the city, but upon its capture, in June, 1734, Stanislaus fled into Prussia, and the Polish aspect of the war was over.

It is needless to point out that the succession to the throne of Poland was not the only, nor even the chief, question at issue in the War of the Polish Succession. The alliance of France and Spain in 1733, known as the First Family Compact, was concerned with common action against Great Britain and the Emperor quite as much as with Poland. In addition to the mutual guarantee of their possessions against attack by either Great Britain or the Emperor, the Bourbon powers undertook to support Don Carlos in Parma and Piacenza and to recognise his right to the succession in Tuscany. Commercial privileges were conceded by each to the other, and they undertook not to make peace nor to negotiate about the Pramatic Sanction separately.

The allies met with a considerable degree of success in the war in the west of Europe. The Sardinians overran the Milanese, and Don Carlos marched through the Papal States and conquered the kingdom of Naples, following up his victory with the annexation of Sicily. Further fighting occurred in the north of Italy and on the Rhine, but in 1735 negotiations for peace between France and the Emperor were begun. Before the end of the year the Third Treaty of Vienna was signed, though it was not ratified until 1738 and was not accepted by Spain and Naples until 1739.

Augustus III was recognised as King of Poland, and Stanislaus withdrew his claim. Certain territorial rearrangements in the west of Europe were made. It was assumed by French diplomats that the Emperor's daughter, Maria Theresa, would marry Francis Stephen, Duke of Lorraine, and that in due course he would be chosen Emperor. The possession of Lorraine by the Emperor would be a menace to France, and it was decided that at the death of the Grand Duke of Tuscany Francis should succeed him and surrender Lorraine, which would be given to Stanislaus for the term of his life as compensation for the loss of Poland. Stanislaus was to receive the duchy of Bar at once, and at his death Lorraine and Bar were to be annexed to the crown of France. Don Carlos, to whom the Tuscan succession had been promised, was to be confirmed in possession of the kingdom of the Two Sicilies, which he had already conquered. Parma and Piacenza were to be surrendered to the Emperor, who was to recover the Milanese, except Tortona and Novara, which were to be ceded to the King of Sardinia. France undertook to guarantee the Pragmatic Sanction.

The treaty might be regarded as satisfactory to most of the powers engaged in the war. The Emperor's candidate had gained the Polish throne, and Charles had secured important guarantees—France, Poland, and Saxony—for the Pragmatic Sanction. Though he had lost the kingdom of the Two Sicilies he had gained Parma and Tuscany, and the change was in the direction of consolidation of his Italian possessions. The ultimate gain of Lorraine by France was to the advantage of that country, and the establishment of Don Carlos as King of the Two Sicilies gratified the pride of Spain in the virtual recovery of a lost possession, besides enhancing her reputation as a great power.   Elizabeth Farnese, indeed, was angry at the conduct of France in hastening on the peace negotiations and at the abandonment of Parma and Piacenza.   This aspect of the settlement caused for a time an estrangement between Spain and France.

Some other features of the war deserve attention.   The close alliance of Russia and Austria was important, and the emergence of Russia as a European power was demonstrated to all.   The weakness of Poland was equally evident, and it could be only a matter of time before she would be partitioned.   Sardinia was a power of steadily increasing importance.

One other aspect of the settlement deserves notice.   It has often been remarked that the sovereigns of Europe in the eighteenth century looked upon their territories as their private estates, and that they exchanged them without regard to the interests or wishes of their people.   Kingdoms and provinces were passed from hand to hand; no thought of the desires or the welfare of the people whose allegiance was thus transferred from one potentate to another was permitted to influence the course of negotiations.   In no treaty of the eighteenth century is this characteristic more clearly exemplified than in the Third Treaty of Vienna.

CHAPTER IX

THE AUSTRIAN SUCCESSION

THE year 1740 is a landmark in the history of modern Europe. The persons who occupied the European stage in the generation following the Peace of Utrecht were replaced then, or soon after, by others, whose attention was engaged by new problems. The long reign of Philip V of Spain was drawing to a close, and his wife, Elizabeth Farnese, ceased to exert a dominating influence upon the course of events. Walpole, whose influence had for some time been declining, fell from power at the beginning of 1742, and Fleury, whose authority at the French court had long been overshadowed by that of younger men, died a year later. Three European sovereigns—the Emperor Charles VI, Frederick William I of Prussia, and the Empress Anne of Russia—died in 1740.

A period of war followed, which lasted with little inter-mission until 1763. Great Britain and Spain had already, in 1739, drifted into war in connection with abuses arising out of Central American trade, and the rivalry of Great Britain and France in India and North America and elsewhere led them into a prolonged and determined struggle for colonial, com-mercial, and naval supremacy. The accession of Maria Theresa to the Austrian dominions afforded an excellent opportunity to the enemies of her line to attempt a partition of the heterogeneous Hapsburg lands. The long-drawn-out Franco-Austrian rivalry might now end with the downfall of the Hapsburgs. Spain was ready to carry her Italian schemes to their logical completion. Prussia embarked upon that contest with Austria for supremacy in Germany for which she had long been preparing—a struggle which was to be carried on intermittently for a century and a quarter.

Charles VI succeeded his brother Joseph I as Holy Roman Emperor in 1711. He had no son to carry on his line, and his hopes were concentrated on the succession of his daughter

Maria Theresa. Not long after her birth, he drew up a document, the Pragmatic Sanction, by which he recognised her as his rightful successor in all the Hapsburg dominions, and much of his diplomatic and military activity in the latter part of his reign was directed to the acquisition of guarantees of this arrangement from the powers of Europe. Recognition of the Pragmatic Sanction was accorded by the Estates of the Emperor's dominions—of Austria in 1720, of Hungary in 1722, and of the Austrian Netherlands in 1724. In 1725 the Pragmatic Sanction was guaranteed by Spain in the First Treaty of Vienna. Russia followed in 1726, and by the Treaty of Wusterhausen in the same year Prussia gave her adhesion. Great Britain's guarantee was included in the Second Treaty of Vienna, 1731, and the Diet of the Empire assented to the Pragmatic Sanction in 1732. In 1733 the Elector of Saxony, in order to gain the Emperor's support in his candidature for the throne of Poland, dropped his wife's claim to the Austrian dominions and assented to the Pragmatic Sanction. The Third Treaty of Vienna, in 1738, secured a limited recognition from France, and when, in 1739, Sardinia and Spain acceded to the treaty they, too, accepted the Pragmatic Sanction.

In the pursuit of these paper guarantees Charles neglected more important affairs, and he remained unconvinced by Eugene's advice that the best guarantee of Maria Theresa's succession would be a strong army and a full treasury. At his death his list of guarantees was long, and he was probably convinced that he had done all that was humanly possible to secure the peaceful succession of his daughter to his dominions.

The Imperial Crown could not be disposed of in this way. It was no concern of the powers of Europe, but of the Electors. There was no precedent for the choice of a woman to occupy the Imperial throne, but in 1736 Maria Theresa had married Francis Stephen, Duke of Lorraine, who a year later became Grand Duke of Tuscany. Charles hoped that at his death the Electors would choose his son-in-law as Holy Roman Emperor, so that the Imperial Crown might remain in the Hapsburg family, although in the female line.

On the death of Charles VI in October, 1740, Maria Theresa was proclaimed Archduchess of Austria, Queen of Bohemia, and Queen of Hungary. She named her husband Francis Stephen as co-regent in her dominions, and she received the recognition of Great Britain, the United Provinces, Russia,

Prussia, Venice, Saxony, and the Pope. By some other states recognition was withheld. France delayed on a trivial pretext; Spain wished to recover the Duchy of Milan; the King of Sardinia hoped to secure an extension of territory. The Elector of Bavaria asserted a claim, through both himself and his wife, to the whole Hapsburg inheritance.

The Bavarian claim deserves examination. Leopold I at

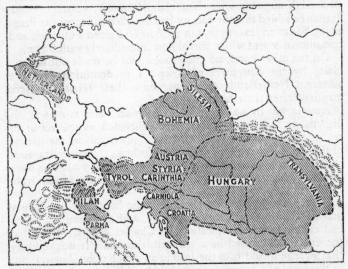

HAPSBURG DOMINIONS IN 1740

his death in 1705 left two sons, Joseph and Charles, who successively occupied the position of Emperor. Joseph had two daughters, Maria Josephine and Maria Amelia, who at his death were passed over in favour of their uncle Charles, as next male heir. Maria Josephine had married Augustus III, Elector of Saxony and King of Poland, who, as stated above, had renounced her claim; Maria Amelia was the wife of Charles Albert, Elector of Bavaria. Charles VI was now dead, and had left only a daughter, Maria Theresa. The Bavarian contention was that the daughter of the younger brother ought not to have prior rights over the daughter of the elder; Maria Amelia's claim to Hapsburg territories was at least as strong as Maria Theresa's, and Charles Albert had as much right as Francis

Stephen to consideration by the Electors as a candidate for the Imperial Crown. It was also contended on behalf of the Elector of Bavaria that the Emperor Ferdinand I, at his death in 1564, had arranged for the reversion of his lands, in the event of a failure of male heirs, to his daughter Anne and her descendants. Charles Albert was descended from Ferdinand through Anne, and so might establish a title independent of that derived through his wife. This claim, however, was not pressed. It may be added that the Elector had declined to accept the Pragmatic Sanction (except that in 1726 he had given a guarded and conditional assent which was almost immediately withdrawn).

On the other hand, no good case could be made out for any claim by the daughters of Joseph I to dominion over the Austrian Netherlands or Milan, since these territories were acquired after their father's death.

Austria was by no means ready for war. Her army was ill-organised, and her finances were exhausted as the result of recent unsuccessful wars—with the Turks, and in the matter of the Polish Succession. The Archduchess, though courageous and able, was young and inexperienced, while her advisers were senile. The greatest danger to be apprehended was from France and Prussia.

France had guaranteed the Pragmatic Sanction, but Fleury had pursued a double line of policy, and at various times he had encouraged the aspirations of Charles Albert. Now that the crisis had arrived he acted with caution. It was unlikely that France would take the lead in an attack upon Austria, but in the event of a scramble she would be willing to take part in it.

Frederick the Great succeeded to the throne of Prussia a few months before the death of Charles VI. He possessed a large and well-trained army, the finances of Prussia were in a satisfactory condition, and he was a military commander of outstanding ability. He resolved to seize Silesia. Pretexts were, of course, not wanting, but of real justification for this act of violence there was no trace. In an age characterised by utter lack of scruple in international relations the invasion of Silesia stands almost without parallel.

The attack which took place in December, 1740, was so sudden and unexpected that Frederick met with no serious resistance, and by the end of January, 1741, the conquest of the province was practically complete. Maria Theresa made vigorous preparations for its recovery. An Austrian army marched into Silesia, but it was defeated by Frederick at Mollwitz. The importance of this battle lay not merely in the failure of the Austrians to recover Silesia but in the encouragement afforded to the enemies of Maria Theresa to attack her. Spain, Sardinia, Saxony (whose Elector withdrew his recognition of Maria Theresa), Bavaria, and France all joined in the scramble for Austrian provinces.

In the light of subsequent events it cannot be asserted that either side followed the best possible course. The action of France was bound to cause resentment in Great Britain and to bring the entente of a quarter of a century's duration to an end. It involved her, moreover, in European complications for many years, during which her resources would have been more profitably employed in contesting Great Britain's claims to predominance in North America and India and on the sea. Nor was the action of Maria Theresa calculated to serve her own interests. Her resentment at the faithlessness of the Prussian King blinded her to the wisdom of making terms with him on the basis of the cession of Silesia. Had she done this, an alliance of Austria, Prussia, Great Britain, and the United Provinces—a revival of the Grand Alliance of the Spanish Succession—would have placed France and Spain in very great difficulty.

For the moment French policy met with a good deal of success. Frederick was too cautious to assent readily to a course of action which might result in a strengthening of French influence in the Empire, but in June, 1741, an alliance was formed. France was to recognise the Prussian possession of Lower Silesia and to support the candidature of Charles Albert to the Empire. She was to induce Sweden to declare war on Russia, in order that Maria Theresa might not receive help from her eastern neighbour, and it was understood that she was to seize the Austrian Netherlands. Sweden declared war on Russia, and the accession of Elizabeth, daughter of Peter the Great, to the Russian throne, brought about the downfall of that party in Russia which was in favour of intervention on behalf of Maria Theresa. France took up arms as the ally of Prussia and Bavaria, and did not at this time make any formal declaration of war. A French army entered the Empire and co-operated with the Bavarians in an invasion of Upper Austria. Saxony joined the allies at this time, and Spanish troops landed in Italy with a view to an attack upon Milan.

The dominions of Maria Theresa were thus subject to attack in several quarters, and for a time she was unable to rely upon the fidelity of Vienna. In the autumn of 1741 she appeared in person before the Diet of Hungary and secured the enthusiastic support of the Magyar nobles, a factor of no slight importance in the course of the war. She profited, too, by the mistakes and dissensions of her opponents. After the Franco-Bavarian army had captured Linz it might have advanced upon Vienna; instead of doing so, it invaded Bohemia and captured Prague. Frederick the Great disapproved of this move, and, before Prague had fallen, he abandoned his allies and came to a secret arrangement with Maria Theresa by which he was to receive Neisse and to retain Silesia. The possession of Neisse strengthened his strategic position, and he occupied the province of Glatz, in Bohemia. Having gained his ends by his faithlessness to his allies, he now deserted Maria Theresa and turned again to the French and Bavarians, by whom he was utterly distrusted. He invaded Moravia and moved into Bohemia, where an indecisive action was fought at Chotusitz.

Meanwhile the Austrians recovered Linz and invaded Bavaria. Charles Albert was elected Emperor, as Charles VII, early in 1742, and on the day of his coronation at Frankfort his capital, Munich, fell into the possession of the Austrians, so that the new Emperor became a fugitive from his hereditary territories. The accession of Carteret to power in Great Britain in place of Walpole was the prelude to more vigorous British participation in the struggle, and at the same time the King of Sardinia, Charles Emmanuel, changed sides and agreed to assist Maria Theresa in the defence of Austrian possessions in North Italy. Don Carlos, King of Naples, was threatened with the bombardment of Naples by an English fleet, and, being compelled to withdraw from the war, was unable to support the Spanish in the north of Italy. The Russian preoccupation with the Swedish war ended with the Treaty of Abo in 1743, and for a time France and Russia were not on good terms. Vigorous Austrian action against the French in Bohemia resulted in the capture of isolated detachments and garrisons and the isolation of the remnant in Prague.

Frederick realised that no good purpose would be served by a continuance of the war in the company of allies who were meeting with such ill-success, and in the face of enemies of increasing strength. He had gained his ends and was willing

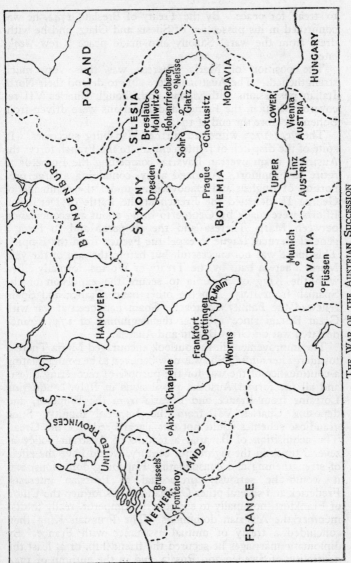

The War of the Austrian Succession

to treat for peace. By the Treaty of Breslau, 1742, he was
confirmed in his possession of Silesia and Glatz, and he withdrew from the war. Saxony also made peace a few weeks
later.

The position of Maria Theresa was thus very much
strengthened. The Austrians were able to defend their North
Italian possessions with vigour, and, though Charles VII recovered Munich, the French and Bavarians were driven from
Bohemia before the end of 1742.

The year 1743 witnessed further Hapsburg successes. In
spite of the dispatch of reinforcements to the French forces the
Austrians again overran Bavaria, compelling the Emperor to
retire to Frankfort. A mixed army, containing a large proportion of English and Hanoverians, under the command of
George II, defeated the French at the Battle of Dettingen.
Efforts were made by George to bring about a reconciliation
between Maria Theresa and the Emperor and to form a
general German league to expel the French from the Empire.
This move was not successful, but before the end of the year
Maria Theresa had, by the Treaty of Worms, formally allied
with the King of Sardinia to secure the expulsion of the
Spanish from Italy. On the other hand, France and Spain
renewed the Family Compact. Spain had been at war with
Great Britain since 1739; at the beginning of 1744 France
declared war on Great Britain and Austria.

The improvement in the outlook encouraged Maria Theresa
to enlarge her aims. She was now believed to be contemplating
a continuance of the war for the purpose of recovering Silesia
and all the former Austrian possessions in Italy, conquering
Lorraine from France and Bavaria from the Emperor, and
deposing Charles VII from the Imperial dignity. Such
grandiose schemes could not but alarm Frederick the Great.
The acquisition of Bavaria, a feature of Austrian policy at
several times in the eighteenth century, would have the effect
of strengthening and consolidating Hapsburg dominions, and
it would be seriously prejudicial to Prussian interests.
Frederick and several other German princes formed the Union
of Frankfort, nominally to support the Emperor, really to dis-
member the Austrian dominions. The Prussian King then
concluded a treaty of mutual assistance with France. By
diplomatic marriages he secured the friendship, or at least the
neutrality, of Sweden and Russia, and in the autumn of 1744

he felt strong enough to begin the Second Silesian War. He invaded Bohemia and took Prague, but, advancing southward towards Vienna, he found himself in difficulties. Austrian forces converged upon him, the French gave no material assistance, and he was forced to retire into Silesia.

Early in 1745 Charles VII died, and the ostensible object of the Union of Frankfort disappeared. The Union had not received widespread support; nevertheless, it had provided Prussia with some sort of moral basis for her action which she no longer possessed. The new Elector of Bavaria, Maximilian Joseph, was only eighteen years old. He was anxious for peace and declined to put himself forward as a candidate for the Imperial Crown in succession to his father. There were thus no serious questions at issue between Austria and Bavaria, and, though in the spring of 1745 part of Bavaria was occupied by Austrian troops, terms of peace were arranged. By the Treaty of Füssen Maximilian Joseph was left in possession of his electorate, and in return he recognised the Pragmatic Sanction and promised his vote for Francis Stephen. Maria Theresa shortly afterwards made the Treaty of Warsaw with the Elector of Saxony, arranging for joint action against Prussia, and securing the promise of the Saxon vote for Francis Stephen. Frederick was thus practically isolated in Germany, though his alliance with France continued.

The military position in 1745 was affected by the victory of Marshal Saxe and the French over the British and Hanoverian army under the Duke of Cumberland at Fontenoy and by the subsequent withdrawal of British forces from the Continent to meet the menace of a Jacobite revolt. Frederick had to face an invasion of Silesia by Austrian and Saxon armies, which he defeated at Hohenfriedberg. He followed up his success with an invasion of Bohemia, but his position was still serious. His finances were exhausted, and the French withdrew from Germany. The Convention of Hanover, between Frederick and George II, guaranteed his possession of Silesia in return for an undertaking not to attack Hanover, but English efforts to bring about a general peace met with no success.

In September, 1745, Francis Stephen was chosen Emperor, and Maria Theresa now prepared to make a big effort for the recovery of Silesia. Frederick retired from Bohemia after inflicting another defeat on the Austrians at Sohr. A joint Austro-Saxon invasion of Brandenburg was planned, but

Frederick anticipated it by invading Saxony and occupying Dresden. Both sides were now ready to treat, and by the Treaty of Dresden, in December, 1745, Frederick's right to Silesia was acknowledged, he recognised the election of Francis Stephen as Emperor, and the Convention of Hanover was confirmed.

For the remainder of the war the combatants were Austria, Great Britain, the United Provinces, and Sardinia against France and Spain, and the fighting was confined to Italy and the Netherlands. In Italy the Spanish had captured Milan in 1745, and it was the news of this reverse which had convinced Maria Theresa of the necessity of coming to terms with Frederick. The loss of Milan weakened the Austro-Sardinian alliance for a time; Charles Emmanuel felt that he was not being adequately supported by Austria and was being left to defend Austrian possessions as well as his own against Franco-Spanish attack. Negotiations for a Franco-Sardinian alliance were proposed by d'Argenson, the French foreign minister, but the arrival of Austrian reinforcements in Italy caused him to decline the French overtures. Milan was recovered, and in the course of 1746 the French were expelled from Italy.

In the Austrian Netherlands the French met with greater success. Marshal Saxe captured Brussels, and this was the prelude to a series of victories which resulted in the entire occupation of the Austrian Netherlands by the French before the end of 1746. They followed this up by an invasion of the United Provinces in 1747, but by this time Great Britain was prepared to intervene with vigour in the war, and at sea some British successes were gained over the French.

Russia had taken no active part in the campaigns, but the attitude of Elizabeth had not been without effect. As early as 1745 she had concluded with Maria Theresa an alliance of mutual defence against Prussia, a circumstance which induced Frederick to agree the more readily to the Peace of Dresden. The Treaty of St. Petersburg in December, 1747, provided for active Russian assistance, and this prospect induced France to accelerate peace negotiations.

Most of the parties to the war were by this time desirous of peace. France was exhausted, and her commerce was ruined. Holland was in danger of French conquest; the policy of Spain under Ferdinand VI, who succeeded Philip V in 1746, was no longer dominated by Elizabeth Farnese, and Great Britain, under Henry Pelham, felt that she was unlikely to derive benefit from a continuation of her financial sacrifices. Maria Theresa alone wished to carry on the struggle, but she recognised that with the defection of Great Britain and the United Provinces she could not defend the Netherlands, nor without the aid of Sardinia would she conquer Italy.

The Peace of Aix-la-Chapelle (Aachen) was agreed upon in the year 1748. Prussia was to retain Silesia and Glatz, the Spanish prince Don Philip was to receive Parma and Piacenza, and Sardinia received a portion of the Milanese, but with these exceptions the Pragmatic Sanction was confirmed. Other conquests were to be restored, the French retiring from the Austrian Netherlands and restoring the barrier fortresses to the Dutch. In India Madras, which had been captured by the French in 1746, was restored to the English East India Company, while in North America Louisburg, which had been taken by the New England colonists, was given back to the French. The Asiento, which had been interrupted in 1739 on the outbreak of war between Great Britain and Spain, was renewed for a period which would complete the original term of thirty years. France agreed to expel the Pretender and to dismantle the fortifications of Dunkirk, and the powers recognised the election of Francis Stephen as Emperor.

The Peace of Aix-la-Chapelle offered no real settlement of the chief questions at issue. Maria Theresa was not reconciled to the permanent loss of Silesia, and her future policy, framed with a view to its recovery, would inevitably lead to a renewal of war with Prussia. Nor was the colonial and commercial rivalry of Great Britain and France brought to an end. In the Far East the seventeenth-century rivalry of English and Dutch had been followed in the eighteenth century by a Franco-British struggle for supremacy, in which the French under Dupleix were so far fully holding their own. In North America the balance in the struggle was inclining in favour of the British. In both regions the ultimate issue was likely to be decided by supremacy at sea, and the French navy had almost ceased to exist. Nevertheless, the struggle was not over, and the position seemed to point to its early renewal.

Yet it would not be right to regard the struggle of the Austrian Succession as without result. The settlement in Italy remained substantially unchanged until the French Revolutionary War, and the Prussian hold upon Silesia was not relaxed. In the main, the Pragmatic Sanction had been vindicated, and was not again challenged. Austria emerged from the war stronger than she entered it. Her military prestige had been strengthened, and the courage of Maria Theresa had called forth the loyalty and enthusiasm of her subjects.

For the rest, it may be pointed out that Russia, which had made her influence felt in European affairs in the Polish Succession War, had given further proof of her importance as a European power, that Sardinia had strengthened her position in the north of Italy, and that the aims of Elizabeth Farnese had advanced a further step in that both her sons were now ruling princes in Italy.

France had been deeply involved in the war and had expended large sums of money and sacrificed thousands of men. She had gained nothing, not even an acre of territory. She had emerged from the war exhausted, while Austria, despite her territorial losses, was strengthened and was of far greater account in Europe at the end than at the beginning of the struggle. The action of France, in fact, was not truly consonant with her interests. Obsessed by age-long notions of exercising influence in Germany and Italy, she wasted treasure and blood in this war and the next in order to intervene in the rivalry of Austria and Prussia, while Great Britain, with a keener realisation of where her interests lay, took advantage of the opportunities overseas which France neglected.

CHAPTER X

THE DIPLOMATIC REVOLUTION AND THE SEVEN YEARS' WAR

IT has been shown that the Treaty of Aix-la-Chapelle failed to settle the major points at issue among the powers of Europe. The colonial and commercial rivalry of France and Great Britain continued unabated, and Maria Theresa could not regard as satisfactory a peace which left Silesia in the possession of Prussia. The treaty restored peace for the moment, but it could not establish amity. Maria Theresa was inclined to blame Great Britain for her misfortunes, in spite of battles fought on her behalf by British and Hanoverian troops and of the naval activity which had reduced Don Carlos to neutrality. Maria Theresa's hatred of Frederick the Great was shared by Elizabeth of Russia. The alliance of France and Prussia was cooling; each of them felt that the other had been guilty of desertion at a critical moment. The period 1748–56 was occupied by the powers in preparing for the next war.

For some years after 1748 there was little indication of the imminence of a Diplomatic Revolution. Maria Theresa was engaged in a series of internal reforms in the Austrian dominions. Administrative reorganisation was effected with a view to diminishing the power of the Austrian nobility and centralising the government. The courts of justice also were reorganised and made more efficient for their purpose. The revenue was augmented by the imposition of an income-tax and a poll-tax, by enquiry into exemptions, and by the checking of corruption. Trade was stimulated by the abolition of some of the customs between province and province, by the improvement of road and canal communication, by the enlargement of the port of Trieste, and by an increase in the merchant fleet. The army was enlarged, improved conditions were established for the comfort of the men, training schools were set up for officers, and the artillery, in particular, was strengthened.

The foreign policy of Maria Theresa during this period was

directed towards obtaining alliances of greater value to her than that of Great Britain and the United Provinces had been in the late war. Her ministers, indeed, with one exception, advised a continuance of the existing diplomatic system. The exception was Kaunitz, who had already proved his ability in the sphere of diplomacy. He held that, Great Britain's interests falling in the main overseas, she could not be relied on to plunge with energy into a war for the recovery of Silesia, while Holland would inevitably follow the British lead. On the other hand, though Austria and France had been at the opposite poles of the European system for nigh upon three hundred years, there was now no vital ground of disagreement between them. He advocated the opening of negotiations for a Franco-Austrian alliance.

It is unnecessary to trace the course of European diplomacy during the next few years in detail. Frederick was suspicious of Austro-Russian designs upon his dominions, and George II, who did not like the Prussian King, was restrained from joining a combination hostile to Frederick only through fear for the safety of his electorate. Meanwhile, Kaunitz was for three years Austrian ambassador at Versailles, but at this time he met with little success; uncertainty as to the attitude of Great Britain kept Louis XV faithful to the Prussian alliance.

In 1755 Great Britain, realising the imminence of war, formally proposed a renewal of the Austrian alliance. Kaunitz, now Chancellor, returned an evasive answer, and British statesmen turned to Russia. An agreement was reached by which, in return for British subsidies, Hanover was to be defended by Russian troops. This decided the issue for Frederick. He had little to fear from an alliance of Austria and France, since they were too remote from one another to act in concert, and he thought he could defeat them separately. But if Russia joined his enemies he would be encircled, and in great danger. Now, however, that Russia and Great Britain had come to terms he was eager for the British alliance, since this would guarantee him immunity from Russian attack. The Treaty of Westminster, early in 1756, arranged an offensive and defensive alliance between Great Britain and Prussia and provided for the defence of Hanover by Prussian troops.

The Treaty of Westminster threw French and Austrians into one another's arms. Yet agreement was not reached at once, and it is possible that it was the influence of Madame de

Pompadour, the mistress of Louis XV, who was equally attracted by the personal charm of Kaunitz and incensed at the reported references of Frederick to herself, that turned the scale. The Treaty of Versailles (in actual fact, three distinct treaties) bound France and Austria in offensive and defensive alliance which lasted until the French Revolution.

News of the Westminster agreement was received by Elizabeth of Russia with great indignation. She denounced the arrangement of 1755 with Great Britain, and prepared to co-operate with Austria in an attack upon Prussia. The factor which had induced Frederick to seek the British alliance thus disappeared. The Diplomatic Revolution was now complete; Great Britain and Prussia were allied against France, Austria, and Russia in the Seven Years' War.

The questions at issue were twofold, and they were entirely distinct. On the one hand, there was the rivalry of Austria and Prussia for supremacy in central Europe, of which the possession of Silesia was the immediate symbol. On the other hand, France and Great Britain were engaged in a contest for maritime supremacy and colonial empire. France was outwitted by Kaunitz. Her interests required her to keep aloof from a European war in which she was concerned in only a minor degree in order to concentrate on the struggle overseas. By plunging into the European vortex she played the game of Britain and Austria, and so contributed to her own downfall.

Elizabeth adhered to the Treaty of Versailles in January, 1757, and shortly afterwards she entered into a close alliance with Austria. In the course of this year a second Treaty of Versailles between Austria and France provided for the partitioning of Prussia, while France succeeded in bringing Sweden into the war. Spain under Ferdinand VI remained neutral, on account of the English sympathies of the Queen, formerly a Portuguese princess. Several of the German states joined the coalition against Frederick, who was placed under the ban of the Empire.

The object of the coalition was, as stated above, to reduce the power of Prussia and partition her dominions. If the allies were successful, the territories of Frederick would be reduced to, at the most, the original electorate of Brandenburg and the kingdom of Prussia. Austria would recover Silesia and Glatz, and Eastern Pomerania would be restored to Sweden. France would be compensated for her efforts by receiving a part of the Austrian Netherlands, the remainder of which would be assigned to Don Philip, who would be expected to resign Parma and Piacenza to Austria. The achievement of these aims depended on the close and cordial co-operation of the allies, and this, as events proved, was lacking.

Frederick anticipated attack by invading Saxony in the autumn of 1756. His object was twofold; he dared not leave behind him a hostile Saxony when he attacked Austria, and he hoped to discover in Dresden documents which would compromise the allies and afford a justification of his action. Dresden did not fall at once, however; the Saxons put up an unexpectedly obstinate resistance, which enabled the Austrian Government to complete its mobilisation. The Austrian army which marched north to reinforce the Saxons was checked at Lobositz, and the Saxon army was compelled to capitulate at Pirna. Dresden was now occupied by the Prussians, and the honours and advantages of the opening campaign lay with Frederick. After the fall of Dresden he issued to every court in Europe a defence of his proceedings which, though it gained him no immediate advantage, has tended to vindicate him in the eyes of posterity.

In the year 1757 Frederick resolved to repeat his strategy of the previous year and to meet attack by anticipating it. He invaded Bohemia and defeated an Austrian army before Prague. The Austrians retired into the city and were besieged there until the arrival of a relieving force under Daun, which defeated Frederick at the Battle of Kolin, raised the siege, and drove the Prussians out of Bohemia. While this was happening the Duke of Cumberland was defeated by the French at the Battle of Hastenbeck and forced to agree to the Convention of Klosterseven, by which Hanover was left in the hands of the French. Soon afterwards, a Russian army under Apraksin invaded East Prussia and defeated the Prussians at Gross-Jägerndorf. Swedes invaded Pomerania and Austrians over-ran Silesia, and in October the Austrians entered Berlin.

These disasters might have proved fatal to Frederick's cause had his enemies acted with vigour and in concert. But Daun failed to follow up his victory at Kolin, and Apraksin, believing that the Tsaritsa Elizabeth was about to die, and knowing that her heir, the Grand Duke Peter, was an admirer of Frederick, made no attempt to follow up his victory. Pitt, who became Secretary of State in Great Britain at this time, declined to recognise the Convention of Klosterseven, and he appointed

Ferdinand of Brunswick to the command of the British and Hanoverian Army.

Frederick acted with rapidity and decision. On 5th November, 1757, he inflicted a heavy defeat on the French at the Battle of Rossbach, and forced them to retire across the Rhine, and exactly a month later he defeated a large Austrian army at Leuthen and recovered the province of Silesia. These events served fully to restore Frederick's military prestige, to establish his position as a German national hero, and to strengthen the alliance with Great Britain. The French were expelled from Hanover, and Pitt promised an annual subsidy from Great Britain to Frederick.

Frederick's strategy in the spring of 1758 was on similar lines to that of the two previous years; he resolved to attack rather than defend. He invaded Moravia and besieged Olmütz, hoping, after its fall, to be able to advance upon Vienna. Olmütz was saved by Loudon, an Austrian general of Scottish ancestry, and Frederick was compelled to retire into Silesia, which he did in good order. Meanwhile, the Russians were on the move. Apraksin had been superseded by Fermor, who overran East Prussia, which was too far off for Frederick to defend, and prepared to invade Brandenburg in conjunction with the Swedes in Pomerania. Frederick met the Russians at the Battle of Zorndorf, and drove them back with heavy losses. In the autumn Austrian armies invaded Saxony and Silesia. Frederick moved with great rapidity against them, and, though he was defeated by Daun at the Battle of Hochkirch, he compelled his enemies to retire from both provinces.

During this year the French failed to make any great effort, on account of the incapacity of ministers and generals. A French army under the Count of Clermont was defeated by Ferdinand of Brunswick at the Battle of Krefeld, and though some successes were achieved elsewhere by the French they were over small forces and were not of great importance.

By the end of 1758 it seemed more than ever unlikely that the foes of Prussia would be able to overwhelm her. France had been reduced to impotence, and Frederick had shown himself able to keep Austria and Russia at bay. The inability of his enemies to act in concert had again been demonstrated, and there seemed on their side to be little advantage in continuing a war which could not be brought to a decisive issue. That

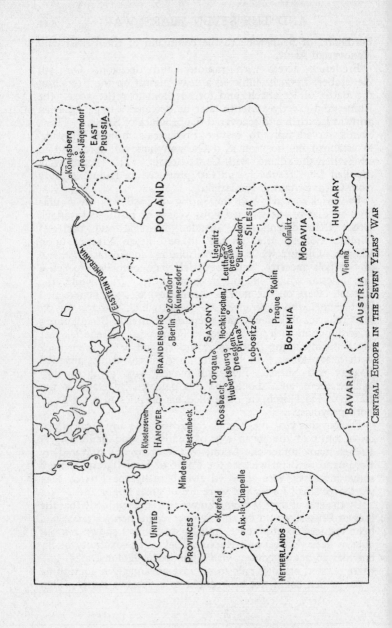

CENTRAL EUROPE IN THE SEVEN YEARS' WAR

no move for peace was made at this time must be ascribed to Madame de Pompadour, who secured the retirement of Bernis, Minister for Foreign Affairs, and his replacement by the Duke of Choiseul. Choiseul was the ablest French statesman of the time, and he devoted himself with vigour to the prosecution of the war. He made a new treaty with Austria by which neither power was to make a peace which did not include the other. He planned to send additional forces to the assistance of Austria, to conquer Hanover, to invade England, and to organise a Russo–Swedish descent upon Scotland.

These ambitious projects were not realised. The British fleet, after its initial reverse at Minorca in 1756, had been reorganised and strengthened by Pitt. Competent admirals

FRANCO-BRITISH NAVAL WARFARE, 1756-61

and captains were appointed, and a close watch was being maintained on French ports. Choiseul's plan of effecting a junction of the Toulon and Brest squadrons, which were to proceed to Havre and convoy a fleet of transports across the Channel, was foiled by the victories of Boscawen at Lagos and of Hawke at Quiberon Bay. This series of British successes was completed by the destruction of the transports at Havre by Rodney, and for the remainder of the war France was practically without a fleet. The destruction of French naval power resulted in the capture of Quebec in 1759 and of Montreal in 1760, in victories in the West Indies, and in the capture of

Belle Isle, off the Breton coast, in 1761. French power in India had already received a shattering blow by Clive's victory at Plassey in 1757, and its destruction was completed by Coote's defeat of Lally at Wandewash in 1760, an event which was followed by the capture of Pondicherri.

The year 1759 was no more successful for France on land than at sea. Some small successes were gained in the west of Germany, but the great event of the year was the victory of Ferdinand of Brunswick over the French at Minden, which saved Hanover from invasion. Nor was Choiseul's scheme of a Russian invasion of Scotland destined to be put into operation. Russia was not at war with Great Britain, and the Tsaritsa declined to listen to the French proposals. The year was not so successful for Frederick as for his ally. At the Battle of Kunersdorf he was defeated by combined Russian and Austrian armies, and if the victors had taken advantage of their success he must have been overwhelmed. But Daun contented himself with the recovery of Dresden, and the Russian general Soltikoff, expecting the early death of Elizabeth and the accession of the Grand Duke Peter, which would inevitably bring about a change of Russian policy, retired into Poland.

During the winter of 1759–60 Choiseul made renewed efforts to secure the close co-operation of the three principal enemies of Prussia. But Louis XV followed a policy which was independent of that of his ministers; he had no desire to see Russian territory extended at the expense of either Prussia or Poland, and he gave instructions to the French ambassador at St. Petersburg which conflicted with those issued by Choiseul. The minister's plans, therefore, fell to the ground.

Further desperate fighting occurred in the year 1760. Frederick was again exposed to Russian and Austrian attack. He defeated Loudon at the Battle of Liegnitz, in Silesia, but he was unable to prevent the Russians entering Berlin. The Austrians occupied Saxony, but Frederick inflicted a heavy defeat on Daun at Torgau and recovered possession of most of Saxony, though not of Dresden. In the west Ferdinand defeated the French at the Battle of Warburg, and Hanover remained inviolate.

The fighting in 1761 was less strenuous; differences between Austrians and Russians prevented their effective co-operation, and it was not until the autumn that they were able again to advance into Silesia. A further French attempt to attack Hanover was repulsed by Frederick.

The ill-success which had attended French arms in the war led Choiseul to consider fresh measures. He began a policy of naval construction which, though valueless in the Seven Years' War, was destined to become a vital factor in the War of American Independence. Further, he opened negotiations with Spain for a new Family Compact. On the death of Ferdinand VI in 1759, his half-brother, Don Carlos, King of the Two Sicilies since 1735, succeeded to the throne of Spain as Charles III. (The Neapolitan kingdom was surrendered by Charles to his son Ferdinand IV.) The Family Compact was concluded in August, 1761; it provided that Spain should declare war on Great Britain on 1st May, 1762, unless peace had already been reached between France and Great Britain before that date, and France promised to give Minorca, captured from the British in 1756, to Spain. The intervening period was designed for Spanish military and naval preparations. The Compact was to be kept secret, lest Great Britain upon learning of it should declare war upon Spain before she was ready for it. This, in fact, happened. Pitt received early information of the Compact and wished to declare war upon Spain. George III professed to doubt the reliability of Pitt's information, and this difference between the King and his minister led to the latter's resignation. His successor, Bute, was compelled to recognise the soundness of Pitt's views, and war was declared on 2nd January, 1762.

The fall of Pitt was followed by the discontinuance of the Anglo-Prussian alliance and of the subsidy, and this might have been a fatal blow to Frederick had it not been counterbalanced by the death of Elizabeth of Russia in January, 1762. The new Tsar, Peter III, made peace with Frederick and restored all conquered territories, and soon afterwards he made an offensive and defensive alliance with Prussia against Austria. Sweden at the same time withdrew from the war. The Russian alliance was of little value to Frederick, since Peter was overthrown in a few weeks, and his wife ascended the throne as Catherine II. She decided to withdraw from the war, but before the actual departure of his Russian allies Frederick defeated the Austrians at Burkersdorf and recovered possession of Silesia. Skirmishes in various parts of Germany preceded the termination of the Seven Years' War.

The Franco-Spanish alliance proved to be valueless. Havana in the West Indies and Manila in the Philippine Islands were captured by British fleets, and an attempted invasion of Portugal by a Franco-Spanish army was foiled by the dispatch of a British force to Lisbon.

Two treaties of peace were negotiated. Terms agreed upon by Great Britain, France, Spain, and Portugal were included in the Treaty of Paris, while the settlement between Prussia, Austria, and Saxony was embodied in the Treaty of Huberts-burg. Both these instruments were signed in February, 1763.

Various territorial arrangements between France and Great Britain were embodied in the Treaty of Paris. In India all French possessions, except Pondicherri and two other factories, were ceded to Great Britain. Great Britain acquired also the French possessions east of the Mississippi, together with Senegal in West Africa and several islands in the West Indies. Minorca was restored to Great Britain, and Belle Isle to France, and the French undertook once more to dismantle the fortifications of Dunkirk. Both powers withdrew from the continental war.

Great Britain restored Havana and Manila to Spain, and received the peninsula of Florida in return, so that the eastern half of the mainland of North America became entirely British. Though the right of French fishermen to continue the exercise of their industry in the Gulf of St. Lawrence was recognised, the Spanish renounced their claim to participate in it, and they acknowledged the British claim to cut log-wood in Honduras. Spain and France agreed to withdraw their troops from Portuguese territory.

By the Treaty of Hubertsburg, Maria Theresa recognised the right of Frederick to Silesia and Glatz, so that the King of Prussia emerged from the struggle without loss of territory. Frederick promised to give his vote to the Archduke Joseph, the son of Francis I and Maria Theresa, at the forthcoming Imperial Election, and it was arranged that the electorate of Saxony should be restored intact to Augustus III.

In view of the magnitude of the attack upon Prussia the issue of the war must be regarded as a personal triumph for Frederick the Great, whose position as a German national hero and a great military captain was established for all time. Victory was due primarily to his genius, his energy, and his perseverance in the face of difficulties that would have overwhelmed a lesser man. His skill in forestalling the attacks of his enemies, and his vigour in marching to meet them separately, contributed to his success. He was fortunate in being able, by making use of interior lines of communication, to move his troops rapidly from one front to another. The allies suffered from inability to communicate with one another speedily, and they frequently failed to co-operate in attack, while the Prussian campaigns were planned by a single commander. Finally, in estimating the causes of Frederick's victory, the assistance, military and financial, afforded by Great Britain must be given due weight, while the balance was finally turned in his favour by the withdrawal of Russia.

Important results followed from the Seven Years' War. The struggle between Great Britain and France for supremacy in the field of colonisation ended decisively in favour of Great Britain, and, although only fifteen years elapsed before France embarked upon a war of revenge, the British position was too strong to be overthrown. The British victory was due, on the one hand, to the genius of Pitt, who made effective use of British naval and financial strength in the prosecution of the war, and, on the other hand, to the mistaken policy of France in permitting herself to be committed to a continental war in which her interests were involved to only a minor degree. France during the war possessed neither able captains nor wise statesmen; the only French minister to see the situation in true perspective was Choiseul, and his efforts were thwarted by the independent diplomacy of Louis XV and the intrigues of Madame de Pompadour. The great effort of the enemies of Prussia to destroy her power and partition her territories had failed, and she was recognised henceforth as one of the great military powers of Europe. Neither Prussia nor Austria had crushed the other, and their rivalry for leadership in Germany was destined to continue for a century. Russia, if she had failed to exert a decisive influence in the war, stood forth definitely as a European power to be reckoned with in all future wars and diplomatic arrangements.

The alliance of France and Austria was not terminated by the war. It was never popular in either country, and though it was cemented by the marriage of the future Louis XVI with Marie Antoinette, the daughter of Maria Theresa, it was broken by the revolutionary Government of France.

Frederick was bitterly incensed by what he regarded as the

desertion of Great Britain. But Bute's withdrawal of the subsidy could be defended on several grounds. The debt of Great Britain had been more than doubled during the war, and the financial position was causing alarm. Great Britain was faced with a new war, against Spain, at the moment when Frederick was relieved of the worst of his difficulties by the death of Elizabeth. It might reasonably be argued that the support of Great Britain was no longer so vital to him as in the critical years of the war. The reflection that he himself in the course of his reign had been guilty of the desertion of allies did not in any way serve to modify his denunciation of the conduct of Great Britain. He resolved never to enter into alliance with her again. For the next twenty-five years Great Britain was in a state of diplomatic isolation.

CHAPTER XI

BENEVOLENT DESPOTISM

ONE of the most remarkable features of the history of Europe in the second half of the eighteenth century was the existence of a type of government commonly known as benevolent despotism. Absolute monarchy prevailed nearly everywhere in continental Europe. The monarchs of Europe recognised, however, that government ought to exist for the benefit of the governed, and they were eager to initiate reforms in order that the internal condition of their dominions might be as nearly perfect as possible. They held that reforms should spring from the will of the ruler, and they hardly conceived the possibility of their originating from the people themselves. Though government was to be for the people it certainly was not to be by the people. To describe the attitude of the eighteenth-century despots as liberal would involve a misuse of the term. Liberalism implies some degree, at least, of popular participation in the work of government, and the good intentions of the benevolent despots certainly did not go so far as to invite the people to take any part in the direction of public affairs. It should be added that in some states the work of reform was carried on by ministers who might be called benevolent statesmen.

This philosophy of government was not inconsistent with the trend of thought among people of culture in the eighteenth century. There was a higher conception of human dignity than in former times, and this led to a belief in the essential equality of men. But it was hardly thought possible that men should order their own government, and it was felt that in no better way could social inequality be destroyed, poverty decreased, the way to fortune opened to the adventurous, and public virtue maintained, than by the activities of absolute monarchs.

Benevolent despotism was faulty in many ways. Reforms which sprang from the whim of a ruler were not necessarily permanent. They had no roots; they could be maintained only by constant watchfulness on the part of their originator, and when his attention was turned to other matters officials might grow careless and edicts might be neglected. His successor might have other views, and his work might be reversed. Proposed reforms were often inoperative from the beginning through the non-existence of effective administrative machinery. More lasting results might have been achieved through the co-operation of monarch and people. Any eighteenth-century king who had invited the participation of his subjects in putting his proposals into effect might have created an interest among them which would have been of lasting value. Nor were the reforms themselves always well thought out. They did not go to the root of existing evils. To the student of eighteenth-century history it would seem that the most urgent need of the period was the abolition of serfdom. Some of the enlightened rulers issued edicts touching the worst abuses of serfdom, but they had little effect. The enforcement of such edicts was usually in the hands of nobles and officials who were interested in the maintenance of the abuses which were being attacked. No sweeping edict of emancipation (other than an abortive attempt by Joseph II, referred to below) was made before the French Revolution. A review of the work of the benevolent despots leads to the conclusion that in the main it failed to confer lasting benefit upon the people.

The achievements of some of the benevolent despots, notably Frederick the Great and Catherine II, are described in other chapters; some other monarchs of the time deserve special notice. Maria Theresa is usually classed with the group. She certainly did much to improve the Austrian administrative system and to sweep away abuses, and her measures for the reinvigoration of Austrian industry and commerce increased the prosperity of the country. It may be pointed out, however, that her motive, in the earlier years of her reign, at least, was not so much to bring about improvement in the condition of the people as to strengthen Austria in preparation for a renewal of the struggle with Prussia.

Charles III, King of Spain from 1759 to 1788, affords a better example of the enlightened despot. Already, as King of Naples, he had done something for the improvement of that kingdom, and in Spain, with the aid of a succession of able ministers, he carried on work which had been begun by his father and brother. Restrictions were imposed on ecclesiastical privilege, attempts were made to develop natural resources, and trade was encouraged. Charles was vigorous and healthy, cheerful and active, a striking contrast to his gloomy and half-mad predecessors. He was one of the best kings who ever sat upon the throne of Spain. That his efforts were not more successful was due to the fact that the evils which he attacked were too deeply rooted to be readily eradicated. Centuries of oppression by Church and nobles had reduced the peasantry to a condition of superstition and degradation which was not to be remedied by the issue of a few well-meant edicts.

The work of reform in Portugal was carried on by a minister of King Joseph I, Pombal, who was in office from 1750 to 1777. He endeavoured to foster Portuguese trade by founding trading companies, and he did something to stimulate agriculture. Order was restored in the finances of the country; public expenditure was reduced, and corruption in the collection of taxes was checked. Noble privileges were reduced, and an attempt was made to improve the education and culture of the younger nobles. Perhaps the most important achievement of Pombal's ministry was the expulsion from Portugal of the Jesuits, the opponents of social progress and the champions of ecclesiastical privilege. Pombal's measures had at the time some effect in galvanising the country into a semblance of vigour and prosperity, but, as with the reforms of Charles III in Spain, they had no lasting effect. The people were too slothful and unintelligent, too ignorant and superstitious, to be rescued from their degradation by the efforts of a single statesman in a single generation.

The efforts of Tanucci in Naples, under Don Carlos and Ferdinand IV, were equally without permanent result. Naples was one of the most backward countries of Europe. Tanucci attacked ecclesiastical privileges and exemptions, and he attempted to reform the judicial system of the kingdom. Educational and financial reforms were begun. Industry and commerce revived, and a determined effort was made to put an end to brigandage. After the fall of Tanucci in 1776 these measures were allowed to lapse, and in the first half of the nineteenth century Naples resumed its unenviable distinction of being the worst governed kingdom in Europe.

Louis XV cannot be included in the list of benevolent despots, and Choiseul is the only French minister of the period with any claim to be regarded as a reformer. But the philosophy which inspired many of the reforming rulers had its origin in France. The work of Montesquieu, Voltaire, Rousseau, the Encyclopaedists, and the Physiocrats is referred to elsewhere. It should be noted that these advanced thinkers were unsparing in their criticism of the *ancien régime*, in France and elsewhere, and in their advocacy of reforms. These philosophers, other than Rousseau, had no belief in democracy; as is indicated above, they looked to monarchy as the source of reform, and they must be ranged with the champions of benevolent despotism. The Government of France, if it failed to follow the fashion in promoting positive reforms, was not intentionally oppressive; it was well-disposed towards the people, who suffered more from the maintenance of aristocratic privilege than from actual state tyranny.

The perfect type of the benevolent despot was Joseph II, Holy Roman Emperor from 1765 to 1790. The formal election of Joseph as King of the Romans occurred in 1764, and he became Emperor on the death of Francis I a year later. But he did not at this time obtain full control over the Hapsburg possessions, in which he was only co-regent with his mother, Maria Theresa, until her death in 1780. Such attempts at reform as were made by him during this period met with the opposition of Maria Theresa and Kaunitz, and it was only with difficulty that Joseph was able to bring about a measure of military reorganisation and some improvement in the condition of the serfs. His opposition to religious persecution in Moravia almost resulted in an open breach with his mother. In his Imperial capacity Joseph attempted some reform in the Imperial Chamber and the Aulic Council.

The efforts at reform in the Hapsburg dominions which are associated with his name were really limited to the ten years of his independent rule. He was a man of marked ability, who was attracted by the philosophic ideas prevalent in Europe at this time. Reason became his watchword; he was impatient of the continuance of any institution, any custom, any law, which was bound up with tradition or privilege and which could not be defended on grounds of reason. He was well-meaning, and he worked hard, but he attempted far too much. In a short reign he tried to carry out a many-sided policy which might have taxed the energies of a succession of statesmen throughout a century.

The dominions to which the Emperor succeeded were of the most varied character. They were occupied by peoples of many races and languages, each with its own laws and traditions, and with no common economic interests, and they were not even geographically contiguous. In the main, the peoples of the Hapsburg dominions professed the Catholic religion; apart from this, their only common tie was subjection to the same sovereign.

Joseph's aim was to transform his scattered and varied possessions into a single consolidated, homogeneous state, in which existing nations should be merged and existing privileges levelled. He resolved to establish uniformity of laws, of justice, and of social conditions, and this was to be accompanied by religious toleration. He determined to make a clean sweep of the antiquated privileges, exemptions, and disabilities which existed in infinite variety amongst various classes and in different provinces of his dominions. His attempts to bring about an exchange of the Austrian Netherlands for Bavaria, and their failure, are recorded elsewhere. His measures of internal reform remain to be considered.

The whole of the Emperor's dominions, even including Lombardy and the Austrian Netherlands, were now proclaimed to consist of a single state divided into thirteen districts, each of which was placed under the rule of a governor. Diets were no longer to be summoned, save by the Emperor's express command, and municipal privileges were abolished. The German language alone was recognised as the official tongue. Edicts, imperfectly understood and only partially enforced, were issued for the abolition of serfdom; peasants were directed to pay to their lords money rents for their holdings instead of rendering personal service. Codes of civil and criminal law were drawn up, and their application was ordered in every part of the state. Legal costs were reduced; torture was abolished; the death penalty was reserved for the most serious crimes; marriage became a civil contract. The system of courts was revised; appellate tribunals were established and were made subject to a final High Court at Vienna.

An Edict of Toleration was issued in 1781 which, while recognising the Roman Catholic faith as the religion of the state, allowed freedom of worship and organisation and the right of holding property to all forms of religion. This toleration was extended, with some restrictions and conditions, even to the

Jews. Dissenters became eligible for public appointments and sundry restrictions upon their liberty were removed. Heresy ceased to be a crime, and orthodoxy of belief was no longer regarded as an essential test of good citizenship. The special privileges of the Church of Rome were severely curtailed. Appeals from Austrian courts to the court of Rome were forbidden; payments of money to Rome were to cease; monasteries were forbidden either to pay tribute or to render obedience to alien superior authority; many religious houses were abolished, and the remainder were directed to engage in philanthropic or other charitable work; regulations were framed for the education and training of aspirants to the priesthood.

Social and economic reforms were undertaken by the Emperor. Exemptions from taxation were annulled, and the whole fabric of Austrian finance was overhauled. Harbour works were undertaken at Trieste and Fiume, and vigorous efforts were made to develop Austrian trade in the Mediterranean, commercial treaties being concluded with Russia and Turkey.

Joseph's reforming activity evoked opposition from well-nigh every class of his subjects. This he considered to be unreasonable, since his proposals were based upon reason. Conscious of his own beneficent intentions, he expected an immediate and cordial response from his people. Opposition could be explained only by ill-will, which deserved censure and suppression. He was unhesitating in his resolution to put down resistance to his will, whether it emanated from nobles or Church, burghers or peasantry, or from other German princes.

The Emperor's efforts to eliminate distinctions of race and language never had any real prospect of success; small races which existed under Hapsburg rule were tenacious of their distinctive characteristics and their language, and they resented attempts at absorption into a single nation.

Joseph's ecclesiastical policy was not well thought out. Since he wished to unify his dominions it was unwise to attack the single feature which was already common to most of the races under his rule. A shrewder statesman than Joseph would have considered the possibility of maintaining friendly relations with the Church and winning its support for his other measures. Even a visit of Pope Pius VI to Vienna in 1782 failed to deflect the Emperor; the Pope was received with courtesy and reverence, but his admonitions were disregarded. Nevertheless, the presence of the Pontiff stimulated the religious enthusiasm of the people, and strengthened them in their attitude of hostility to the attack upon ecclesiastical privilege.

It has been pointed out that Joseph attempted too much in too short a time; it may be added that he was ill-advised in trying to forward ambitious schemes of foreign policy at the same time as plans for internal reform. His suggestions for the exchange of the Austrian Netherlands for Bavaria met with the opposition of the German princes, from whom discontented races and classes within the Austrian dominions might expect to receive some measure of support.

Between 1787 and 1790 much of the Emperor's attention was given to the Austrian Netherlands, where, for centuries, provinces and cities had enjoyed privileges and immunities which had been conferred upon them, individually, by former rulers. (It will be remembered that the infringement of local privileges had been a factor in inspiring the provinces to revolt against Spanish rule in the sixteenth century.) Joseph disregarded the lessons of history, and in a series of edicts he annulled local charters, abolished provincial Estates, insisted upon ecclesiastical reform, and set up a new judicial system. Insurrection followed, and by 1790 the revolted provinces had followed the example of the United States by declaring their independence and proclaiming a federal republic. This was the most serious, but not the only, indication of revolt which the Emperor had to meet; rebellions were imminent in Hungary, Bohemia, and Galicia. His enemies, especially Frederick William II of Prussia, prepared to attack him, and there seemed every likelihood of a European war.

The revolutionary movements among Joseph's subjects at this time were not in any way comparable with that which was about to appear in France. They were not inspired by the philosophy of reasonableness; they were reactionary in character, having as their aim the restoration of the *ancien régime*. The revolutionary was Joseph himself. The course of modern history provides many examples of the inability of sovereigns to prevent revolution when the people are determined to bring it about; the career of Joseph demonstrates the impotence of a ruler to force revolutionary ideals upon unwilling and unprepared peoples. Joseph seems to have realised this during the last few months of his life. A week before his death he revoked the bulk of his reforms, ordering the restoration of conditions which existed at the death of Maria Theresa.

Yet the work of Joseph II did not pass for nothing. His Edicts of Toleration remained, and some part of his work for the alleviation of the condition of the serfs was permanent. His economic reforms — the stimulus afforded to agriculture, industry, and commerce—were of lasting value. It may be asserted that his work was a failure only in the sense that it was premature, and that he succeeded in proposing ideals which future reformers might try to realise.

When the Emperor Francis I died in 1765 the Grand Duchy of Tuscany was assigned to his second son Leopold, under whom Tuscany became one of the best-governed states in Europe. The system of local government was remodelled, and some judicial reforms were introduced; torture was abolished, the application of the penalty of death was reduced, corruption was checked, and legal procedure was simplified. The worst features of serfdom were remedied, and agrarian improvements were undertaken. Some monopolies were abolished, and new industries were set up. Taxation was reduced; yet, with the increasing prosperity of the state, its finances were in excellent order.

Some measure of ecclesiastical reform was undertaken. Many religious houses were suppressed; others were reformed, and were placed under episcopal jurisdiction. The Inquisition was abolished, and the authority of the ecclesiastical courts was limited to purely spiritual affairs. In many ways the authority of the papacy in Tuscany was limited.

The excellence of Leopold's intentions did not serve to commend his reforms to his subjects. The common people were too ignorant and superstitious to appreciate the value of his measures, and the aristocracy and the clergy naturally resisted attacks upon their privileges. The reign of Leopold in Tuscany is interesting in the history of benevolent despotism as an example of the attempt of a man of high ideals to establish perfect administration in a small state. No permanent success was achieved, for the reasons which were responsible for the failure of benevolent despotism elsewhere.

Leopold succeeded Joseph as Emperor in 1790. In his short reign he showed that, while he shared his brother's high ideals, he was Joseph's superior in discretion and tact.   By judicious concessions he brought about the collapse of the revolt of the Netherlands and restored his authority there.   He came to an understanding with the King of Prussia, and in 1791 he agreed to the termination of the war between Austria and Turkey by the Treaty of Sistova.   Unfortunately, the reign which began so auspiciously was cut short by Leopold's death in March, 1792.

CHAPTER XII

THE CHURCH AND THE JESUITS IN THE EIGHTEENTH CENTURY

THE superstition and corruption which characterised the Church in the later Middle Ages led to the great revolt against ecclesiastical authority known as the Reformation. Protestantism, though it earned the right to survive, failed to overwhelm the Church. By the end of the sixteenth century the Church had reformed itself — in part, at least—and during the seventeenth century it more than held its own. In the eighteenth century it was called upon to face new attacks.

The autocratic sovereigns of the eighteenth century, even those who professed Catholicism, were disinclined to sanction the continuance in their states of a power which was not under their control. The political influence of the Church had by this time sunk almost to insignificance; papal sanction to international treaties was not sought, papal censure was disregarded. Nevertheless, the influence of the Church upon the common people in Catholic countries was still considerable and was a factor to be taken into account by monarchs who wished to introduce changes among their subjects. Other restrictions upon royal authority—noble independence, popular assemblies, and the like—had been suppressed, and it was felt that ecclesiastical power also should be brought into subjection.

Jansenism was another factor in the attack upon the Church. The movement had been decisively condemned by the Bull *Unigenitus*, and the French Government had set its face against it. Nevertheless, many moderate Catholics felt that the condemnation of Jansenism had been excessive. The theological questions which had been in dispute fell into the background and, in the eighteenth century, were well-nigh forgotten, but the continuance of the movement, which was not limited to France, was a challenge to the Church.

The philosophy of the eighteenth century, based on the appeal to reason, was definitely ranged against the Church. Authority and tradition, upon which the ecclesiastical system was based, were not accepted by the philosophers, who attacked the whole conception of revealed religion. Their influence was considerable with the cultured classes, among whom atheism steadily spread.

There was one branch of the ecclesiastical system which all these forces inimical to the Church—monarchs, reformers, atheists—were agreed in attacking. The Society of Jesus was rich and powerful, often opposed to reforming activity, and always devoted to the maintenance of papal authority. It had been extraordinarily successful—too much so, in fact, and the eighteenth-century autocrats felt that the Jesuits should be brought more definitely into subjection to the civil authority. The Order had lost its early popularity and had become an object of hatred nearly everywhere in Europe. The system of casuistry commonly associated with the Jesuits (whether rightly or wrongly) did nothing to enhance their reputation with the spiritually minded. Above all, the Order had embarked upon commercial enterprises which might be unexceptionable in themselves but could not be regarded as the peculiar function of a body of priests; this type of activity aroused the envy of commercial companies which resented the appearance of the Jesuits as their competitors. Within a period of less than twenty years the Jesuits were attacked in nearly every Catholic country in Europe, and the Order was suppressed.

The first blow fell in Portugal. Jesuit rule had long been established in Paraguay, and when this region was ceded by Spain to Portugal in 1751 the fathers organised resistance to the change which was not fully overcome for some years. Pombal, the leading minister of Joseph I, took energetic measures against the Jesuits in Portugal, and he complained to the Pope, Benedict XIV, of their American trade. The Pope ordered Cardinal Saldanha, a friend of Pombal, to investigate the complaint, and meanwhile issued an order limiting the activity of the fathers. Benedict died before the issue of Saldanha's report, which was hostile to the Order, and Pombal found fresh ground of attack in an attempted assassination of the King of Portugal, which, it was asserted, was instigated by the Jesuits. The new Pope, Clement XIII, tried to protect the Jesuits by forbidding their trial in Portuguese courts; Pombal's answer, in 1759, was to deport the Jesuits from Portugal and its colonies. Two hundred of them were cast into prison on suspicion of being concerned in the assassination plot; the remainder, over six thousand in number, were sent to the Papal States. The Pope retaliated by expelling all Portuguese from his dominions; Pombal's action in reply was the confiscation of Jesuit property in Portugal.

The attack on the Jesuits extended to France, where several circumstances contributed to intensify the animosity with which the Order had been faced for many years. As has been indicated elsewhere, Jansenist feeling existed in greater or lesser degree throughout the reigns of Louis XIV and Louis XV, and Jansenists and Jesuits were bitter opponents. The Parlements, jealous of Jesuit power, tended to support Jansenism, and had no kindly feelings towards the Order. The philosophers of the eighteenth century, too, could not but be hostile to an organisation pledged to support authority and tradition, the very negation of the principles which commended themselves to the rationalists. Nor was Jesuit influence unchallenged at court. The Queen and the Dauphin supported them; some of the ministers of Louis XV, among them Choiseul, were hostile, while the influence of Madame de Pompadour was exerted against them. The event which brought matters to an issue was the bankruptcy of Father Lavalette. This Jesuit had undertaken commercial operations in the island of Martinique, but the capture of a number of merchantmen laden with his goods involved him in financial difficulties. He was unable to meet his obligations by an amount exceeding two and a half million livres. His creditors, merchants of Marseilles, brought an action against the Society of Jesus, which repudiated responsibility, asserting that in this matter Lavalette had acted in his private capacity and not as the representative of the Order. The Jesuits lost their case in the local court, and their General, Ricci, appealed to the Parlement of Paris. The Parlement ordered an investigation of the constitution of the Society of Jesus, and, as a result, confirmed the decision of the lower court. Louis XV at the same time appointed a commission for the same purpose. It was determined as a result of these inquiries that the absolutism of the General of the Jesuits was inconsistent with the paramount authority of the King in France, and it was suggested that Jesuits in France should be subject to a French Vicar-General independent of the General and of the papacy. Ricci refused to accept the proposal, in words which have become famous: *Sint ut sunt, aut non sint.* The Parlement thereupon ordered the confiscation of the property of the Jesuits, dissolved their educational establishments, and prohibited French subjects from joining the Order. In 1764 a royal edict ordered the suppression of the Society of Jesus in France. Members were permitted to remain in France as secular priests provided that they renounced the Order. The issue in 1765 of a papal Bull which declared the innocence of the fathers and extolled their services to the Church failed to secure any modification of the policy of the French court.

Charles III of Spain was devout. At first he entertained no hostile feelings towards the Jesuits, and he even gave shelter to some of the exiles from France. The case was different with his minister, Aranda, who was resolved to overthrow the Order. He succeeded in convincing the King that the Order was plotting against his authority and his life. Charles was determined to maintain absolutism in his kingdom, and he concurred in a plan for the expulsion of the Jesuits. Secret orders were dispatched to all parts of Spain, and, on an appointed day, members of the Society were arrested and conveyed to the coast, where they were placed on board ship and sent to the Papal States. The arrival in the Papal States of so many priests caused some embarrassment to the Pope, and he refused admission to the Spanish Jesuits. They were at length given a refuge in Corsica by the Genoese, to whom the island belonged, but upon its acquisition by France in 1768 they were again expelled, and the Pope reluctantly permitted them to settle in his dominions.

The smaller Bourbon governments imitated the larger. Jesuits were expelled from Naples through the influence of Tanucci. The Duke of Parma became involved in a quarrel with Clement XIII, in the course of which the Pope threatened him with excommunication and deposition. The Duke replied by expelling the Jesuits from his dominions, and the Bourbon governments united in demanding the withdrawal of the papal threat to depose the Duke. Clement unwisely refused, and was faced with war with all the Bourbon powers. His effort to secure the support of Maria Theresa failed. The French seized Avignon, and the King of Naples occupied Beneventum. Charles III, on behalf of all the Bourbon powers, presented a formal demand for the abolition of the Society of Jesus. The Governments of Modena, Venice, and Bavaria followed the example of the Bourbons in expelling the Jesuits.

These events were too much for the Pope, who died of apoplexy early in 1769.

The conclave which followed was of unusual importance, since upon the personality of the Pope to be elected would depend the fate of the Order. Cardinal Ganganelli, a Franciscan, was chosen, and assumed the name of Clement XIV. He had little sympathy with the Jesuits; yet he was reluctant to take the final step. But the unpopularity and friendlessness of the Jesuits continued, and in 1773 Clement issued the Bull *Dominus ac Redemptor*, by which the Society was abolished. Its property was confiscated, and its General, Ricci, was imprisoned in the Castle of St. Angelo, where he died. In the following year Avignon and Beneventum were restored to the papacy. Most of the members of the Order received pensions and were permitted to return to their homes as secular priests.

In so far as the Order had lost sight of its spiritual function and had become absorbed in the pursuit of wealth, it deserved its fate. But, although its commercial success aroused the animosity of its competitors, it may be doubted whether this was the real cause of its collapse. It has been argued that the Order had changed its aim—that it had been founded to fight the Reformation and to recover for the Church what had been lost to the Protestants, and that it had abandoned this field of action in order to support every reactionary and autocratic cause. If, however, the Jesuits might regard the defence of the Catholic faith, with which they associated the papacy, as their *raison d'être*, they were justified in opposing Protestantism in the sixteenth century, Jansenism in the seventeenth, and rationalism in the eighteenth, without being exposed to the charge of change of aim. Their aim was constant; it was the attack upon the Church which changed its form from time to time. The fall of the Jesuits deprived the papacy of its stoutest guardians; it was the heaviest blow the Church of Rome had received since the Reformation of the sixteenth century.

After the issue of the Bull of dissolution some of the Jesuits found a refuge in Prussia, and others were welcomed by Catherine II in Russia. These members of the Order maintained its organisation, and even elected Vicars, who were Generals in all but name, to rule it. Early in the nineteenth century the Society secured a limited degree of papal recognition; its existence was sanctioned in Russia, and, shortly afterwards, in Sicily. In 1814 the Bull *Dominus ac Redemptor* was revoked, and the Society of Jesus was formally reconstituted. Pius VII, however, avoided even the appearance of censure upon his predecessor, by making no attempt to refute the charges brought against the fathers in the Bull of 1773.

The Order had a chequered existence in the nineteenth century. In various countries it was admitted, expelled, readmitted, restricted. It secured great influence with the papacy, and it was able to affect the policy of one pope after another. It remains to the present day the most ultramontane influence at Rome, the most determined bulwark of papal absolutism, and the most resolute of opponents to modernist tendencies in the Church.

CHAPTER XIII

POLAND

THE reign of John Casimir, King of Poland from 1648 to 1668, opened with a serious Cossack and Tartar revolt. The Poles were defeated at Pildawa, and for a time the Cossacks of the Ukraine were practically independent. They were ultimately routed at Berestecsko, in 1651. The chief importance of the revolt lay in its evidence of Polish weakness. From 1654 to 1667 Poland was at war with Russia, and in 1655 Charles X of Sweden invaded and overran the country. John Casimir retired into Silesia, while Charles besieged Danzig. The conduct of Frederick William of Brandenburg at this time is described elsewhere. By the Treaty of Wehlau, 1657, he offered to ally with Poland against Sweden in return for the recognition of his full sovereignty over East Prussia. The war with Sweden was ended by the Treaty of Oliva, 1660. John Casimir was forced to renounce his claim to the Swedish throne, to cede Livonia to Sweden, and to confirm the independence of Frederick William in East Prussia, which henceforth ceased to be a part of the kingdom of Poland.

The war with Russia was now prosecuted with some vigour and success; nevertheless, the Treaty of Andrussowa, 1667, registered further territorial losses. This was the last time Poland and Russia were involved in war. The weakness of Poland was such that the Tsars were able to exert continuous and increasing influence on its affairs without the necessity of resorting to fighting.

Poland was rapidly becoming moribund. The invigorating effect of the religious revival of the sixteenth century had long since spent itself. Foreign influence, often corrupt, prevailed in the country; Polish nobles and statesmen did not hesitate to accept the gold offered by foreign potentates, especially the rulers of France and Russia. The selfishness and cupidity of the landed aristocracy, and their carelessness of any interests but their own, found formal expression in the *liberum veto* in the

Diet. This extraordinary privilege of members of the Diet
reduced the feeble constitution of the country to a condition
which can be described only as organised anarchy. By the
exercise of the *liberum veto* any member of the Diet could
prevent the passage of a measure, so that for the enactment of a
law unanimity of assent was necessary. An overwhelming
affirmative vote was of no avail against a single franchise cast
in opposition. Moreover, any deputy could suspend the Diet
and compel the submission of measures already accepted to
a subsequent Diet for approval. This remarkable state of
affairs was firmly established by the middle of the seventeenth
century. It is not to be assumed that so extravagant a power
was kept by deputies in reserve, to be used only upon grave
constitutional issues. In course of time it was used frequently
and recklessly, and sometimes without reference to the merits
of the measure under consideration. A state which permitted
such proceedings in its legislative assembly was evidently far
advanced on the road to ruin.

The most notable of Polish kings in the latter part of the
seventeenth century was John Sobieski (1674–1696). The
general history of his reign is a record of failure, and he is to
be commended only for his military exploits. These, indeed,
were considerable, and he deserves a place of honour in the
history of Europe on account of his magnificent and successful
effort to save Vienna from the Turks in 1683, when even so
mighty a king as Louis XIV was prepared to leave the Emperor
to his fate. His attempt to reform the constitution of Poland
ended, as did those of abler men, in failure, and throughout his
reign Lithuania remained in chronic revolt. The war with the
Turks which began in 1683 dragged on until after his death; it
was ended by the Peace of Carlowitz, 1699.

After the death of John Sobieski the Elector of Saxony,
Augustus II, was chosen to fill the throne of Poland. He was
soon involved in a war with Charles XII of Sweden, in which
he was hopelessly defeated. The Swedish King held an
assembly of notables at Warsaw at which Augustus was deposed,
and Stanislaus Leszczynski, a creature of Charles, was chosen
King in his place. The reign of Stanislaus lasted only as long
as he remained under the protection of Charles; with the overthrow of the latter by Peter at Pultava, Stanislaus was forced to
fly and Augustus recovered his throne.

The death of Augustus II in 1733 was the signal for another

attempt by Stanislaus Leszczynski to obtain the Polish throne. He was now the father-in-law of Louis XV, and his candidature was supported by France. Russia and Austria resented French interference in Poland, and they prepared to assist Augustus III, the son of the late King. Stanislaus was elected in September, 1733, but he realised the impossibility of holding the country without French assistance and retired to Danzig, while Augustus was put in possession of Poland by Russian forces. The main interest of the war lay elsewhere than in Poland, and by the Third Treaty of Vienna Augustus was recognised as King, Stanislaus being compensated with the duchies of Lorraine and Bar.

Augustus III was indolent and pleasure-loving, and he left the government of Poland in the hands of the Czartoryskis, a noble family of great wealth. The aim of the Czartoryskis was to reform the constitution of the country by securing the abolition of the *liberum veto*. In no other way could Poland be rescued from anarchy. But her neighbours—Russia, Prussia, and Austria—were unwilling to sanction a revival of Polish vigour, and it was likely that they would oppose any action undertaken to that end. Augustus approved of the Czartoryski aim, but, fearing that he might be deprived of his crown by the greater powers, he refrained from giving them active support. During the Seven Years' War the belligerents crossed and recrossed Polish territory, utterly disregarding the neutrality of the country and adding to its misery. The Czartoryskis, failing to stimulate Augustus to assist their plans, hoped to come to terms with Russia, and they sent a young relative, Stanislaus Poniatowski, as Polish ambassador to St. Petersburg. Stanislaus acquired influence with the Grand Duchess Catherine, who in 1762 became Tsaritsa.

Augustus III died in 1763. Catherine was naturally disinclined to forward the Czartoryski plans for a stronger Poland, and she entered into an agreement with Frederick the Great to place on the vacant throne her favourite Stanislaus, through whom she expected to exert a controlling influence in Polish affairs. The two monarchs were resolved not to permit the Polish monarchy to become hereditary nor to sanction the abolition of the *liberum veto*. They desired, in short, the continuance of the existing disorder.

The Czartoryskis continued to press for reform, hoping to strengthen the monarchy by making it hereditary and reducing the power of the nobles. They were opposed by the Potockis, who wished to maintain noble power and privilege, and were supported by both Catherine and Frederick.

Pretexts for the intervention of Catherine and Frederick were to be found in the condition of religious affairs in Poland. The majority of the Poles were Catholic, but there were substantial minorities of Protestants and of Orthodox Christians. Any grievance, real or fancied, of these Dissident minorities could be used as ground for interference; Frederick was ready to protect the Protestants, while Catherine posed as the champion of the Orthodox.

A demand for full political rights for the Dissidents was refused by the Polish Diet, which was strongly Catholic, in 1766. The Dissidents in the following year formed the Confederation of Radom, and Russian troops marched to their support. A further Diet was overawed by the Russians into granting Dissident demands, and in a treaty between Russia and Prussia in 1768 it was agreed that the *liberum veto* should be maintained, that the monarchy should continue to be elective, and that Dissident rights should be respected.

Such undisguised aggression on the part of the neighbouring powers aroused intense indignation among the Catholic nobles, who formed the Confederation of Bar in 1768 and appealed to France for support. The most effective means open to France to assist the Polish nobles appeared to be to bring about a Russo-Turkish war. In this, French diplomacy was successful, and the Sultan declared war on Russia "in defence of Polish liberty." The course of the war went in favour of Russia, which gained substantial victories in the Danubian provinces of Turkey. Austria was alarmed at the extent of Russian successes, and in 1771 she concluded a treaty with Turkey by which she agreed to take up arms against Russia. Frederick the Great, realising that Austria would not consent to a large extension of Russian territory in the direction of Constantinople, suggested that Catherine should give up her conquests and accept compensation at the expense of Poland. Catherine agreed, and, though Maria Theresa was reluctant, the Emperor Joseph II and the Austrian Chancellor Kaunitz concurred in the plan. A Treaty of Partition was agreed upon, and the consent of the Polish Diet was extorted under threat of the conquest of the whole country.

In the First Partition of Poland Russia annexed the province of White Russia, with the territory which lay between the Dwina and the Dnieper; Austria received the regions known as Red Russia and Galicia; Prussia secured West Prussia, Ermeland, and Kulmerland, with the exception of Danzig and Thorn.

The Partition of Poland has been characterised as a great

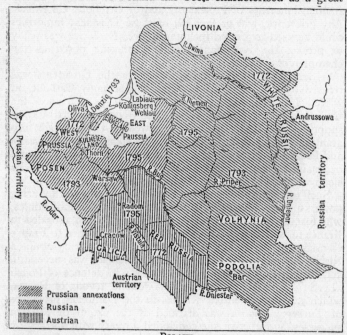

POLAND

international crime, and it has been asserted that the three powers introduced into European politics the principle of undisguised aggression against the territories of a weaker neighbour. It was certainly not a new principle; the history of Europe in the first three-quarters of the eighteenth century shows several similar, though not equally successful, examples of the violent aggression of the strong against the weak. It is difficult to see any difference of principle between Frederick's annexation of Silesia and of West Prussia. This, of course, is no defence of the Partition of Poland. Nevertheless, it may be noticed that many of the people of West Prussia were German in race and language, and that White Russia was inhabited by Russian-speaking people the bulk of whom were adherents of the Orthodox faith.

The true cause of the Partition lay less in the circumstances of the moment than in the anarchic condition of Poland. The attitude of the Polish nobility had prevented the consummation of any scheme of reform; the selfishness of the Diet in refusing to vote the necessary supplies had prevented the organisation of adequate defences; the existence of a system of serfdom under which the mass of the nation was kept practically in slavery prevented the development of any genuine national feeling. The bulk of the people felt no resentment at the Partition; those who were transferred to a new allegiance benefited by the change. To represent this and the subsequent Partitions as the brutal extinction of the independence of a brave, liberty-loving nation is an absurd travesty of the facts.

Catherine's wisdom in agreeing to the Partition is open to question. With her favourite Poniatowski on the Polish throne her influence was dominant throughout the country, and it might have been better for her to defend the integrity of the country, with a view to its annexation at a convenient time. On the other hand, her refusal to accede to the plan would probably have been followed by Austrian intervention in the war with Turkey, with consequences that could not be foreseen. That the Partition was to the advantage of Prussia cannot be doubted. The acquisition of West Prussia was an important step in the linking up of the scattered dominions of Brandenburg-Prussia, which was a feature of Hohenzollern policy in the eighteenth and nineteenth centuries. It may be added that Frederick acted energetically in developing the resources of his new province and increasing its prosperity.

The remainder of the story is soon told. It was not yet too late for Poland to reform herself, and Stanislaus made some proposals to the Diet. That body was long unwilling to consider the only reforms worth consideration, the establishment of hereditary monarchy and the surrender of the *liberum veto*. Not until the Diet of 1788–91 were effective measures taken, when the more intelligent and patriotic of the Poles hoped to take advantage of the Russian preoccupation in a war with Turkey by introducing reforms in their own land. A new constitution was established, by which the monarchy was

F 1643–1843

henceforth to be hereditary, the privileges of the nobles were to be curtailed, and a legislature of two chambers was to be set up. The religious question was to be settled by the retention of Catholicism as the state religion, toleration being granted at the same time to the Orthodox and the Lutherans. Serfdom, however, was not abolished, although some efforts were made to diminish its burdens.

The course of events in Poland was pleasing to neither Frederick William nor Catherine. The hereditary crown of Poland was offered to the Elector of Saxony, and a united kingdom of Saxony and Poland would be a serious menace to Prussia. The maintenance of Russian influence in Poland depended upon a continuance of the old disorder; for that reason Catherine viewed the new constitution with disfavour, and she hastened on her peace with the Turks in order that she might be free to deal with her neighbour. But Leopold II was disposed to support the new order of things for precisely the reason that led Frederick William to frown upon it—that it would provide a check upon Prussian power. Austria, however, was too fully occupied with the French war at this time to intervene effectively, and early in 1793 Russia and Prussia carried out the Second Partition. Prussia received Thorn, Posen, Danzig, and other territories, while Russia annexed Volhynia and Podolia. Austria received no share.

Polish patriots under Kosciuszko now organised a rising to undo the work of this Second Partition and to restore the Polish kingdom to its former limits. Kosciuszko met with some initial successes. He seized Cracow and Warsaw, but the struggle was bound to fail. The nobles were alienated by Kosciuszko's concessions to the peasants, and the townsmen held aloof. A Russian army defeated the brave Kosciuszko and recovered Warsaw. Prussian and Austrian armies invaded Poland, and the Third and final Partition was agreed upon. Russia seized the lands between the lower Dwina and Galicia. Prussia took the region between the Bug and the Niemen, including Warsaw, and Austria annexed a stretch of territory south of Warsaw. Poland as an independent state ceased to exist.

CHAPTER XIV

SWEDEN

THE Peace of Westphalia marked the zenith of the greatness of Sweden; it remained to be seen whether she could maintain the position she had attained. For several reasons this proved to be impossible. Her population and her material resources were too small, and her strategic position too remote, to enable her to exert a commanding influence in European affairs. Her Baltic territories were as much a source of anxiety as of strength; behind them lay powerful neighbours, whose pressure it would be impossible to resist. Within much less than a century the greater part of the Baltic lands of Sweden had passed into the possession of Russia, Prussia, and Hanover, and Sweden had ceased to count as a great power.

During the minority of Christina, who succeeded Gustavus Adolphus in 1632, the government of Sweden was vested in the great officers of state, of whom Oxenstjerna, the Chancellor, was the most powerful. The oligarchy which ruled the country profited from the minority of the Crown and the continuance of the war, but heavy taxation impoverished the peasants, and the drain of man-power prevented the expansion of industry and commerce.

The vexed question of the Sound was still unsettled. The Danes still held the province of Halland, and their attempt to place heavy tolls on Swedish shipping resulted in war between 1642 and 1645. The Danes, taken by surprise, were defeated, and by the Treaty of Brömsebro, 1645, Swedish shipping was freed from tolls in the Sound and Halland passed into Swedish possession. These gains were of greater practical advantage to Sweden than the more spectacular acquisitions under the Treaty of Westphalia.

For ten years, from 1644 to 1654, Christina ruled Sweden in person. She was a woman of great political ability, intellectual strength, personal charm, and force of character. She established her ascendancy over the oligarchy which had seized power during her minority. In 1654 she embraced the

Roman Catholic faith, and, realising the impossibility of a
Catholic queen ruling in Lutheran Sweden, she abdicated in
favour of Charles Gustavus, who took the title of Charles X.

The new King was soon involved in a war with Poland,
whose King, John Casimir, refused to recognise the right of
Charles X to the Swedish crown. Charles, an able soldier,
invaded Poland by way of Eastern Pomerania, defeated John
Casimir, and laid siege to Danzig. Frederick William of
Brandenburg, the Great Elector, attempted to form a triple
alliance of Brandenburg, Poland, and Denmark, against Sweden,
but Charles X abandoned his enterprise at Danzig, and marched
into East Prussia, which was under the Elector's rule. By the
Treaty of Königsberg Frederick William was forced to acknowledge Swedish suzerainty over East Prussia, to add a contingent
of Brandenburg troops to the Swedish army, and to give
Charles free passage through his dominions.

Charles renewed his attack on Poland and inflicted a further
defeat upon John Casimir at Warsaw in 1656. At this time
Russia declared war and sent forces into East Prussia, while
a Danish invasion of Sweden was being planned. Charles
retired from Poland, and, after releasing Frederick William
from his vassalage in the Treaty of Labiau, sailed for Denmark.
He inflicted heavy defeats on the Danes, and his death in 1660
was followed by the conclusion of peace. By the Treaty of
Oliva between Sweden and Poland, John Casimir renounced
all claim to the Swedish throne. The Treaty of Copenhagen
restored peace between Sweden and Denmark, the latter power
surrendering its remaining footholds in Sweden. The Treaty
of Kardis ended the war between Sweden and Russia.

The new King, Charles XI, was a child, whose mother acted
as Regent. As was the case during the minority of Christina,
real power was wielded by an oligarchy of great nobles, who
enriched themselves by seizing Crown lands and accepting the
bribes of Louis XIV. Sweden was thus committed to a French
alliance, and though she joined the Triple Alliance of 1668 her
defection was only temporary. Charles XI came of age in
1672 and supported his ally in the Dutch War. He invaded
Brandenburg in 1675, but was decisively defeated by the
Great Elector at Fehrbellin. Frederick William followed up
his victory by overrunning Western Pomerania, so that the
Swedish gains on the Baltic at Westphalia would have been
utterly lost had not Louis stood by his ally. By the Treaty of

St. Germain-en-Laye, 1679, the King of France compelled the Great Elector to restore Western Pomerania to Sweden.

From 1679 until the death of Charles XI his country was at peace. He was able to reduce the power of the nobles by ordering the restoration of the alienated Crown lands, and he reduced their share in the government. Abuses were corrected, and prosperity returned.

In 1697 Charles XII, at the age of fifteen, succeeded his father. Other Baltic powers thought that his accession provided an opportunity for a war of aggression against Sweden, and an alliance of Denmark, Poland, and Russia was formed in 1699. They had no idea of the military capacity of their young antagonist. Without waiting to be attacked he sailed for Copenhagen. Frederick IV was not ready to defend his capital, and was forced to accept the terms offered by Charles. He made peace and withdrew from the war.

Meanwhile, Peter the Great was besieging Narva, and Charles sailed to its relief. He routed a Russian army many times the size of his own, and marched southward into Poland. He captured Warsaw in 1702 and defeated Augustus, King of Poland, and in the following year he took Thorn and Danzig. In 1704 Charles arranged a meeting of Polish nobles at which Augustus was deposed and Stanislaus Leszczynski was chosen King in his stead. Fighting continued until 1707, when Augustus was forced to agree to the Treaty of Altranstadt, by which he recognised Stanislaus as King of Poland.

In the winter of 1707-8 Charles was at the zenith of his career. He had defeated all his enemies, and for the moment his sword was in its sheath. But the war in which he had been engaged was not the only one which was being waged at this time. Western Europe was deeply involved in the War of the Spanish Succession, and both sides in this struggle looked to the King of Sweden. Louis XIV sought an alliance with Charles on the ground of the long friendship of France and Sweden in the seventeenth century. This might have appealed to the young King had not the Spanish Succession war borne in his eyes a religious aspect. Louis was persecuting Huguenots, and it was inconceivable that a king of the Swedish House of Vasa should fight on behalf of the Counter-Reformation against Protestants. Marlborough, a soldier as renowned as Charles, visited the young King at Altranstadt and flattered him into a benevolent neutrality. Further, Charles's interests lay elsewhere than on the Rhine, and he was determined to push his war with Russia to a successful issue.

Nothing went right with him after this. Disregarding Peter's operations in Ingria and Carelia, Charles marched towards Moscow. He allied with Mazeppa, a Cossack chief, but he was unable to effect a junction with his auxiliaries. The march was continued under inconceivable difficulty and with heavy losses throughout the winter of 1708–9, and in June, 1709, Charles was overwhelmed by Peter at Pultava. The Swedish army as a fighting force ceased to exist. Those Swedes who were not slain in the battle were forced to surrender, and Charles himself fled southward into Turkish territory. The provinces of Esthonia and Livonia fell into Peter's possession, and Swedish predominance in the Baltic came to an end.

Charles lived for some years at Bender, in Turkey, and in 1710 he induced the Sultan to take up arms against the Tsar. The Turks met with some successes, and made an advantageous treaty in 1713 by which Charles was permitted to return to Sweden, from which he had been absent for many years.

As might be expected, he found the country in great disorder. Sweden in his absence had been at war with her old enemies, Denmark, Poland, and Russia, and Finland had been lost. Further fighting occurred after Charles's return, and in a war with Norway he was killed at the siege of Fredrikssten. He was succeeded by his sister Ulrica, under whom negotiations for peace were begun. By two Treaties of Stockholm, in 1719 and 1720, between Hanover and Sweden, Bremen and Verden passed to the electorate, and Prussia obtained Stettin. The Treaty of Frederiksborg, 1720, marked the conclusion of peace between Sweden and Denmark. Denmark surrendered certain conquered territories, but retained Schleswig, and Sweden relinquished her exemption from tolls in the Sound. The unwillingness of Sweden to surrender her provinces to the east of the Baltic postponed the conclusion of the treaty with Russia. British efforts to secure a modification of Russian demands in favour of Sweden met with no success, and a Russian descent upon the coast of Sweden reconciled her to the inevitable. By the Treaty of Nystad, 1721, Russia secured Esthonia, Livonia, Ingria, Carelia, and part of Finland, with the fortress of Viborg. In return, she surrendered Finland west of Viborg.

A new constitution was promulgated in Sweden in 1720. All power was vested in the Riksdag, or Diet, which consisted of four estates—nobles, clergy, citizens, and peasants—sitting and voting independently of one another. The assent of any three of the estates was sufficient for the passing of a law; it was

THE BALTIC

thus possible for legislation to be enacted by the combination of three estates to the detriment of the interests of the remaining class. While the Diet was in session a secret committee, consisting of fifty nobles, twenty-five clergy, and twenty-five citizens, and from which peasants were excluded, exercised a great deal of power. It nominated ministers, exercised judicial functions, and prepared legislation for the Diet. When the Diet was not in session the executive power was vested in a Senate of twenty-four members. Under this constitution the power of the Crown was reduced to insignificance.

The defects of the constitution did not become apparent at first. For many years Sweden was under the rule of Count Horn, a wise statesman who kept on friendly terms with Great Britain and gave his country twenty years of peace. In course of time an opposition to Count Horn sprang up under the leadership of Count Gyllenborg and Count Tessin. These men advocated a return in foreign policy to the traditional alliance with France. They despised the peaceful Horn and his followers, whom, in contemptuous reference to their political somnolence, they nicknamed the Night-Caps. This term was soon popularly shortened to Caps, and the adherents of Tessin called themselves the Hats.

Corruption was prevalent in Sweden, and the French ambassador distributed bribes among members of the Diet, with the result that in 1738 the Caps were defeated, and Count Tessin succeeded Horn at the head of the administration. An alliance with France followed, and the Hats prepared to carry on an aggressive policy abroad. War was declared on Russia in 1741 for the purpose of recovering the lost provinces to the east of the Baltic, but the Swedish forces met with no success, and the Russians overran Finland. Peace was concluded by the Treaty of Abo in 1743; the greater part of Finland was restored to Sweden, and it was agreed that Adolphus Frederick of Holstein, a relative of the Russian Empress Elizabeth, should be selected as Crown Prince of Sweden.

Adolphus Frederick, who married a sister of Frederick the Great, succeeded to the throne in 1751, and he reigned rather than ruled until his death in 1771. This was a period of utter corruption in Swedish politics. The rivalry of the Hats and the Caps reached its height; the Hats were in the pay of France, while the Caps looked to Russia for payment. By each party in turn the Crown was subject to great humiliation. The Hats were in power from 1738 to 1765, and fell into disfavour only because of their disastrous intervention in the Seven Years' War at the bidding of France. When the Caps assumed office they initiated a policy of retrenchment in public finance which made them unpopular, and they entered into an alliance with Catherine II of Russia which was against the best interests of the country. By 1769 they were defeated, and the Hats returned to power. In 1771 Adolphus Frederick died suddenly, and was succeeded by his son Gustavus III, who proved to be worthy of his name.

Gustavus, twenty-five years of age at his accession, was a man of outstanding ability who was determined to rescue the country from the corrupt factions which were bringing her to ruin. Sweden was sinking into a condition of anarchy similar to that of Poland, and there was some possibility of the policy of partition being applied to her by Frederick the Great and Catherine. His attempts to reconcile the two parties in Sweden meeting with no success, Gustavus resolved upon a *coup d'état*. With the aid of loyal partisans and guards, he made himself master of Stockholm and overawed the Diet, in whose presence he promulgated a new constitution, by which his power, though not unlimited, would be substantial. He recovered for the Crown the right of appointing ministers and senators and of summoning the Diet. He obtained the command of the forces. The rights of legislation and taxation remained with the Diet, whose consent was necessary to a declaration of war. Judges were made independent and irremovable, except upon impeachment, as in Great Britain.

Gustavus was responsible for many reforms in the state. Finance was established on a sound basis, the administration of justice was purified, the strength and efficiency of the army was increased, and the navy was augmented. Although these measures were to the advantage of the country Gustavus met with a good deal of resistance from his Diets, and when, in 1788, he embarked upon a war with Russia without the consent of the Diet he was faced with a mutiny of the army. His position was critical, but a Danish declaration of war and invasion of Sweden proved to be his salvation. The peasantry rallied to his support; the Danes were defeated and driven out, and Gustavus was able to face the Diet in 1789 as a victor in war.

He now succeeded in carrying the Act of Union and Security, by which his power was very greatly increased and noble privileges and exemptions were substantially curtailed. The Crown of Sweden henceforth enjoyed almost absolute power. The war with Russia was pursued with vigour and success and was ended in 1790 on terms favourable to Sweden. In the following year a definite alliance was concluded between Catherine and Gustavus, to whom the Empress agreed to pay an annual subsidy.

The attitude of Gustavus III to the French Revolution was

one of hostility, and he tried to induce the great powers to co-operate in its suppression. His efforts met with no success. Before the joint invasion of France in 1792 by Austria and Prussia had begun, Gustavus was assassinated as the result of a conspiracy of nobles.

His son, Gustavus IV, was a minor, and did not assume the direction of affairs until 1796. In the interval the regency was in the hands of the Duke of Sudermania, who reversed the foreign policy of Gustavus III by entering into friendly relations with the Jacobins of France. This attitude was not maintained by Gustavus IV after he took control of the government. He adhered to the Armed Neutrality in 1800, but in 1805 he joined the Third Coalition against Napoleon. His intervention in the war was too slow to be effective, and its chief result was the occupation of Pomerania by the French. The reconciliation of Napoleon with the Tsar at Tilsit was followed by a war between Sweden and Russia in 1808. The Swedes met with no success, and the Russians conquered Finland, which was thus finally lost to Sweden. The disasters which his policy had brought upon the country led in 1809 to his deposition and the exclusion of his descendants from the throne.

The crown was conferred on Charles XIII, the former Duke-Regent. By this time he was feeble and incapable, and, as he was childless, the Swedish nobles in 1810 offered the succession to one of Napoleon's marshals, Bernadotte. Bernadotte accepted, against the wish of the French Emperor, and from the time of his recognition as Crown Prince he exercised a commanding influence in Swedish affairs. He was popular and able, and he devoted himself to the interests of his new country, to the utter disregard of those of his former master. He frankly recognised that Finland was lost irretrievably and that it was not worth while to attempt its recovery. He preferred, instead, to consider the possibility of obtaining Norway from Denmark as compensation for the loss of Finland. This opened the way to friendly relations with Russia, with whom he made an alliance in 1812. He joined the Fourth Coalition and assisted the allies at the Battle of Leipzig, but while they were following the defeated Napoleon into France Bernadotte carried on an independent campaign against Denmark, which resulted in the conquest of Norway. The Congress of Vienna recognised the claim of Sweden to Norway and left Finland in Russian possession.

Bernadotte became King of Sweden in 1818 as Charles XIV, and he ruled until his death in 1844. He followed a policy of peace and he promoted internal reforms, so that his reign was of lasting benefit to the country.

It is unnecessary to follow the history of Sweden and her kings throughout the nineteenth century. Sweden ceased to be recognised as one of the powers of Europe, and she no longer concerned herself with the questions which agitated the Continent. Her recent history can be described as peaceful and uneventful, and the condition of her people as prosperous.

CHAPTER XV

THE ANCIEN RÉGIME IN FRANCE

FRENCH society in the eighteenth century, like that of other continental countries, was characterised by rigid caste distinctions. Traditionally, the people of France were classified in three estates—the clergy, the nobles, and the third estate. The clergy and the nobles were the privileged classes, the third estate (mainly the peasantry), the unprivileged. In the seventeenth and eighteenth centuries an additional group—of officials and professional men and others—came into existence. This class was smaller in numbers than the others; its members enjoyed privileges in certain directions, though in strict law they belonged to the third estate.

The nobles in France were much more numerous than the peers of Great Britain. In Great Britain the sons of a peer were, and are, legally commoners, though they may enjoy "courtesy" titles; upon the death of a peer his eldest son succeeds to his rank, but his other sons remain commoners. In France the nobility formed a hereditary caste; all the sons of a noble were noble, and all enjoyed the privileges referred to below. It has been estimated that, immediately before the Revolution, this, the second estate of the realm of France, included 140,000 persons. Only a small proportion of these men could be classed as nobles in the English sense. These great nobles owned large estates, from which they drew substantial incomes. They lived at court, however, and many of them were attached to the households of the King, the Queen, or some other member of the royal family. They were gay, witty, cultured, and extravagant, and it may be asserted that their existence, as a class, was of no advantage to France. They rarely or never visited their estates, which were managed by bailiffs whose function was to extort for the benefit of their masters the maximum from the peasantry that law or custom or economic circumstance permitted. There was no personal tie between noble and peasant, and this accounts in no small degree for the bitterness of the peasantry towards the aristocracy at the time of the Revolution. The lesser nobles were men of some property who could hardly be described as rich and who lived on their estates—men who in England would be classed as country gentlemen. There were also many poor nobles who in economic position were indistinguishable from the peasantry, from whom they were divided socially by the titles and exemptions to which they clung.

The privileges of the nobles originated in a time when some justification might have been found for them. In the Middle Ages a powerful lord established and maintained order in his district, and afforded protection from violence to his underlings. All such political power had been wrested from the nobility by successive Bourbon rulers, and the privileges of the lords had long outlasted their obligations. They possessed the sole rights of hunting, fishing, and shooting, and they alone on their domains were entitled to provide certain services for the people, so that the peasant was bound to grind his corn at the lord's mill, to kill his cattle in the lord's slaughter-house, to press his grapes in the lord's winepress, and to bake his bread in the lord's oven, and in connection with each of these obligations he had to pay a toll. Nobles were entitled to levy certain dues on the produce of the peasant's land, and they enjoyed exemption from service in the ranks of the army, from forced labour on the roads, and from payment of the land-tax, or *taille*.

As in the case of the nobility, some justification might have been found in earlier times for the privileges of the Church. In the Middle Ages the Church was the guardian of morality, and it stood for the advance of education and civilisation; it kept learning and culture alive in times of violence and brutality; it protected the weak and relieved the poor; it tended the sick and sheltered the homeless. By the eighteenth century it had ceased to be useful; it was corrupt; it had lost the respect of the people; it was concerned mainly with the retention of its privileges. The clergy were exempt from ordinary taxation, and they were entitled to collect tithes. By its control of education and of the censorship of the press, the Church still wielded great power.

The middle class, to which reference was made above, consisted of lawyers, state officials, merchants, and wealthy gildsmen. With these may be associated the tax-farmers and other financiers who lent money to the state. People of this class enjoyed a considerable degree of wealth. In their tastes and style of living, many of them were the equals of nobles, but they were debarred from intercourse on equal terms with nobles by reason of the privileges enjoyed by the aristocrats and from which they were excluded. On account of their wealth they were hated by the poor, and during the Reign of Terror they, as well as the nobles, were the objects of popular attack.

The great mass of the French people belonged to the peasant class. They bore the burdens of the state and were subject to irritating restrictions. The plight of the French peasant in the eighteenth century has often been depicted; it is difficult to describe his condition without falling into exaggeration. In most parts of France the peasant was not a serf; only in the east and north-east, on the borders of the Holy Roman Empire and the Netherlands, did serfdom survive. Yet many of the vexatious accompaniments of serfdom—payment of sundry dues to the lord, attendance at the seigneurial court, service in the lord's household—remained. Again, the typical peasant was not a landless labourer but a landed proprietor, though in the north and north-west of the country the tenancy system prevailed. Further, it is undeniable that the condition of the French peasantry improved during the eighteenth century. Their wealth increased, as is proved by the fact that they were able to purchase land from the nobles, and it is possible that the poverty which was observed by many travellers was more apparent than real; it was unwise for a peasant to appear to be prosperous when the bailiff or the tax-collector was in the neighbourhood.

When full allowance is made for these facts it remains true that the condition of the French peasant was anything but enviable. Living in primitive huts, wearing rough woollen clothing, and subsisting on the coarsest of food, the peasants, men and women, toiled hard in the fields and became prematurely aged by fatigue, exposure, and privation. Methods of tillage were medieval, and the improvements which were being introduced into English agriculture had no parallel in pre-revolutionary France. Though in good years the produce of the soil was sufficient, after the demands of the lord, the Church, and the state had been met, to afford subsistence to the people, in times of deficient harvest they suffered from famine.

Peasants were not permitted to drive the lord's pigeons from their crops, and nobles were entitled to ride across growing crops in pursuit of game; in such ways serious loss was caused to cultivators. Peasants were required to labour on the public roads for periods varying from one to six weeks in the year. This labour was unpaid, and the obligation was bitterly resented. The unmarried peasant was liable to be conscripted into the army, and early and improvident marriage was resorted to as a means of evading military service.

Industry in the towns was controlled, as in the Middle Ages, by gilds which were dominated by wealthy manufacturers and merchants. It was carried on by hand, and was subject to a mass of vexatious restrictions. Trade was hindered by the existence of customs barriers at every provincial frontier.

Paris was the centre of national life. The administration was so highly centralised that large numbers of officials lived in the capital. Paris, too, was the most important manufacturing city in France, and it contained a large industrial population prone at times to violent outbreaks. The city was a centre which attracted the discontented, the destitute, and the turbulent from other parts of France. These formed the nucleus of a rabble ready to follow any demagogue who might harangue them; during the Revolution the mob exerted a marked influence upon the course of events.

The government of France in the eighteenth century was a highly centralised, albeit inefficient, despotism. There were, indeed, in some parts of the country traces of the survival of local liberties. In certain provinces, known as the *pays d'état*, local assemblies still retained some right of control over taxation; some towns possessed privileges guaranteed by their charters; here and there were nobles who retained remnants of ancient jurisdictions. But all the essential features of the government depended upon the Crown. The actual work of administration was entrusted to ministers appointed by and responsible to the King. (These included the First Minister, though this post was not always filled; the Controller-General, who supervised national finance; and four Secretaries of State—for foreign affairs, the royal household, war, and the navy.) Taxation and legislation were by royal edict alone. Justice was administered by close corporations of lawyers known as Parlements; of these the Parlement of Paris was the most important, and there were about a dozen provincial Parlements which usually followed the lead given by the Paris Parlement.

It was held that an edict was not effective unless it had been registered by the Parlements, and the Parlement of Paris occasionally offered resistance to an oppressive edict by refusing registration. This could always be overcome by the King attending the Parlement in person and holding a *lit de justice*, at which he might order registration to be made. The effectiveness of this check upon despotism was not very great, but if the provincial Parlements also declined to register an unpopular decree it might be necessary for the King to make a tour of the country, lasting a year or more, in order to secure registration and observance in every part of the land. As such a journey might be inconvenient to the King, it was sometimes possible for the Parlements to secure a modification of an edict as a condition of registration. The supervision of local affairs was entrusted to the Intendants, who collected non-farmed taxes, maintained order, enforced military service, and exercised judicial authority which might conflict with that of the Parlements.

The revenue of the government of France was derived from a multiplicity of taxes, of which the *taille* was the most important. It was a land-tax levied on the produce of non-noble lands. (Noble and ecclesiastical lands were exempt.) The tax was burdensome, and became unnecessarily so by reason of exemptions, inequalities of assessment, and the vagaries of collectors. With the *taille* was usually demanded a poll-tax which increased the total yield by fifty per cent. The *vingtième* was an income-tax of five per cent, from which, also, privileged persons could secure exemption. Customs and excise duties and inter-provincial customs added to the revenue while hindering the trade of France. Perhaps the most vexatious of all French taxes was the *gabelle*, or salt-tax. The sale of salt was a government monopoly, and as the tax varied enormously in different provinces there was a strong temptation to smuggle salt across a provincial boundary, an offence long punishable with service in the galleys.

Certain of the taxes were farmed. Capitalists, known as farmers of taxes, made contracts with the Government for a period of years; in return for a sum of money paid down they received the privilege of collecting a tax, and the difference between the sum collected and that paid for the privilege represented their profit. Tax-farmers were among the wealthiest and most hated men in France.

The condition of French finance in the eighteenth century was deplorable. Through exemptions, inequalities of assessment, the extortions of the tax-farmers, and the corruption of collectors, the amount received by the state was much less than that paid by the people. No proper system of accounting was employed, and no effective audit existed. The wars which occurred from time to time involved a heavy drain upon state resources, and at all times the lavish expenditure of the court caused serious embarrassment to finance ministers. The state debt was steadily augmented, until charges for interest absorbed more than half the national income. French finance could have been restored to a satisfactory condition only by a statesman of the ability and determination of Walpole or the younger Pitt. The only French financier in the eighteenth century capable of grappling with the problem was Turgot, and, as narrated below, even his preliminary measures of reform met with such opposition that he was speedily dismissed.

The eighteenth century in France was distinguished by great intellectual activity. The abuses which were inherent in the *ancien régime* invited attack, which developed against every aspect of authority and tradition. There was a strong tendency to re-examine the basis of authority and to repudiate everything that could not be justified by an appeal to reason. It was inevitable that the Church, which of all existing institutions was most completely based on authority, should be the object of the fiercest onslaught, and the moral and intellectual condition of the clergy was such that they were an easy mark for their critics. Only here and there among the ecclesiastics was to be found a man capable of joining in the controversies which arose, and more often than not such a man would range himself with the attack rather than the defence. Philosophical speculation was not limited to religion and theology, however; it concerned itself with politics, economics, and jurisprudence, and ranged itself over the whole field of science, physical, mental, and moral.

The movement (if such a term may be applied to this outburst of intellectual activity) was in the main destructive. It was superficial and imaginative, resting upon no true basis of historic fact, and lacking many of the elements of reasoned criticism. The philosophers had little knowledge and understanding of the past, and their speculations have failed to stand the test of subsequent investigation and criticism. To pour contempt upon the Church, the monarchy, the financial system, and the privileges of the aristocracy was easier than to propound alternatives based on sound principles. The antagonism of Great Britain and France in the eighteenth century did not prevent French philosophers expressing their admiration of English institutions. They were ready to acknowledge the superior stability of the constitution of Great Britain, the excellence of her financial system, the absence of caste privilege, and the prosperity of the British people. They advocated the imitation, in various respects, of British institutions; yet they often failed to understand what they most admired. Nor did they realise that the political and social condition of Great Britain was the product of centuries of evolution under conditions markedly dissimilar to those which prevailed in France, and that its transplantation would not necessarily have been attended with success.

Montesquieu, a lawyer by profession, belonged to the first half of the eighteenth century. He was one of the most serious and profound thinkers of his time. His *Lettres Persanes*, published in 1721, purported to contain the observations of two Persian merchants visiting Europe on the customs and political system of France, a literary form which gave full opportunity for witty and penetrating satire. Montesquieu's greatest work was *L'Esprit des Lois*, an important contribution to the political science of the eighteenth century. It contained a ruthless analysis and criticism of the French system and a eulogy of that of Great Britain, where the author had resided for some time. Montesquieu attributed much of the success of the British constitution to the application of the doctrine of the separation of powers—executive, legislative, and judicial. It is true that the judiciary in Great Britain is free from external influence (though the Lord Chancellor, who is the head of the judiciary, is also a member of the Cabinet and is Speaker of the House of Lords, so that he participates in all three forms of constitutional activity), but a longer and closer acquaintance with the working of the British constitution might have convinced Montesquieu of the close interdependence of the executive and legislative powers. Nevertheless, the doctrine of the separation of powers played its part in the controversies of the constitution-makers at the time of the French Revolution. (Its influence is to be observed, also, in the constitution of the United States.)

The influence of Voltaire extended over many years. He was not a systematic nor even an original thinker, and he made no effort to put forward a reasoned system of philosophy. His views are to be found in numerous essays, poems, dramas, pamphlets, and philosophical and historical works which streamed from his pen during a period of more than half a century. He was effective less on account of the profundity of his thought than by reason of his style, which was gay, epigrammatic, and witty. If any principle can be traced as continuously applied throughout his works it is the appeal to reason. Everything which conflicted with the dictates of human reason earned his unsparing condemnation. He denounced the Church as the citadel of privilege and the enemy of progress and enlightenment, and he desired its overthrow. Yet he was not an atheist, and he taught the existence in mankind of a divinely implanted sense of justice and goodness that would triumph over evil.

Voltaire in his works recommended many specific reforms, such as the abolition of serfdom and feudal privilege, of the use of torture, and of exemptions from taxation. But he made no proposal for a radical change in the constitution of France. He was no democrat, and if he cherished any hope that his ideals would ever be realised he expected them to be put into operation by the monarchy.

The *Encyclopaedia*, a compilation in twenty-eight volumes which professed to cover the whole range of human knowledge, was issued between 1751 and 1765. Many of the philosophers of the time, including Diderot, d'Alembert, Rousseau, Voltaire, Turgot, and Mirabeau (father of the more famous Mirabeau of the Revolution), contributed to it. Its importance in connection with the philosophical movement lay not so much in positive contributions as in its tone. It was in form respectful to, though critical of, Church and state, but it expressed contempt of tradition and the supernatural, and based its conclusions upon reason. It thus denounced many of the prevalent abuses, and strengthened the attitude of criticism of existing institutions which was becoming so widespread in France.

The Physiocrats, of whom the most prominent were Quesnay, Turgot, Mirabeau, Dupont de Nemours, de la Rivière, and Le Trosne, were less concerned with the political than the economic structure of society. They envisaged a "natural order" of society which contrasted emphatically with the artificial structure

of society then existent in France.   They contended that this
natural order could be restored only by the abolition of the
restrictions and regulations which had grown up, and they
therefore advocated what has since been termed *laissez-faire*.
They regarded agriculture as the sole source of wealth.   Only
in tillage, they asserted, was more received than was expended.   Commerce and manufacturing industry might be
necessary, but, in the opinion of the Physiocrats, they added
nothing to the wealth of the nation; the goods produced by the
manufacturer could not exceed in quantity the raw material
used, while the merchant could only exchange goods for goods.
In neither case was there any "natural increase."   Such
occupations were sterile, and elaborate systems for the direction
and control of industry and commerce were not worth while,
since national prosperity could not be augmented by such
means.   These arguments were, of course, fallacious, but the
Physiocrats made a useful contribution to the science of
political economy in that they drew attention to the importance
of agriculture and advocated free trade, in these respects
preceding and inspiring Adam Smith.   In their criticisms of
the existing trade gilds, industrial and commercial regulations,
and customs system, they launched an attack upon these
institutions from a new angle.

The one real revolutionary among the philosophers was Jean
Jacques Rousseau, if, indeed, he is to be classed as a philosopher
at all, and not as a romantic.   It is impossible to give here more
than the barest outline of his ideas, which were expressed in
several works, but especially in his *Contrat Social*, published in
1762.   Rousseau, like many other political speculators from the
sixteenth to the eighteenth century, asserted that civil society
originated in a contract.   Primitive man, he contended, lived
in a "state of nature," which continued until an agreement was
reached for the formation of a political society.   This conception of a Social Contract had been used by Thomas Hobbes in
the seventeenth century in order to provide a defence of
absolute monarchy, and at the end of the seventeenth century
by John Locke as a justification for the English Revolution.
Since it was purely speculative, resting on no historical basis
whatever, it could obviously be framed in any way which would
buttress the conclusions which the writer wished to draw.
Hobbes held that by the original contract men bound themselves to obey an absolute monarch, and that the contract itself

was irrevocable; Locke maintained that the contract was between king and people, and that if the king violated its terms the people were at liberty to depose him; Rousseau asserted that the original contract was drawn up at the instance of the wealthy, and that its object was the defence of property. The poor were thus outwitted, since they possessed little or no property, yet were engaged in its defence. Such a contract was evil, in that it confirmed the rich man in his wealth and the poor man in his poverty. The remedy, in Rousseau's view, was to be found in the termination of the existing contract and the drawing up of a new one on fairer terms. Between the destruction of the old contract and the establishment of the new, men would revert to the state of nature, and "Back to Nature" became the slogan of the followers of Rousseau. In plain terms, Rousseau advocated not so much the reform as the utter destruction of existing institutions as a preliminary to the setting up of a new heaven upon earth.

The overthrow of the contract was justifiable, according to Rousseau, since ultimate sovereignty rested with the people as a whole, and could not be alienated. Rulers did not receive their power from God but from the people, and they were entitled to retain it only so long as the people willed that they should do so. When the people were dissatisfied with their ruler they might depose him and appoint another, or they might change the form of government altogether. This, Rousseau proclaimed, should now be done. "Man is born free, and is everywhere in chains." It was time for the chains to be struck off. It is easy to see that such doctrine was acceptable to extreme revolutionaries, and that the *Contrat Social* became the Bible of the Jacobin party during the French Revolution.

The influence exerted by Rousseau was much greater than that of other writers of the eighteenth century. They had attracted the attention of the cultured and educated classes; Rousseau appealed to the mass of the people, and it is hardly possible to overstate the effect of the *Contrat Social* as a factor contributory to the French Revolution.

The account of French society given in the foregoing pages should not mislead the reader into thinking that conditions were worse in France than elsewhere. In some ways the reverse was the case. Serfdom survived in most parts of central and eastern Europe, and, though some of the enlightened despots had taken measures to protect the serf from gross oppression, his lot was still grievous. In some countries peasants had to cultivate the lands of their lords; they had no rights that could be upheld in courts of law; they could not sell their plots of land without the lord's consent; they might be evicted; the right of succession might depend upon the whim of the lord; they bore the burden of taxation and of numerous feudal obligations; they were at the mercy of the lord in the matter of capital or corporal punishment. Nobles enjoyed vast wealth and great privileges; they were exempt from most of the obligations that bore heavily upon the peasant; they exercised jurisdiction over the people living on their estates.

In Great Britain, on the other hand, the Revolution of 1688–9 had established the supremacy of Parliament and the universal rule of law. All men were equal before the law, and no class enjoyed special privileges. Every man was personally free. Serfdom had been extinct for centuries, and if some ancient feudal dues survived, such as the quit-rents payable by copy-holders, they were not in any way onerous. If the burden of taxation was heavy it was well-distributed, and there were no exemptions. Until the imposition of the assessed taxes by Pitt the only direct tax of any importance in eighteenth-century England was the land tax, which bore most heavily upon the landed gentry. The finances of the country were well-ordered. Agriculture was more advanced than in any other country of Europe. Nor were the landed gentry out of touch with the peasantry. Country squires lived upon their estates; even if they went to London for the meeting of Parliament they spent some months of every year in the country. They were personally acquainted with tenant-farmers and even with labourers, and there was little trace of hostility between men of different classes. In Ireland, however, many great estates belonged to English absentee landlords who were represented by agents who rackrented the peasantry in much the same way as did the estate bailiffs in France. There was an absence of personal contact between landlord and tenant, and an antagonism of interest existed which led to the development of the Irish agrarian problem of the nineteenth century.

This brief review of conditions outside France is sufficient to indicate that the state of the common people in that country was not more desperate than in other parts of the Continent. The Revolution did not occur first in France because the Frenchman was more oppressed than anyone else. On the contrary, he was sufficiently emancipated to desire a further measure of freedom. He was not so utterly steeped in ignorance and superstition as to be incapable of aspiring to a better state of things. He was not insensible to the currents of revolutionary thought that existed around him. He was not unaware of the revolt of the American colonies of Great Britain against an oppression that, by comparison with his own lot, must have appeared trivial.

The earlier part of the reign of Louis XV, who reigned from 1715 to 1774, has been described in another chapter. The decay of the French monarchy was accelerated in his later years. He was absolute—yet he was too indolent to rule and at the same time too greedy of power and too suspicious to be willing to entrust the work of administration to capable ministers. The financial difficulties of France inspired in him no thought of economy. He was recklessly extravagant, wasting vast sums on his personal pleasures. He was grossly immoral, the history of the court being little more than the record of a succession of mistresses, some of whom were able to exercise definite influence upon the course of French policy. The French monarchy was far gone in degradation when the decision of a vital point of foreign policy, as in 1756, depended in the main on the whim of a courtesan.

Opposition to the monarchy developed during the reign. The growth of public opinion, guided by the philosophers, against the existing system has already been described. After the middle of the eighteenth century the Parlement of Paris (which for nearly a century after the Fronde had been the obedient tool of the monarchy), privileged and unrepresentative as it was, became the organ of constitutional opposition to the Crown, and in its attitude it was supported by the provincial Parlements. The Parlements protested against fresh proposals of taxation, and the remnants of the Jansenist controversy sufficed to provide other grounds of disagreement. Protests were not very effective, but *lits de justice* were more frequently needed. Riots sometimes occurred, and blood was shed. Such proceedings, within and outside Parlement, indicated the growth of public dissatisfaction.

Towards the end of the reign, d'Aiguillon, Governor of Brittany, was summoned to trial before the Parlement of Paris for misgovernment. The King intervened to stop the proceedings; the Parlement protested, and in January, 1771,

its members were exiled to various parts of France. Despite
the protests of the provincial Parlements the counsellors of the
Paris Parlement were not recalled nor was their tribunal reconstructed until after the death of Louis XV, which occurred
in 1774.

The prestige of France sank low in the latter part of the
reign. During the Seven Years' War she lost her possessions
in North America and in India, and she experienced the
mortification of being defeated by Great Britain at sea and by
Prussia on land. By far the ablest and most patriotic of Louis's
later ministers was Choiseul, who was in office from 1758 to
1770. His achievements were considerable; that they were
not greater was not his fault but that of the King, who was
unwilling to give his full confidence to any minister. Choiseul
remodelled the French army, introducing the Prussian system
of drill, which, if it was unpopular, certainly tended to efficiency.
He restored the French navy, building a large number of ships,
with the result that in the American War the French fleet was
for a time able to control the North Atlantic. His foreign
policy was based upon hatred of Great Britain; after the Seven
Years' War he looked forward to a war of revenge, and with
this in mind he maintained the close connection of the Bourbon
courts of France, Spain, and Naples. He maintained also the
alliance with Austria, and arranged the marriage of the Dauphin
with Marie Antionette.

During Choiseul's term of office Lorraine passed under the
French Crown by the death of Stanislaus Leszczynski in 1767.
Choiseul was responsible for the purchase of Corsica from the
republic of Genoa in 1768 (so that it happened that Napoleon
Bonaparte, who was born in 1769, was a Frenchman). Choiseul
had many enemies at court, among them Madame du Barry,
whose advancement he had consistently opposed. With the
growth of her influence at court his fall was inevitable; at the
end of 1770 he was dismissed from office. The administration
of France during the last three years (1771–4) was in the hands
of a group of ministers—d'Aiguillon, Terray, and Maupeou—
known as the Triumvirate, but the chief influence over the
King was exercised by Madame du Barry.

The accession of Louis XVI was greeted with relief and even
with enthusiasm. He was in most ways a much better man
than his grandfather. He was unique among the Bourbon
kings of France in leading a strictly moral life, and, in an age of

agnosticism, when among the upper classes Christianity was commonly treated as an outworn superstition and the Church as a convenient institution for teaching the poor their duty towards their betters, he was a sincere Christian. Yet France has rarely had a king less fitted for his duties, less suited to the times, than Louis XVI. That his intentions were good is undeniable. But he possessed neither capacity nor strength of character; he was slow of thought and hesitant in reaching decisions; he was lacking in the qualities which make for leadership. He did not realise the gravity of the problems which demanded his attention; he was neither able to direct affairs nor willing to leave them to competent advisers. In private life, as a country gentleman addicted to sport and not concerned with politics, he might have been successful; as King he was unequal to his position.

As in the reign of Louis XV, feminine influence was strong at court; while the old King had been guided by his mistresses the young King submitted to the advice of his wife. Marie Antoinette exhibited some of the qualities which Louis lacked. She was not without capacity, and she was energetic and of definite personality. But her influence over the King was rarely exercised for good. She was in temperament essentially an aristocrat, and she despised the common people. She was a foreigner who never understood the French. She was not an agnostic, but the observances of religion sat more lightly upon her than upon her husband. She was even believed to be vicious and immoral, though it is proper to state that such charges against her have been fully refuted. Rumours derogatory to her personal character no doubt owed their origin to her unpopularity, and must be treated as entirely without foundation, though some colour was given to them in her own time by her love of display and her extravagance. Her advice to the King was usually in the direction of the maintenance of privilege and the suppression of signs of discontent, and it must be admitted that she failed to foresee the coming storm.

The reign of Louis XVI opened with the dismissal of the Triumvirate and the removal from court of Madame du Barry. The Count of Maurepas was appointed First Minister, a post which he held till 1781. He was a courtier rather than a statesman, and the direction of affairs soon passed into stronger hands. His most important achievement was the restoration of the exiled Parlements, a measure popular but of doubtful wisdom. Vergennes became Minister for War and retained the post until 1787. The most important appointment was that of Turgot, as Controller-General of the Finances.

Turgot was one of the greatest financiers ever produced by France, and was certainly the only man in France at this time capable of dealing with the financial situation. He attacked the extravagance of the administration; he scrutinised the list of pensions, many of which he reduced and some of which he abolished; he even made some effort to limit the expenditure of the court. The *corvée* was abolished, and in its place an impost was established on all landed property, noble and non-noble alike. Turgot abolished the gilds which still controlled town industry on medieval lines. He established internal free trade in corn and wine by the abolition of interprovincial customs duties on these commodities. He could not touch the exemption of noble lands from the *taille*, but he investigated various illegal exemptions, and he insisted on the payment of the *capitation* by all, noble and non-noble, alike. He proposed to set up a system of schools staffed by lay teachers, thus attacking the clerical monopoly of education. He contemplated the establishment of an elaborate system of councils (to be known as *municipalités*) in parishes, *arrondissements*, and provinces, with a *Grand Municipalité* to represent the nation as a whole. The franchise would be limited to landowners, but in view of the extent of the system of peasant proprietorship this would include the bulk of the peasantry. These councils would have little actual power, but they would enjoy freedom of debate and might be valuable as organs of public opinion. The scheme is of some interest in that it resembled, superficially at least, the system of local assemblies established in the early days of the Revolution. Certain measures in the direction of religious toleration were projected, such as the recognition of the validity of Protestant marriages.

The opposition of nobles and clergy to proposals which entrenched upon their privileges and exemptions and monopolies was to be expected. Opposition was experienced also from the Parlements, and Turgot's first batch of edicts was registered only in a *lit de justice*. Turgot was in office less than two years. While he retained the support of the King he was able to press his reforms forward. But the opposition, reinforced by the Queen, became too strong, and Louis was induced to dismiss his ablest minister. From that time the Revolution became inevitable.

Turgot was succeeded as Controller-General by Clugny, whose only title to fame lies in his efforts to undo Turgot's work. He revived the *corvée*, the gilds, and the internal customs on corn and wine, and he attempted to raise money by the institution of a state lottery. He died in 1777, and was succeeded by Necker, a Genevan banker. (Necker was a Protestant, and, though he controlled the finances, he was legally ineligible for appointment to the post of Controller-General.) He was honest and a good man of business, but he was timid and irresolute. He could devise expedients to meet the exigencies of the moment, but he was incapable of recasting the whole financial system, and still less of embarking upon wide schemes of political and economic reform. His period of office corresponded closely with that of French intervention in the War of American Independence.

The republicanism of the Americans was not to the liking of the King, who regretted the popular enthusiasm for the war. News of the surrender of Burgoyne at Saratoga in 1777 was received in Paris with delight; a treaty was concluded with the Americans, and in 1778 war was declared against Great Britain. The greater part of the fighting between British and French was naval. The work of Choiseul now bore fruit. French fleets dominated the Channel, and an invasion of England was threatened. This did not take place, but the strength of the fleets of d'Estaing and de Grasse in the North Atlantic prevented the arrival of the British fleet to relieve Cornwallis at Yorktown. Several islands in the West Indies were captured by the French; Minorca was taken; Gibraltar was besieged. British command of the sea was restored only by the victory of Rodney over de Grasse in the Battle of the Saints.

Victory in war did not avail to avert the fall of the French monarchy. Even the glory of victory was a little dimmed by the defeat of de Grasse. The war had added to the financial embarrassments of the French Government. Necker had succeeded in raising fresh loans, and, in order to revive the waning credit of France, he published in 1781 the *Compte Rendu au Roi de l'État des Finances*. This was not a budgetary statement but a review of the resources of France, designed to inspire confidence in the financiers to whom the government looked for further support. In this it was successful for the time being, but, in drawing attention to their exemptions from taxation, Necker aroused the hostility of the privileged classes, and he was compelled to resign.

The post of Controller-General was held by two or three nonentities for short periods in rapid succession, until the appointment of Calonne, who held office from 1783 to 1787. Calonne made no real attempt to grapple with the difficulties of the position. The accounts would not balance, and were made to do so by means of loans. He even encouraged the extravagance of the court on the ground that lavish expenditure was good for trade and that an appearance of wealth would inspire that confidence without which loans could not be raised. For about three years the Government was carried on in this way, but the end was in sight. By the end of 1786 the treasury was empty, and no further loans could be raised. France was bankrupt.

By Calonne's advice the King summoned an Assembly of Notables to consider the position. The Controller-General explained the financial position to the magnates, and stated that the only remedy was the imposition of a new land tax from which there should be no exemptions. The Notables were unwilling to sacrifice themselves for the public good. They censured Calonne, and instead of accepting his proposals they demanded the production of public accounts. They thus succeeded in posing as reformers while acting in defence of privilege.

Calonne was dismissed from his office, which was given to Loménie de Brienne, Archbishop of Toulouse, and a Cardinal. Public excitement and discontent was now intense, and the history of Brienne's ministry is a confused story of shifts and expedients. Edicts were issued abolishing the *corvée*, instituting provincial assemblies which should limit the power of the intendants, and establishing interprovincial free trade in corn. These were accepted by the Parlement, but a further proposal of a new land tax from which there should be no exemptions was hotly contested. The King summoned the Parlement to Versailles and held a *lit de justice* for the registration of the edict.

The Parlement declared the registration illegal, and in consequence it was exiled to Troyes. Public opinion supported the Parlement in its opposition to the Government, in spite of the fact that it was defending privilege and resisting necessary reforms. The attitude of Parlement throughout the reign demonstrated the unwisdom of Louis XVI in recalling it at his accession, and the clamour of the mob in this incident showed how far its opinion was from being thoughtful and intelligent.

The Parlement was recalled, and the edicts relating to new taxation were put before it in a modified form; even then they were registered only in a *lit de justice*. In May, 1788, the Parlement was again summoned to Versailles, where in a *lit de justice* a whole series of edicts, drastically revising the judicial system and curtailing the powers of the Parlement, was placed before it for immediate registration. The members of the Parlement took an oath to resist the new proposals, and from every class and every quarter there was a demand for the convocation of the States-General. At length Louis yielded. The States–General was summoned to meet on 5th May, 1789, at Versailles. Brienne was dismissed, and Necker was reappointed to the control of the finances.

The position was now desperate. Bad harvests had brought famine in some parts of France, and starving peasants made their way into Paris throughout the autumn and winter of 1788–9. The mob from the slums of Paris was thus reinforced by hordes of hungry and homeless country folk. The very appointment of Necker improved the credit of the Government, and he was able to borrow a few millions of livres to meet its most pressing needs.

As there had been no meeting of the States-General since 1614 there was much uncertainty as to the method by which elections should be held. The King ordered that a search should be made into precedents; this was interpreted as a relaxation of the press censorship, and the months immediately preceding the meeting witnessed the publication of a large amount of electioneering literature. Two questions called for settlement in connection with the elections. The first was whether the three orders should have equal representation or whether the third estate should have greater representation than the other two. It was decided that France should be divided into constituencies each of which should return four deputies (or a multiple of four), one to represent the clergy, one the nobles, and two the third estate; the representation of the common people would thus equal that of nobles and clergy combined. The other question, whether in the States-General voting should be *par tête* or *par ordre*, was not settled until after the deputies had assembled. It provided the occasion for the first great struggle between the orders, in which the victory of the third estate turned what might have been a movement for constitutional reform into a Revolution.

CHAPTER XVI

THE FRENCH REVOLUTION

THE States-General assembled at Versailles in May, 1789. It did not meet with the intention of overthrowing the Government of France and destroying the monarchy and nobility, but it was resolved to remodel the constitution of the country. It expected to be called upon to sanction reforms which would enable the Government to be carried on more efficiently and which would restore order in the finances. It looked to the Government for leadership, and if ministers had been prepared to suggest a scheme of reform there is little doubt that the States-General would have discussed it, perhaps modified it, and finally adopted it. But the Government had no proposals to make. It gave no lead to the States-General, and the deputies, entirely without political experience and lacking leaders of their own, were uncertain how to proceed.

When the States-General met the deputies did not know whether the three orders were to sit together or apart, and after the formal opening ceremony a royal command was issued that they should sit in separate chambers. The advantage expected by the third estate from its superiority in numbers would thus be lost, and it resolved to resist the proposal. For nearly two months the point was contested. At length the third estate resolved to call itself the National Assembly, to invite the other orders to join it, and, whether they did so or not, to proceed with the work of framing a constitution for France. The immediate consequence of this bold action was that the deputies were excluded from the hall in which they had been meeting. They assembled hastily on a Tennis Court and solemnly swore not to separate, unless dispersed by force, until they had drawn up a new constitution. Within a few days the other orders gave way and joined the third estate. The King sanctioned the joint meeting, and the National Assembly prepared to begin its work.

The court speedily regretted its concession, and troops were massed at Versailles and near Paris. The intention of the Government, if any clear intention can be traced in this time of hesitancy and indecision, was to overawe the Assembly. Meanwhile, the Paris mob was active. The city was crowded with refugees from the nearer provinces, where, owing to the failure of the harvest of 1788, famine threatened. The streets were filled with poverty-stricken people who were hoping for much from the Assembly. There was much political excitement; demonstrations and riots were of daily occurrence. The authorities seemed powerless to suppress disorder. The Parisians, becoming impatient of the debates in the Assembly, and being suspicious of the intentions of the Government towards it, at length burst into revolt. The Bastille, a great fortress and prison in Paris, was popularly supposed to be filled with the victims of state tyranny, and on 14th July, 1789, the mob attacked it and, despite the resistance of the guard, captured it. Only about half a dozen prisoners were found within it, but the taking of the Bastille was felt to be the symbol of the overthrow of the *ancien régime*. For the purpose of protecting property in the city from pillage, a citizen army, known as the National Guard, was organised in Paris and was placed under the command of the Marquis de Lafayette, who had been distinguished in the American War.

Rioting was not limited to Paris. Outbreaks occurred in towns and villages in every part of France. Mobs of peasants stormed and burned châteaux, customs-houses, monasteries, and government offices, and wherever official records of feudal obligations were found they were destroyed. Troops ordered out to suppress disorder made common cause with the rioters. The Government was powerless, and the very framework of local administration — intendants, law-courts, officials — disappeared. The utter collapse of the existing structure of society seemed to indicate that France was conforming to Rousseau's precepts by returning to a "state of nature." The general feeling of alarm and insecurity which resulted from these outbreaks led to a reaction during which volunteer forces, similar to the Parisian National Guard, came into existence to restore order and protect property, while in some of the towns unofficial committees of leading citizens tried to re-establish some sort of administrative machinery.

These events alarmed the court, which abandoned its attempt to overawe the Assembly at Versailles. Necker, who had been dismissed from office a few days before the taking of the Bastille, was restored to it a few days after. The Assembly continued its debates, but it gave proof of its inexperience by its failure to deal at once with urgent problems. It spent some weeks in considering a Declaration of the Rights of Man. However desirable it might appear, in theory, that reforms should be based on sound principles, it was essential that they should be produced at once; the statement of principle might be postponed to some less pressing occasion. This the deputies failed to understand. However, on one memorable day, or rather night, 4th August, 1789, the Assembly decided upon the abolition of all traces of serfdom, all tax exemptions, and all noble privileges.

The mob in Paris was still on the verge of starvation. Distress, in fact, was increasing, for many of the Parisians gained a living by ministering, in a hundred ways, to the wants of the upper classes. But numbers of wealthy people, in alarm at the turn of events, were quitting the capital, and unemployment was increasing. It was commonly supposed that food was plentiful in Versailles, where the court was in residence. Early in October a crowd of women marched from Paris to Versailles, where they swarmed into the palace and forced the King and Queen to accompany them back to Paris. The National Assembly also moved to Paris, and for the next two years it was occupied in making reforms and drawing up a new constitution for France.

The old provinces of the kingdom were replaced by departments, which were divided into districts (*arrondissements*), these into cantons, and these again into communes. This new system of local government areas survived all later revolutionary changes and exists in France at the present day. The Parlements and the subordinate courts were abolished, and a new system of courts was set up for departments and districts. The evils of the old system were removed, but there were grave defects in the new. Judges were elected by the people for limited periods, and when the time for new elections was reached they might be turned out in favour of others if their conduct had not pleased the populace. Judges were thus encouraged to bid for popular favour rather than to administer justice without fear or prejudice.

To meet pressing financial needs the Assembly confiscated the property of the Church and ordered it to be sold. The

Church was reorganised as a department of the state. No change was made in its doctrine or ritual, but all bishops and priests were required to swear obedience to the Civil Constitution of the Clergy, which converted them into officials with salaries fixed and paid by the state. Many refused to do so; they were not removed from their posts at once, however, and for some time both constitutional and non-juring priests continued to exercise their functions. A new system of taxation was established, but was enforced with difficulty. The Assembly discovered that reforms could not be carried through without heavy expenditure, and, as taxation was unpopular, paper money was printed and was issued in such excessive quantities that in course of time it became practically valueless. The proceedings of the Assembly were conducted in public; outsiders were admitted to its meetings, and its decisions were influenced by the clamour of the mob.

The King disliked much of the work of the Assembly, and he consented only with great reluctance to the Civil Constitution of the Clergy. He wished to leave Paris and pass the Easter of 1791 at St. Cloud in order to avoid the ministrations of the constitutional clergy in the capital, but he was prevented by the mob from leaving the Tuileries. He felt henceforth that he was a prisoner in Paris, and he determined to escape. Plans for a flight were made, and the King and Queen actually reached Varennes, within a short distance of the frontier, before they were overtaken and compelled to return. The flight was treated officially as an "abduction," and the King was allowed to remain at the head of affairs, though for a time he was little better than a prisoner.

The Assembly, which by this time was commonly called the Constituent Assembly, continued its work of constitution-making. The King's power was very much reduced; laws were to be made and taxes levied only by the Assembly. By September, 1791, the constitution was completed and was placed before the King for approval or rejection. He accepted it, and the Constituent Assembly, after passing a decree that none of its members was to be elected to the new Assembly, was dissolved.

It is impossible in this short sketch to do full justice to the work of the Assembly, and space will not permit reference to the many interesting personalities within it. Two of them may be mentioned briefly. Lafayette was popular, brave, and incorruptible. He was ambitious, but he was not sufficiently statesmanlike to direct the course of the Revolution. The greatest politician in the National Assembly was undoubtedly Mirabeau. He was less concerned than most of the deputies with abstract theory. He attacked the abuses of the *ancien régime*; he was eager to abolish privilege and inequality. But he realised the necessity for a strong Government in France, and his aim was to induce the King to put himself unreservedly at the head of the party of reform, and so to bring about the closest possible co-operation between King and Assembly. He opposed anarchical attacks on life and property, and he despised rhetorical appeals to liberty and equality when they were not associated with practical proposals. At a time when he was the dominant figure in the Assembly he remained in touch with the court. It is doubtful whether he could have brought the two into harmony, but it is certain that no other man could have done so. His death in 1791 ended all possibility of a reconciliation.

The Legislative Assembly, which succeeded the Constituent Assembly, was elected in 1791. Though the majority of the deputies were moderate men who did not wish the Revolution to go farther, the Assembly contained a considerable minority of men of republican views. Of these the Girondins were the more numerous; they were so called from the fact that several of them represented the department of the Gironde. The Jacobins, who in course of time became the bitter and determined opponents of the Girondins, were at this time in alliance with them against the constitutional party, the Feuillants, in the Assembly. The organisation of the Jacobin party was far more thorough and complete than that of any other group in French politics at this time. The Jacobin Club had been established in the early days of the Revolution; it was so called because it met on the premises of a former Jacobin convent. Hundreds of provincial clubs were formed and affiliated with that parent body. When the Jacobin Club in Paris decided upon a line of policy or a course of action it secured the support of the provincial clubs, and resolutions passed by them were sent to Paris. This organisation of opinion gave the Jacobins greater influence than might have been expected from their numbers alone. There was little difference of principle between Jacobins and Girondins. The Girondins were more refined than their rivals, and held higher ideals; the Jacobins, on the other hand, relied for the success of their cause on brute force, as represented by the people of the capital. From the first the Girondins were at the disadvantage that their real support lay in distant provinces and was not so well organised as was that of their rivals; the Jacobins were aided by the municipal council of Paris and were applauded by the mob.

The early part of the Revolution had been mainly political, and it had succeeded in its aims. The *ancien régime* had been destroyed. Freedom had been gained, privilege and inequality had been swept away. But prosperity had not made its appearance. The poor were no better off than before. There was still danger of famine in parts of France. Employment was difficult to obtain. Industry seemed almost at a standstill. The poorer classes felt that the benefits of the Revolution had passed them by, and that a new Revolution was needed, which should do for them what the first Revolution had done for the bourgeois. This feeling played into the hands of the Jacobin party, whose ultimate aim was the utter overthrow of the existing structure of society and its replacement by a commonwealth organised in the interests of the sovereign people.

Friction developed between the Legislative Assembly and the King. Since the early days of the Revolution many nobles had fled abroad—some to England, but many into the Empire. It was the aim of these *émigrés*, among whom were the Counts of Provence and Artois, the King's brothers, to induce foreign powers to intervene in French affairs with a view to suppressing the Revolution and re-establishing the King's authority. The Assembly threatened the *émigrés* who remained near the frontiers of France with forfeiture of their lands and with death unless they returned, but the King vetoed the decree. He vetoed another decree of the Assembly directed against the non-juring clergy, who were causing trouble in many parts of France. The Assembly contended that its decrees were justified by the fact that the activities of *émigrés* and non-jurors were dangerous to France; in defence of the King's veto it was argued that the *émigrés* had broken no law, and that priests who had refused to take the oath to the Civil Constitution had now been deprived of their posts and so had paid the penalty for their disobedience to the law. In any case, the constitution of 1791 had left the power of veto in the hands of the King, and he was entitled to use it. These disputes between King and Assembly indicated that the new constitution was not working well and that, since they looked at public affairs from opposite points of view, agreement was not likely to be reached.

In the spring of 1792 war was declared against Austria and Prussia, and although this was done on the King's proposal he was believed to be secretly in sympathy with the enemies of France and to expect that in the turmoil of war the royal authority would necessarily be recovered. This belief was strengthened by a declaration of the Duke of Brunswick, commander of the Prussian army, that he would punish the city of Paris if any injury or insult were offered to the King. On 10th August, 1792, the King was suspended from his functions, and, when the Parisians learned that French soil was invaded and that some victories had been gained by the enemy, panic prevailed. Early in September the mob broke into the prisons of Paris, and some hundreds of Royalist prisoners were massacred. In the same month the Legislative Assembly was dissolved and was replaced by the Convention. The King was deposed, and France became a republic.

During the first weeks of its existence the Convention was the scene of a contest for power between the Girondins and the Jacobins. The struggle occurred over the trial of Louis XVI, who was charged with intriguing with foreign powers against France. In this the Jacobins were successful, and the King was condemned to death, though by a majority of only one vote. The Girondins did not really wish for the King's death, but voted for it in order to bid for Parisian support and to clear themselves of all suspicion of lukewarmness in the cause of the Revolution. Louis was a simple, well-meaning king, who certainly was not responsible for the evil plight of France in his time, though it is not unlikely that he was in sympathy and even in communication with the invaders of his country. He suffered for the faults of his predecessors, who, by their wars, their misgovernment, and their extravagance had brought French affairs to such a condition that the Revolution was inevitable.

The death of the King was a victory for the Jacobins. The Girondins might have recovered their influence if the war had been attended with success, but the defeats suffered by the French in the Netherlands and elsewhere in the early months of 1793 increased their unpopularity, and at the end of May the Paris mob broke into the Convention and a number of Girondin deputies were arrested.

The Jacobins completed their triumph over their rivals by the organisation of the Terror. The Terror was based on the principles that in the national emergency treachery should be punished, and that the whole nation would be inspired to a desperate courage against the enemy if it felt that there was no possibility of its efforts being brought to naught by traitors in the rear. A Committee of Public Safety and a Revolutionary Tribunal acted against suspects in Paris, while the Terror was spread to the provinces by "Deputies on Mission." Hundreds of suspected persons were hurried off to execution after trials in which there was no possibility of acquittal. In October, 1793, Marie Antoinette, who had been subject to every indignity and insult while in prison, was brought to the guillotine. At first the victims of the Terror were aristocrats and priests, men and women who were known to be supporters of the *ancien régime*, but as the supply of noble victims ceased others were found. Wealthy men were accused in order that their fortunes might fall into the hands of the revolutionaries. In course of time some of those who had inspired the Terror became its victims. Danton, who had been a prominent figure in the Revolution since its outbreak, was guillotined, and Robespierre, who became the leader of the Terrorists after Danton, was overthrown and put to death.

While this was going on churches were closed and the practice of the Christian religion was restricted, and in its place the worship of Reason was established, Notre Dame becoming a Temple of Reason. The use of the calendar, which was associated with the Christian religion, since the years were numbered from the birth of Christ, was discontinued, and a new calendar was drawn up. In the republican calendar the years were numbered from the establishment of the republic; months were named after natural processes and were subdivided into periods of ten days. But people in all parts of France continued to reckon by the old calendar; its successor was used chiefly in legal documents and official announcements. Its use was discontinued in 1806, shortly after the establishment of the Empire.

The orgy of bloodshed died down in course of time, and reaction succeeded the Terror. Whatever justification might have existed for it while the country was in danger and the aristocrats were suspected of being in league with its enemies had long since ceased. The Revolutionary Tribunal and the

Committee of Public Safety were reorganised, and trials (chiefly of former Terrorists) became fewer and fairer. The Jacobin Club was closed, and the Convention, which had exerted little authority over the Terrorists, recovered control of the Government of France.

While the Terror was proceeding a good deal of useful work was accomplished by the Convention. A system of education was planned, and laws were modernised and codified, a task which was completed by Bonaparte as First Consul. The metric system of weights and measures was introduced, and attention was given to the relief of the poor and to the condition of agriculture.

In 1795 the Convention drew up a new constitution for France. It was felt that some safeguard ought to be introduced against a repetition of the Terror and the overthrow of the constitution by a small group, as had been done in 1793–4. This might best be done by a division of authority, and by the new constitution the country was to be ruled by a Directory of five members, who were to hold office for five years, one director retiring each year. The Legislature (unlike the three bodies which had existed between 1789 and 1795) was to consist of two chambers, one of which, the Council of Five Hundred, was to propose legislation which the other, the Council of Ancients, was to accept or reject. Since it was feared that the Royalists might gain a majority in the Councils it was further ordered that two-thirds of their members should be selected from the members of the Convention; the election of a majority of Royalists was thus rendered impossible.

The new constitution was accepted by the people of France in a referendum in which few took the trouble to vote. The "Law of Two-Thirds" was unpopular in Paris, however, and the people launched an attack upon the Tuileries, where the Convention was sitting. But the Convention was ready for the attack, and a body of troops, with field guns and under the command of General Bonaparte, repulsed the crowd with a "whiff of grapeshot." The effect of the incident was remarkable. The mob, which for years had been a factor in determining the course of events, was dispersed, and lost its political importance. It is not too much to assert that the Revolution was over. With the establishment of the Directory constitutional government seemed to be restored, a fact recognised even by the enemies of France.

The rule of the Directory lasted four years. It was neither popular nor efficient. It was unable to cope with provincial risings or with the revival of Royalist feeling, or to prevent the renewal of Christian worship. It was afraid of brilliant generals such as Bonaparte, and sent them on expeditions abroad. It was corrupt and weak. The early defeats of the French in the war with the Second Coalition brought matters to a head. The need for a stronger Government became so overwhelming that in November, 1799, by the Revolution of Brumaire, the Directory was overthrown. A provisional Consulate was established, which within a few weeks gave place to the permanent Consulate, and in both of these Bonaparte, the victor of Italy, was First Consul. Only ten years had elapsed since the meeting of the States-General at Versailles; if monarchy was not yet restored it was at least in sight.

From the fact that the first French Republic lasted only a few years the Revolution might seem to have been a failure. Such was far from being the case. Though France reverted to monarchy she retained many of the best results of the Revolution. Feudal privileges were not revived, and the Church did not recover the power it possessed under the *ancien régime*. The administration was carried on efficiently, and the peasants were much better off than before. Justice was open to all, and taxation was levied on a fair basis.

The effects of the Revolution were not confined to France. Agitation spread to other countries, where Governments became alarmed lest the course of events in France should be imitated in their own dominions. For many years it became the common practice of European Governments to suppress all traces of revolutionary sentiments and to punish severely persons who attempted to spread them.

CHAPTER XVII

THE FRENCH REVOLUTIONARY WAR

To the statesmen of Europe it did not seem likely that the outbreak of the French Revolution would lead to a general European war. France, apparently fully occupied in reorganising her government, was in no condition to make war upon her neighbours, and no cause of conflict could be perceived. The chief effect, indeed, of the internal troubles of France appeared to be the complete, if temporary, extinction of her influence in international affairs. Spain, which, through the Family Compact, had been in close alliance with France, became involved in 1790 in a dispute with Great Britain over the seizure of some ships in Nootka Sound, and found that she could no longer rely upon the support of her neighbour. Austria had been friendly with France since 1756, and now found that the moral support of her ally counted for nothing in the Turkish war which was still being waged. France had ceased to be a factor in European affairs.

After the flight of Louis XVI to Varennes and his return to Paris some concern began to be felt for the safety of the French King and his family. The Emperor Leopold II, brother of Marie Antoinette, felt that the time had come for the powers of Europe to act together in support of Louis XVI. He suggested that the authority of the French King should be restored and the Revolution restrained by the joint action of other states. Though Great Britain was unwilling to intervene, Leopold met the King of Prussia, Frederick William II, at Pillnitz, in August, 1791. The difficulties in the way of co-operation were considerable. The two monarchs were suspicious of each other on the Polish question, and they feared that their preoccupation in a French war would be to the advantage of Russia. They were more ready to threaten than to strike; yet they were urged by French émigré princes and nobles to take action, and a Declaration was issued expressing the view that the authority of the French King ought to be restored and the hope that other states would not refuse to co-operate in re-establishing it. If other powers would associate themselves with the enterprise, Austria and Prussia would undertake to employ an adequate force for this purpose. The exact intention of the two monarchs in issuing the Declaration of Pillnitz was by no means clear. Since, however, Great Britain was known to be averse to intervention, it is probable that the Declaration meant, and was intended to mean, very little. Resentment was aroused in Paris, but when news of the acceptance of the constitution of 1791 by Louis XVI reached Leopold he withdrew the Declaration.

More serious matters of difference soon arose between France and the Central Powers. *Émigré* princes and nobles were living in the Rhenish provinces of the Empire. They made extreme demands and tried to induce German princes to fight against the Revolution. They were armed, and under the leadership of Condé they tried to organise at Coblentz an army for the invasion of France. The French were alarmed, and their relations with the German princes became unfriendly. Some of these princes, moreover, possessed lands in the east of France, and their rights had been affected by the decrees of the Constituent Assembly. Negotiations were carried on, but took an unsatisfactory course, and by the beginning of 1792 war was certain. An Austro-Prussian alliance was formed in February, and in April, on the proposal of Louis XVI, France declared war against Austria. It is possible that in taking this step Louis believed that France would be speedily defeated and that the Assembly would be compelled to strengthen his hands. By his action, however, he made his own dethronement certain.

It is useless to discuss the rights and wrongs of the outbreak of war. It may be contended that France had a right to settle her internal affairs without foreign interference, while, on the other hand, it is reasonable to assert that the Emperor and the King of Prussia (who regarded the French declaration of war against Austria as applicable also to himself) were entitled to prevent the spread of the Revolution to their own people. From both points of view, revolutionary principles were incompatible with absolute monarchy, and war was inevitable.

The French army at the outbreak of war was ill-equipped and badly organised. Recruiting was unsatisfactory, and discipline was lax. The allies, on the other hand, were little better prepared for waging war, for they distrusted each other, and both feared the activity of Catherine II in eastern Europe.

The campaign did not open in earnest until July. As already stated, the commander of the Prussian army issued a manifesto calling upon the French people to restore the authority of their King and threatening to punish the city of Paris if any insult should be offered to him. This ill-advised document was really inspired by Frederick William, and its effect was the reverse of what was intended. From its tone the Parisians assumed that Louis was in secret touch with the enemies of France. Events moved to a crisis; on 10th August the King was suspended from his functions, and shortly afterwards he was deposed.

An Austrian army invaded France from the north-east and besieged Lille, while the Prussians crossed the border into Lorraine and captured the fortresses of Longwy and Verdun. Panic prevailed in Paris, and in September, 1792, some hundreds of prisoners opposed to the Revolution were put to death in the prisons of the capital. But Kellermann and Dumouriez withstood the Prussians at the Cannonade of Valmy, and the invaders, abandoning Longwy and Verdun, retreated across the frontier. They were followed by a French army which captured Worms and Mainz and for a time occupied Frankfort, which had to pay a heavy ransom.

Before the end of the year Dumouriez was able to relieve Lille and invade the Austrian Netherlands, the population of which was discontented with Austrian rule and had been, a few years earlier, in actual revolt against the Emperor Joseph II. The Austrians were defeated at Jemappes, and the country was easily overrun. At the same time another French army annexed Savoy and Nice. These provinces had hitherto formed part of the kingdom of Sardinia, which by this time was at war with the republic.

Although, at the outbreak of war, the French had disclaimed all thought of conquest, these easy and rapid successes, gained by them in the name of liberty, led to a desire for military glory and perhaps inspired the Edict of Fraternity, of 19th November, 1792. The Convention, by this pronouncement, promised French aid to all the oppressed peoples of Europe who wished to recover their freedom and, by a further decree of 15th December, announced that in all territory occupied by

French armies feudal rights would be abolished and republican institutions established. These edicts were a challenge to every European power, and a war in which France would be opposed to a European coalition could no longer be averted.

Pitt long hoped that war between Great Britain and France might be avoided, and, though the French afterwards regarded

THE EASTERN AND NORTH-EASTERN FRONTIERS OF FRANCE, 1792–5

him as their most implacable enemy, he laboured to the uttermost to maintain peace. The French invasion of the Austrian Netherlands was viewed in Great Britain with uneasiness, but Pitt considered this action against the territory of a power which had invaded France to be no sufficient ground for war. But English opinion was hardening. The deposition of Louis XVI and the September massacres destroyed the sympathy which many Englishmen had hitherto felt for a people struggling for liberty. The Edict of Fraternity might have resulted in war, but Maret, an unofficial French agent in London, offered an explanation of the Edict which postponed the crisis. The execution of Louis XVI, however, in January, 1793, and the opening of the Scheldt to navigation, in defiance of an agreement included in the Peace of Westphalia and other treaties, made a conflict unavoidable. At the beginning of February, 1793, France declared war against Great Britain and Holland.

In the course of 1793 France found herself at war with fifteen states, of which the most important were Great Britain, Austria, Prussia, Holland, Spain, and Sardinia. Dumouriez invaded Holland, but, fearing Austrian attack on his flank, retreated, and was defeated by the Austrians at Neerwinden. He was suspected of treasonable designs against the republican Government, and messengers were sent by the Convention to arrest him, whereupon he fled to the enemy. A British army under the Duke of York now joined the Austrians in the Netherlands, drove the French back, invaded France, and besieged Dunkirk. A Spanish army invaded Roussillon, in the south-west, and a British naval force occupied Toulon. A royalist revolt broke out in La Vendée. Invasion by Prussians and Austrians was threatened again from the east, where Mainz was recovered from the French.

France proved equal to the emergency. The people rallied with intense enthusiasm to the defence of their land, for they realised that the victory of the enemies of France would be followed by the restoration of the *ancien régime*, with all its burdens, its oppression, and its injustice. A *levée en masse* was ordered, and the new forces were organised by Carnot. All men of suitable age were conscripted for the army, and even women and children were assigned work of national importance. Austrians and Prussians were driven back, the Duke of York was forced to abandon the siege of Dunkirk, the Vendéan insurrection was checked (though it was not entirely suppressed for some time), and the English were compelled to leave Toulon.

In 1794 the tide of battle ran even more definitely in favour of the French. The Spaniards were driven back across the Pyrenees, and Catalonia was invaded. A new and irresistible attack was launched against the Austrian Nether-lands. The Austrians were defeated by Jourdan at the Battle of Fleurus, and the Duke of York was driven into Holland, whence he was soon afterwards recalled to England. Austrian and Prussian forces were withdrawn from western Europe and diverted to Poland, the final partition of which was about to take place. In a naval battle off Ushant, the "Glorious First of June," a British fleet under Lord Howe defeated the French, but the corn ships which were being convoyed from America to France succeeded in reaching port.

In the winter of 1794–5 French armies overran Holland and compelled the Dutch to accept a humiliating peace. An indemnity was to be paid, territory was to be ceded, and an alliance, offensive and defensive, was to be accepted. The Dutch undertook to equip and maintain a body of French troops quartered in their own land. The Stadtholder refused to agree to these terms and fled to England, and with his sanction Great Britain annexed the Dutch settlement at the Cape of Good Hope. The French sugar islands in the West Indies were also captured by the British fleet, but in Europe Prussia made peace and ceded certain of the Rhenish territories to France by the Treaty of Basel, on 5th April, 1795. Spain made peace by another Treaty of Basel, on 22nd July, 1795, and by a further treaty (San Ildefonso) in August, 1796, she entered into an alliance with France.

By the beginning of 1796 the only states of importance remaining in arms against the French republic were Austria, Sardinia, and Great Britain. Negotiations for peace between Great Britain and France were attempted, but without result. Now that peace had been concluded with Spain and Prussia the republic was free to concentrate her military forces against Austria and Sardinia. A threefold attack upon Austria was planned by Carnot, the French Minister for War. Jourdan and Moreau were to invade Austrian territory by way of the Rhine, while Bonaparte was to attack Austrian power in northern Italy. This young general had already attracted notice, and in the Italian campaign of 1796 he was to distinguish himself alike as a strategist and as a tactician. His troops depended little upon long baggage trains and lived by seizing provisions and other stores wherever they went. He thus moved his armies rapidly, making surprise attacks after long marches. He demoralised the enemy by cannon-fire, and by his charges he drove wavering troops from the field, Much of his success was due to his attention to detail and to his capacity in selecting efficient staff officers.

Entering Italy between the Maritime Alps and the sea, Bonaparte, by defeating the Sardinians and Austrians five times within a month, prevented the junction of their armies. Detaching a small force to cover the Austrian army, he drove the Sardinians back towards Turin. He thus forced Victor Amadeus to agree to the Treaty of Cherasco, by which peace was made and Savoy and Nice were left in French hands.

Bonaparte then marched to the south-east of Milan, which the Austrians abandoned, retreating towards Mantua. By defeating them at Lodi he became master of Lombardy and was able to enter Milan, which, although it welcomed him as a deliverer from Austrian rule, was compelled to pay a large indemnity and to surrender a number of pictures from Milanese churches and galleries. The French were hated, however, by the country-folk of Lombardy, on account of their systematic plundering of the countryside. A rising of the peasants occurred; some French soldiers were killed, and the insurgents sheltered in Pavia, which was taken by the French and sacked.

The Austrians prepared to make a stand at Mantua and Peschiera, on the border of Venetian territory, but Bonaparte defeated them at Peschiera, and laid siege to Mantua. A short expedition to the Papal States compelled the Pope, who had sided with the Austrians against France, to agree to an armistice by which he yielded pictures and other works of art and paid an indemnity to his conquerors.

The arrival in Italy of Austrian reinforcements in two divisions caused Bonaparte to raise the siege of Mantua, but the new-comers were defeated separately, and other Austrian armies which were poured into Italy met with a like fate. The siege of Mantua was renewed and pressed vigorously, and the city fell into French hands in February, 1797. Before the end of 1796 Bonaparte had united the duchy of Modena with certain provinces of the Papal States and had established the Cispadane Republic, in alliance with France.

Bonaparte was now master of the whole of northern Italy. Invading the States of the Church a second time on account of papal intrigues with the Austrians and Venetians, he forced the Pope to agree to terms of peace at Tolentino.

Meanwhile the Archduke Charles had defeated Jourdan and forced him to retreat, and in consequence of this Moreau, who had gained some successes in Bavaria, was compelled to fall back. But early in 1797 Bonaparte defeated Charles at the Tagliamento and invaded Carinthia. Austria was beaten, and the Treaty of Campo Formio was concluded.

By the terms of the peace Lombardy and the Austrian Netherlands were ceded to France. Lombardy was now joined with the Cispadane Republic to form the Cisalpine Republic, in alliance with France, and this new organisation

NORTH AND CENTRAL ITALY, 1796-1800

was recognised by Austria. As some compensation for her losses Austria was permitted to annex that part of Venetia which lay east of the Adige, together with Istria and Dalmatia. The Venetian Republic thus came to an end. A Congress was to be held at Rastadt to arrange terms of peace between France and the Holy Roman Empire, and the Emperor promised to use his influence at the Congress to secure the cession of all territory west of the Rhine to France. Earlier in the year Genoa had become the Ligurian Republic. At the Congress of Rastadt, which opened in December, 1797, it was agreed to yield the left bank of the Rhine to the French and to compensate the dispossessed princes with grants of ecclesiastical lands elsewhere in the Empire.

The successes of France thus resulted in immense territorial gains. The French boundary now reached the Rhine, the Austrian Netherlands were annexed, and in the north of Italy were vassal republics which were French territory in all but name. Yet Austria, which had suffered heavy defeats, had lost little. She had given up the Austrian Netherlands and Lombardy, but she had obtained Venetia and other lands as compensation, and the change was in the direction of the consolidation of her dominions. She had pursued a selfish policy, seeking her own interests instead of acting in defence of Germany. The conclusion to be drawn from a consideration of four years of warfare was that neither of the two great military monarchies of the Holy Roman Empire was prepared to put Imperial interests before its own.

In 1797 Great Britain alone remained at war with France, and France was no longer without allies. Holland and Spain had both declared war on Great Britain, whose position was extremely serious, since her freedom from invasion depended on the superiority of her fleet, and each of her enemies was a naval power of importance. An attempted invasion of Ireland by the French in 1796 had failed only through bad weather conditions. It now became the object of British naval strategy to prevent a concentration of enemy fleets, and, in spite of mutinies in the navy, this was achieved. Jervis and Nelson defeated the Spanish fleet at the Battle of St. Vincent, and some months later Duncan defeated the Dutch at the Battle of Camperdown. By the end of the year Great Britain was as assuredly supreme at sea as France was dominant on land.

On account of his successes in Italy, where he had acted with little regard for the Directory, Bonaparte's reputation now stood high in France. The Directors feared that he might use his power to overthrow them, and he obtained their ready consent to undertake a new expedition in 1798. He sailed from Toulon with a fleet and an army, and after capturing Malta from the Knights of St. John he reached Egypt, a province of the Turkish Empire. No certain knowledge exists of his ultimate aims. It is probable that he intended to conquer Egypt and continue his course to

India.   He would thus inflict a heavy blow upon British prestige
and British trade and might compel Great Britain to submit
to peace on French terms.   It is possible, too, that he contemplated the conquest of Turkey and the liberation of the
Christian peoples in the Balkan peninsula.   With their aid he
might deliver a fresh attack upon Austria from the south-east.

Although there was no British naval base east of Gibraltar
a small fleet with Nelson in command had been watching

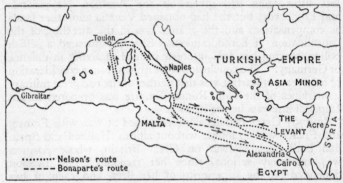

THE MEDITERRANEAN, 1798-1800

Toulon.   The British admiral was driven out to sea by stress
of weather; he was compelled to put in at a Sardinian port,
and was unable to prevent Bonaparte's departure.   Nelson
had no certain information of the plans of the enemy, but,
after receiving reinforcements, he sailed to the east and reached
Alexandria before the arrival of the French.   Not finding them
there, he cruised about the Levant for a month in search
of them.   Upon returning to Alexandria he discovered the
French fleet at anchor and, in the Battle of the Nile, he destroyed
it.   Bonaparte, who had defeated the Mamelukes, a body of
Circassian cavalry, in the Battle of the Pyramids, was now cut
off from France, and the re-establishment of his communications
became an urgent matter.   He marched into Syria, but he
was checked at Acre, which was strongly held by the Turks,
reinforced by an English naval brigade under Sir Sidney
Smith, and he withdrew to Egypt.   At length news of the
formation of the Second Coalition and of French defeats in
Italy reached him.   Before long he received instructions to

return home, and, abandoning alike his enterprise and his army, he embarked for France.

Early in 1798 the constitution of the Batavian Republic (as the United Provinces had been known since their conquest) was remodelled on that of France. Soon afterwards the French made war upon the Swiss, whose ancient form of government was destroyed; in its place the Helvetic Republic was formed. In the same year a French army attacked Rome, removed the Pope to Valence, on the Rhône, and established the Roman Republic.

Austria was dissatisfied with the settlement at Campo Formio and now determined upon a renewal of the war. A Second Coalition of European powers was formed against France, and it secured from the Tsar, Paul I (son of Catherine II, who died in 1796), the promise of aid. The King of Naples resented French action in the Papal States and joined the alliance, to which Great Britain promised financial assistance.

Naples was conquered by the French early in 1799, and in the place of the monarchy the Parthenopean Republic was established, but a Russian army passed through Austrian territory and, with the Austrians, entered northern Italy, easily overrunning it and occupying Milan. The French abandoned Naples and Rome and were defeated by the allies at Novi. The Cisalpine Republic was overthrown and the French retreated into the Ligurian Republic (Genoa); they were saved from utter disaster only by dissensions among the allies. The Austrians were jealous of Russian victories, while the Tsar was annoyed at the lack of Austrian co-operation. Masséna was able to defeat another Russian army at Zürich, in Switzerland, and the Tsar soon afterwards withdrew from the war.

In November, 1799, Bonaparte became First Consul, and in 1800 he took the field against the Austrians in Italy. Moreau was sent at the same time into South Germany to occupy the south bank of the upper Danube in order to prevent additional Austrian forces being moved into Italy. Bonaparte crossed the Alps by the Great St. Bernard Pass and entered Milan. Masséna, who had been left in command of the French remnant in Italy, had been blockaded in Genoa and starved into surrender, but a few days later the Austrians were defeated by Bonaparte at the Battle of Marengo and were compelled to retreat east of the Mincio. Piedmont was occupied, the

Cisalpine Republic was restored, and French troops again entered the south of Italy, though the Parthenopean Republic was not revived. Negotiations followed, and by the Treaty of Lunéville, 1801, Austria repeated the Treaty of Campo Formio and agreed without further demur to the settlement reached at Rastadt—that French territory should extend to the Rhine and that the dispossessed princes should be compensated out of other German lands with the sanction of the Consulate. The effect of this arrangement was that Germany would be reconstructed in accordance with French ideas. The Emperor also agreed to recognise the Batavian and Helvetic Republics. Peace was made with Naples at about the same time.

With the collapse of the Second Coalition Great Britain for the second time stood alone against France. The Tsar had by this time become very unfriendly towards Great Britain. He had assumed the Grand Mastership of the Knights of St. John, and he resented the British capture of Malta, which had occurred in September, 1800. Moreover, the determination of the British to maintain a blockade of French ports and to exclude from them neutral ships which carried contraband wheat, timber, and other things, led to friction with a number of the states of northern Europe. A Northern League (a revival of the Armed Neutrality of 1780), consisting of Russia, Prussia, Sweden, and Denmark, to resist by force British interference with neutral vessels, was formed in December, 1800. A British fleet was sent to Copenhagen under the command of Parker and Nelson in 1801, and it succeeded in crippling the Danish fleet. The Tsar Paul was assassinated at this time, and Great Britain found it possible to come to terms with his successor, Alexander I, on the question of contraband. With the withdrawal of Russia the Northern League collapsed.

Both sides were weary of a war in which there seemed to be no prospect of a decisive victory being obtained by either. Great Britain was definitely successful at sea; the French were triumphant everywhere on land, except, indeed, in Egypt, where the French army had been defeated by Sir Ralph Abercromby. Negotiations for peace were begun, and by the Treaty of Amiens Great Britain undertook to restore to the French the captured West Indian Islands and to the Dutch the Cape of Good Hope, but she retained Trinidad, captured from Spain, and Ceylon, taken from the Dutch. Malta was to be restored by Great Britain to the Knights of St. John, and the French agreed to retire from the Papal States and Naples. British and French troops were to leave Egypt, which was to be restored to the Turkish Empire.

The treaty was more favourable to France than to Great Britain. The latter gave back many important conquests. The First Consul yielded only Egypt, which he had already lost and could not recover, and central and southern Italy, which he could recover whenever he wished. Great Britain, moreover, had entered the war in 1793 in order to maintain the existing system of states in Europe against French attack, and, by making a peace which left the French in possession of the Rhine boundary, with vassal republics in Holland and northern Italy, she had failed to secure her main object in the war.

The war was remarkable, perhaps, for the success of the French. When hostilities began France was distracted and nearly bankrupt. Her armies were ragged and undisciplined and were opposed to the trained levies of the powers of central Europe. By all the recognised rules of warfare the struggle ought to have been short and, for France, inglorious. But the enthusiasm of the French troops, fighting for the ideals of the Revolution, enabled them to carry everything before them and to force the monarchs of Europe to accept humiliating terms of peace from the republic they hated and despised. The system of benevolent despotism was, in fact, played out, and it was bound to suffer defeat when it was opposed to revolutionary ideals. Great Britain allied herself in the First and Second Coalitions with these despotic monarchies, and her escape from similar humiliation was due only to her special geographical position and to the strength of her navy.

CHAPTER XVIII

NAPOLEON'S RULE IN FRANCE

By the establishment of the Consulate in 1799 and the appointment of Bonaparte as First Consul a notable step was taken, only ten years after the beginning of the Revolution, towards the re-establishment of monarchy in France. The new constitution provided, indeed, for government by three Consuls, but the whole power of the state, including military command, was confided to the First Consul, to whom the Second and Third Consuls were assistants rather than colleagues. The new monarchy thus established was fully as despotic as that of the Bourbons, although its character was to some extent veiled at first under constitutional forms. (Even these were modified or discarded in course of time.) It was a despotism, however, which in many respects contrasted strongly with the inefficient despotism of the last Bourbons. It was vigorous and ruthless where theirs was mild and feeble; they were overwhelmed with a load of debt and an antiquated financial system, while the Consulate was run economically and on sound financial principles; the old Government was unable to cope with its work, while the new administration was in every way efficient.

The ease with which the change from the Directory to the Consulate was effected may be accounted for by the disgust of the nation with the inefficiency and corruption of the Directors. The only chance of a strong Government appeared to lie in the elevation to a position of supreme authority of a general who had won fame for the republic. The French had tasted of liberty. Not for the last time in their history they showed their preference for glory.

An elaborate organisation was set up to conceal the fact that legislation and administration alike were subject to the will of the First Consul. The Council of State dealt with administrative matters, but its members were appointed by the First Consul and, presumably, were expected to act in

accordance with his views. The Senate, which was partly
appointed by the First Consul and partly co-opted, was entrusted with the appointment of the tribunes and legislators.
Legislation was proposed by the Council of State, was discussed by the tribunes, and was voted upon by the body of
legislators. Councillors and tribunes might argue for and
against the proposals before the Legislative Corps. In practice
this elaborate organisation, most of the members of which were
supporters of the First Consul, existed to carry out his will,
and it is to be presumed that, if any part of it had attempted
serious opposition to him, the First Consul would have suppressed it or would have ridden rough-shod over it. In the
early days of the Empire the Tribunate was, in fact, abolished,
and the Senate and the Council of State were brought more
strictly under the Emperor's control.

The policy of the Consulate may be described as one of
centralisation, sound finance, and conciliation. The over-
centralisation of Bourbon government had been followed,
in the early days of the Revolution, by the establishment of
a new and elaborate system of local government, and for a
time France suffered from excessive decentralisation. This
was now corrected by Bonaparte. The local government
divisions, of which the most important were the department
(roughly equivalent to an English county) and the commune
(or parish), were retained, but they became subject to prefects
and mayors, the nominees of the First Consul instead of to
elected officials. Paris was divided into twelve districts,
each under a mayor, while the city as a whole was under the
authority of a prefect of police.

French finance was in no better condition in 1799 than it had
been ten years earlier. The enormous masses of paper money
issued in the earlier years of the Revolution had been repudiated in 1797. Under revolutionary conditions the collection
of the revenue had presented great difficulty, and by the
time of the establishment of the Consulate it was three or four
years in arrear. The lists for the current year had not even
been prepared. Bonaparte, besides economising in public
expenditure and declining to fall back upon loans, put the
collection of taxes upon a businesslike footing. Arrears were
collected, and current and future lists were prepared, in
order that collection might henceforth be made at the proper
time. The establishment of a Bank of France on the

model of the Bank of England strengthened the credit of the country.

Bonaparte endeavoured to deal in statesmanlike manner with some of the problems left over from the Revolution. Many thousands of *émigrés* were still living abroad, where they were a source of disaffection towards France and of friction between France and the countries which gave them shelter. The First Consul invited them to return to their native land, and restored their estates to them if these had not already been sold. As evidence of his good intentions towards those who had hitherto opposed the Revolution he released large numbers of political prisoners (including many non-juring clergy), and he annulled the laws which debarred the relatives of *émigrés* from holding office in the state.

More serious than the question of the *émigrés* was that of religion. Many people, especially in the country districts, adhered to the old Church, whose clergy regarded the Count of Provence as Louis XVIII. Bonaparte was anxious to weaken the Bourbons by undermining the support they received from this source. He endeavoured, therefore, to bring about an agreement with the Pope which should settle the ecclesiastical question in such a way as to satisfy the Roman Catholic Church, the people of France and the Government of France. Non-juring priests were released from prison, those who had fled were permitted to return, and many churches were reopened. Negotiations were opened with the Pope (Pius VII), and agreement was reached in 1801, though it was not in full working order till April, 1802.

By the Concordat the Roman Catholic religion was recognised as the religion of France. Bishops were to be appointed by the First Consul and instituted by the Pope, and parish clergy were to be appointed by the bishops. No claim was to be made for the restoration of Church property, but salaries were to be paid to the clergy by the state, and cathedrals and churches were to be restored. It was agreed that forms of service should contain prayers for the republic and the Consuls.

In order to bring the new arrangements into effect it was necessary to induce existing bishops, both constitutional and non-juring, to resign. Little difficulty was experienced with the former, but many of the latter refused, and it became necessary for the Pope to depose those who stood out for their former rights. New appointments were made, mainly from the ranks of the non-juring bishops, but the constitutional clergy (bishops and priests) were received again into the Church. The schism was regarded as healed, and Bonaparte was hailed as a second Constantine.

The original appointment of Bonaparte as First Consul was for a period of ten years, but in 1802 he became First Consul for life. France was still regarded as a republic, and, indeed, this term was not dropped until 1809, several years after the establishment of the Empire, but the Government had become a monarchy in fact though not in name, since its head held office for life and was empowered to name his successor. From this time Bonaparte assumed, in royal fashion, the style of "Napoleon."

The renewal, in 1803, of the war with Great Britain strengthened Napoleon's position, and the discovery of plots, royalist and republican, against his life stimulated his supporters to propose the final change. Little opposition was experienced, and on 18th May, 1804, a decree was issued by the Senate announcing that "the Government of the Republic is entrusted to an Emperor." Napoleon assumed the title of "Emperor of the French." That this step did not meet with the entire approval of his veterans is indicated by the remark, at once contemptuous and sorrowful, of one of his officers, "He is Napoleon, and he becomes—Emperor."

Recognition of Napoleon's new dignity was obtained easily in France, where a plebiscite was taken; the people confirmed it by a practically unanimous vote (3,572,329 to 2,569). Difficulties were experienced abroad, however. Francis II, the Holy Roman Emperor, assumed the style of "Hereditary Emperor of Austria," and he demanded and received recognition of this in exchange for his recognition of Napoleon's new dignity. (Within a couple of years Francis laid down the title of Holy Roman Emperor, and the ancient Empire came to an end.) Great Britain was already at war with France and never formally recognised the Empire. Prussia and many other German states, however, readily recognised Napoleon as Emperor. The Tsar was at this time opposed to France and was soon afterwards at war; he was not on cordial terms with Napoleon until after the meeting at Tilsit. But the Pope was induced to acknowledge the French Emperor, at whose coronation he was present. Napoleon, however, placed the crown on his own head—a fitting act by one who was the architect of his own fortunes and who, in his rise, owed nothing to the favour of priest or pope.

In many ways Napoleon showed a desire to make his Empire a real and vigorous successor to the Roman Empire. It was developed from a republic, as was the Empire of the Cæsars, and in both cases the term "Republic" remained in use long after the rule of an Emperor had been established. Napoleon imitated Charlemagne, the founder of the Holy Roman Empire, by establishing dominion over vast territories, with subject peoples and vassal kings. Charlemagne and other Holy Roman Emperors had been crowned by the Pope; the Pope was present at Napoleon's coronation. The successors of Charlemagne had designated their heirs "Kings of the Romans"; Napoleon conferred on his son (born in 1811) the title of "King of Rome." For centuries the Roman Empire had existed in two divisions, Eastern and Western; by the Treaty of Tilsit Napoleon contemplated a similar partition of Europe between himself and the Tsar. By his marriage in 1810 with Marie Louise, daughter of Francis I of Austria, Napoleon allied the House of Bonaparte with that of Hapsburg, so that his descendants might claim connection with the old Imperial line.

If liberty had been the keynote of the republic, glory was the dominant characteristic of the Empire. A magnificent court was established, with numerous dignified officials. A new nobility was brought into existence, the passport to which was not birth only, but ability and merit. In the army a body of Marshals was set up, and promotion was granted to soldiers according to capacity alone. A Legion of Honour, which was founded in the time of the Consulate, was continued under the Empire, and the distinction was awarded alike for civil and military services to the state.

It has been contended that, apart from any other title to fame, Napoleon is worthy of remembrance on account of his Codes. The Civil Code, which had been begun by a committee of the Convention, was completed by a commission of lawyers while Napoleon was First Consul. The whole body of French civil law was revised and codified, and, though the Code was open to criticism in some ways, it has remained the basis of French law ever since. Nor would it be right to assert that Napoleon merely gave his name to the work of other men. He took an active and intelligent part in the task of revising the final draft of the Code. Other Codes, of Civil Procedure, of Crime, of Criminal Procedure, and of Commercial Law, followed in course of time, and, though they were not of equal importance or influence to the Civil Code, they strengthened Napoleon's reputation as a modern Justinian. As his conquests extended, the Codes were introduced into other lands, so that his legal work exercised an influence far beyond the borders of France.

Soon after the establishment of the Empire a conflict arose between Napoleon and the Pope. Pius VII was annoyed with his treatment at the Emperor's coronation, and before long he contended that various acts of Napoleon violated the rights of the Church. When Napoleon conquered southern Italy and appointed his brother Joseph to the throne of Naples the Pope revived a claim, which his predecessors in the Middle Ages had enforced, to the overlordship of that kingdom, and he refused to recognise the new king unless the claim was admitted. Napoleon replied with a demand that one-third of the body of cardinals should be French. The Pope ceased to institute to vacant sees in France the bishops named by Napoleon in accordance with the Concordat. The Emperor annexed the papal territories, and the Pope pronounced excommunication against all who were concerned in this act of violence, though he did not mention Napoleon by name. The climax came with the Pope's arrest.

This did not solve the problem. Catholic opinion everywhere was shocked, and Napoleon realised that it was to his interest to bring about a settlement. The Pope continued to refuse institution to French bishops, and the Emperor's efforts to circumvent him on this matter were fruitless. Attempts at compromise were made, but they failed, and the Pope was brought a prisoner to Fontainebleau, where he remained for some years.

The sound financial policy of the Consulate was continued for some years under the Empire. Government was conducted efficiently and with economy. Land was reassessed for purposes of taxation, and some of the former indirect taxes, such as those on salt and tobacco, which had been abolished by the Constituent Assembly, were reintroduced. But the most remarkable feature of Napoleonic finance was the establishment of a special fund under the Emperor's personal control and known as the Extraordinary Domain. Into it were paid indemnities from conquered countries and tributes from subject states, and the expenses of new expeditions were paid from it. The cost of war was thus made to fall upon the enemy, and French finance was not subject to excessive military burdens.

Napoleon was not disposed to allow much liberty to the press, which he viewed with suspicion. A censorship was established, and only certain papers were permitted to appear. An official journal, *Le Moniteur*, was issued, and published news in such a way as to extol and glorify the Emperor.

There was an advance of material prosperity in France in the earlier years of Napoleon's rule. French boundaries were pushed forward, and the country was free from invasion. Industry flourished, and, in imitation of Great Britain, machinery was introduced, though not at first to any great extent. Improvements were made in agricultural methods. Fallows were discontinued, a better rotation of crops was devised, and more land was brought under cultivation. Prosperity, however, was not maintained. The effect of the British blockade was severely felt in the latter years of Napoleon's reign, and cessation of imports combined with failure of crops to cause distress among the poor.

Enough has been written to show that Napoleon was something more than a great conqueror. He was a great organiser and a great administrator. In France, and elsewhere, he established government on sound principles in place of corruption and inefficiency. He disregarded privilege, and though he had some regard for tradition he transformed it and used it for his own purposes. Old problems were solved by him, and he worked for the prosperity of France. His achievements as a conqueror came in the end to nothing; his Empire was overthrown. But his work as an administrator was too solid to be discarded; his system of government survived him, and he must be given credit for much that is of permanent value in French life to-day.

CHAPTER XIX

War between Great Britain and France was renewed in May, 1803, after an interval of only thirteen months. The Peace of Amiens appears to have been regarded by both countries merely as a temporary stoppage of the war. Ill-feeling remained, and each side soon began to complain of the conduct of the other. Great Britain was slow to begin the evacuation of Malta, and in fact, never left the island at all; it was believed that the First Consul was contemplating the revival of his Eastern schemes and that he would not hesitate to seize the island again after the British had restored it to the Knights. Yet the retention of the island afforded to Napoleon an opportunity of charging Great Britain with bad faith; if the treaty had been observed and the French had afterwards seized Malta, the charge of bad faith might have been brought against them, while the recovery of the island by a British fleet would have presented little difficulty.

Alarm was felt in Great Britain at the continued growth of Napoleon's influence in various parts of the Continent. He annexed Piedmont and controlled Genoa. He became President of the Cisalpine Republic, which he renamed the Italian Republic. The Helvetic Republic was remodelled as the Swiss Confederation, in alliance with France. The work of reorganising the western part of the Holy Roman Empire, which had been begun by the Congress of Rastadt, was completed under French direction. Many of the small states and most of the Free Cities were merged into the territories of their more important neighbours. The Batavian Republic also was reorganised, the country was occupied by French troops, and it was feared that the closing of Dutch ports to English trade was contemplated. The First Consul refused to renew the commercial treaty which had existed between Great Britain and France before 1793 and imposed a high tariff on British goods, which made a renewal of trade practically impossible. References to him in the British press were hostile and insulting, and he resented the cartoons which continually held him up to ridicule. Finally, as stated above, suspicion was aroused that the First Consul intended to revive his designs upon Egypt, and the British Government refused to discuss the question of Malta until he had given satisfactory assurances upon this matter. Negotiations were conducted with increasing bitterness and anger upon both sides and ended with a declaration of war by Great Britain.

The struggle which began in 1803 differed in character from that which preceded it. In the French Revolutionary War Great Britain was allied with the eighteenth-century despotic monarchies against a nation inspired with revolutionary ideals. In the Napoleonic War the position was to a considerable extent reversed. In the earlier war the French had appeared everywhere as liberators. They had spread revolutionary principles and had established sound and satisfactory government in the territories which they conquered. But the nations of Europe were now called upon to withstand the advance of a tyranny harsher than that of their former rulers, and in course of time Napoleon was opposed by popular enthusiasm and determination in every part of Europe. In the first war France was the champion of freedom against despotism; in the second war she fought under a tyrant against the freedom and independence of other nations.

In 1803 Napoleon sent troops to occupy Hanover, whose Elector was King George III. Prussia regarded herself as the protector of all the North German states; Frederick William III protested against the French invasion of Hanover, but took no further action. Great Britain thereupon blockaded the Elbe and the Weser, with serious effects upon Prussian trade, and Frederick William asked Napoleon, but without effect, for an assurance that he would do nothing further which might be harmful to German interests.

In spite of the fact that Naples was not at war with France, troops were sent into that country to occupy its ports, though it seemed uncertain whether Napoleon's intention was to use these places as bases of attack upon Malta or upon Egypt. By threats Spain and Portugal were compelled to pay subsidies to France, and the Dutch and the Swiss were ordered to contribute troops. These measures were intended by Napoleon as preliminaries to an invasion and conquest of Great Britain;

by them, however, he aroused resentment and alarm in various parts of the Continent, and before long it became possible for Great Britain to organise a Coalition against him.

In 1804 Napoleon assembled a large army at Boulogne, apparently for the invasion of England. A fleet of transports was assembled, and troops were practised in embarkation and landing. Alarm was felt in England, and energetic measures were taken to repel the French. An army of volunteers was

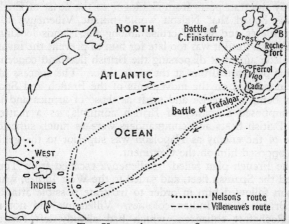

THE NORTH ATLANTIC, 1805

enrolled, the militia was strengthened, Martello towers were built, and a system of semaphore signalling was installed. Arrangements were made to transfer, if necessary, the court and the treasury from London to a city in the Midlands; artillery and other stores were to be removed from Woolwich to the interior of the country; districts threatened with invasion were to be stripped of everything which could be of use to the enemy.

The obstacle to an invasion was, of course, the superiority of the British fleet and the certainty that the French transports would be captured or sunk in mid-Channel. Napoleon hoped to slip across the Channel in a fog, but for many months the sea was clear of all but the slightest of mists. At length, weary of waiting, he evolved a plan for assembling in the Channel a fleet powerful enough to overcome that of Great Britain, and in this he was assisted by the fact that Spain had, in 1804, entered the war against Great Britain. He directed the Toulon fleet, under Villeneuve, to evade Nelson's blockade, to make a junction with the Spanish fleet at Cadiz, and to sail for the New World. A squadron from Rochefort had already escaped from blockade and was attacking British commerce in the West Indies. Villeneuve was expected to unite with the Rochefort fleet and to return speedily to European waters and, in conjunction with the Brest fleet, to sail up the Channel and convoy the transports from Boulogne to the coast of England. It was hoped that Nelson would pursue Villeneuve to the West Indies and would cruise among the islands looking for the French until it was too late for him to prevent the invasion. Napoleon aimed at dispersing the British fleet and concentrating his own squadrons at the same time. The success of the plan depended on the movements of the French and Spanish fleets being as precise and swift as those of armies and upon the supposed stupidity of British admirals; as a matter of fact, British fleets and commanders were as much superior to those of the enemy as Napoleon was superior to the generals who opposed him on the Continent.

The French plan failed. Villeneuve escaped from Toulon, joined the Spanish fleet, and sailed to the West Indies, whither Nelson followed him in order to frustrate possible attacks on the British West Indian colonies. Villeneuve did not meet the Rochefort squadron, which had already left American waters, and he failed to shake off Nelson, who divined his intention of returning to Europe. The British admiral sent a fast brig home to inform the Government of the state of affairs, and he followed with his fleet. Villeneuve, on reaching European waters, was attacked by Sir Robert Calder off Cape Finisterre, and after the battle he retreated towards Ferrol. Moving southwards, he put in at Vigo, and when at length he ventured out he retreated to Cadiz. Calder was court-martialled and censured for not acting with greater vigour against the enemy. Had Nelson been in command of Calder's fleet it is certain that Villeneuve would have suffered greater loss. Yet it should be remembered that Calder had engaged twenty ships of the line, two of which he captured, though he had no more than fifteen vessels in his squadron.

Meanwhile, Nelson was back in the Channel. Napoleon was angry at the collapse of his scheme and censured Villeneuve for not pressing on to the Channel after the Battle of Cape

Finisterre. The French admiral now left Cadiz, determined to show his eagerness to meet the British fleet. At the Battle of Trafalgar the French and Spanish fleets were destroyed as a fighting force, though in Great Britain the victory was felt to be dearly bought at the cost of the life of Nelson. The proposed invasion of England had to be abandoned, and the camp at Boulogne was broken up.

Some students of military and naval strategy have doubted whether Napoleon ever meant to invade England. The risks were enormous, and the success of the naval plan depended to a great extent upon luck and upon the supposed incompetence of British admirals. The alternative view is that Napoleon intended the proposed invasion to be a pretext for the formation of a camp where a huge army might be concentrated—an army which would be ready to strike at any possible enemy on the continent of Europe. Yet it cannot be doubted that victory over Great Britain was desired by Napoleon beyond anything else, and his preparations were on so vast a scale and appeared to be directed so completely to one end that it is difficult to regard them as mere bluff. It should be remembered, moreover, that, if British admirals had been less acute, the scheme of concentrating a large French fleet in the Channel might have succeeded, and it can hardly be doubted that in that event the invasion would have been attempted.

Meanwhile, after lengthy negotiations, a new Coalition had been formed against France. Agreement was reached between Great Britain and Russia early in 1805. Napoleon, perhaps recognising the absurdity of the Emperor of the French being President of the Italian Republic, converted this republic into a kingdom with himself as King, and Austria, desirous of recovering Lombardy and being alarmed for the safety of her remaining Italian possessions, joined the Coalition a few months later. For the time being, Prussia remained neutral.

The Austrians placed two armies in the field. One, commanded by the Archduke Charles, attacked the new kingdom of Italy, while the other, under General Mack, awaited in Bavaria the arrival of the Russians in South Germany. But Napoleon marched with extraordinary rapidity from Boulogne to the Danube and took Mack in the rear, compelling him to surrender at Ulm. Charles withdrew from Italy, but he was too far off to save Vienna, which Napoleon entered unopposed. The Austrian forces in the neighbourhood of Vienna retreated in order to join the approaching Russians. Napoleon pursued them, but was unable to prevent the junction.

Bernadotte, the commander of the French army in Hanover, moved south to join Napoleon. In the course of his march he crossed Anspach, a Prussian province, without permission, and Frederick William prepared for war. In an agreement with the Tsar it was arranged that the King of Prussia should

CENTRAL EUROPE IN 1806

offer his services to Napoleon as mediator and that he should join the allies if his proposal was not accepted. If he had acted with vigour, Napoleon's position would have been critical. But before he could move the French Emperor encountered and defeated the combined Austrian and Russian armies at the decisive Battle of Austerlitz, on 2nd December, 1805. Russian troops withdrew from Austrian territory, the Emperor Francis sued for peace, and the Prussian King explained away his recent treaty and formed an alliance with Napoleon, in connection with which he was permitted to occupy Hanover.

By the Treaty of Pressburg, 1805, Austria was compelled to yield the last of her Italian possessions, Venetia, Istria, and Dalmatia, to the kingdom of Italy, though she was permitted to retain Trieste. Tyrol was ceded to Bavaria, and other lands to Baden and Würtemberg. Bavaria and Würtemberg were recognised as kingdoms, over which the Austrian Emperor renounced all rights.

About this time the French Emperor began the policy of establishing vassal states under the rule of members of his family. The King of Naples was deprived of his throne, which was allotted to Joseph Bonaparte, although the deposed Ferdinand continued to reign in Sicily, which was beyond Napoleon's reach. The Emperor's sister Élise was made Princess of Lucca, his brother Louis was appointed King of Holland, his brother-in-law, Joachim Murat, became Grand Duke of Berg, and his stepson, Eugène de Beauharnais (son of the Empress Josephine by her former marriage), acted as the Emperor's viceroy in the kingdom of Italy.

It had for some time been one of Napoleon's aims to create, as a counterpoise to Austria and Prussia, a third powerful state in Germany. He was now in a position to carry out this idea, and he formed the Confederation of the Rhine. A number of petty states were absorbed into their larger neighbours, and these, sixteen in number, formed a Confederation which passed under the "protection" of Napoleon, and was bound, upon demand, to supply him with an army of 63,000 men. The states of the Confederation were governed despotically, but efficiently. Old feudal privileges were abolished, and the burden of taxation was distributed fairly. The armies of the Confederation were organised and trained by French officers. The Confederation formally announced its withdrawal from the Holy Roman Empire. Francis II thereupon laid down the title of Holy Roman Emperor, and the antiquated Empire came to an end.

Friction soon developed between Napoleon and the King of Prussia, who was hoping to form a North German Confederation similar to the Confederation of the Rhine. Napoleon at this time was negotiating for peace with Great Britain on the basis of the restoration of Hanover, which had been promised to and occupied by Prussia. Frederick William allied with the Tsar, who was still at war with France, and demanded that Napoleon should withdraw his troops to the west of the Rhine. The Emperor's answer was to march against Prussia. One Prussian army was overwhelmed by Napoleon at the Battle of Jena on the same day as another was beaten by Davoust at Auerstadt. Before Russian assistance could be obtained other Prussian armies and fortresses surrendered in rapid succession, and Napoleon entered Berlin as a conqueror.

Frederick William still held out east of the Vistula. Napoleon marched against the Russians and Prussians, but, with an ever-lengthening line of communications, his position was dangerous, and, if Austria had attacked him and England had sent an expedition to the Baltic at once, he might have been overcome. An indecisive and bloody battle was fought at Eylau early in 1807, but in June of that year Napoleon was able to strengthen his forces and inflict a decisive blow on the Russians at Friedland.

Peace was now proposed and was arranged by the two Emperors in person at Tilsit, on the river Niemen. Alexander was delighted to find that Napoleon did not demand of him any sacrifice of territory and that he even suggested the extension of the Russian boundaries at the expense of Turkey and Sweden. Prussia, however, was to lose heavily, and Napoleon only consented to the restoration of any of his lands to Frederick William on the direct intercession of the Tsar. The Prussian share in the Partitions of Poland (except part of West Prussia) was to be formed into the Grand Duchy of Warsaw, with the Elector of Saxony (now called King of Saxony), an ally of Napoleon, as Grand Duke. The Prussian territory west of the Elbe was surrendered, part of it being formed into a new kingdom of Westphalia, for Napoleon's brother Jerome. Saxony and Westphalia joined the Confederation of the Rhine. Various territorial adjustments were made, and the Tsar agreed to support the Continental System, which was being established by Napoleon against Great Britain. In a separate treaty between France and Prussia the latter was to support an army of occupation until a war indemnity, the amount of which was not fixed, was paid off, and her army for the future was to be limited to 42,000 men.

Napoleon was at the zenith of his power. The Tsar was his ally. Prussia was crushed so completely that for some time she ceased to be a factor in European affairs. Austria was afraid to move. Napoleon was not only supreme in a greatly enlarged France but he had established a number of vassal kingdoms and tributary states, so that his will was paramount everywhere in western and central Europe.

But he had not conquered Great Britain.

CHAPTER XX

THE DECLINE OF NAPOLEON'S POWER

WITH the collapse of the Third Coalition and the conclusion of the Treaty of Tilsit in 1807 Great Britain stood alone against France for the fourth time in ten years. Napoleon, realising that British resistance was based on naval power and that Great Britain supported her navy out of the profits of her trade, concluded that if British commerce were ruined Great Britain would be compelled to reduce her fleet. He thought that, if the market for British exports were cut off while imports continued, the balance of trade would turn heavily against Great Britain, and that she would find herself in such serious financial difficulties that she would be glad to treat for peace.

While he was at Berlin in 1806 he issued the Berlin Decree, and in the following year he put forth a supplementary edict at Milan. These decrees began what is called the Continental System. Napoleon declared the British Isles to be in a state of blockade and forbade France and her allies to trade with this country. He further ordered that all European ports from the Vistula to the Adriatic were to be closed to British ships and, in order that British goods should not find their way into Europe in neutral ships, that neutral vessels which visited the Continent after having touched at a British port were to be confiscated as prizes. British merchandise, wherever found, was to be destroyed. The British reply was contained in the Orders in Council by which the ports of France were declared to be in a state of blockade. Neutral ships were forbidden to go to the Continent, and those on the way thither were to be diverted to British ports. In substance, Napoleon ordered that the Continent should not buy British goods; Great Britain determined that if the Continent would not buy British goods it should buy goods of no other country.

This commercial warfare continued till the fall of Napoleon. The Continental System inflicted much damage upon British trade by the closing of European markets to British goods, and, though no French fleet existed by which the blockade of Great Britain could be enforced, a large number of privateers inflicted heavy losses upon British merchant shipping. It was feared that Napoleon might seize the Danish fleet and use it against Great Britain, but a British squadron visited Copenhagen in 1807, bombarded the city, and captured the Danish fleet. But the counter-blockade of the Continent by Great Britain caused much greater loss and suffering to the French and to other peoples subject to Napoleon. British industrial supremacy was by this time so well established that British products were really needed upon the Continent, and a good deal of smuggling went on. Napoleon himself had to issue licences for the admission of British goods of various kinds. The earlier conquests of Napoleon had resulted in his new subjects enjoying prosperity and good government. The hardships now caused by the Continental System, especially to the middle and lower classes, reacted against him and caused widespread resentment, which developed into hatred of him and his rule.

The success of the Continental System depended upon its being applied universally; if any port on the Continent was open to receive British merchandise the system was bound to fail. Portugal, which had always been friendly with Great Britain, was reluctant to exclude British trade, and Napoleon determined to enforce the system in that land. A treaty for the partition of Portugal was concluded between France and Spain, and troops of both countries, under Junot, invaded Portugal. Junot reached Lisbon only to find that the court had fled to Brazil, a Portuguese colony.

Even before Junot's entry into Lisbon Napoleon had taken action which he had been contemplating for some time against the King of Spain. Summoning Charles IV and his son Ferdinand to Bayonne he induced them, by threats or other means, to resign their rights to the Spanish crown. He thereupon appointed his brother Joseph to the vacant throne, and Murat was awarded the crown of Naples, now laid down by Joseph. Napoleon thus completed the dethronement of the Bourbons in Europe (with the exception of the Neapolitan Ferdinand in Sicily). Monarchs of this line had held the crowns of France, Spain, and Naples, which were now worn by Napoleon himself, his brother, and his brother-in-law. But

he had overreached himself.   The Spanish people were indignant at his high-handed action, and before long the country was
in revolt against its new King.   The Peninsular War had begun.

Napoleon under-estimated the strength of Spanish national
feeling, and he sent an army of raw conscripts under Dupont
to restore order.   The surrender of 18,000 of these men, with
their general, at Baylen enheartened the Spaniards, and convinced the British Government that their resistance to Napoleon
was not merely formal, but was a general national uprising.
Great Britain was already morally bound to support Portugal
in its resistance to the Continental System, and she now realised
that an opportunity had arisen for conducting a land campaign
against Napoleon with some prospect of success.   Sir Arthur
Wellesley was sent to Portugal in command of an army which
defeated Junot at Vimiero.   Unfortunately, Wellesley was
superseded during the battle by Sir Harry Burrard, who in
his turn gave place to Sir Hew Dalrymple.   Dalrymple signed
with Junot the Convention of Cintra, by which the French
were permitted to return to France with the spoils of war
instead of being compelled to surrender unconditionally.   The
generals were ordered home to England to defend their action
before a court-martial, and Dalrymple and Burrard, though
acquitted, were not sent back.   Wellesley was held not to have
been responsible and was restored to his command.

Joseph Bonaparte reached Madrid in 1808, but the hostility
of his subjects and the news of Dupont's surrender to Spanish
rebels at Baylen compelled him to withdraw beyond the Ebro.
He was joined by Napoleon, who with an army of veteran
troops recovered Madrid.   When Sir John Moore, who was
at this time in command of the British forces, advanced from
Portugal into Spain, Napoleon turned towards him.   Moore
retreated towards Corunna, and Napoleon relinquished the
pursuit to Marshal Soult, returning to Paris in January, 1809.
Before embarking on the transports which were sent to receive
them, the British had to beat off Soult's attack at Corunna,
where Moore was slain.

Saragossa, which was besieged by the French, held out
for some weeks at the beginning of 1809 and surrendered only
after the most desperate resistance.   Soult invaded Portugal
and occupied Oporto, but Wellesley, upon his return from
England, recovered it.   By a brilliant march he threatened
Soult's communications, and the French marshal retreated

into Spain with the loss of fifty-eight guns. Wellesley marched farther east and defeated Marshal Victor and King Joseph at the Battle of Talavera; Soult, however, received reinforcements, and Wellesley retired into Portugal.

In 1810 a large French army under Masséna marched towards Lisbon, but was checked by a triple line of fortifications across the Peninsula between the Tagus and the sea. These lines of Torres Vedras, covering a front of nearly thirty miles and

THE PENINSULAR WAR

defended by hundreds of guns, formed the basis of British strategy in the war. Wellesley, who became Viscount Wellington after the Battle of Talavera, had constructed these lines secretly, and behind them he was able to receive reinforcements and equipment from Great Britain and so to build up a mighty army which ultimately drove the French back beyond the Pyrenees. The region in front of the lines had been cleared of supplies, and Masséna, after vainly trying to find a weak spot in the fortifications, retired into Spain early in 1811. Wellington ventured out and defeated Masséna at Fuentes d'Onoro, while Beresford besieged Badajos, a border fortress. He repulsed Soult at Albuera, but even with Wellington's aid he could not take Badajos, and the British withdrew into Portugal for the winter.

Early in 1812 the border fortresses of Ciudad Rodrigo and Badajos were taken by storm, and shortly afterwards the

French forces in the Peninsula were seriously weakened by the withdrawal of troops which were required to take part in the Russian expedition. Wellington advanced into Spain and defeated Marmont, who had replaced Masséna, at Salamanca. This victory was regarded as the turning-point in the Peninsular War. Wellington, who had been made an earl after the fall of Ciudad Rodrigo and who now became a marquis, entered Madrid, but a fresh concentration of French armies compelled him to move back to Ciudad Rodrigo for the winter.

The victories of Wellington in 1812 encouraged the Spanish to look forward to the time when their land would be free from the French. But although their triumph over the invaders would involve the restoration of Ferdinand VII, they had little love for that monarch. A Cortes, or Assembly, met at Cadiz and drew up a constitution which declared the sovereignty of the people and drastically reduced the authority of the king. The constitution of 1812 was of little immediate importance, for the country was not yet delivered, and when Ferdinand was restored he resolved to disregard it. But it formed an ideal for which Liberals in several countries in the south of Europe strove in the years to come.

In 1813 the French fought a losing campaign. Napoleon withdrew more troops for the war in Germany. Joseph abandoned Madrid and retreated towards the Ebro. At Vittoria, Joseph and Marshal Jourdan suffered a crushing defeat, with the loss of a hundred and fifty guns, and their shattered troops fled in great disorder. The veteran Soult replaced Jourdan, but he was compelled to fall back, and after desperate fighting he was driven from the border fortresses of Pampeluna and San Sebastian into France. Wellington was now able to invade France, and early in 1814 he inflicted further defeats on Soult at Orthez and Toulouse. The Peninsular War was over. The French had been expelled from Portugal and Spain, and the adventure had cost the Emperor the lives of 200,000 men.

While the Peninsular War was in progress Napoleon was engaged in campaigns elsewhere. The early disasters to the French in the Peninsula, at Cintra and Baylen, had somewhat dimmed Napoleon's prestige. He arranged a meeting with Alexander at Erfurt in 1808, and the alliance of the two Emperors was renewed, but in 1809 the Austrians, thinking that Napoleon would be unable to spare a large army to fight

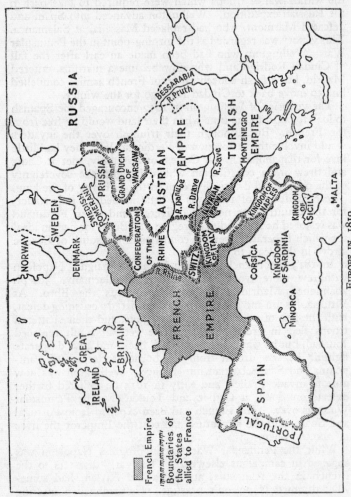

against them, declared war for the fourth time in less than twenty years. But Napoleon marched against them with large forces and occupied Vienna. The main Austrian army, under the Archduke Charles, lay on the northern bank of the Danube. A few miles below Vienna the stream of the Danube is divided by the island of Lobau. Napoleon decided to cross the river at this point. He found no difficulty in crossing the southern branch and occupying Lobau, but after 40,000 men had reached the northern bank of the Danube they were attacked by the Austrians and were hard pressed. They were reinforced next day, and the village of Aspern was captured and recaptured several times. Napoleon ultimately withdrew his men to Lobau, having suffered at Aspern a serious check. He made elaborate preparations for his next effort, and six weeks after the Battle of Aspern he succeeded in transferring an immense force from the south to the north bank of the Danube. The Battle of Wagram followed, and though victory rested with the French the Austrians retired in good order and with no greater losses than their enemies.

But the Emperor Francis feared to continue the war, and peace was made by the Treaty of Vienna. Austria was compelled to pay a large indemnity and to reduce her army to 150,000 men. She had to cede Galicia to the Grand Duchy of Warsaw and the Illyrian provinces (Carniola, Trieste, and Fiume, and parts of Carinthia and Croatia) to France. The French Empire, with the kingdom of Italy, now stretched without a break as far as the border of Turkey, and Austria was cut off from the sea altogether. The peace was followed by the marriage, in 1810, of Napoleon to Marie Louise, daughter of Francis I.

The Tsar supported Napoleon in the Austrian war of 1809, but by the following year friction began to develop between them, and in course of time war became inevitable. Alexander was displeased by the French annexation of the duchy of Oldenburg, whose Duke was his uncle, and also by the addition of Galicia to the Grand Duchy of Warsaw. The Tsar feared that Napoleon might be contemplating the revival of the kingdom of Poland, including those parts now Russian, and he made overtures to Austria. He suggested the cession of Galicia in exchange for certain Danubian lands, but the proposal met with so little favour that the Austrians opposed Russia in the war which followed. But the real reason for a breach between the two Emperors lay in the attitude of Alexander to the Continental System. Great harm was being done to Russian trade, and the Tsar issued decrees which placed heavy duties on French wines and silks and permitted the import of British colonial produce in neutral ships. Such a leak in the Continental System would jeopardise the whole scheme, and Napoleon determined on war.

He believed the opportunity to be favourable, on account of Russian preoccupation with a war against Turkey, but the conclusion of peace between these two powers in May, 1812, released a large Russian army for action against the French. In April, 1812, the Tsar came to an understanding with Bernadotte, Crown Prince of Sweden, who had formerly been one of Napoleon's marshals. Sweden renounced her claim on Finland, and in return she was to receive Norway at the peace. As Norway was at this time ruled by the King of Denmark, an ally of France, this arrangement was a further defiance of Napoleon.

On his side Napoleon made treaties with both Prussia and Austria. A Prussian army of 20,000 men was to march with Napoleon and under his command, and other Prussian troops, under French orders, were to guard communications. Austria, distrusting the Tsar's intentions with regard to Poland and receiving from Napoleon a promise of the restoration of the Illyrian provinces, agreed to contribute 30,000 men (but under Austrian command) to the expedition. But neither Prussians nor Austrians could be trusted to exert themselves to the uttermost against the Russians, nor, if Napoleon should meet with defeat, to continue the fight at all.

Last-minute negotiations for peace between the two Emperors were attempted, but, though agreement might have been reached on other points, the Tsar's attitude towards the Continental System made peace impossible. With reserves and auxiliaries Napoleon's forces in eastern Germany amounted to fully 600,000 men, of whom 100,000 were cavalry. In June, 1812, without formal declaration of war, the Emperor crossed the Niemen with about two-thirds of this vast host. It was too large. Depots of food had been prepared, but commissariat arrangements broke down. Transport wagons could not keep pace with the army, desertion began, and thousands of men fell sick. The rough pasture afforded by the Russian plains proved unsuitable to the horses, and large numbers of them died.

Napoleon pushed on, and hoped to overtake the main
Russian army under Barclay de Tolly before it could effect a
junction with a second army from the south, under Bagration.
But the Russians retreated before him, drawing him ever
farther east, and the two Russian armies united at Smolensk.
Napoleon's original intention had been to limit the campaign
of 1812 to the occupation of Poland and Lithuania and to embark upon further conquests in 1813. This course would have

THE CAMPAIGN OF 1812

presented difficulties, especially of commissariat, but it is
possible that the ultimate result of the campaign might have
been very different. It could hardly have been worse.

On the Russian side the strategy of Barclay de Tolly had its
critics. He abandoned Smolensk, to the great dissatisfaction
of his men, and soon afterwards he was superseded by Kutusoff,
who resolved to make a stand and give battle to the enemy.
The Battle of Borodino resulted in immense losses on both
sides, but it failed to stop Napoleon's march, and Barclay's
policy of retreat and devastation, was justified. At length the
weary French reached Moscow, only to find the city almost
deserted and bare of supplies. Fires broke out, no appliances
were available for their extinction, and a large part of Moscow
was destroyed. Napoleon had marched six hundred miles
into a hostile country and had lost 200,000 men, and he had
gained a city in ruins!

Napoleon expected that the Tsar would ask for terms of peace, and he waited for five weeks in the ancient capital of Muscovy. But Alexander was determined to make no peace while a single French soldier remained in arms on Russian soil, and though negotiations were opened by Kutusoff they appear to have been carried on chiefly in order to detain the French in the heart of Russia until the beginning of winter. If the return journey had been begun in the middle of September it might possibly have been completed without serious disaster; the start was delayed until the third week in October, and, although the weather remained fine for two or three weeks longer, the winter set in early in November. Napoleon attempted to return by a more southerly route in order to avoid the devastated country through which he had passed already, but Kutusoff was too strongly entrenched, and the Emperor was forced to take the road by which he had come.

Men half-starved and inadequately clad were subject to the ceaseless attacks of the Russians, and only the heroic efforts of Marshal Ney, "the bravest of the brave," in command of the rear-guard, prevented the utter extermination of the rapidly dwindling remnant of the Grand Army. The river Beresina had to be crossed by temporary bridges under the fire of Russian cannon. One bridge collapsed, and large numbers of men were slain or drowned. At length Napoleon left his army and pushed on to Paris in order to raise fresh levies. A mere remnant of 20,000 men under Murat recrossed the Niemen at the end of the year, and when other straggling groups reappeared less than 50,000 men emerged of the 600,000 who had started on the venture.

The disasters of 1812 led to the formation in 1813 of the Fourth Coalition and to the War of Liberation. By anticipating the conscription Napoleon enrolled mere boys in his ranks and was again at the head of an army. He was still powerful. Italy and the Confederation of the Rhine remained faithful to him, and Austria had not yet broken her alliance. But Prussia saw an opportunity of escaping from the heavy yoke imposed upon her in 1807, and she allied with Russia by the Treaty of Kalisch. At Lützen Prussians and Russians were checked by Napoleon, and he repeated his victory at Bautzen, though the allies retired in good order. Meanwhile the Austrian Government hoped to secure for itself a commanding position in the affairs of Europe and offered its mediation

to Napoleon.   But the French Emperor had no intention of
accepting terms from a power to which in the past he had
dictated them, and he preferred to fight.

Austria now joined the Coalition, which was financed by
Great Britain, but an allied army was severely defeated at
Dresden.   At the same time, however, other French armies
were defeated by Bernadotte, who had joined the Coalition,
and by the Prussian marshal Blücher.   Large allied armies
converged on Leipzig, and Napoleon had to fight a battle on
unfavourable ground.   The conflict raged for three days,
and it resulted in disaster for the Emperor, who retreated into
France, having lost in 1813 nearly as many men as in 1812.

Napoleon's supremacy in central Europe was overthrown.
Austria recovered the Illyrian provinces, Holland revolted from
French rule, the Confederation of the Rhine collapsed, and
Jerome's kingdom of Westphalia came to an end.   In Italy
all was confusion.   Murat hoped by abandoning Napoleon's
cause to become King of Italy, but had to retire to Naples.
Eugène de Beauharnais retained Lombardy as long as possible,
but at length he was compelled to retire to France, leaving
northern Italy in Austrian possession.

Yet if Napoleon's diplomacy had been as sound as his
strategy he might have retained his throne.   The allies offered
him terms of peace by which France would have remained in
possession of her "natural boundaries," the Rhine and the
Alps, provided that she acknowledged the independence of
Holland and Germany, Italy and Spain.   By the objections
which he raised Napoleon practically rejected these terms, and
the allies prepared to renew the war.

Early in 1814 three separate invasions of France occurred.
As already stated, Wellington (on whom a dukedom was conferred at this time) advanced from Spain into France.   The
Austrians under Schwarzenberg entered by way of Switzerland, and Blücher with the Prussians crossed the Rhine.   But
the allies were suspicious of one another.   The Tsar, who
wished to be regarded as the liberator of Europe, was annoyed
at the possibility of Blücher reaching Paris before the arrival of
Russian troops; Prussians and Austrians feared that the Tsar
was contemplating the establishment of Bernadotte on the
French throne.   Napoleon took advantage of these dissensions
to defeat Blücher on the Marne.   Other desperate battles were
fought, in some of which Napoleon was victorious, in others

defeated. But the allies pressed on to Paris. France was exhausted; resistance was at an end. Napoleon was deposed by the Senate, and a few days later he signed an act of abdication. He was permitted to retire to the island of Elba and to retain the title of Emperor. Louis XVIII, brother of Louis XVI, was restored to the throne of his ancestors, and it was with him that peace was made.

By the First Treaty of Paris France was reduced to the

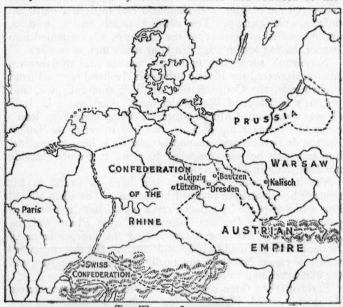

THE WAR OF LIBERATION

limits of 1st January, 1792 (with a slight frontier rectification towards Savoy). This implied the retention of Avignon and some other regions annexed in revolutionary times, but involved the loss of German, Dutch, Belgian, and Italian conquests. Most of the French colonies which were conquered during the war by Great Britain were restored, the only exceptions being Mauritius, Seychelles, Tobago, and St. Lucia. The balance of the indemnity due from Prussia under the treaty of 1807 was cancelled, but no indemnity was demanded of France, and no army of occupation was to be maintained within her borders.

Nor, with few exceptions, were the works of art taken by Napoleon from conquered cities reclaimed. It was arranged that Holland should be restored to the House of Orange, that Germany should consist of a confederation of independent states, and that Italian princes should be restored.

These terms were regarded by the French as hard; discontent was felt in Great Britain at their moderation. France lost the conquests of twenty years; yet she was left larger than before the Revolution. She had bled Europe of treasure for many years; yet restitution was not required of her. She had elaborated a system for the destruction of British commerce; by the restoration of French colonies Great Britain made possible the resumption of French overseas trade.

The settlement of Europe after the disturbances of twenty years presented numerous and difficult problems which it was decided to discuss at a Congress to be held at Vienna. The results of the deliberations at Vienna will be considered in another chapter, but it may be stated that at the Congress dissensions appeared of so serious a character that it seemed possible that further fighting might take place among the victorious powers. Napoleon at Elba watched with keen interest the course of events at Vienna, and hoped that the differences among his conquerors might be turned to his own advantage.

At the end of February, 1815, he left Elba and landed in the south of France with about a thousand men. In his march towards Paris he met with little opposition; regiments sent to oppose him fell in behind his standard; the peasants throughout the countryside welcomed him, and with a considerable force he reached the capital a day or two after Louis XVIII had fled. He declared that he wanted nothing but peace and expressed his intention of honouring the Treaty of Paris and of ruling as a constitutional monarch. But the allies at Vienna pronounced him to be an outlaw and a public enemy. They felt that Napoleon, if granted an interval of peace, would use it merely to consolidate his position and to prepare his forces for future wars. In the general interest it was necessary to crush him forthwith. Russia, Prussia, Austria, and Great Britain concluded a treaty by which each power agreed to contribute 150,000 men to the common cause, and other states joined the alliance.

A double attack upon France was decided upon. Russians

and Austrians were to enter by the east, British and Prussians by the north-east. The latter danger appeared to Napoleon to be the more pressing. Before Wellington and Blücher could invade France, he marched against them with an army of 120,000 veterans, many of whom had been prisoners of war;

Brussels

Wellington's route >······>···
Blücher's route ----→-

Waterloo

La Haye Sainte

Quatre Bras

Ligny

THE WATERLOO CAMPAIGN

they had been released at the fall of Napoleon, and they now rallied to the banner of their old leader.

Napoleon's aim was to prevent a junction of British and Prussians and to defeat them separately. He attacked Blücher at Ligny, while Ney engaged the British at Quatre Bras. Blücher was driven back, and Wellington, though he had repulsed the French at Quatre Bras, was compelled by Blücher's retirement to fall back to Waterloo. Blücher's retreat, however, was on a line parallel to the road taken by Wellington, and though Grouchy was ordered to pursue the Prussians he was too far behind them to prevent the junction which took place on the field of Waterloo.

The Battle of Waterloo was fought on 18th June, 1815. Napoleon did not expect the Prussians to come up, and his aim was to capture La Haye Sainte and break through the British left, thus placing himself between the British and Prussian armies and destroying all hope of their junction. The British troops steadily and stubbornly defended contested points against repeated attacks, and though ground was yielded at La Haye Sainte the line as a whole held firm, even against the onslaught of the Imperial Guard. The arrival of the Prussians and the general advance of the British line decided the battle. The French ranks broke, retreat became general, and pursuit was undertaken by the Prussian cavalry. Guns and equipment were abandoned. Napoleon himself fled to Paris, whither he was followed by the allies. His efforts to organise further resistance failed, and he retired to Rochefort. He embarked on a French frigate, but he surrendered a day or two later to Captain Maitland of the *Bellerophon*. On the order of the British Government he was transferred to the *Northum-*

berland, upon which he was conveyed to St. Helena, where he died in 1821.

The allies insisted on the restoration of Louis XVIII, it being felt that Bourbon rule in France was the best guarantee of peace. The Second Treaty of Paris, signed in November, 1815, while not so severe as the Prussians desired, was necessarily more drastic than that of 1814. France was reduced to the boundaries of 1790, except that she was permitted to retain Avignon. An indemnity of 700,000,000 francs (£28,000,000) was exacted, and an army of 150,000 men under the command of the Duke of Wellington was to be stationed in the north-east of France for a period of five years. Works of art taken by Napoleon from conquered European cities were to be restored.

Napoleon's fall was due to many causes. The almost unbroken succession of victories which marked the earlier years of his career was due not merely to inborn military genius but to careful planning and accurate foresight. He was less careful in these respects towards the end, and the members of his staff were of opinion that in the Russian campaign and the War of Liberation the qualities which distinguished him ten or fifteen years earlier were lacking. Nevertheless, many competent military critics hold that this view was mistaken and that Napoleon had lost none of his military skill with the passage of time.

His failure in the end was due to wider causes than this. France was exhausted by the strain of constant warfare. Conscription was rigorously enforced, and the nation poured forth its manhood until there was no more to give. Enormous losses were experienced in the Peninsula, in the Russian campaign, and in the War of Liberation, and this wastage of life could not be made good.

As the years rolled on and the burden of the Continental System was felt in every part of Europe, Napoleon became more and more disliked. The peoples of Europe regarded him as a despot whose yoke became year by year more burdensome. Spanish and Portuguese in the south-west, Germans in central Europe, Russians in the east, were at one in their determination to free themselves from Napoleon's tyranny.

And throughout the long struggle Napoleon was faced by the might of Great Britain. The British fleet exercised ceaseless vigilance, enclosing the Continent in a stranglehold from which there was no escape. Behind the fleet British industry developed and British commerce throve, and the increasing wealth of the country enabled it to hold on until Napoleon's career was ended. The British navy, indeed, contributed in no small degree to his failure. In the early part of the war the skill of admirals and the bravery of seamen achieved the destruction of enemy fleets and freed the country from the fear of invasion. Enemy colonies were captured and enemy trade was strangled, while, despite the depredations of privateers, the seas were kept open for British trade. Wellington in Spain remained in uninterrupted communication with Great Britain, and the fleets kept him regularly supplied with the reinforcements and equipment which enabled him to build up the magnificent army with which he drove the French from Spain.

The career of Napoleon has been described as meteoric, but the adjective is inadequate. He was more than a flash across the European sky; his career left lasting effects, some good, some bad. As the nineteenth century rolled on, Europe presented to an increasing extent the appearance of an armed camp. Every continental power maintained a huge conscript army. It can hardly be doubted that this high degree of military activity was stimulated by the example of Napoleon.

In other and better respects also the nineteenth century owed much to Napoleon. In his conquests many an ancient throne crashed, many a petty despotism was destroyed. Highly efficient French rule replaced the old autocracy in many parts of the Continent. Feudal privileges and feudal burdens disappeared wherever Napoleon held sway, and in their place were set up the principles of the *Code Napoléon*. Public finances were put in order, communications were improved, trade was developed, education was encouraged, corruption, if not absent, was checked. And though Napoleon's rule was overthrown, a higher standard of administration was set up, which provided an example for later rulers.

The spirit of nationality was awakened in every part of Europe by the tyranny of Napoleon. In the earlier part of his career he had appeared as a liberator, freeing subject peoples from oppression; in course of time they found that their new "freedom" was more burdensome than their former serfdom. And, as the years passed and the iron hand of Napoleon pressed ever more heavily on them, Prussians and Austrians, Italians and Spanish, became conscious of their nationality as they had never been before. This national spirit contributed to the downfall of Napoleon, but, when that result was achieved, the national spirit continued to exist and had further effects. An ancient despotism could not maintain itself permanently over people who were fully aware that they were of one blood and one language, and who aspired to freedom. Outbreaks occurred, and sooner or later constitutional liberty was secured. Such countries as Italy and Germany, which had been divided and subdivided for centuries, achieved unity and became great powers. Others, such as Belgium and the Balkan States, secured independence of alien rule. These and similar examples indicate that the spirit of nationality aroused by Napoleon became a vital factor in the development of modern Europe.

CHAPTER XXI

PRUSSIA, 1740–1815

Frederick II, commonly known as Frederick the Great, succeeded his father as King of Prussia in 1740, and he ruled until his death in 1786. The first half of his reign was occupied by wars with Austria; the second half of the period was almost entirely peaceful. The special characteristics of the eighteenth century are exemplified to the full in his reign.

The eighteenth century was an age which exhibited international relations in their most unlovely aspect. Monarchs were selfish and greedy, and their territories were treated as private estates, which could be passed from one to another without the smallest regard to the wishes and well-being of the common people. Lip-service was paid to the principle of the Balance of Power. The implication of this doctrine was that no state ought to become so powerful as to be a menace to the security of its neighbours. If there were signs of such a development of the power of any one state, it was natural for others to draw together in a combination against it. Hence the frequency with which the acquisition of some new province by a powerful state was met with claims of "compensation" by others. But, in the eighteenth century, the doctrine of the Balance of Power appeared in a perverted form. It was not the strength, but the weakness, of a state which attracted the attention of its neighbours, and on several occasions in the course of the century the weakness of a country was held to afford not only an opportunity but a justification for stronger states to combine to partition it. The classic example of such action was the Partition of Poland, but every great European war of the period affords an example of the working of this policy. In the Spanish Succession War Spain, in the Austrian Succession War Austria, in the Seven Years' War Prussia, in the War of American Independence the British Empire, were attacked by hostile combinations the members of which hoped to gain spoils for themselves. The monarchs of Europe were ready at all times to seize the territories of their neighbours. In none was this disposition more fully present than in Frederick the Great, as is shown by a consideration of the wars and diplomacy of his reign.

Another feature of the government of European countries in the eighteenth century was benevolent despotism, which has been considered in some detail in another chapter. Rulers recognised that government ought to exist for the good of the governed, and most of them tried to introduce reforms in administration, in finance, and in social and economic conditions for the benefit of the people. But if they were benevolent they were also despots. It was held that all reform should spring from the good-will of the monarch, with whose authority no interference could be tolerated. The reforms of the period were not in the least a symptom of the growth of democracy, and it was inevitable that in the monarchs of the time despotism should outweigh benevolence. This characteristic of the age was as fully exhibited in the dominions of the King of Prussia as elsewhere. The reforms which were brought about in Frederick's reign were initiated by him; he interfered in every department of national life, and, as was to be expected, when his strong personality was withdrawn and he was succeeded by weaker men, his system collapsed.

A third characteristic of eighteenth-century Europe was the decay of religious belief and the advance of agnosticism. European politics were dominated by questions of religion in the sixteenth century, and this was the case to a great extent in the seventeenth. But in the eighteenth century the motives of political action were territorial greed and commercial advantage. Men had ceased to believe; the Church, though in many countries still privileged and wealthy, lost influence, and was the object of attack; the papacy was disregarded. In this respect, also, Frederick was the child of his age. He patronised French philosophy and corresponded with Voltaire. He was as familiar with the French language as with German, and he encouraged the spread of French culture in his dominions. It was in this direction that he discovered a basis for his reforming activity. It was founded not on religious or moral but on philosophical principles.

The first half of Frederick's reign has been described in other chapters, and it is sufficient here to recapitulate his military achievements in outline. Taking advantage of the death of the Emperor Charles VI in 1740 he invaded and conquered Silesia, and, by the Treaty of Breslau, 1742, wrested from Maria Theresa a reluctant recognition of his right to his prize. Fearing for its safety, and perhaps coveting Bohemia, he renewed the war in 1744 and received confirmation of his possession of Silesia by the Treaty of Dresden in 1745. He was utterly regardless of the interests of his allies on both occasions; yet the Peace of Aachen recognised anew his sovereignty over Silesia.

Expecting another war within a few years, Frederick, no less than Maria Theresa, made military and diplomatic preparations for it. He knew that negotiations were proceeding between France and Austria, but he was less concerned with the attitude of France than with that of Russia, and when the latter power reached an understanding with Great Britain he accepted the British alliance. This did not prevent Elizabeth of Russia withdrawing from the agreement with Great Britain and making war on Frederick, who, in the Seven Years' War, was called upon to defend his scattered possessions against the combined attack of a ring of great powers. The vigorous support afforded him by Pitt, in the form of an annual subsidy and a British army under the command of Ferdinand of Brunswick, was a material factor in enabling him to hold his own. The defection of Great Britain after the fall of Pitt was balanced by the withdrawal of Russia, after the death of Elizabeth, from the coalition of his enemies, and when the Treaty of Hubertsburg was concluded Frederick emerged from the struggle without loss of territory.

The second half of Frederick's reign was peaceful. The alliance of Prussia with Russia, which began after the death of Elizabeth, continued until 1781, and until his death Frederick kept aloof from Great Britain, which for some years counted for very little in continental affairs. War broke out between Russia and Turkey in 1768; the Russian successes were viewed with apprehension by Austria, and Frederick feared the possibility of a renewal of European war. To avert this, he propounded a plan by which each of the eastern powers should receive a slice of Polish territory. Personal meetings took place between Joseph II (Emperor after 1765) and Frederick, and the Emperor was won over to the plan, although his mother and co-regent, Maria Theresa, agreed to it only with some reluctance. Catherine was induced to relinquish her Turkish conquests in return for a Polish province, and the first Partition of Poland took place in 1772. Frederick annexed the provinces of West Prussia, Ermeland, and Kulmerland; this was the smallest of the three shares, but the most important, since it was the most populous, it included a stretch of Baltic coastline, and it established territorial connection between East Prussia and Brandenburg.

The death of the Elector of Bavaria in December, 1777, brought grave danger of a new war between Prussia and Austria, and, possibly, of a general European war. The heir to Bavaria was Charles Theodore, the Elector Palatine, who was induced by Joseph to renounce his claim. The Emperor's aim was to incorporate Bavaria in the Hapsburg dominions, and he sent Austrian troops into the electorate. Frederick was alarmed, and prepared to support the claim to Bavaria of the Duke of Zweibrücken, next heir to the Elector Palatine. Prussian and Austrian armies entered Bohemia, and faced one another for some time, and fighting seemed to be inevitable. Joseph appealed for assistance to France, but without success. He even offered to exchange the Austrian Netherlands for Bavaria, a move which would have been valuable to him as tending to the consolidation of Hapsburg territories, but France declined to endorse the proposal. An appeal to Catherine of Russia was equally fruitless, and she prepared to assist Frederick. The Emperor had to give way, and the questions at issue were settled in the Treaty of Teschen, 1779. Charles Theodore was recognised as Elector of Bavaria, though a small slice of Bavarian territory was ceded to Austria. This result was eminently satisfactory to Frederick the Great. The union of Bavaria and the Palatinate created a new South German state able to some extent to act as a counterpoise to the power of Austria, while the prestige of Frederick himself, as the defender of the rights of the lesser princes against Imperial aggression, was strengthened.

Prussia followed Catherine's lead in joining the Armed Neutrality against Great Britain in 1780, but this was the last occasion in this period on which the two powers were able to co-operate. The alliance of Prussia and Russia came to an end with the dismissal, in 1781, of Catherine's foreign minister, Panin, and her subsequent alliance with the Emperor. Frederick had been persistently hostile to Great Britain since the conclusion of the Seven Years' War. He now found himself as isolated as Great Britain among the powers of Europe, and it is possible that he might have been willing to modify his attitude towards his former ally. But no new alliance with Great Britain took place.

Joseph II attempted to take advantage of internal dissensions in Holland and of the exhaustion of Great Britain after the American War to revive his scheme of an exchange of the Austrian Netherlands for Bavaria and the Palatinate. The possible hostility of France was to be bought off by the cession of Luxemburg and Namur. Charles Theodore of Bavaria and his heir, the Duke of Zweibrücken, were to be induced to agree to the exchange by the offer of the title of King (of Burgundy). These proposals were put before the Elector and the Duke; the latter appealed to Frederick as protector of the Imperial constitution, and both Frederick and the Duke sent protests to Austria, France, and Russia. Charles Theodore thereupon denied knowledge of the scheme, and Joseph, alarmed at the opposition thus evoked, withdrew it.

Frederick had for some time been considering the formation of a League of Princes, and Joseph's action provided the necessary stimulus for the project. In March, 1785, the *Fürstenbund*, or League of Princes, was established. It was joined by many of the most powerful of the princes, including some of the Electors. Its aim was to maintain the constitution of the Empire as settled at Westphalia, and to resist Imperial action against princely independence. It cannot be asserted that the *Fürstenbund* exercised any profound influence upon the course of events in the Empire; its chief importance lay in its potential opposition to any future Austrian plan for the absorption of Bavaria.

After 1763 Frederick sought to repair the havoc wrought in his dominions during the Seven Years' War. Of simple tastes, he cared little for ceremonial; he was a hard worker, attending to the business of state early and late. Towns and villages were rebuilt, farms were restocked, war-horses were harnessed to the plough, waste land was brought into cultivation, parts of the royal domain which were of small value were converted into fertile land by drainage operations, and communications were improved. The coinage, which had become depreciated during the Seven Years' War, was restored (although base coin was called in at its real and not its nominal value, to the great loss of the people). The Bank of Berlin facilitated the financing of industrial and commercial undertakings. The whole financial system of Prussia was reviewed. French revenue officials, specially trained in tax-collection, were appointed, and the burden of taxation remained heavy. A huge treasure was accumulated and kept in reserve for use in any future war. Some parts of Frederick's territories which had especially suffered from the war were granted remissions of taxation. The immigration of artisans was encouraged in order that manufacturing industry might be developed, while hundreds of thousands of foreigners were settled in the more sparsely populated provinces, where they were given grants of land, usually of inferior quality, which they were expected to improve by their industry. The population of the Hohenzollern dominions increased during the reign from two to six millions; a substantial part of this increase was due to the acquisition of new provinces, but the growth of population was considerable in every part.

An important feature of Frederick's work was the codification of Prussian law, a task which he entrusted to a body of jurists (and which was not completed until the reign of his successor). The law-courts also were reorganised. Unfortunately, Frederick occasionally interfered with the work of the courts, even to the extent of overriding and reversing judicial decisions. There was no ground for supposing the King's views to be closer to the ideal of absolute justice than were those of his judges. If he had any ground for regarding his judges to be corrupt or incompetent he should have removed them and appointed others; to annul their judgments, often from a partial or mistaken view of the circumstances of a case, was not conducive to the maintenance of justice.

Frederick was as notable for what he failed to do as for what he did. The Prussian social system was based upon a division of the people into three orders—nobles, burghers, and peasants—which were kept rigidly apart. The nobles formed the privileged class, exempt from most of the taxation. To them the King looked for officers for his army and for rulers for his towns and villages, and they filled the most important posts in the government service. The citizens were, in the main, free from military service and were engaged in commerce and industry, the latter being under the control of gilds which were medieval in outlook and organisation. The peasants, for the most part, were serfs, who were subject to conscription for the army. They bore the weight of taxation and were subject in many ways to the nobles. To some extent they could rely upon royal support against intolerable oppression, since it was to the King's interest to protect the source of military recruitment. The division of society into these three castes was so thorough and complete that land in the possession of a member of one class could not pass to a person of another class. Frederick did nothing towards the diminution of these social distinctions, which militated seriously against the development of a real feeling of nationality.

The Prussian administrative system was developed during the reign, and its efficiency made it possible for the King to put his reforms into effect. The administration was carried on under his personal supervision, and this was at once its strength and its weakness—its strength, since his oversight of officials prevented slackness and inefficiency—its weakness, because there was no room in it for individuality and initiative. Ministers were mere clerks; officials, and the people in general, were so much accustomed to submission that they were helpless when the master-mind was removed. At Frederick's death his system fell into decay. If the advance of Prussia in the eighteenth century was due to the genius and vigour of Frederick the Great, it is equally true that he cannot be absolved from responsibility for its temporary eclipse in the early years of the nineteenth century.

Frederick William II (1786-97), the nephew of Frederick the Great, though kindly and well-meaning, was a man of weaker character than his uncle. He was addicted to pleasure rather than business, and he was incapable of carrying on the government with his predecessor's vigour. The weakness of the King was at once reflected throughout the state; abuses developed, though for some time the growing weakness of Prussia was not apparent to her neighbours.

Frederick William in 1787 intervened with some success in the affairs of Holland, where friction between the burgher party and the Stadtholder had become acute. The Stadtholder, William V, had married the sister of the King of Prussia, who sent an army into Holland to support his brother-in-law. Great Britain was prepared to approve this line of action, and in 1788 a Triple Alliance of Great Britain, Prussia, and Holland was formed for mutual defence and for the maintenance of the Stadtholder in his position.

Frederick William was not at first alarmed at the outbreak
of the French Revolution. It is probable that he regarded the
troubles in France as important mainly because, while they
lasted, they would render France powerless to influence the
course of European affairs. The state of Poland occupied his
attention. He suspected the intentions of Catherine II with
regard to that country and did not wish to be involved in a war
with France while the Polish situation remained uncertain.

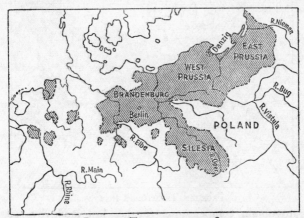

PRUSSIAN TERRITORIES IN 1789

Leopold II, who became Emperor in succession to his brother
Joseph in 1790, met Frederick William in 1791 at Pillnitz,
where *émigré* nobles and princes exhorted the two monarchs
to restore order in France. The Declaration of Pillnitz
probably meant little to either of them, since the suggestion of
intervention was conditional upon other states being associated
with it, and it was most unlikely that Great Britain would move
in the matter.

But events moved rapidly, and when, in April, 1792, France
declared war against Austria, Frederick William treated the
declaration as applying to him also. Prussian forces under the
Duke of Brunswick invaded France and captured Longwy and
Verdun, but they were defeated at Valmy and soon withdrew
across the frontier. France was threatened with invasion
again in 1793, but the allies were suspicious of each other.
The Austrian alliance was distasteful to Prussian officers who

had fought under Frederick the Great and had always regarded Austria as the enemy of their country. The allies failed to co-operate, and soon retired. Prussia, with her eye on Poland, took little further part in the war, and in 1795 peace was concluded by the Treaty of Basel. France was to retain certain Prussian territories west of the Rhine, but agreed not to make war against states north and east of a line agreed upon. Prussia

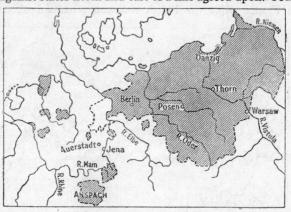

PRUSSIAN TERRITORIES IN 1795

was to obtain compensation for her lost lands by seizing territories farther east.

In 1793 the Second Partition of Poland occurred, and Prussia was enlarged by the addition of Danzig and of a stretch of territory which included Posen and Thorn. From the final Partition, in 1795, Prussia obtained Warsaw and the region south and west of the Niemen.

The Treaty of Basel had the merit of giving peace to North Germany for several years. Prussia took no part in the war of the Second Coalition. In 1797 Frederick William II died and was succeeded by Frederick William III, an abler man than his father, who remained on outwardly friendly terms with France for the first few years of his reign. He continued the work of Frederick the Great in improving the condition of the peasants, and the process of transforming them from serfs into landed proprietors began. Some reforms were made in the government of certain of the Prussian provinces. Tariffs were rearranged, and some internal customs were abolished.

Frederick William was offended by the high-handed action of Napoleon during the war of the Third Coalition. In their march against Austria French troops had crossed the Prussian province of Anspach without permission, and this happened at a time when Frederick William, as a neutral, was refusing passage to the Tsar's troops in the east. He now agreed with the Tsar to offer mediation and to join the Coalition if Napoleon declined the proposal. But the French victory at Austerlitz altered the situation, and Frederick William allied with France, being permitted to occupy Hanover. The Prussian King did not wish to offend Great Britain, and proposed to make the occupation only provisional until a general peace was established, but Napoleon insisted upon Prussia annexing the province. Not long afterwards Napoleon was negotiating for peace with the English on the basis of the return of Hanover to them.

This insult to the King of Prussia brought war nearer, and after the formation of the Confederation of the Rhine Frederick William allied with the Tsar and demanded that Napoleon should withdraw his troops west of the Rhine. But Prussia was in no condition to face the French armies. Her military system was antiquated. The noble officers were harsh towards their men, the peasant conscripts were sullen, and discipline was maintained by flogging. Many of the officers, moreover, were old and inefficient. Napoleon moved rapidly against the Prussians before the Russians could march to the assistance of their allies, and he overthrew one army at Jena on the same day as Davoust defeated a second army at Auerstadt. Fortresses surrendered to the French in rapid succession; Napoleon entered Berlin, and Frederick William retired to East Prussia.

Peace was not concluded until after the Treaty of Tilsit. Napoleon at first contemplated the complete destruction of the Prussian kingdom, but in deference to the Tsar's wishes he permitted Frederick William to resume the throne of a much diminished realm. The provinces west of the Elbe and most of the Prussian gains from the Partitions of Poland were lost. A crushing war indemnity, the amount of which was not even fixed at first, was levied. A French army of occupation was to remain on Prussian soil until it was paid off, and the Prussian army was to be limited in future to 42,000 men.

Prussia profited by her misfortunes. The old military

system had broken down utterly, and Frederick William recognised that reform must come. Hardenberg, a Prussian minister who was regarded as friendly to Great Britain, was dismissed at the command of Napoleon, and Frederick William entrusted the task of reorganising the state to Stein, who issued a series of decrees. Serfdom was abolished, and, though certain rights of the lords over their serfs were at first allowed to remain, a subsequent edict (by Hardenberg, who returned

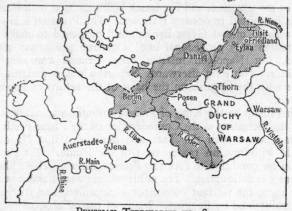

PRUSSIAN TERRITORIES IN 1807

to office in 1810) freed the peasants from their burdens in return for the yielding of one-third of their lands to their lords. The rigid distinctions between the classes of the people were relaxed. Citizens were permitted to hold commissions in the army and were able to purchase the land of nobles. Nobles, on the other hand, were allowed henceforth to engage in trade. Stein denounced the lack of interest exhibited by the Prussian people in the affairs of their country, and rightly attributed it to their exclusion from the work of government. He contrasted the apathy which existed in Prussia with the vigorous public opinion which exercised an important influence on affairs in Great Britain. He did not believe in democracy, but he thought that it would be well for the people to have some interest, however small, in the work of government. Towns were permitted henceforth to choose their own councils, which were entrusted with some features of local government, such as the maintenance of streets and the relief of the poor. The

central Government was reorganised, and a State Council of
ministers was established. The duties of government were
apportioned among ministers on a more satisfactory basis than
hitherto, and the civil service was improved.

Stein held office for little more than a year. He met with a
good deal of opposition in Prussia, especially from the nobles,
who regarded him as a revolutionary. He wished Prussia to
take advantage of the French difficulties in Spain, but Napoleon
suspected his designs, and he was forced to resign. Napoleon
ordered his banishment, and Frederick William dared not
refuse, but his work was carried on by Hardenberg, who
reformed the financial system and freed industry from the
control of the gilds. The great Prussian statesman retired to
Vienna and then to St. Petersburg, and wherever he went he
became the centre of influences hostile to Napoleon. He did
much to arouse in the people among whom he lived feelings of
patriotic fervour. But his greatest work was his regeneration
of Prussia. In a twelvemonth he left an indelible impress on
the Prussian state.

Another notable Prussian minister of this period was Humboldt, who was interested in education. He brought about the
establishment of the University of Berlin, and he reformed the
public schools. The value of his work was seen in the enthusiasm with which the University supported the national
cause in the War of Liberation.

Reform in the Prussian military system was effected by
Scharnhorst and Gneisenau, and it was conducted on principles
similar to those followed by Stein. Commissions were no
longer monopolised by the nobles but were granted to suitable
men of the citizen class. Old and incompetent officers were
removed. The conditions of service in the ranks were improved. Citizens as well as peasants were enlisted, and
imprisonment was substituted for flogging as the normal
method of punishment. By Napoleon's command the Prussian army was restricted to 42,000 men, but Scharnhorst
devised a system by which men were enlisted and trained for
a short period and were then passed into the reserve so that
their places might be taken by others. The stipulated number
was never exceeded; yet in three or four years Prussia had
150,000 trained men at her disposal. New equipment was
provided, and guns of improved pattern were cast.

Frederick William viewed with alarm the prospect of war

between Napoleon and the Tsar in 1812. The Prussian state had been saved in 1807 as the result of Alexander's intercession; if Russia were defeated Prussia might be destroyed altogether. On the other hand, a victorious Russia might annex the Grand Duchy of Warsaw, which consisted largely of the Prussian share in the Partitions of Poland. Frederick William conducted negotiations with both sides. If he could have been certain of Russian assistance he would have declared war

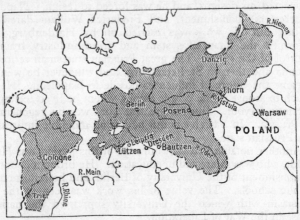

PRUSSIAN TERRITORIES IN 1815

against Napoleon, but the Tsar decided upon a defensive campaign and would not promise to send troops to Prussia. In the end Frederick William was forced to promise assistance to Napoleon to the extent of 20,000 men.

The Prussian corps, under Yorck, formed part of the army of Marshal Macdonald in the siege of Riga. With the retreat of the French from Russia, Macdonald withdrew west of the Niemen, but Yorck, without the sanction of his King, concluded an agreement with the Russians. Frederick William hesitated whether to endorse or to disavow the action of his general, but before long he decided to ally with the Tsar, and Yorck's action was approved.

The part played by the Prussian forces in the War of Liberation is referred to in another chapter. Prussians fought in the battles in Saxony and took part in the overthrow of Napoleon at Leipzig. A Prussian army under Blücher invaded France in 1814 in conjunction with other members of the Coalition, and Blücher shared with Wellington the glory of the final defeat of Napoleon at Waterloo.

By the settlement effected at Vienna Prussia recovered much of her lost territory, and acquired other lands which more than compensated her for the Polish provinces which remained in Russian possession. She was once more a great power, greater than in the days of Frederick. She had benefited by adversity; she had shaken off the trammels of outworn systems; the spirit of the people had been aroused; she was ready to fulfil her destiny in the nineteenth century as the leader of the German nation.

CHAPTER XXII

THE CONGRESS OF VIENNA

THE turmoil of war had left the Europe of 1815 in a very different condition from that of the eighteenth century. Several states had ceased to exist, and the boundaries of many others had been modified again and again. After the fall of Napoleon in 1814 it was decided that a Congress should be held at Vienna to settle the affairs of the Continent. All the great powers and most of the lesser states were represented at the Austrian capital by sovereigns or statesmen. The Tsar, the King of Prussia, the Austrian Emperor, and many lesser potentates were present in person. The French representative was Talleyrand, and British interests were in the charge of Lord Castlereagh, the Foreign Secretary. Metternich, the Austrian Chancellor, was the president of the Congress, and exercised great influence in shaping its policy. The Congress had its social side, and during its meetings, which lasted several months, Vienna was the scene of diversions and festivities which stood in marked contrast with the misery of a blood-stained continent.

Much of the work of the Congress was done through committees, and some parts of the settlement were the results of negotiations and intrigues carried on within smaller groups. Moreover, few of the powers entered upon the discussions with open minds; most of them had already entered into agreements for which they tried to secure the approval of the Congress. Many of the Vienna decisions, therefore, had been reached before the Congress opened.

In making its arrangements the Congress displayed a natural tendency to reward those states which had opposed Napoleon and to penalise those which had supported him. It wished, further, to strengthen the states in proximity to France in order to diminish the likelihood of a renewal of trouble from that quarter, and it sought to take precautions against revolutionary outbreaks in future. It professed to base its decisions upon the principle of "legitimacy," which implied the restoration, as far as possible, of the authority of "rightful" sovereigns. But this principle was applied only in certain cases. Had it been enforced everywhere Europe would have been restored to its pre-war condition, but a return to the state of affairs which was in existence in 1792 would have been satisfactory to few, if any, of the powers represented at Vienna and, in any case, would have been impossible. The Holy Roman Empire had ceased to exist, and this relic of the Middle Ages could not be restored. The Congress viewed republican institutions with such disfavour that the revival of the Venetian and Genoese Republics could hardly be contemplated, and although the Tsar wished to re-establish the kingdom of Poland it was with himself as King.

It was settled that Germany should become a confederation of independent states, under the leadership of Austria. Suggestions for a closer union, which might lead to a strong empire under Prussian control, were opposed by Metternich, and more than half a century was to elapse before German unity was achieved. The Congress recognised the right of Austria to the Illyrian provinces, which had been lost in 1809 and recently recovered. Austria, however, did not desire to recover her former possessions in the Netherlands; she received compensation in the north of Italy, where Lombardy and Venetia were restored to her. The ex-Empress Marie Louise, who, it will be remembered, was the daughter of Francis I, became Duchess of Parma, in which state, therefore, Austrian influence was predominant, though the French system of government was retained.

Prussia left most of her share of Polish territory in the hands of Russia and received in exchange part of Saxony, whose king was punished for his support of Napoleon by the loss of nearly half of his kingdom. Prussia also received Swedish Pomerania and recovered her Rhenish lands, to which were added the greater part of the old electorates of Cologne and Trier. Although the Hohenzollern territories thus remained scattered, the political importance of these arrangements was considerable. The withdrawal of Austria from the Netherlands and the strengthening of Prussia on the Rhine made the latter the natural protector of Germany against France, and this was an important factor in the elevation of Prussia to the leadership of the German Empire in the course of the nineteenth century.

The settlements elsewhere may be noted briefly. The

annexation of Finland by Russia was recognised by the Congress, and Sweden, which lost this province and Swedish Pomerania, was permitted to retain Norway, which she had already received from Denmark (another example of reward and punishment). The Bourbon king, Ferdinand, was restored in Spain. Belgium, formerly the Austrian Netherlands, was

EUROPE IN 1815

joined to Holland, which became a kingdom under the rule of the Prince of Orange. The Swiss Confederation was restored, with the addition of three cantons. The King of Sardinia recovered Piedmont, Nice, and Savoy, and added Genoa to his dominions. (France was thus hemmed in on the east by four important powers, Dutch, Prussian, Swiss, and Piedmontese.) The King of the Two Sicilies recovered Naples, and the Pope's authority was restored over the States of the Church.

Great Britain kept some of her aquisitions overseas, including Malta, Ceylon, Mauritius, and the Cape of Good Hope, but the British Government paid the sum of £6,000,000 to the

King of Holland as compensation for the loss of the Cape and a few minor possessions. Hanover, now recognised as a kingdom, passed once more under the rule of George III.

The obvious criticism of these arrangements is that they were made in the interests of the sovereigns and without consulting the wishes of the peoples of Europe. The Belgians resented their connection with Holland, Norway disliked its union with Sweden, the Poles never forgot their lost independence. Italians wanted a united Italy, Germans a united Germany. Yet Napoleon had been overthrown by the peoples and not merely by the sovereigns of the Continent. While the French Emperor was face to face with the despotic Governments of the eighteenth century he was victorious; when he had to meet the grim and determined opposition of the nations which resented his tyranny he was mastered. He aroused against himself the national spirit in Spain, in Russia, and in Germany, and this proved to be his undoing. But the diplomats at Vienna disregarded the national spirit, and since, during the nineteenth century, popular wishes proved to be more powerful than royal interests, the settlement failed to be permanent. The history of Europe in the nineteenth century is to a large extent the record of the undoing of the work of the Congress of Vienna.

On one matter the policy suggested by Great Britain was accepted by other European powers before the Congress of Vienna separated. The abolition of the slave trade had been decided upon by this country in 1807. At Vienna the other powers, France, Spain, Portugal, and Holland which were interested in this inhuman traffic agreed to end it, although each country was left to determine from what date and under what conditions it should begin to enforce the prohibition.

The Congress of Vienna also considered the question of the Barbary Corsairs and decided that the time had arrived for their extermination. For centuries the commerce of the Mediterranean and the coasts of western Europe had been subject to the raids of the Corsairs, whose captives had been kept in lifelong servitude. It seems incredible that the great powers of Europe should have been indifferent for so long to this menace to the liberty and prosperity of their subjects. A British squadron under the command of Lord Exmouth visited Algiers, bombarded it, and released a large number of Christian slaves.

Before the Congress of Vienna is decisively condemned on account of its adhesion to "legitimacy," its opposition to revolutionary principles, and its disregard of the spirit of nationality, the point of view of its members should be taken into account. Europe had passed through a terrible experience. It had been bled white by more than twenty years of war, which had begun as a result of the French Revolution. The Continent needed peace, and European statesmen thought that the surest way to secure it was to prevent revolution, and if, in spite of their efforts, revolution should appear, to crush it.

The Tsar Alexander I was a man of deep religious feelings, and he proposed that the chief powers should enter into an alliance with a view to conducting the affairs of Europe upon Christian principles—"the principles of that holy religion which the Divine Saviour hath imparted to mankind." Although the respect with which any proposal of the Tsar must necessarily be received was at first tempered with astonishment, the idea took root, and the Holy Alliance of Russia, Prussia, and Austria, with some states of minor importance, was formed. The Tsar's suggestion was, indeed, one which it would have been difficult to decline, for, apart from Turkey, all the powers of Europe were nominally Christian, and they could hardly be expected to declare that they were *not* willing to see European affairs settled upon Christian principles. But men were not all agreed upon the definition of the phrase. It is certain that the Tsar did not, at first, intend the Holy Alliance to be an instrument of repression. He was considering the grant of a constitution to Poland, and he was in favour of the establishment of constitutional government elsewhere. But Metternich saw clearly that the maintenance of absolute monarchy and the suppression of revolutions would be regarded by the monarchs of Europe as entirely in harmony with the doctrines of the Christian religion. The idea of Divine Right, which had been the basis of the Stuart monarchy in Great Britain in the seventeenth century, was, in fact if not in any formal claim, held by the despotic monarchs of central and eastern Europe in the nineteenth century. Metternich, therefore, although he was at first outwardly contemptuous of the proposal, supported it, and for some years the Holy Alliance was on the watch to put down all revolutionary, and therefore unchristian, tendencies in any part of Europe.

Though the Holy Alliance was a league for the suppression of future revolutionary movements it was also a league for the avoidance of wars, and, as pointed out above, the connection between these two ideas was, in the minds of the statesmen of the time, very close; it was the connection of cause and effect. The Holy Alliance presents some points of similarity to the United Nations of the present day. While, however, the United Nations includes many states, large and small, and its Security Council works for the avoidance of war by receiving notice of matters which may endanger peace and trying to settle them, the Holy Alliance included a few great powers which desired to impose their will upon all smaller states. It should be remembered to the credit of the Alliance that the peace of Europe was broken by only minor wars for forty years after the Congress of Vienna.

Lord Castlereagh was by no means in entire sympathy with the policy of repression which was being developed at the Congress. Yet Metternich and the Tsar were anxious to secure the adhesion of Great Britain to the Holy Alliance, and, as stated already, it was not easy to give a direct refusal to the invitation to join. Great Britain was a Christian country with an established Church, and she ought to be in sympathy with the professed ideals of the Alliance. A way out of the difficulty was found in the fact that George III was insane and that his duties were being carried on by a Prince Regent, who wrote to the Tsar that the Holy Alliance had his personal approval and sympathy, but that he had no authority to commit the country to it.

Great Britain agreed, however, to send representatives from time to time to Congresses of the powers whenever important matters should arise which should call for joint European action. A Quadruple Alliance of Russia, Prussia, Austria, and Great Britain was formed. It might appear to be singularly illogical for Great Britain to join the three eastern powers in the Quadruple Alliance and to refuse to enter the Holy Alliance with them. But the Holy Alliance was committed to a definite line of policy; by joining the Quadruple Alliance Great Britain merely promised to meet the other powers whenever necessary and to uphold the terms of the Second Treaty of Paris. She was not committed to the support of a line of policy already decided upon, and she might, and in fact did, oppose

*I 1643–1848

the repressive action which commended itself to the other powers. It is sometimes contended that this reactionary policy was the work of the Quadruple rather than of the Holy Alliance, but, in view of the attitude of Great Britain at the later Congresses, this assertion cannot be maintained. Repression was, indeed, decided upon, but it was supported by the three Holy Alliance powers and was opposed by Great Britain.

CHAPTER XXIII

THE BREAK-UP OF THE CONCERT OF EUROPE

THE primary aim of the Quadruple Alliance was the maintenance of the Second Treaty of Paris. It felt that the Coalition which had succeeded in overcoming Napoleon should be kept in existence in order to check any possible revival of French aggression, and it was arranged that the representatives of the powers should meet from time to time to consider the best measures for the continuance of European peace.

The first of these Congresses was held at Aachen (Aix-la-Chapelle) in 1818. It was decided that the army of occupation might safely be withdrawn from France, and this was done before the end of the year. On other matters differences of opinion appeared. The British proposal that France should be admitted to the Quadruple Alliance was accepted, though with some hesitation. The inclusion of France obviously made some difference to the original aim of the Alliance, which was, in effect, to prevent an increase in French power. The Tsar suggested that it should undertake a general supervision of European affairs and that periodic meetings should be held. Great Britain, however, was opposed to the tendency of the Holy Alliance powers to interfere in the affairs of other states, and, though Lord Castlereagh agreed to send British representatives to future Congresses summoned for specific purposes, he would not assent to periodic meetings. When the next Congress met, in 1820, at Troppau, a more marked divergence of opinion developed between Great Britain and the eastern powers.

In the year 1812 a constitution had been drawn up in Spain by the Cortes, or Assembly. The principles of this document were far too liberal for an ignorant and priest-ridden peasantry, and they were understood and appreciated only by an enlightened minority of the Spanish people. Upon the fall of Napoleon and the expulsion of Joseph from Spain the Bourbon king,

Ferdinand VII, was restored, and, with the approval of the nobles, the clergy and the mass of the people, he declared the constitution void. The Inquisition was re-established, the press was censored, and thousands of the supporters of the constitution were imprisoned.

In 1820 Riego, colonel of a regiment which formed part of a force assembled at Cadiz to undertake the reconquest of the revolted colonies of Spain, led a military rising and proclaimed the constitution of 1812. The effort met with little success in the south of Spain, but it was taken up in the north, and from Corunna to Barcelona the country declared for the constitution. The excitement spread to Madrid, and the King yielded. He restored the constitution, swore to maintain it, and ordered copies of it to be circulated throughout Spain.

The King of Naples was Ferdinand I, also of the Bourbon line. The French system of government, established under Murat, was retained after Ferdinand's restoration, but the administration was corrupt and the peasants were oppressed. There was much discontent in the army, where favour was shown and promotion granted to officers and men who had served Ferdinand in Sicily, while those who had fought for Murat were passed over.

A secret society, the Carbonari, had come into existence during the early years of the century, and though it originated among the charcoal-burners in the kingdom of Naples it now contained men of all classes, including even Government officials, army officers, and priests, and it extended throughout Italy. Though its aims were by no means clearly stated they were certainly revolutionary in character, and its members were prepared to revolt whenever the opportunity should occur. When news of the successful Spanish revolution of 1820 reached Naples a military rising occurred, and Ferdinand assented to the demand of the rebels that the Spanish constitution of 1812 should be applied to Naples.

Metternich, who for many years dominated the Holy Alliance and directed its policy, realised the possibility that revolutionary feeling in the south of Italy might spread to the Austrian possessions in the north, and he was far more anxious to put down the Neapolitan rising than the Spanish, which was too far away to affect the subject-peoples of Austria. A Congress was called to meet at Troppau to consider the condition of the kingdom of Naples. In accordance with the arrangement entered into at Aachen, Great Britain was represented at the Congress, but the British envoy was instructed to report to his Government upon the proceedings and was not entrusted with full powers. The three eastern powers approved of the issue of the Protocol of Troppau, which asserted the right of other states to intervene in order to suppress revolution in any country in which it had broken out. Great Britain protested vigorously, but took no further action.

At a further Congress at Laibach, in 1821, Ferdinand I was present. He had been allowed by his people to leave his kingdom only after he had again sworn to maintain the constitution. At Laibach, however, he disregarded his oath and asked the allies to restore his absolute power. The Congress, despite British protest, authorised Austria to suppress by force the constitutional movement in Naples. The Austrians experienced little difficulty in performing their task, and Ferdinand became once more an absolute monarch.

Before the Neapolitans were finally crushed a revolution was threatened in Piedmont. At the fall of Napoleon Victor Emmanuel I had been restored as an absolute monarch, but in 1821 a constitutional movement was attempted. Its supporters demanded that the Spanish constitution of 1812 should be applied in Piedmont, and they hoped that the King's dislike of the Austrians would influence him to grant it. Victor Emmanuel abdicated, however, in favour of his brother Charles Felix, and as the latter was absent from the country another prince of the royal line, Charles Albert, ruled for a time as regent. He granted the constitution, but Charles Felix, upon his return, annulled it. An Austrian army invaded Piedmont, and, in conjunction with loyal Piedmontese, defeated the revolutionists at Novara. The cause of constitutional freedom was crushed as decisively in the north of Italy as in the south.

The problem of Spain was not yet settled, and a Congress assembled at Verona in 1822 to consider it. Lord Castlereagh died shortly before the date appointed for the meeting but his successor, Canning, adopted as his own the protest which Castlereagh had prepared against the suggested intervention in Spain of the despotic powers of Europe. In spite of the British attitude the Holy Alliance determined to restore the absolute power of Ferdinand VII, and France, in which reactionary influences had for some time been gaining ground,

associated itself with this policy and was authorised to send an
army into Spain. The French overran the country, suppressing
the constitutional party everywhere; the constitution was
annulled, and Ferdinand VII became once more absolute.
Savage reprisals, which disgusted even the French troops
whose success had made them possible, were inflicted upon
the King's opponents.

This was the last important victory of the Holy Alliance,
which now contemplated taking action to recover for Spain
her revolted American colonies. Great Britain, however,
was no longer content with barren protest, and Canning proposed joint action with the United States with a view to the
ultimate recognition of the South American republics. The
United States was unwilling to act in concert with Great
Britain, but President Monroe sent a message to Congress
asserting that the United States did not admit that there was
any further field in America for colonial extension by European
powers and that it would regard with disfavour any attempt
of the absolute powers of Europe to extend their system to the
American continent. This was followed by Canning's formal
recognition of the independence of the revolted colonies.
The Holy Alliance powers protested, but they accepted the
situation.

In connection with Portugal, Great Britain dealt a second
blow at the principles maintained by the Holy Alliance. The
King of Portugal, John VI, had lived for some years in Brazil,
and during his absence a revolutionary party, in 1820, demanded
the grant of the Spanish constitution of 1812. John returned
to Portugal in 1821, leaving his elder son, Pedro, who sym-
pathised with the constitutional party, as regent in Brazil.
The King granted a constitution to Portugal, but his second
son, Miguel, who was supported by the French, led the
reactionary party and revolted against his father. Canning
sent a fleet to the Tagus to give moral support to the King.
Miguel's revolt collapsed and he was exiled.

Brazil in 1822 proclaimed its independence, and this was
recognised by Portugal in 1825, Pedro becoming the first
Emperor of Brazil. When John VI died, in 1826, Pedro,
not wishing to give up the crown of Brazil, granted a new
constitution to Portugal and forthwith resigned the sovereignty
of that country to his young daughter Maria. Miguel's
supporters, with unofficial Spanish assistance, continued their

efforts to put him on the throne, and the regency at Lisbon appealed to Canning for help. British troops were dispatched to Lisbon, and Canning threatened war against any power which attacked Portugal. Spain and France disavowed any intention of supporting the party of Miguel, and for the time being the constitution triumphed.

CHAPTER XXIV

METTERNICH AND THE GERMAN CONFEDERATION

WHEN the Congress of Vienna was called upon to decide the future of Germany it resolved neither to continue the Confederation of the Rhine nor to revive the Holy Roman Empire, but to establish a German Confederation of thirty-eight states. Little was done by the Congress, however, to provide for its internal organisation. A Diet representative of the rulers of the German states was to meet at Frankfort under the presidency of the Austrian delegate, and to this body was left the task of developing the institutions of the Confederation. The Diet was in no sense a Parliament, since it represented sovereigns and not peoples. It was in some respects a conference of ambassadors, who voted in accordance with the wishes of their masters. The members did not possess equal voting rights in the Diet, more votes being assigned to the larger than to the smaller states. Only minor matters might be settled by a majority vote; more serious decisions could be made only by a two-thirds majority; matters affecting the constitution of the Confederation required a unanimous vote.

The thirty-eight states of the Confederation were sovereign in most respects, though not in all. They might wage war, though not against other members of the Confederation. They might make treaties with foreign powers, but not against other German states. If the Confederation should be at war all member-states were expected to support it. In all other respects they were independent.

The policy of the smaller states was to maintain their independence and to guard against any encroachment upon their rights by their powerful neighbours, Austria and Prussia. Proposals which came before the Diet were examined from this point of view, and any suggestion which tended to the strengthening of the Confederation, such as the establishment of central law courts or a federal army, met with sufficient opposition from the minor states to ensure its rejection.

Several of the members of the Diet had interests outside Germany. The greater part of the Austrian Empire was non-German, the King of Hanover (before 1837) was also King of Great Britain, Holstein was a possession of the King of Denmark, Luxemburg of the King of Holland. Even the kingdom of Prussia, though mainly within the Confederation,

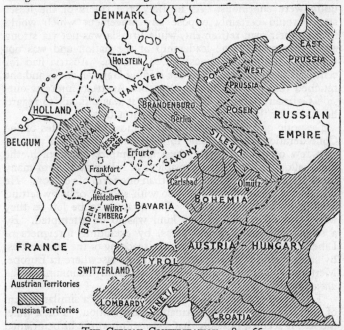

THE GERMAN CONFEDERATION, 1815–66

included provinces outside it. It was obvious that in the Diet the representatives of these potentates would be instructed to vote in accordance with the more important interests of their masters, so that questions affecting Germany might be settled by the German Diet in a manner to the advantage of foreign countries rather than of Germany.

The establishment of this loose Confederation was profoundly disappointing to those German patriots who had hoped that some measure of national unity would be built up out of the disorder of the War of Liberation. A real feeling of German nationality had come into existence and had been a powerful factor in the defeat of Napoleon. Germans were conscious of their kinship and of their common language, and many of them hoped that in the settlement they would become citizens of one German state. But the Congress of Vienna decided otherwise. Moreover, the difficulties in the way of German unity were enormous. As in Italy, the rulers of the lesser states would certainly oppose any movement which would involve their own retirement, while Prussia was not yet strong enough to assume the leadership of the nation and was not willing to resign such a position to Austria. Austria had for centuries been recognised as the leading German state, and she retained that position in the Diet, but Austrian interests outside Germany were so extensive that it was difficult to regard her as fit for the headship of a German nation.

Despotic government prevailed in most of the states of the Confederation, though some form of constitution was granted in a few of them. In the Austrian Empire Metternich, the Chancellor, had to face the problem of ruling peoples of many races and languages and of more than one form of religion. He felt that it was possible to do so with success only by setting himself against any change. Things were to be left as they were, and no reform of any kind was to be attempted. By a strict censorship of the press, by excluding foreigners of Liberal opinions, by controlling the teaching of the universities, by suppressing revolutionary movements elsewhere in Europe, Metternich succeeded for many years in maintaining the *ancien régime*.

To a great extent he succeeded in imposing a similar system of repression upon the German Confederation. For a time, indeed, it seemed possible that a constitution might be granted in Prussia. It had been promised, and a commission was set up to consider the form it should take. But Frederick William III was lukewarm on the matter, and, after certain disturbances, described below, had broken out, Metternich found it easy to persuade him to drop the project.

In October, 1817, a festival was held at Wartburg by a society of university students to commemorate the three-hundredth anniversary of Luther's quarrel with the Church of Rome. There was a good deal of patriotic oratory; aspirations for political freedom and unity were expressed, and some reactionary books were burnt. This was sufficiently alarming to Metternich, and it was followed in March, 1819, by the murder of Kotzebue, a journalist who was suspected of being a Russian spy, by a student of the University of Jena.

In August, 1819, Metternich called a meeting of representatives of certain of the German states at Carlsbad, where decrees were drawn up for the suppression of Liberalism throughout the Confederation. They were submitted to the Diet at Frankfort and, by somewhat irregular means, were carried, in spite of the opposition of some of the smaller states. By these regulations university teaching was placed under close and constant government inspection. Professors and students alike might be expelled if they showed any dangerous tendencies. Student associations were not to be formed except with official permission. The press was to be under strict control, and a special commission was set up to seek out any traces of conspiracy which might be discoverable from time to time.

The Carlsbad decrees were rigidly enforced. Police spies were actively engaged in trying to discover traces, however slight, of Liberal opinions. Men were imprisoned or exiled on mere suspicion. By such means Metternich succeeded in imposing on the German Confederation the system which he had already brought to perfection in the Austrian Empire. Until his fall from power in 1848 his was the controlling mind of the Confederation.

The long period of Metternich's ascendancy over the German Confederation was thus almost without political history. Yet the July Revolution in France and the movements which followed from it in Italy, Belgium, and elsewhere were not altogether without effect in Germany. Constitutions were granted in a few states, of which Hanover and Saxony were the most important; in both of these states the press was granted greater freedom, and trial by jury was established, but the constitutions were not so far-reaching as to deprive the ruler of the control of the affairs in his state. A certain amount of agitation on behalf of freedom and unity led to meetings and speeches, in spite of the rigours of the repressive system. It provided Metternich with a pretext for proposing further restrictions to the Diet, which was empowered to interfere in support of any ruler who was in difficulties with his subjects. Political societies and meetings were forbidden, press restrictions were renewed, and strict control of the universities was revived.

Yet in other respects the government of the Confederation

was not oppressive. Scientific research was encouraged, and industry and trade made progress. Each state, however, had its own tariff system, and in some of the larger states there were internal customs barriers—duties were payable when goods passed from one province to another, or into a city from the surrounding country. Tariff difficulties were especially annoying in Prussia, whose Rhenish provinces were entirely detached from the main part of the state. In 1818 Prussia abolished her internal customs and proposed to her neighbours that a customs union, or Zollverein, should be formed. Duties should be levied on goods entering the union from outside, but tariff barriers between the states of the union should be discontinued. The revenue obtained should be divided among the states of the union in proportion to population.

The smaller states of North Germany were, as usual, suspicious of any suggestion made by their powerful neighbours, but at length they were convinced of the advantages of the proposal, and most of them joined the Zollverein, though Hanover held aloof. A few years later a rival customs union was formed in South Germany under Bavarian leadership, and a third was established in Central Germany on the proposal of Saxony. In course of time these groups amalgamated, and by 1842 the Zollverein, under Prussian leadership, included most of the states in the Confederation. Austria, however, was not a member of this economic league, and it was significant that the members of the German Confederation had been able, for a definite object, to combine independently of the Diet and of Austria and that this combination had taken place under Prussian leadership.

Frederick William III, King of Prussia, died in 1840, after ruling for forty-three years. In the early part of his reign Prussia had been humiliated by Napoleon, had been reduced in extent, had been threatened with extinction. A regenerated Prussia had taken part in the War of Liberation and in the final overthrow of Napoleon, her territories had been restored, additions had been made to them, and she had resumed her place as one of the two leading German states. Liberal hopes had run high in Prussia after 1815. Frederick William had promised a constitution to his people, but nothing came of it. The old King fell more and more completely under the influence of Metternich in the latter years of his reign. Yet he never lost his popularity among the Prussians—a fact which accounted for the absence of Liberal agitation while he lived.

But much was expected from his son, Frederick William IV. His reign began well. He released a number of political prisoners, and the press censorship was relaxed. Provincial assemblies with limited powers already existed, and a demand arose for the establishment of a central Parliament representative of the whole of the Prussian dominions. This, however, the King was not inclined to grant, and though the agitation continued for several years Frederick William would go no farther than the summoning, in 1847, of the provincial assemblies to meet as one body. This United Diet was to have exceedingly limited powers. The King might, but was not bound to consult it on questions of taxation and legislation, but it was to have no control over either. The disappointment of those who had been clamouring for a constitution was intense, and in its first session the United Diet petitioned the King to establish a real Parliament. He refused, and shortly afterwards dissolved the Diet.

Such was the state of affairs at the beginning of 1848.

CHAPTER XXV

THE RESTORED MONARCHY IN FRANCE

AT the fall of Napoleon the Bourbon line of kings was restored in France in the person of Louis XVIII, brother of Louis XVI. But the *ancien régime* was not restored. The privileges of nobles and clergy, abolished at the Revolution, were not revived. It is one of the merits of Louis XVIII that he realised the impossibility of putting back the clock, one of the faults of Charles X that he made the attempt.

Louis XVIII frankly accepted the position of a constitutional monarch, and he issued the Charter in which was embodied the constitution of France until 1848. The power of governing was to be in the hands of the King, and, though in practice it might be exercised by his ministers, it was not contemplated that the King should become a nonentity. The royal power included the command of the army and navy, the right to declare war and conclude treaties, the making of appointments to the public service and to the Chamber of Peers, and the proposing of legislation. A legislature of two Houses was established. The Chamber of Peers consisted of hereditary nobles together with some members appointed by the King for life; the Chamber of Deputies contained members elected for a period of five years, of whom a substantial property qualification was required. Only persons who were forty years of age and who paid at least one thousand francs in direct taxes were qualified for election, and only men of thirty who paid at least three hundred francs were eligible to vote. Laws could be proposed only by the Crown, and they were to be accepted or rejected by the Chambers. No tax might be levied without the assent of the Legislature.

On paper the Charter preserved many of the principles of the Revolution, though it failed to maintain them in fact. Frenchmen were declared to be equal before the law and to be equally eligible for all public positions. Yet this vaunted "equality" of the people did not exist; the right of voting and the right of being elected to the Chamber of Deputies were restricted to men of certain degrees of wealth, so that privilege remained—a privilege no longer of birth but of wealth. In this respect the Charter was based less on the principles of the Revolution than on those of the constitution of Great Britain, where property qualifications were required for membership of the House of Commons and for the exercise of the franchise.

Every Frenchman, when accused, was to be entitled to fair trial before a jury. Freedom of the press was promised, though in a clause whose wording was ambiguous. Those who were in possession of confiscated property were assured that it would not be taken from them. Toleration was guaranteed for all forms of religion, though Roman Catholicism remained the official religion of the state. The nobility created by Napoleon was recognised equally with that of the *ancien régime*, but neither was endowed with pre-revolutionary privileges.

The importance of the Charter lay in two directions. In the first place it accepted, at least in form, much of the work of the Revolution and the Napoleonic *régime*—religious toleration, personal equality, eligibility for office, the *Code Napoléon*, the Concordat with the Pope, a well-organised government system. In the second place, it was not entirely inconsistent with the principle of the Divine Right of Kings, on which the old Bourbon monarchy had been based and which was maintained by the restored kings. The Charter was not imposed by a dominant people on kings who had to be content with such remnant of power as the nation chose to allow them. It was granted by the monarchy, as a gracious concession to the nation, out of the abundance of the power which it possessed.

Louis XVIII was a man of common sense, who realised that it was necessary for him to accept the position of a constitutional monarch. He had endured many years of exile, and he did not wish to lose his throne again. But his return was associated with that of hundreds of the nobles of the *ancien régime*—*émigrés* who had disregarded the invitation of Napoleon to return and resume their share in the national life, men to whom the Revolution and all its results were utterly abhorrent, men who had learned nothing and forgotten nothing. They formed the Ultra-Royalist party under the restored monarchy. They were more royalist than the King; yet they were not conspicuous for their loyalty to him. They aimed at the recovery of all the ancient noble privileges, and at the same time they desired to secure for their class a degree of political power which the nobles of the eighteenth century had not possessed. They recognised the Charter only as a starting point. By strained interpretation of its provisions, and by occasional violations, they hoped to advance their cause to the point at which they could abolish the Charter and reduce the common people to a state of permanent subjection. Essential features of the policy of the Ultras included the revival of the power of the Church and the suppression of the freedom of the press. Their recognised leader was the Count of Artois, the King's brother, to whose accession to the throne they looked forward hopefully.

The most important party opposed to the Ultras was that of the Moderates, who were loyal to the Crown and who based their policy on the maintenance of the Charter. The Moderates consisted, however, of several distinct groups, with varying aims, and their unwillingness to act together in times of crisis was one cause of the progress which was made by their opponents. There was also a party, or a number of parties, of the Left — Republicans, Bonapartists, and other discontented groups. Under the electoral law established by the Charter these were unable to secure substantial representation in the Chamber of Deputies.

A general election was held in 1815, and it resulted in the Ultras commanding a majority in the Chamber of Deputies, although the Moderates prevailed in the Chamber of Peers. The Duke of Richelieu, a Moderate, was the leading minister of France for some years, and he and the King tried to restrain the Ultras in the Lower Chamber. Repressive and revengeful measures, such as the punishment of those who had supported Napoleon in the Hundred Days, were demanded, but, though Marshal Ney was shot, an Amnesty Bill was carried by Richelieu. A new electoral law was put forward by the Government, but the Ultras in the Lower Chamber amended it in such a way as to strengthen their position, and it was rejected only by the Chamber of Peers. The Ultras proposed a partial repudiation of the Napoleonic debt, and in order to curb their excesses the King took the decisive step of dissolving the Chamber.

The new Chamber contained a Moderate majority, and for the next few years the country was ruled on Moderate lines.

Richelieu continued in office until 1818, and during this period France was able to pay off the indemnity imposed by the Second Treaty of Paris. The Government of France appeared to be so stable that the army of occupation was withdrawn by the allies in 1818. An electoral law passed in 1817 was regarded as advantageous to the Moderates. The growing strength of the party of the Left, however, brought about the retirement of Richelieu in 1818, and his colleague Decazes was placed at the head of the Government. In 1819 a new press law was passed, abolishing the censorship and permitting cases in which newspapers were involved to be tried before juries. But this law pleased neither of the extreme parties. It was not advanced enough for the Left, and it angered the Ultras. The Left gained strength at the elections of 1819, and in alarm many moderate men veered round to the Ultras.

The Ultras gained further ground through the murder of the Duke of Berry, son of the Count of Artois, in 1820. They contended that such events were the logical outcome of a Moderate and Liberal policy, and Decazes was forced to resign.

Richelieu returned to office for a short time, but he was unable to stem the tide of reaction which had set in. The electoral law was revised, to the marked advantage of the Ultras, and the press censorship was restored. By the end of 1821 Richelieu gave place to Villèle, an able and cautious statesman but a pronounced reactionary, who held office till the end of 1827.

Villèle's aim was to promote reactionary measures by keeping alive the fear of revolution, and to distract popular attention from encroachments on national freedom by a vigorous foreign policy. The press censorship was strengthened, a new and heavy tariff was drawn up, and public education was placed under the control of the University, which was itself directed by a bishop. Meanwhile, a French expedition, with the sanction of the Holy Alliance, entered Spain and restored the absolute power of Ferdinand VII. France, ever attracted by the prospect of military glory, applauded this adventure enthusiastically, although it was on behalf of reaction and against freedom. But Villèle did not wish to go too far, and he declined to undertake campaigns to recover the Rhine frontier, that vain dream of generations of Frenchmen.

Louis XVIII was succeeded in 1824 by his brother, the Count of Artois, who took the title of Charles X. Although the new King announced his intention of maintaining the Charter, reaction now gained ground at an accelerated pace. It was decided to recompense the *émigrés* for the loss of their lands, and since it was hardly possible to dispossess existing landowners it was decided to reduce the rate of interest on the National Debt and with the money thus saved to award pensions as compensation to the *émigrés*. The power of the Church was strengthened, and Jesuits were permitted to return to France. But Villèle was unwilling to move too fast; by his caution he lost the confidence of the extreme members of the Ultra party, and at the end of 1827 these combined with the Left to bring about his fall.

His successor, Martignac, was faced with a hostile majority in a new Chamber of Deputies. He attempted certain measures of conciliation, modifying the press law and limiting the educational activities of the Jesuits. He thus offended the extremists of the Right without conciliating those of the Left, and the two groups renewed their alliance and drove him from office.

In 1829 Polignac, a former *émigré*, became the leader of the ministry. A vigorous policy of reaction was followed, which aroused such a degree of opposition that the Chamber of Deputies petitioned the King to dismiss Polignac. Charles dissolved the Chamber, but its successor contained a more pronounced majority for the Opposition.

A crisis had arisen. Had Charles dismissed Polignac he might have preserved his crown. He preferred to act under an article of the Charter which empowered him to issue ordinances for the safety of the state. On 25th July, 1830, he published four ordinances. The first prohibited the issue of newspapers without the assent of the Government, the second set aside the recent elections, by the third the electoral law was altered, and in the fourth the date of new elections was fixed.

The journalists of Paris and many of the newly-elected deputies drew up protests. Workmen, especially printers, joined in the agitation, and within a day or two Paris was in revolt. Barricades were erected in the streets, and fierce fighting occurred, in which hundreds of lives were lost. At length the troops were withdrawn, and a Provisional Government, with which Lafayette was associated, was set up. Louis Philippe, Duke of Orleans, was appointed Lieutenant-General of the kingdom. Charles X now withdrew the ordinances, but he was too late. In a letter to the Duke of Orleans he abdicated in favour of the Count of Chambord (who was also known as the Duke of Bordeaux), son of the murdered Duke of Berry, but Orleans announced the abdication without mentioning the condition. Had this been made known it is at least possible that the Count of Chambord would have been accepted as King. Charles withdrew to England and was permitted to reside at Holyrood. He passed the remainder of his life there and in Austria.

Some of the revolutionaries wished for a republic, but others felt that to abolish monarchy would be to establish too close a parallel to the Revolution of 1789–95, and that it would invite the hostility of the powers of Europe. The Duke of Orleans, member of a younger branch of the royal family (he was a descendant of Louis XIII), was invited to become King. He had always seemed to be well-disposed towards Liberal opinions, and he became King "by the grace of God and the will of the people."

The July Revolution involved the overthrow of the principle of Divine Right in France. The changes introduced into the constitution were not sweeping; yet the monarchy depended henceforth on the support of the nation, and if this should be withdrawn it would collapse. The hopes of the Ultras were extinguished, and the influence of the clerical party was lessened; there was no further possibility of building up an aristocratic *régime*. And it must not be overlooked that the July Revolution marks the reversal of one feature of the Vienna settlement.

Louis Philippe, the new King of the French, had had an adventurous career before his elevation to the throne. As a young man he fought with the forces of the republic at Valmy and at Jemappes. He afterwards fled from France and visited various parts of the world, including northern Europe, Sicily, and the United States, and at different times he lived in Switzerland and England. He returned to France at the Bourbon restoration, recovered the family estates, and entered the Chamber of Peers. For some years he affected Liberal opinions and associated with the bourgeois and even with the workmen of Paris. He thus gained the support of people who did not suspect that his profession of democratic and even republican views was merely a cloak for his ambition.

His accession to the throne was acquiesced in rather than welcomed by the mass of the people. Little change was made in the constitution. The royal power of framing ordinances was restricted, the Chambers were empowered to propose legislation, and the press censorship was abolished. In 1831 a new electoral law was passed, but the franchise was only slightly extended and was still open only to the wealthy. The Orleanist monarchy rested, therefore, on the support of the bourgeois, the well-to-do trading and manufacturing classes, and from the first it had to face the opposition of the working classes, who had helped to bring about the July Revolution and were disappointed with its results.

The supporters of the Orleans monarchy were not united in opinions and policy. The Progressive party hoped that a programme of democratic and social reform would be carried out at home and that, abroad, France would pose as the champion of oppressed peoples, such as the Belgians and the Poles, who were struggling for liberty. The Conservative party held that the July Revolution had merely maintained the constitution against a king who plotted its overthrow, and it was opposed to any changes in the direction of democracy. In opposition to the monarchy were the Legitimists, who schemed for the enthronement of the Count of Chambord, the Bonapartists, who revived the memory of the glories of the Napoleonic era, and the Republicans.

Louis Philippe as King was by no means so democratic as he had been as Duke of Orleans, and early in his reign the Conservatives under Casimir-Périer came into power. The minister was a man of great firmness and capacity. Disturbances, caused by political and social unrest, which occurred in the provinces, were vigorously suppressed. The refusal of Casimir-Périer to intervene in the Polish revolt of 1830 was unpopular, but his pacific policy was sound, and his death in 1832 was a misfortune for the country.

The history of the next few years is a record of disturbances— a Legitimist attempt in La Vendée, Republican outbreaks in Paris and at Lyons, strikes of the working classes, attempts on the life of the King. Such events afforded full excuse to the Government for embarking upon a policy of repression. All associations had to obtain the sanction of the Government for their continuance, journalists were prosecuted for the publication of articles which criticised the Government, new courts were set up, and a censorship of plays was established. Many new offences were created, and freedom seemed to be at an end. The Government was unpopular, but for the time being it had little to fear from its opponents.

During the reign of Louis Philippe the "Napoleonic legend" came into existence. Napoleon's achievements were glorified, and the evils of his reign were forgotten. He was regarded as a hero, a regenerator of society; he was looked upon as the personification of national glory. The Orleanist monarchy was not glorious; the growth of the legend could not but emphasise the contrast between the present and the past. Yet Louis Philippe, with a strange blindness to the effect of his action, approved of and patronised the Napoleonic legend. He completed the Arc de Triomphe, which commemorated the Emperor's career, he permitted streets to be named after Napoleon's battles, and he allowed Napoleon's body to be transferred from St. Helena to Paris, where it was reburied with imposing ceremonial. The late Emperor's nephew, Louis Napoleon, made two attempts during the reign to recover his uncle's throne; on the second occasion he was imprisoned, but in 1846 he escaped.

Among the ministers of Louis Philippe during the first half of his reign were Soult, the ex-marshal of Napoleon, Thiers, a Progressive, and Guizot, a historian and philosopher who was the leader of the Conservative party. The King found it no easy matter to follow a sound and consistent foreign policy throughout his reign. The surest way to strengthen a weak Government in France was to pursue a vigorous policy abroad; the French people have always been attracted by *la gloire*. But activity in foreign affairs might arouse the suspicions of the powers, and France might draw upon herself their hostility. Thiers favoured a strong policy abroad, and on his advice Louis Philippe supported Mehemet Ali, the Pasha of Egypt, in his war against the Sultan of Turkey. The revival of French influence in Egypt, which had been destroyed by Nelson's victory at the Battle of the Nile in 1798, seemed to be approaching. But Palmerston outwitted Thiers and formed a Quadruple Alliance of Russia, Prussia, Austria, and Great Britain to support the Sultan, which would have left France isolated in the event of a European war. Thiers was willing to risk war, but Louis Philippe drew back, though at the cost of losing prestige at home and abroad. Thiers was replaced, as the King's chief minister, by Guizot, who held office for the remainder of the reign.

Guizot wished to maintain peace and to cultivate friendly relations with Great Britain; yet these relations were strained by Louis Philippe in his dealings with Spain. In that country the queen, Isabella, and her sister, Luisa, were both unmarried. Louis Philippe wished to extend French influence in Spain through a marriage between Luisa and his son, the Duke of Montpensier. Such a marriage, involving as it did the possibility at some future time of the union of the French and Spanish crowns (which had been forbidden by the Peace of Utrecht), was bound to excite apprehension in Great Britain. Lord Aberdeen, the Foreign Secretary in Peel's second ministry, announced that Great Britain would offer no opposition to the wedding if it were postponed until after the marriage of Isabella and the birth of an heir to the Spanish throne. In spite of this, the two sisters were married on the same day. Palmerston, who by this time had returned to the Foreign Office, was indignant, and remained hostile to the French King until his fall. Louis Philippe gained no prestige in France or elsewhere to set against the antagonism he had aroused. He had sacrificed a good understanding with Great Britain for purely selfish reasons; he had placed the interests of his family before those of the state.

The Government continued its policy of repression at home. No opposition was experienced from the Chamber of Deputies, for the whole parliamentary system was corrupt. Deputies and electors alike were bribed, directly or indirectly, to support the Government. The franchise was limited to the well-to-do, and many of the deputies and electors held official posts.

The needs and the opinions of the working classes were disregarded. France was passing through the Industrial Revolution, and the factory system, with its attendant evils of long hours, starvation wages, and child labour, was being developed. The doctrines of Socialism, advocated by such men as Proudhon, Leroux, and Louis Blanc, spread far and wide among the workers, who were discontented with their low wages and hard conditions of work, with the Government, and with their exclusion from any share of political power.

The King made no effort to meet the growing demand for reform. Agitation was denounced as disloyal, petitions were thrust aside. "Reform banquets" were instituted by those opposed to the Government, and one of these functions, which was to be attended by a number of deputies, was forbidden in February, 1848. Rioting broke out in Paris, and barricades were erected. Troops sent against the people refused to fire. Louis Philippe was now alarmed; he prepared to grant reforms, and he permitted Guizot to resign. But fighting broke out, and the Republicans piled some bodies on a cart which was paraded through the streets in order to rouse the mob. The people called for a republic, and Louis Philippe, after vainly endeavouring to abdicate in favour of his grandson, passed into exile.

The Orleanist monarchy fell because it failed to win the approval of the nation. It relied upon the support of a class, the bourgeois—a class which was numerically small, which was without any moral or historical right to control the government of the state, which was despised by the aristocracy and detested by the masses, and which, moreover, was more intent upon the acquisition of wealth than upon political power. Louis Philippe might have strengthened his position by bidding for popular support through a programme of social and political reform. He might have appealed to French patriotism by a more vigorous policy abroad. But he was misguided enough to allow the Bonapartists to profit by the French passion for glory, while the Republicans took up the cause of reform. He failed to meet the wishes of his people, he made no attempt to win more widespread support for his throne, and his power collapsed.

CHAPTER XXVI

BELGIAN INDEPENDENCE

DURING the Middle Ages the Netherlands had consisted of seventeen provinces which became united under the rule of the Dukes of Burgundy and, later, of the Kings of Spain. In 1572 the provinces revolted against Spanish oppression. The ten southern provinces returned to their allegiance in 1579, but the seven northern states continued the struggle for another thirty years and won their independence. The United Provinces (modern Holland) became an aristocratic republic under the hereditary presidency of the Princes of Orange, who, though they held no higher title than that of Stadtholder, were monarchs in all but name. The southern Netherlands (modern Belgium) remained Spanish until they were conquered by Marlborough in the Spanish Succession War, and at the Peace of Utrecht, 1713, they were assigned to Austria. Early in the French Revolutionary War they were conquered by the French, and they remained part of France for twenty years. Holland also was conquered by the French, and for many years the Stadtholder was an exile in Great Britain, while his country became the Batavian Republic and, later, the kingdom of Holland, under the rule of Louis Bonaparte, brother of Napoleon I.

Before the fall of Napoleon in 1814 the Stadtholder returned to Holland. He was warmly welcomed by the Dutch, and it was felt, by prince and people alike, that the opportunity should be taken to establish a new constitution for the country. Holland became a hereditary monarchy, ruled by the House of Orange. The States-General, an assembly which represented the provinces, was to have certain rights, but the King, William I, retained a large measure of political power.

The Congress of Vienna wished to establish a strong state to the north-east of France, and decided to unite the former Austrian Netherlands (by this time generally known as Belgium) to the newly-organised kingdom of Holland. The union was not popular with the Belgians, though it is possible that a conciliatory policy on the part of the Dutch Government might have broken down prejudices and ensured the continuance of a connection which would have been beneficial to both countries. Dutch and Belgians differed in many ways. They spoke different languages and professed different religions, the Dutch being Protestant and the Belgians Catholic. The Dutch had been a great commercial and colonising race; Belgium was, and had for centuries been, a mining and manufacturing region. The Belgians outnumbered the Dutch, who, with their long record of independence, were inclined to despise their neighbours as a politically inferior race.

A commission was appointed by William I to draw up a constitution for the united kingdom. In spite of Belgian protests the States-General was to be composed of fifty-five members for each part of the kingdom, the Belgian superiority in population being disregarded. A Belgian Assembly rejected the constitution when it was complete, but the King ordered its enforcement.

During the next fifteen years friction was constant. The Belgians resented their exclusion from official posts, to most of which only Dutch were appointed. The States-General invariably met at The Hague, in Dutch territory, and never in Belgium, as required by the constitution. In the States-General the Government was always able to obtain a majority for its proposals, since it received the support of the whole of the Dutch members and of a few Belgians who held official posts. The determination of the Government to make Dutch the official language of the whole of the new kingdom caused further resentment. The financial policy of the Dutch Government was felt to be unjust to the Belgians. The debt burden of the two countries was unequal. Holland had a debt much heavier than that of Belgium—yet taxation to meet debt charges was levied uniformly over the united kingdom, and the imposition in 1821 of new taxes on flour and meat added to the growing irritation.

It was the religious question, however, which separated the two races most completely. At the time of the union the Catholic bishops protested against the grant of religious toleration to Protestants in the united kingdom. The determination of the Church to retain control of education in Belgium was opposed by the resolution of the Government to transfer it

K 1643-1848

to secular hands. The political opposition in Belgium to the Dutch Government was thus strengthened by the attitude of the Catholic Church.

Yet, in spite of the existence of political and religious griev- ances, the union was in another way markedly beneficial to the Belgians. The great manufacturing industries of Belgium flourished, and the foreign trade of the country increased in volume, since Dutch colonies were open to the reception of Belgian products.

An industrial exhibition was held in Brussels in the summer of 1830, and large numbers of visitors were attracted to the city. When news of the July Revolution in Paris reached Brussels great excitement prevailed. A revolutionary demon- stration, which began in an opera house, spread to the streets and soon developed into a riot. The royal forces in the city were insufficient to restore order, and the King's eldest son, the Prince of Orange, who was popular in Belgium, attempted without success to bring about a reconciliation of the rebels to the Government. The King resolved to suppress the out- break by force and sent an army of 10,000 men to Brussels. It was driven out and retired to Antwerp. This employment of an inadequate force was worse than useless. It not only failed in its task of restoring order but it aroused the national spirit of the Belgians. A National Congress met at Brussels which declared the country to be independent of Holland and decided to elect a new king.

Since 1815 several revolutionary movements in Italy and Spain had been suppressed by the Holy Alliance, and it was to be feared that the three eastern powers would intervene in Belgian affairs in order to restore the authority of the King of Holland. That they did not do so was due to the outbreak of a serious rebellion in Poland in November, 1830. The Tsar was fully occupied in its suppression, while Prussia and Austria, with fighting going on so near their own borders, were dis- inclined to interfere in the affairs of the Netherlands. Austria, moreover, had reason to fear an outbreak in North Italy. The powers of the Holy Alliance were, therefore, unable to move. Meanwhile, Palmerston in Great Britain and Louis Philippe in France were well-disposed towards the new kingdom. At a conference of the powers held in London towards the end of 1830 it was decided to recognise the separation of Belgium from Holland and to guarantee its independence and neutrality.

Early in 1831 the Belgian National Congress offered the new crown to the Duke of Nemours, son of Louis Philippe. The French King dallied with the proposal, but its acceptance would bear the appearance of a revival of former French schemes of territorial extension to the north-east. Palmerston hinted that Great Britain would resist by force any such extension of French influence, and the offer was declined. On the advice of Palmerston, the Belgians now chose Leopold of Saxe-Coburg as their King, and in the course of the year this prince accepted the crown and was received in Brussels.

William I had not yet abandoned hope of recovering the revolted provinces. A Dutch army under the Prince of Orange invaded Belgium in July, 1831, and Louis Philippe sent an army to aid the Belgians and to preserve their country from reconquest. But both armies withdrew, although the Dutch retained Antwerp for some years. At length Great Britain and France determined to settle the Belgian question. Antwerp was invested by sea and land by a British fleet and a French army, and in due course it surrendered. In 1839, by the Treaty of London, the independence and neutrality of the kingdom of Belgium were solemnly recognised and guaranteed by all the powers, including Holland. It may be observed that it was the breach of this treaty by Germany which was the immediate cause of the entry of Great Britain into the European War of 1914.

CHAPTER XXVII

ITALY IN THE FIRST HALF OF THE NINETEENTH CENTURY

METTERNICH on one occasion referred to Italy as a "geographical expression." Hemmed in on the north by mountains and bounded elsewhere only by the sea, Italy seemed to be more favourably placed than most of the countries of Europe for the attainment of unity and independence. Yet since the early Middle Ages she had been from time to time the battle-ground of the greater powers, and her territory had been split up into many small states which had fought one another, been conquered or annexed, recovered separate existence, been enlarged or diminished in extent, in a bewildering succession of events.

Yet throughout these kaleidoscopic changes it is remarkable that Italian nationality persisted. At different times parts of the peninsula had been under Spanish, French, Austrian, or German rule, but the subject people had not become Spanish or French or Austrian or German; they had remained Italian. North of the Alps, even as late as the middle of the nineteenth century, a man was Bavarian or Saxon or Prussian, rather than German. In Italy, though men were Neapolitans or Florentines or Venetians they were also Italians. This sense of nationality, fostered by common language and religion and by some recollection of the greatness of Imperial Rome, lay dormant, but not extinct, in the eighteenth century, and it was revived by the conquests of Napoleon in the Italian peninsula. The petty despotisms of the eighteenth century were swept away; efficiency and vigour replaced corruption and oppression. Unity, indeed, was not established. Part of the country was annexed to France, the kingdom of Italy occupied the north and centre, and the kingdom of Naples remained in the south. But a system by which Italy was divided among only three Governments, all of which were dominated by the mind of one man, approached more nearly to unity than anything which had existed in the land for centuries.

The Congress of Vienna decided to restore, in Italy, the

old divisions, and in most of them, though not in all, the old rulers, and the hopes of the more enlightened Italians—that the fall of Napoleon would be followed by the establishment of a single Government for the whole country—were dashed to the ground. For the next forty-five years there were eight separate political units in Italy. In the southern part of the peninsula was the kingdom of Naples, which included the island of Sicily. It was still largely feudal in character, its people were lazy and ignorant, and its administration was corrupt. North of the kingdom of Naples and Sicily (often known as the kingdom of the Two Sicilies) lay the States of the Church, which stretched like a saddle across Italy and extended along its eastern coast as far north as the Po. The Papal States, which included Romagna, the marches of Ancona, Umbria, and the Patrimony of St. Peter, were under the rule of ecclesiastics, and corruption, oppression, and incompetence prevailed. West and north of the Papal States lay the Grand Duchy of Tuscany, under a prince of the House of Hapsburg, whose rule was enlightened and who encouraged the imitation in Tuscany of the material progress which was being made elsewhere in Europe in agriculture, industry, and commerce. Lucca was now a small duchy to the north-west of Tuscany. Parma and Modena were two duchies on the south bank of the Po. The former was assigned to the ex-Empress Marie Louise, who, although she was of Austrian birth, retained in her duchy French methods of government. In Modena, on the other hand, which also was ruled by a Hapsburg prince, the principles of eighteenth-century benevolent despotism were restored. North of the Po and east of the Ticino lay the provinces of Lombardy and Venetia, which had been assigned to Austria by the Congress. The administration was efficient, but it was autocratic. The Metternich system was in full play in these provinces, and its influence was felt in other parts of Italy. Piedmont, with Savoy, in the north-west of Italy, formed with the island of Sardinia the kingdom of Sardinia, and, in course of time, it was upon this kingdom that the hopes of Italian patriots were concentrated. It will be observed that the republics, Lucca, Genoa, and Venice, which had formerly existed in Italy, were not restored. Lucca became a duchy, Genoa was added to Piedmont, and Venice was annexed by Austria as compensation for the loss of the Netherlands.

The problem with which Italian patriots were faced in the nineteenth century was the establishment of unity and constitutional government in a land which contained many petty states, in all of which absolute government prevailed. The

ITALY

obstacles to success appeared to be insuperable. It was to be expected that every ruler would oppose any scheme of Italian unity which would involve his own retirement. The Governments were mostly corrupt, and the people were ignorant and superstitious; they had not learned the necessity for concerted action, and many of the early risings were merely local and were easily suppressed. But, apart from the antagonism of the lesser rulers and the indifference of the people, the greatest difficulties to be overcome by those who schemed for Italian unity were the power of Austria and the power of the Pope. Austria was immensely strong, and she held that she was entitled, by reason of her possession of Lombardy and Venetia and of her indirect control of the central duchies, to exercise influence over every state in the peninsula. Although his military resources were trivial, the Pope presented, perhaps, an even more formidable obstacle to unity, since any attempt to deprive him of control over the States of the Church might be met with spiritual penalties, and excommunication presented real terrors to an ignorant peasantry. Further, any action against the authority of the Pope would certainly arouse Catholic antagonism in all parts of the world.

The various despotic Governments did not allow of any public expression of the discontent which soon became widespread. Newspapers were censored, and, indeed, would have had little influence among an illiterate people. Public meetings were suppressed, and agitation was necessarily carried on in secret. The society known as the Carbonari (charcoal-burners), which sprang up in the kingdom of Naples and spread throughout Italy, has been described elsewhere. It was, of course, secret, and was not well organised. It attracted to itself all the discontented elements in the land, but it had no clear and definite aim, and it was quite unsuitable as an instrument for the attainment of Italian unity and independence. The value of the movement lay in its keeping alive and extending the revolutionary spirit among the common people.

In 1820, following the outbreak in Spain, revolutionary movements occurred in Naples and Piedmont. In both states they were for a time successful, and constitutions were granted. But in both states Austrian troops intervened on behalf of the monarchy, the constitutions were annulled, and despotism was re-established. The failure of these efforts was due not merely to this interference from outside but to lack of sound leadership and support from within. The lesson to be learned from them was that the time was not yet ripe—that the ground must be more thoroughly prepared.

The wave of revolution in Europe in 1830, when Charles X lost the throne of France and Belgium declared herself independent of Holland, encouraged renewed outbreaks in Italy. On this occasion disturbances occurred in central Italy. The rulers of Parma and Modena were expelled, and a considerable rising broke out in the Papal States. The Italians for a time hoped for French support, but Louis Philippe was disinclined to risk his newly-won crown in a war with Austria, whose prompt action was again successful in putting down the rebels. It was again made clear that local risings, of indefinite aim and with limited support, would be powerless to achieve Italian unity and independence.

The work of preparing for a more successful effort was undertaken by a number of literary men, of whom Joseph Mazzini was the most famous. It was he who inspired his countrymen with a passionate longing for liberty that in the long run would not be denied. He was no statesman, like Cavour, no general, like Garibaldi; he was the poet, the idealist, the apostle of the movement. Most of his life was spent in exile, but from France and England he by his writings kept alive and fanned the flame which he had started. He founded a new society, Young Italy, secret, indeed, but differing from the Carbonari in that it had definite objects and was not merely destructive of existing institutions. The great aim of Young Italy was the expulsion of the Austrians from the peninsula. This must be done by Italians alone, without foreign aid, and in Mazzini's view it could be done if Italians would only combine to do it. The expulsion of the foreigner would be followed by the collapse of the petty Governments which had been kept alive by Austrian support, and the way would be clear for the establishment of an Italian republic.

The republicanism of Mazzini, however, did not commend itself as an ideal to all Italian patriots. Gioberti, a priest, in *The Moral and Civil Primacy of the Italians*, advocated that the Austrians should be expelled and that the existing Italian states should form a federation under the presidency of the Pope—a solution of the problem that would meet some of the difficulties referred to above. Gioberti's idea, however, was open to the objection that of all the existing states in Italy the Pope's possessions were almost the worst governed. Other writers put forward the view that unity might best be achieved by the annexation of other states to the kingdom of Piedmont (or Sardinia). Though, at first, this idea was not attractive to the more fervid patriots, the course of events in years to come proved its essential soundness.

In 1846, with the election of Cardinal Mastai Ferretti to the papacy as Pius IX, the Italian Question entered upon a new phase. Pius IX was kindly and well-intentioned, qualities which have often been observed in the occupant of the throne of St. Peter, but he was suspected of more than this. He was believed to be well-disposed to the ideas of the patriots and to lean definitely towards Liberalism. Metternich regarded a Liberal Pope as an impossibility—but Pius released political prisoners in his dominions and set on foot a number of reforms. Great enthusiasm prevailed among the Romans, who were permitted to enrol themselves in a civic guard. The Pope's example was followed in some other Italian states, notably in Piedmont, where the King, Charles Albert, abolished the censorship of the press in 1847 and proclaimed a constitution in March, 1848, and in Naples, where, in January, 1848, Ferdinand II was forced to grant a constitution.

Early in 1848 the Austrian Government was seriously embarrassed by revolutionary movements in many provinces of the ramshackle Empire. Italian patriots had been greatly enheartened by what had happened since the elevation of Pius IX, and they felt that the moment had come for striking a decisive blow at Austrian power in Italy. In Lombardy the Milanese resolved to abstain from smoking, since the Austrian Government derived a large revenue from the taxation of tobacco. In the tobacco riots which followed, Austrians who were observed smoking were attacked in the streets. Austrian military power, however, was strong enough to restore order in Milan. Venetia, under the leadership of Daniele Manin, declared itself to be a republic once more, and the province of Lombardy was invaded by the Piedmontese, who received assistance from Tuscany, the Papal States, and Naples, states in which absolute government had been, for the time being, overthrown. The conditions seemed to be more favourable for success than ever before. Austrian power was attacked at a moment when the Austrian Government was preoccupied with troubles nearer home. Italian patriotic feeling was at fever heat, and for the first time the rising appeared to be national rather than local in character. The situation was saved for Austria by the aged Radetzky, who abandoned all military posts of less importance and concentrated his forces on the Quadrilateral, the four fortresses of Legnano, Peschiera, Verona, and Mantua. Here he waited for dissensions to appear in the Italian ranks, and he had not to wait long. The troops from Naples and the central states were withdrawn, and Charles Albert was left to carry on the struggle against Austria alone. He was defeated by Radetzky at Custozza, and the Austrians re-entered Milan and recovered Lombardy.

The vigorous stand made by the old Austrian field-marshal in the Quadrilateral proved to be the critical point in the conflict between revolution and reaction in Europe. By his

THE QUADRILATERAL

victory Radetzky not only preserved Austrian power in northern Italy but contributed to the revival of absolute power in most parts of the Continent.

Meanwhile, the Pope had become alarmed at the trend of events. He had no wish to be drawn into a war with a state so consistently Catholic as Austria, and he withdrew many of his early concessions. His minister, Rossi, was murdered, and a rising in the city of Rome was so far successful that a republic was established under the temporary rule of a Triumvirate, one member of which was Mazzini. Pius fled to Gaeta, in the kingdom of Naples. In Tuscany, also, a republic was proclaimed, and the Grand Duke fled into Naples, where, by this time, the constitution had been annulled and despotism restored.

The Austrian victory at Custozza had been followed by an armistice, but early in 1849 hostilities between Piedmont and Austria were renewed. At the Battle of Novara the Piedmontese were utterly defeated, and this last effort of Charles Albert to free Italy from the Austrian yoke failed. The three "republics" were all overthrown in the course of the year

1849. The Grand Duke easily recovered Tuscany. To conciliate Catholic opinion in France the President, Louis Napoleon, sent a French army in April, 1849, to re-establish the Pope in Rome. (A French garrison was retained in Rome and the Patrimony of St. Peter for more than twenty years.) The Austrians recaptured Venice. Austrian power seemed to be more firmly entrenched in the peninsula than ever, and Liberal ideas and movements were strictly suppressed throughout the length and breadth of the country.

CHAPTER XXVIII

RUSSIA

FOR many centuries the history of Russia had little connection with that of the rest of Europe. In the thirteenth and four-teenth centuries the country was under Mongol and Tartar domination, but by the end of the fourteenth century the princes of Moscow, of the House of Rurik, had undermined Tartar power and built up an autocratic rule in Russia. Ivan IV, the Terrible (1533–84), assumed the title "Tsar of all Russia" and extended his territories and increased his power. With the death of his son Theodore in 1598 the line of Rurik came to an end, and for some years there was danger that Russia would fall under Swedish or Polish control. In 1613, however, Michael Romanoff was chosen to fill the throne, which he retained till his death in 1645.

The country was still, and remained for some time longer, Asiatic rather than European in character. It was cut off from the Baltic, whose eastern shores were held by Sweden and Poland, and from the Black Sea, whose northern coast was in the possession of Turkey. In the seventeenth century a good deal of trouble was experienced with the Cossacks of the Ukraine, who acknowledged no authority but that of their own chiefs. A Polish attempt to bring them into subjection met with stubborn resistance, in the course of which the Cossacks appealed to the Tsar, Alexius, for assistance. A lengthy war between Poland and Russia followed, in which the Russians met with some success, and by the Treaty of Andrussowa,1667, the Dnieper was recognised as the boundary between the two countries.

The reign of Alexius (1645–76) was marked by a struggle for supremacy between the Tsar and the Patriarch of Moscow. While the Roman Empire of the East existed the Patriarch of Constantinople was held to be head of the Orthodox Church, but after the fall of Constantinople the princes of Moscow regarded themselves as the successors of the Byzantine Emperors, and a new patriarchate was established at Moscow.

Nikon, Patriarch in the time of Alexius, a zealous ecclesiastical reformer, put forward excessive claims on behalf of the spiritual authority, asserting its equality with, and even superiority to, the temporal power. His pretensions and personal arrogance at length exhausted the patience of the Tsar, who deposed him and confined him within a monastery. Henceforth the patriarchate was definitely subordinate to the Tsardom.

After the short reign (1676–82) of Theodore III, the eldest son of Alexius, the second and third sons, Ivan V and Peter I, were proclaimed joint-Tsars. Their sister Sophia ruled as Regent until 1689, when Peter deprived her of power and sent her to a convent. Ivan lived till 1696, but took no part in public affairs after the fall of his sister, and from 1689 Peter was in effect sole Tsar.

Peter's early amusements—sailing boats, drilling boys, organising sham fights—appear to have been those of a boy rather than a man, but he soon turned these occupations to serious purpose. He realised the necessity to Russia of securing an outlet. The White Sea was useless, the Caspian was land-locked, Sweden controlled the Baltic coast, Turkey that of the Black Sea. In 1695 he resolved to attack Azov, but he was unsuccessful. During the winter skilled workmen were imported from Prussia and Austria, and a fleet was built on the Don. In the spring of 1696 the attack on Azov was renewed, and the fortress was captured.

It was unlikely that the Turks would suffer the loss of their outpost without making an effort to recover it, and Peter resolved to organise a crusade against them. Their expulsion from Europe could not fail to be to the advantage of Russia. For a year and a half he toured the countries of western Europe, travelling incognito as a member of the suite of his own ambassador. He learned much—technical details of navigation, shipbuilding, and various industrial processes, and, what was much more important, the political situation in Europe and the aspirations of the powers. He learned that France was the ally of the Sultan and would be unlikely to join in a crusade, that England and Holland were absorbed in questions nearer home, and that Austria, with the problem of the Spanish Succession in view, wanted peace with Turkey. From Augustus II, King of Poland, he found that Poland and Denmark were contemplating an attack on the outlying provinces of Sweden, which had just passed under the rule of the boy-King, Charles XII. Peter eagerly embraced the opportunity to take part in the projected partition, and henceforth the Baltic and not the Black Sea became his objective. Nevertheless, by the Peace of Constantinople between Russia and Turkey in 1700 Peter retained Azov.

The war with Sweden which began in 1700 lasted till 1721. None of the conspirators could have foreseen the amazing energy and ability of Charles XII, whose early victories were entirely unexpected. Peter, with an army of 40,000 men, was routed at Narva by Charles with no more than 8,000. The blow was not fatal, perhaps not even serious. The Tsar in the following years reformed his troops and trained them thoroughly. While Charles was engaged in military operations in Poland, Peter conquered the province of Ingria and laid the foundations of St. Petersburg, his "window to the west"; much of the manual labour was supplied by Swedish prisoners of war. Too late, in 1709 Charles invaded Russia and met with utter disaster at Pultava.

The flight of Charles to Turkey and his residence at Bender involved Russia in a new war with the Turks. Peter advanced to the Pruth, and was caught in such an unfavourable position that, if the Grand Vizier had pressed his advantage, he must have been compelled to surrender. He was spared this humiliation, but as the price of peace he had to surrender his early conquest, Azov. Russian schemes for the acquisition of the northern shores of the Black Sea did not come to fruition until the time of Catherine II.

Peace was not made with Sweden until 1721, three years after the death of Charles XII. By the Treaty of Nystad, Peter acquired Ingria, Carelia, Livonia, Esthonia, and part of Finland, and Russia henceforth possessed a substantial stretch of Baltic coastline.

Peter is equally famous for his internal reforms, the general aim of which may be described as the westernising of Russia. As the result of his observations during his travels he had become convinced that western ideas of progress were preferable to eastern notions of tradition and ancient usage. He has been criticised for his insistence upon trifles, apparently unimportant, such as the shaving of beards, the unveiling of women, and the wearing of western costume. It is suggested that he would have been wiser to leave such external matters untouched and to attend to more vital reforms. But neither

Peter nor his people viewed these things as unimportant. The Tsar felt that the retention of traditional forms and customs would hinder the progress of the people towards the goal which he had marked out; their discontinuance was essential to the success of his plans.

It is impossible to do more than indicate the scope and variety of Peter's reforms. He introduced many industries from the west, and he attempted to improve the standard of education in Russia, encouraging in particular the study of science and mathematics. Realising, perhaps, the impossibility of enforcing obedience to his edicts in the absence of an efficient administrative system, he created a vast army of officials. He adopted the western practice of beginning the year in January instead of, as hitherto in Russia, in September; yet he made no attempt to introduce the Gregorian calendar.

He carried to its logical completion the work of Alexius in bringing the Church into complete subjection to the state. Upon the death of the patriarch in 1700 he made no new appointment, but established a Holy Synod, under the direction of a Procurator who was a layman, to control the Church. The Holy Synod was practically a government department.

In the course of his reign Peter assumed the title of Emperor. This was the cause of a good deal of diplomatic friction throughout the eighteenth century. Other countries, and especially Austria, resented the presumption of this semi-oriental potentate in taking a title which involved a claim of equality of status with the Holy Roman Emperor. Peter and his successors persisted, and the title at length secured recognition.

Peter's reforms were directed against the slothfulness, idleness, ignorance, and corruption of Russian life. His edicts did not appear merely as autocratic commands emanating from the whim of the ruler; as a rule he gave reasons for his orders, explaining why the new was better than the old. He was often high-handed and violent—yet without violence he would have achieved nothing. As it was, he did not achieve a great deal. He was unable to change the nature of his people. Inefficiency and corruption and carelessness of the public welfare continued to characterise Russian officials. Nevertheless, if the result of his efforts was not all that he could have wished, he at least turned the face of Russia to the west and compelled other countries to recognise her as a member of the European family of nations.

Peter was an extraordinary man. He was at one and the same time an idealist and a barbarian. In his paroxysms of rage he behaved as a maniac and a monster; in much of his administrative action he stands forth as a man of no ordinary capacity. There was nothing small about him. His anger was colossal, his revenge terrific; his executions were massacres; even his meals were debauches. His qualities, good and bad, were great.

Peter the Great died in 1725. For the remainder of the eighteenth century the throne of Russia was occupied by female and male rulers alternately. The reigns of the Tsars were short and insignificant, and the history of Russia in the eighteenth century is the history of her Tsaritsas.

The son of Peter, Alexius, had been put to death by his father, and Peter nominated his second wife, Catherine, as his successor. In 1727 she retired in favour of Peter II, the son of Alexius, but he died in 1730, and the throne was offered to Anne, Duchess of Courland, a daughter of Ivan V. Anne, whose reign lasted for ten years, cared little for the work of government, and she left the administration in the hands of her favourite, Biren, who ruled despotically in German style and with German officials. Anne was succeeded in 1740 by her great-nephew Ivan VI, a child, who in the following year was deposed in favour of Elizabeth, daughter of Peter the Great and Catherine I. Elizabeth had no liking for German methods of administration and appointed Russians to official posts. She ruled Russia energetically for twenty years, on lines of which her father would have approved. She was hostile to Frederick the Great, and took part in the Seven Years' War against Prussia. At her death the throne passed to her nephew, Peter III, who was German by upbringing and inclination. Peter was an admirer of Frederick the Great, and at the crisis of the Seven Years' War relieved that monarch by changing sides. This was unpopular in Russia, and the Tsar was deposed and murdered. He was succeeded by his wife, Catherine II, who held the throne from 1762 to 1796.

Catherine was the greatest ruler Russia had had since Peter the Great. Like Peter, she was anxious to advance her realm on western lines. But while Peter imitated western methods of government, western industries, and western customs, Catherine wished to introduce western culture. She patronised the philosophers. Voltaire visited her court, and she offered protection to the compilers of the *Encyclopaedia*. French was spoken at court, and Russian nobles were encouraged to take an interest in French literature. A Russian Academy, in imitation of the French Academy, was founded at St. Petersburg.

Administrative and judicial reforms were undertaken, and some progress was made in the establishment of an educational system, whose scope was necessarily limited. Catherine conceived the idea of emancipating the serfs, but did not proceed with it. Such a measure would have alienated the nobles and might have resulted in her deposition. Russia was not ready for it, and, however desirable it might have been on grounds of justice and humanity, it could only have produced political and economic confusion.

The object of Catherine's foreign policy was the extension of Russian boundaries at the expense of her weaker neighbours. Peter had forced his way to the Baltic; Catherine resolved to establish her power on the shore of the Black Sea, and also to acquire at least a part of Poland.

During her reign the Duke of Courland was deposed and replaced by Biren, the minister of the Tsaritsa Anne. He, and his son after him, ruled as the creatures of Catherine, and in 1795 Courland was formally annexed to the Russian Empire.

Catherine's policy with regard to Poland has been referred to elsewhere. It is sufficient to indicate here that all three Partitions took place during her reign and that she secured the lion's share of the spoil.

Her policy towards Turkey also has been described in another chapter. The reader is reminded of the Russo-Turkish War of 1768-74, in which the Russians were victorious. Catherine was induced to renounce her conquests in order to allay Austrian apprehensions, and to accept compensation at the expense of Poland. But the Treaty of Kutchuk-Kainardji established a vague Russian right of intervention in Turkish affairs which was likely to provide pretexts for future aggression. In that treaty, also, the Crimea was pronounced to be independent, and within a few years Catherine annexed it. She now hoped to bring about a partition of Turkey, in which Russia would annex Black Sea territories while Austria would seize provinces contiguous to her dominions. Wallachia, Moldavia, and Bessarabia would be formed into an independent Kingdom of Dacia, which would obviously be a dependency of Russia, and the expulsion of the Turks from Constantinople was to be followed by the revival of the Byzantine Empire under Catherine's grandson. These grandiose schemes were not realised. In the war of 1787–92 Russian arms met with success, but the outbreak of the Revolutionary War in western Europe induced Catherine to withdraw from Turkish complications in order that she might be free to deal with Poland at a convenient moment.

Catherine's patronage of French philosophy failed to produce in her any sympathy with its practical application in the French Revolution, to which she was stoutly opposed. Nevertheless, she took no part in the War of the First Coalition, preferring to take advantage of her remoteness from France by keeping clear of entanglements which were occupying other powers, in order that she might profit from the state of affairs.

Catherine was succeeded in 1796 by her son Paul, who was as capricious and incapable as his mother was far-seeing and clever. He attempted to reverse some of Catherine's measures of internal reform; he merely succeeded in dislocating the administrative machinery. He joined the Second Coalition against France, but quarrelled with his allies and came to terms with Bonaparte. His reign had no lasting effect upon Russia. He was assassinated in 1801 and was succeeded by his son, Alexander I.

At the beginning of the nineteenth century Russia, despite the efforts of Peter the Great and Catherine II, was still medieval rather than modern, and Asiatic rather than European. Two-thirds of its people were Slavs, who were adherents of the Orthodox Church, but the Russian Empire included Finns, who were Lutheran, and Poles, the majority of whom were Roman Catholic, besides people of other races and religions, especially in the south and south-east. The mass of the people were serfs who were compelled to live and work on the estates of their lords; although they held from their lords grants of land large enough to provide them with the means of living, they were practically without rights and were at times subject to brutal ill-treatment. They were heavily taxed, they might be compelled to undertake any kind and any amount of labour, they might be sold, flogged, exiled to Siberia, conscripted for the army, imprisoned, chained, or otherwise maltreated, and they had no means of redress. They were said to be ignorant, superstitious, idle, and drunken; the discredit for their vices

RUSSIA

(The shaded areas represent Russian acquisitions from the death of Peter
the Great in 1725 to the year 1848.)

should be assigned to their oppressors rather than to themselves. Much of the land in Russia belonged to the Crown; serfs on the Imperial estates were in substantially better condition than those in private ownership. The nobles were the privileged class. They were exempt from much of the taxation; they held commissions in the army; they possessed land, and were wealthy through the labour of their serfs. Yet agriculture was so backward and servile labour so inefficient that many of the nobles were in financial difficulties, and their estates were mortgaged.

Some of the events of the reign of Alexander I have been noticed in other chapters. The reader is reminded of the participation of Russia in the War of the Third Coalition, of Alexander's agreement with Napoleon at Tilsit in 1807, of their subsequent estrangement and the Moscow expedition of 1812, and of the Russian share in the War of Liberation.

Alexander was of deeply religious temperament and was inclined to follow a policy of reform. At the time of the Congress of Vienna he was looked upon as the most liberal-minded of the monarchs of Europe. It was he, indeed, who suggested the Holy Alliance, but the alliance which he conceived was far from being the instrument of repression which it afterwards became in the hands of Metternich. He was known to be in sympathy with the granting of constitutions to the nations of Europe; he set the example to other monarchs by granting a constitution to Poland, which was made a separate kingdom with himself as King and was connected with Russia only through his own person. An elected Diet was established in Poland and was endowed with extensive powers, and for a time the country enjoyed institutions almost as free as those of Great Britain.

In his government of Russia the Tsar wished to improve the state of the country. He recognised the evils which existed; he tried to check corruption among public officials; he realised the necessity of improving the condition of the serfs. But he accomplished almost nothing. He found that, opposed by the passive resistance of the officials in his Empire, even a Tsar could do little. And he soon ceased even to wish to undertake reforms.

Metternich at length won the Tsar over to the side of repression. He pointed out to Alexander the dangers of a Liberal policy; he exaggerated the importance of such trivial incidents as the Wartburg Festival and the murder of Kotzebue. The Tsar was converted. He acknowledged that Metternich was right and that he had been wrong. Henceforth he was an autocrat. Restrictions were reimposed, even in Poland, and the last few years of Alexander's reign were reactionary.

Alexander I was succeeded by his brother Nicholas I in 1825. A military revolt was attempted in December, but it was easily crushed, and the leaders of the Decembrist movement were put to death or exiled to Siberia. The reign of Tsar Nicholas thus began with repression, and this policy continued for thirty years. Rigid censorship of the press was maintained throughout this period, and forbidden books might be neither printed nor imported. Even to be in possession of forbidden literature was punishable with exile. An organisation of secret police, known as the Third Section, was active in seeking out and punishing all persons suspected of disaffection in any form. Foreign travel was forbidden, even to the wealthy, except under rigid conditions, and education was discouraged.

For some years the Poles had been discontented, and in 1830 a Polish insurrection broke out. A revolutionary Government was set up, and for a short time it was master of the country. But Russian troops stamped the revolt out ruthlessly. The Polish constitution was abolished, and in 1832 the country was united with Russia, although the Polish administrative, judicial, and local government systems remained distinct from those of the rest of the Empire.

Yet even so autocratic a potentate as Nicholas I twice made war upon Turkey—on the first occasion in support of the Greeks in their struggle for independence, and in 1853 in order to enforce his claim to be regarded as the protector of Christian peoples in the Ottoman Empire. Such a man as the Tsar can hardly have been moved by the gallantry of the Greeks or by the sufferings of other Christian peoples at Turkish hands, and it must be assumed that he was influenced by the fact that he and they professed the same religion and by the hope that he would be the gainer if the Turkish Empire were weakened. In other directions he was invariably on the side of absolutism, though he was never so completely under the influence of Metternich as his brother had been. Russia was untouched by the wave of revolutionary enthusiasm which rolled over Europe in 1848, and it was due to Russian intervention that the Hungarian revolt was crushed in 1849.

Till the Crimean War the Russian army had been recognised as the most powerful in Europe. In that war the Russian losses were enormous. The troops were badly equipped and badly led, and they were defeated. The prestige gained in 1812 was lost in 1854. Reform was evidently necessary, but Nicholas did not live to carry it out.

The history of Russia after the reign of Nicholas I is beyond the scope of this book, but the trend of events may be indicated in outline. Between the death of Nicholas I and the Bolshevik revolution the throne of Russia was occupied by three Tsars. Alexander II (1855–81) freed the serfs; he suppressed a rising of the Polish nobility; and he fought a successful war with Turkey in 1877–8, though the powers of Europe assembled at Berlin in 1878 deprived him of the fruits of victory. The reign of Alexander III (1881–94) was, politically, a period of reaction, but, economically, a time of progress; a beginning was made of the industrialisation of Russia. Under Nicholas II (1894–1917) the Dual Alliance of France and Russia, which lasted until the fall of the monarchy, was formed. Some constitutional experiments were made which proved to be of little value, and the disasters suffered by Russian troops in the course of the European War were the immediate cause of a revolution in which the Tsardom was swept away.

CHAPTER XXIX

THE TURKS

THE earlier part of the seventeenth century—the period of the Thirty Years' War in the Empire—was a time of peace between the Ottoman and the Christian powers. Feeble and effeminate Sultans were incapable of taking advantage of the anarchy within the Empire. Occasional revolts of the Janissaries weakened their authority, and, so far as they roused themselves to action, their attention was directed towards the prosecution of wars in other parts of their dominions.

The reign of Mohammed IV (1648–87) witnessed a remarkable revival of Turkish activity, which was due to the energy and ability of the Grand Viziers of the time, men of the Kiuprili family. War with Venice had broken out in 1644, and for twenty years Venetians and Turks contended for possession of Candia, on the island of Crete. A Venetian admiral, Mocenigo, sailed through the Dardanelles and threatened Constantinople.

Mohammed Kiuprili, already an old man, became Grand Vizier in 1656, and in the remaining five years of his life he reinvigorated the administration and restored discipline in the army and navy. Before his death Mocenigo was driven off, and Lemnos and Tenedos, islands of the Aegean which had been lost to the Venetians, were recovered by the Turks. Within the short period of five years this remarkable man had inspired the Turks with new enthusiasm, purified the government, and reunited the Ottoman Empire for aggressive war against Christendom.

Ahmed Kiuprili, Grand Vizier from 1661 to 1676, was a man of great capacity. In a war with the Emperor the Turks were defeated in 1664 at the Battle of St. Gothard, a circumstance which was mainly due to the superiority of Austrian tactics. The Imperialist forces had profited by the lessons of the Thirty Years' War, while the Turks had made no advance in the art of war since the time of Suleiman the Magnificent. In spite of their defeat the Turks were able to extort a peace upon almost equal terms. By the Treaty of Vasvar, Transylvania, though they were to evacuate it, was to remain tributary to them.

The Venetian war lasted until 1669, when peace was made and Crete, except for two or three fortresses, was yielded to the Turks. A short war with Poland took place in 1672; events favoured the Turks, to whom the province of Podolia was ceded and a tribute promised. John Sobieski, who became King of Poland at this time, refused to recognise the treaty. He continued the war until 1676, when it ended on substantially similar terms, except that the tribute clause was abrogated.

Kara Mustafa, the brother-in-law of Ahmed Kiuprili, and Grand Vizier from 1676 to 1689, was less capable than his predecessors. He renewed the war with Austria, after reviving the Turkish alliance with France in order that the Empire might receive no help from Louis XIV. In 1683 the Turks repeated their achievement of a century and a half earlier by advancing to Vienna, to which they laid siege. The position was serious. The Emperor's only ally was John Sobieski, who made great efforts to raise forces. He advanced towards Vienna, near which he routed the invading army and relieved the city after it had endured a siege of two months' duration.

The retreat of the Turks from Austria was followed by an alliance of Pope, Emperor, Venice, and Poland against them. The Venetian Morosini gained successes in the Morea, the Russians advanced in the Crimea, and the Austrians poured across Hungary to Belgrade, which was taken in 1688. The Sultan was deposed in 1687 and was succeeded by Suleiman II.

Kara Mustafa was succeeded as Grand Vizier in 1689 by Mustafa Kiuprili, who displayed the vigour which had characterised other members of the family. Discipline was restored in the army, and for a time the tide of fortune in war turned in favour of the Turks. Belgrade was recovered in 1690, and victories were registered over both Venetians and Russians. In 1691, however, at the Battle of Szalankemen, the Turks were routed by the Imperialists, and the Grand Vizier was killed.

The war dragged on with varying fortune until, at the Battle of Zenta, in 1697, Prince Eugene inflicted a heavy defeat on a Turkish army commanded by Sultan Mustafa II in person. Under Hussein Kiuprili, Grand Vizier from 1697 to 1702, peace was made—at Carlowitz in 1699 between the Turks on the one hand and Austria, Venice, and Poland on the other, and in 1700 at Constantinople between the Turks and Russia. The Emperor recovered the whole of Hungary (except the Banat of Temesvar, which was retained by the Turks), and most of Croatia and Slavonia, and he was recognised as overlord of Transylvania. Poland recovered Podolia and the Ukraine, but restored her conquests in the Turkish province of Moldavia. Venice retained her conquests in the Morea and in Dalmatia, and the Russians retained Azov.

The early part of the reign of Ahmed III (1703–30) was peaceful, but the entry of Charles XII of Sweden into Turkey in 1709, after his defeat at Pultava, led to an outbreak of war between Turkey and Russia in 1710. Peter the Great was entrapped on the Pruth, and might have been captured or overwhelmed with his whole army. He was able to offer to his opponents terms which proved acceptable to them. By the Treaty of the Pruth, in 1711, Azov was ceded to the Turks, and Peter, in addition to demolishing some newly-erected frontier fortresses, renounced any claim he might have to Poland or to the Crimea. The Russian gains by the Treaty of Constantinople were thus lost, but Peter was fortunate not to have been penalised more severely.

Hostilities broke out once more with Venice in 1715 and with Austria in 1716. The Turks overran the Morea, but at the Battle of Peterwardein they were heavily defeated by the Austrians, who overran the Banat of Temesvar and captured Belgrade. Peace was concluded in 1718 by the Treaty of Passarowitz, on the basis of the existing state of affairs. The Turks retained the Morea, and the Greeks remained under Ottoman rule for more than a century. The Venetians held certain places in Albania and Dalmatia. Belgrade and Temesvar remained in Austrian possession.

For some years relations between Turkey and Russia were strained, but at length they found ground for agreement and an outlet for their activity in the anarchic condition of Persia. By the Treaty of Constantinople, 1724, the two powers agreed on what was virtually a partition of Persia; Russia was to seize certain Caucasian and Caspian territories, while the Turks would annex Georgia and Azarbijan.

In the subsequent fighting Russia took little part, and soon withdrew, but Turkey became involved in a war with Persia which lasted until 1736. Though at first the Persian kingdom seemed moribund, it experienced a remarkable revival under an adventurer, Nadir Shah, who preserved the independence of the country and drove the Turks out with heavy losses. When peace was made at Erzerum in 1736 the Turks were compelled to surrender their claims to Georgia and Azarbijan; they were weakened by the long struggle, and they had failed to realise that its protraction had enabled their real enemies, Russia and Austria, to develop plans for an attack upon Ottoman dominions.

In 1726 a treaty of mutual assistance in the event of a Turkish war had been signed between Austria and Russia. For some years neither power was quite ready to act, but the question of the Polish Succession having been settled by the Third Treaty of Vienna, 1735, they were ready to put their schemes for a partition of Turkey into effect. The war which followed was the beginning of a systematic and determined attempt by Russia to secure the shores of the Black Sea and to advance towards the Mediterranean. The idea of attacking Turkey was equally attractive to the Emperor, whose plans for Austrian predominance in Italy had been checked by the re-establishment of Spanish power in the kingdom of Naples and who now hoped to obtain compensation in the Balkan peninsula. The allies expected some advantage from risings of the subject Christian races in the Balkans and from the fact that peace had not yet been concluded between Turkey and Persia.

The war opened with Russian attacks on Azov and the Crimea. Azov was captured by one army and the Crimea was overrun by another. Disease caused heavy losses in the Russian ranks, and they withdrew from the peninsula. The Turks had attempted little in defence of their possessions, and in the autumn of 1736 they appealed to Austria to mediate in the war. They appear to have been unaware of the close understanding between Austria and Russia; though the Emperor had not yet taken up arms and even professed to accept the Turkish invitation to arrange terms of peace, the agreement of 1726 was confirmed in 1737, and Austrian forces attacked the Danubian provinces of Serbia, Wallachia, and Bosnia.

After the formal conclusion of peace with Persia in September, 1736, the Turks showed remarkable vigour in withstanding this new onslaught. Although the Austrians gained some initial successes they were driven back in the autumn of 1737, and though the Russians again entered the Crimea during the year they were again compelled to withdraw. In the year 1738 the Turks continued to hold their own. A further Russian invasion of the Crimea was unsuccessful, and the balance of fighting in the Balkans was in Turkish favour.

In 1739 the line of Russian attack was changed. An army was sent into Moldavia and defeated the Turks at Chocsim. The Turks, however, more than held their ground against the Austrians, and they formed the siege of Belgrade. The stubbornness of Ottoman resistance now began to cause alarm to the allies, who had expected the war to be short and easy. Russia, moreover, was apprehensive of an attack from Sweden, since by the accession of the Hats to power at this time there was some prospect of an alliance between Sweden and Turkey through French agency. The Emperor, always bearing the Pragmatic Sanction in mind, did not wish to leave his dominions embarrassed and exhausted by a continuance of the Turkish war. All parties, therefore, were willing to consider proposals of peace.

By the Treaty of Belgrade, 1739, Turkey recovered Belgrade and some other places lost to her by the Peace of Passarowitz, while Austria surrendered her hold on part of Wallachia but retained the Banat of Temesvar. Russia, by the Treaty of Constantinople in the same year, retained Azov on condition that its fortifications should be destroyed and that surrounding territory should be devastated in order that the Crimea should be protected from future Russian attack. Russian troops were to withdraw from the Crimea and Moldavia, and an undertaking was given that Russian warships should not be maintained on the Black Sea.

The peace was a severe check to Russian and Austrian aspirations. Turkey had shown wholly unexpected vigour in defence of her territories. Not only had the projected partition of her Empire not been achieved but she had recovered territories formerly lost. The conclusion, in 1740, of a treaty of alliance between Turkey and Sweden imposed a further difficulty in the way of future Russian aggression. Much of the credit for Turkish success was due to France, which, by diplomatic action in Sweden, had added to the embarrassments of the Russian Government. This was recognised in Constantinople, and was followed by a grant of trading privileges in the Levant which strengthened French influence in the East.

Except for a short Persian war, Turkey enjoyed nearly thirty years of peace, and the Ottomans were roused against Russia only as the result of the intrigues of that power in Poland and among the Christian races of the Turkish Empire. In 1768 the Sultan declared war, nominally in defence of the liberty of the Poles. The war proved that the process of decay had gone far in Turkey, and a series of Russian victories was registered. The Crimea and the Danubian provinces of Moldavia and Wallachia were overrun by the Russians. A Russian fleet which sailed from the Baltic to Turkish waters in the hope of rousing the Greeks to revolt destroyed a Turkish fleet at Tchesmé. The difficulties of the Ottoman Government were increased by the outbreak of risings in Syria, Egypt, and the Morea, and an appeal to France for assistance brought little response.

The successes of the Russians alarmed both Austria and Prussia, and for a time there seemed to be some prospect of an Austro-Turkish alliance against Russia. A treaty to this effect was actually concluded in 1771, and a European war seemed likely. Frederick the Great suggested that a peaceful solution of the problem of Eastern Europe might be found in the Partition of Poland. Austria would not consent to the retention of Moldavia and Wallachia by Russia; if Catherine would consent to forgo her conquests on the Danube and accept compensation at the expense of Poland, peace might be preserved. Austria and Prussia would, of course, receive equivalent shares of Polish territory. This course was followed, and the First Partition of Poland took place in 1772.

Negotiations were opened for peace between Russia and Turkey, but the Russian terms were regarded by the Sultan as too onerous, and the war continued. The Turks maintained a stubborn resistance, and Catherine, hampered at this time by a Cossack rising, at length agreed to terms which were acceptable to her opponents.

By the Treaty of Kutchuk Kainardji, 1774, the bulk of the Russian conquests, including Georgia, Moldavia, Wallachia, and Bessarabia, were restored to Turkey. Certain territories, however, including Azov, were retained by her. The Crimea, one of the objects of Russian ambition, was declared to be independent under a Tartar Khan. The Black Sea was to be open to the navigation, commercial and naval, of both nations. The part of the treaty most pregnant of trouble for the future was the recognition of the right of Russia "to make representations" on behalf of the Christian subjects of the Sultan, a provision which was in after years interpreted by Russia as a right of general protection.

The Treaty of Kutchuk Kainardji was a landmark in the history of Eastern Europe. The power of Turkey had long been in decline; nevertheless, the Turks had from time to

TURKISH DOMINIONS IN THE EIGHTEENTH CENTURY

time shown that they had not altogether lost the military qualities for which they had been famous, and they had offered stubborn, if not always successful, resistance to attack. Henceforth the Ottoman Empire was in a moribund condition, continuing to exist less by reason of its strength than on account of the inability of the powers of Europe to sink their rivalries and act in concert for its extinction. With the Treaty of Kutchuk Kainardji the Eastern Question of the nineteenth century had its beginning.

The ultimate aim of Russia in the years that followed was the
expulsion of the Turks from Europe, with the consequent
liberation of the Christian races from Mohammedan domination. Catherine II entertained fanciful notions of the re-
establishment of a Greek Empire with its capital at Constantinople, but if such a state had ever come into existence it would
have been politically dependent upon Russia, and it would
have served merely to veil Russian expansion towards the
Mediterranean. Such a policy was bound to arouse the
apprehensions of the western powers, which would offer
strenuous opposition to the establishment of Russia as a
Mediterranean power.

Catherine's immediate policy was directed towards securing
the Crimea. Schahin, the Khan of the Crimea, was her
dependant, and the annexation of the province could not be
long delayed. As early as 1781 Catherine entered into an
alliance with Joseph II with a view to joint action against
the Turks. That the Emperor was unwise in reversing the
traditional hostility of his House to Russian attempts at expansion at the expense of Turkey can hardly be doubted.
Possibly he himself felt uncertain about the matter, for when,
in 1782, Catherine put forward a scheme for the erection of
a Danubian principality in the region of modern Roumania,
Joseph demurred, and demanded certain territories as compensation. It was evident that the interests of the allies were
not sufficiently in harmony to make close co-operation possible
at this time, and the plan was dropped.

In the Crimea some fighting occurred between the partisans
and the opponents of Russian annexation. Catherine sent
troops into the peninsula, and in 1784 Schahin was deposed
and the Crimea was formally annexed. In 1787 the Tsaritsa
and the Emperor, with brilliant retinues, and accompanied by
the ambassadors of several European powers, visited the Crimea
and made a journey through it. The tour was a kind of pleasure
party of some political importance, since it was designed to
advertise to the world the development of Russian power
towards the south. It was completed at Sebastopol, where a
fine harbour gave shelter to a newly built Russian fleet.

The Sultan was indignant at the anti-Turkish activity of the
Tsaritsa, and in 1787, hoping for the assistance of Sweden, he
declared war upon Russia. The Emperor, true to his engagement of 1781 with Catherine, immediately attacked Belgrade,

though his declaration of war was not made till the spring of 1788. The attack on Belgrade was unsuccessful, and the Turks invaded and ravaged Hungarian territory as far as Temesvar.

The Russian campaign of 1788 was more successful than the Austrian. A Turkish fleet was shattered, and Ochakov was captured after a long siege. The Turks, however, had not calculated in vain when they looked for support from Sweden. Gustavus III feared the designs of Russia on Swedish independence, and he judged the moment to be favourable for an attack. The disloyalty of Swedish officers in Finland robbed him of any chance of success, but his intervention served to hinder the Russians from pressing their advantage against the Turks for the time being.

The campaign of 1789 witnessed signal successes for Russia and Austria. The Turks were defeated in several pitched battles and were driven from the Banat of Temesvar. While the Russians overran Moldavia and Bessarabia, the Austrians captured Belgrade and Bucharest and invaded Wallachia, and the end of Ottoman rule in Europe appeared to be in sight.

This was not yet to be. Austria was embarrassed by a revolt in her Netherlands provinces, while the successes of the allies had alarmed other powers; Frederick William II of Prussia, in particular, schemed to bring into existence a European combination against Austria. He evolved a plan by which he hoped to compel Austria to retrocede Galicia to Poland in order that the latter power might consent to yield Danzig and Thorn to Prussia. He failed to secure the support of the maritime powers, and Poland declined to consider the proposal. At this juncture Joseph II died and was succeeded by his brother, Leopold II. Leopold announced his determination to retain Galicia and his willingness to grant the reasonable demands of the Netherlands; at the same time he was willing to make peace with Turkey without demanding excessive territorial compensation. This attitude satisfied Great Britain; Prussia found herself isolated, and the danger of a general European war was averted. By the peace made between Austria and Turkey at Sistova in 1791 the Austrian conquests, including Belgrade, were restored to Turkey. Austria retained, however, the district of Orsova.

Catherine continued the war and gained further victories. The course of events at this time in western Europe made her anxious to bring the war to an end, in order that she might be free to deal with Poland in the event of Prussia and Austria becoming entangled in a war with France. By the Treaty of Jassy, in January, 1792, the Turks recognised the Russian annexation of the Crimea and the district of Ochakov, so that the Russian boundary was advanced to the Dniester. In other respects the Treaty of Kutchuk Kainardji was confirmed.

During the earlier part of the reign of Selim III, Sultan from 1789 to 1807, military and naval reforms were attempted within the Turkish Empire. By the French invasion of Egypt in 1798 Turkey became involved in the War of the Second Coalition against France, in which she was in alliance with Great Britain, Russia, Austria, and other powers. Peace between Turkey and France was restored by the Treaty of Constantinople, 1802.

The event showed that Turkey had more to fear from her friends than her enemy. Russia, in return for her assistance in this war, demanded further concessions in regard to Moldavia and Wallachia, over which Christian governors were now appointed. These officials furthered the interests of Russia rather than those of their nominal superior, the Sultan, and, being suspected of participation in revolutionary intrigues, were dismissed. A Russian threat of hostilities brought about their restoration, but this was insufficient to avert war, which broke out in 1806. Disasters followed, and the Sultan was deposed.

The short reign of Mustafa IV was followed by the accession of Mahmoud II, Sultan from 1808 till 1839. The Russian war continued until 1812, when, owing to the imminence of a French invasion of Russia, the Tsar made peace by the Treaty of Bucharest. Russia was left in possession of Bessarabia, the boundary now being fixed at the Pruth.

The Congress of Vienna provided the powers of Europe with an opportunity of discussing and settling the Eastern Question. Discussion took place, but the conflict of interests of the powers was acute. The return of Napoleon from Elba caused consideration of the Question to be postponed, and when the Congress resumed it was tacitly avoided. The Act of Vienna, therefore, contributed nothing to its settlement, and it remained one of the outstanding features of the European political situation in the nineteenth century.

At this point it is appropriate to consider exactly what was meant in the nineteenth century by the expression, "the Eastern Question." (It should not be confused with the Far Eastern Question, which is concerned with matters arising during the nineteenth century from the awakening of Japan and China to the influences of European civilisation.) The Eastern Question consisted of a group of problems arising out of the decay of the Turkish Empire.

The Balkan Peninsula contained several Christian races—Greek, Roumanian, Bulgarian, Serbian—subject to the Sultan. Turkish rule was characterised by occasional outbursts of barbaric savagery upon these unfortunate people. Under the terms of the Treaty of Kutchuk Kainardji, referred to above, Russia claimed a general right of protecting the Christian subjects of the Sultan. But other powers were unable to regard Russian action in the Balkans as disinterested, and viewed any attempt by the Tsar to champion the cause of the oppressed peoples in the south-east of Europe as a move in the Russian policy of securing an outlet to the Mediterranean. Whenever Russia was willing to take up arms on behalf of the Christians the statesmen of western and central Europe were prepared to support the Turkish Empire as a barrier against Russian advance. The problem which Europe was called upon to solve in the nineteenth century was that of obtaining for the small Christian races relief from Turkish misrule without sanctioning an extension of Russian influence, and it was complicated by the jealousies and suspicion existing among the great powers, and, later, among the Balkan nations.

The Serbs were the first of the subject races to rise against Turkish misrule in the nineteenth century. A struggle began in 1804 under the leadership of Karageorge, a man of peasant birth, and the movement was supported by Russia until the conclusion of the Russo-Turkish War in 1812. The Turks recovered Serbia for a time, but the rising was renewed under Milosh Obrenovitch, who in 1820 secured recognition from the Sultan as "Prince of the Serbians." Backed by Russia, he continued to press for Serbian independence. By 1830 Serbia's connection with the Ottoman Empire had become no more than nominal, and the country was henceforth under the rule of princes of the Obrenovitch line ruling by hereditary right.

The Greeks of the early nineteenth century were the degenerate descendants of the noble race of ancient times. They suffered from Turkish oppression, being subject to heavy taxation and brutal treatment, though they were permitted to practise their religion. With the decline of Turkish power in the eighteenth and early nineteenth centuries occurred a revival of the Greek national spirit. Ancient Greek literature was read, and an attempt was made to restore the classical Greek language in place of the corrupt dialect spoken by the people. Interest in the intellectual glories of their ancestors stimulated the national consciousness of the Greeks, and a longing for independence arose. In 1814 a society, the *Hetairia Philike*, was formed by some Greeks at Odessa; it aimed at freeing the Greeks from Turkish rule, and, ultimately, at expelling the Turks from Europe. It became widespread and powerful, and in 1821 war broke out in the Morea.

The Greeks hoped that the movement might be led by Capodistrias, a friend of the Tsar, but he declined, and Prince Alexander Ypsilanti headed the revolt. The War of Greek Independence was fought with great ferocity on both sides. The Greeks attempted to make it a war of extermination against their oppressors, and in revenge for Greek massacres of Turkish peasantry the Turks hanged the Patriarch of Constantinople, the head of the Greek Church, in his robes, at the gate of his palace, on Easter Day, 1821. For some years both sides carried on the conflict with the utmost barbarity. European sympathy was with the Greeks, and in many countries societies were formed for the purpose of assisting them with money and troops. Thousands of volunteers fought for the Greeks, and without their assistance it is probable that the rebellion would have collapsed.

In 1825 the Sultan obtained help from Mehemet Ali, the Pasha of Egypt, and a fleet and an army were sent under the command of Ibrahim to assist in the suppression of the revolt. For a time the intervention of the Egyptians appeared to be decisive. The Morea was recovered, and few places remained to be conquered.

The Governments of Europe were perplexed by the Greek revolt. It was exceptionally difficult for the principles of the Holy Alliance to be applied to it. In other cases the Alliance had been willing to assist a despotic monarch to suppress a revolutionary outbreak, but it could not be maintained that it would be in accordance with Christian principles to help a Mohammedan Sultan to put down a revolt of his Christian

subjects. On the other hand, Greek success would encourage restless and discontented people elsewhere in Europe
to rise against their rulers, and the Alliance existed to put down
such attempts. This point of view appealed to Metternich,
who was not interested in the Greeks as Christians and who
detested them as rebels. For some years his influence was
used to prevent assistance being given to them, but the growth
of sympathy with them brought the question of intervention
to the front.

Nicholas I succeeded his brother Alexander as Tsar in 1825,
and, although he had no sympathy with the rebellion as such,
he was known to be in favour of assisting the Greeks on
account of their professing the same form of Christianity as the
Russians. But European statesmen felt that, if the Tsar intervened to secure for the Greeks their independence, Russian
influence would be extended in the Balkan peninsula, and a
movement would begin which might culminate in Russia
securing an outlet to the Mediterranean. For this reason
Canning, the British Foreign Minister, did not wish to see the
Turkish Empire weakened, but the cruelty of Ibrahim in the
Morea convinced him that intervention could be delayed no
longer. He felt that on grounds of humanity it would be
hardly possible to object to Russia taking up arms, and he sent
the Duke of Wellington to St. Petersburg to arrange for joint
Anglo-Russian action. It was agreed that the two powers
should offer to mediate between the Sultan and the Greeks,
and when the Sultan declined the proposal more drastic steps
were considered. The French Government indicated its
approval of Anglo-Russian policy, and in 1827, by the Treaty
of London, the three powers agreed to compel the Sultan to
accept their mediation and to recognise the autonomy of the
Greeks. The Sultan again refused, and the three powers sent
their fleets to Turkish waters. They encountered the Turkish
and Egyptian fleets in the Bay of Navarino, and, although no
state of war existed between the three powers and the Ottoman
Empire, a chance shot brought about a battle in which the
Turco-Egyptian fleet was destroyed.

The Battle of Navarino was almost accidental, but it was
decisive; though Greek independence was not yet won it was
no longer in doubt. The Sultan, indeed, demanded and was
refused reparation. Great Britain, under the premiership of
Wellington, who described the Battle of Navarino as an

"untoward event," withdrew from participation in Eastern affairs. But Russia declared war against Turkey in 1828, and a Russian army invaded Turkish territory and marched towards Constantinople. The Sultan was compelled to give way.

By the Treaty of Adrianople, in 1829, Greece was recognised as a self-governing state under Turkish overlordship. The Greeks, however, refused to accept this as a solution of the

TURKISH DOMINIONS IN EUROPE
AFTER 1832

problem, and in 1832 the kingdom of Greece was recognised as fully independent, with Otto of Bavaria, who reached the country at the beginning of 1833, as King. The provinces of Moldavia and Wallachia were, at the same time, freed to a considerable extent from Turkish control.

It had been Canning's object to prevent Russia from acting by herself on behalf of the Greeks, lest she should gain an accession of influence in the Balkans; by Wellington's change of policy Canning's plan was

frustrated. Through the withdrawal of Great Britain from the settlement of Greek affairs Russia scored a diplomatic triumph. Her prestige increased, and the Greeks felt that it was to her rather than to any other power that the success of the struggle was due. Moldavia and Wallachia, too, felt that they ought to be grateful to Russia; the Tsar's influence was definitely on the increase in the Balkan Peninsula.

The Sultan was unwilling to grant to Mehemet Ali the province of Syria, which the Pasha expected as a reward for his assistance against the Greeks. In 1832 Egyptian troops overran Syria and invaded Asia Minor. To prevent Constantinople from falling into the hands of the rebels the Sultan, failing to obtain help from other powers, accepted a Russian offer of assistance. In return he agreed to the Treaty of Unkiar Skelessi (1833), by which, in effect, the Dardanelles were to be closed in time of war to the warships of all nations except

Russia. By this arrangement Russian vessels, in any future war, would be permitted to emerge from the Black Sea and to operate in the Mediterranean and, if necessary, to withdraw into the Black Sea without fear of pursuit. Russia appeared to have gained complete ascendancy at Constantinople. Great Britain, France, and Austria protested, but without avail. Strong suspicion of Russian designs was aroused in Great Britain, suspicion which affected British policy for many years. Meanwhile, peace was patched up between the Sultan and the Egyptian Pasha, by which the latter retained Syria.

Turco-Egyptian fighting in Syria was renewed in 1839, and the Egyptians were again successful. France under Louis Philippe and Thiers backed Mehemet Ali. Palmerston, who at this time was Foreign Secretary in Great Britain, realised that, in the absence of British intervention, a Turkish victory would further extend Russian influence over the crumbling Empire, while an Egyptian victory would go far towards establishing that French influence in Egypt and Syria which was threatened forty years earlier and which was prevented by Nelson's victory at the Battle of the Nile. He decided, by supporting Turkey, to deprive Russia of that accession of power which she would have gained if she had been allowed to act by herself. Since the Treaty of Unkiar Skelessi had been signed the Tsar had realised that an attempt to control Constantinople in Russian interests alone would sooner or later lead to war with Great Britain and, probably, with all the other European powers. He was, therefore, by no means unwilling to come to a good understanding with Great Britain. He accepted the association of other powers with Russia in the settlement of the question, and he virtually abandoned the Treaty of Unkiar Skelessi. Austria and Prussia assented, and the four powers in 1840 formed a Quadruple Alliance to bring about a settlement of the Syrian Question by offering terms to Mehemet Ali, and, if necessary, compelling him to accept them. Supported by the French, the Pasha refused, but Acre was captured and the Egyptians were expelled from Syria.

By the Treaty of London, 1841, Mehemet Ali was compelled to renounce his claim to Syria, and, in return, his position as hereditary Pasha of Egypt, under only the nominal overlordship of the Sultan, was guaranteed by the powers. France was isolated from the rest of Europe and found herself powerless to save her ally, and, in consequence, her prestige was lowered.

Later in the year, however, she joined the other powers in signing the Convention of the Straits, by which the Dardanelles and the Bosphorus were to be closed to the warships of all nations, so that the Treaty of Unkiar Skelessi ceased to be effective.

The settlement of the Syrian Question must be regarded as a diplomatic triumph for Palmerston, despite criticisms called

THE LEVANT, 1840-1

forth at the time. Had he withdrawn, as Wellington did in 1828, the position of either France or Russia would have been strengthened. Palmerston's intervention prevented either power from unduly extending its influence, and the Sultan learned to rely less completely for protection upon Russia.

No further development of the Eastern Question occurred for several years, but it engaged the attention of the powers of Europe from time to time during the nineteenth and early twentieth centuries and was responsible for several further wars. The Treaty of Lausanne, which was drawn up some years after the European War of 1914-18, may, it is to be hoped, be regarded as a final settlement of this vexed problem.

In reviewing this short account of Turkish activity in south-eastern Europe it may be observed that Turkish success in the century following the capture of Constantinople was due to the lack of unity in Christendom, to the inability of Christian princes to realise the gravity of the Turkish menace, and to their disinclination to subordinate or postpone the settlement of their local quarrels until the safety of Europe from Moslem conquest had been assured. Francis I did not hesitate to ally with the Sultan against the Emperor, and, a century and a half later, Louis XIV, if he did not give actual help to the Turks at the time of the peril of Vienna, held coldly aloof, and left to a

Polish king the glory of saving Christendom. The work of opposing forces that long seemed invincible and overwhelming was left to the peoples more immediately concerned—Serbs and Albanians, Hungarians and Austrians, Poles and Venetians.

The failure of the Turks to consolidate their conquests and occupy them permanently was due to their own inherent defects. They overwhelmed the civilisation of the countries they occupied, but they did not destroy it. Though they imposed their own government they failed to root out native customs and laws and religion. The Turks were strong only while advancing. When the tide of conquest had reached its height the ebb began at once, and national life which had been submerged, but not destroyed, reappeared with renewed strength. Further, the Turks were not good administrators. Much of the territory conquered by them was left under native rulers who were required to pay tribute but who, in other respects, were allowed to retain a large measure of independence. Even in regions more directly under their rule the work of government was entrusted to officials largely drawn from the conquered races. The Turks themselves, when not engaged with vigour upon military enterprise, sank into idleness, ease, and luxury. Their finer qualities were obscured, and the race declined.

CHAPTER XXX

THE YEAR OF REVOLUTIONS

THE year 1848 was distinguished by political disturbances in several countries of Europe. Most of these outbreaks aimed at the overthrow of existing forms of government, and the year is commonly referred to as the Year of Revolutions.

The movement began in France, where, as narrated in another chapter, a Parisian rising in February brought about the fall of the Orleanist monarchy. The French Revolution of 1789 had been directed against the absolute monarchy of the *ancien régime*, that of 1830 against the efforts of the Ultra-Royalists to recover aristocratic privilege and to obtain political power. The Revolution of 1848 aimed at the overthrow of bourgeois rule and its replacement by a democratic government based on universal suffrage. The republic which was then established lasted nearly five years.

For the first few weeks of its existence the Second Republic was administered by a Provisional Government which held office until a National Constituent Assembly could be elected. In the Provisional Government were two elements. The larger, the Republican, was concerned merely with the abolition of the monarchy and the substitution for it of a republic. The other group consisted of Socialists, of whom the most famous was Louis Blanc, and it aimed at a complete reconstruction of society with a view to improving the condition of the working classes. The Socialists contended that all men had a "right to work," and they advocated the establishment of co-operative workshops, for which the state should provide the capital, but of which the control was to be in the hands of the workmen themselves. Friction soon developed between Republicans and Socialists, and, as the press censorship had been abolished, newspapers and pamphlets put forward the views of these and other groups.

In order to deal with the prevalent social distress the Government opened National Workshops, at which work was provided for all who wanted it. The work was generally unproductive and unsuitable, and the number of applicants rapidly increased. The scheme became unpopular, and the opponents of Louis Blanc pointed to it as evidence of the foolishness of his ideas. Yet it was not his scheme. In the co-operative workshops which he proposed, every man would have been employed on his own trade; the National Workshops were mere relief works in which all, skilled and unskilled alike, were set to perform rough and unnecessary tasks.

The National Constituent Assembly replaced the Provisional Government in May, 1848. Socialist measures had already ceased to be attractive, and the Assembly contained a large majority of moderate Republicans. It resolved to close the National Workshops, and the disappointed workmen in Paris revolted against the Government. Street fighting lasted for several days, and some thousands of people were killed before order was restored.

The Assembly then proceeded to draw up a Constitution. It was decided that the republic should be governed by a President elected for a period of four years; he was to be disqualified, however, for immediate re-election at the close of his term of office. Louis Napoleon, the nephew of Napoleon I, was chosen President, and he resolved to use his position as a stepping-stone to the re-establishment of the Empire. During his presidency he took measures against Socialists and Republicans, some of whom were imprisoned, and in 1852 he was proclaimed Emperor, with the title of Napoleon III.

In no part of Europe were the risings of 1848 more serious than in the Austrian Empire, the centre of the policy of repression which had prevailed since the Congress of Vienna. Francis I, under whom the Austrian Empire, as distinct from the Holy Roman Empire, came into existence, died in 1835 and was succeeded by Ferdinand I, a man of little capacity or inclination to rule. The work of government continued to be carried on by a group of ministers, of whom Metternich was the chief. They did not work well together, however, and their departments were so little inclined to co-operation with one another that neglect crept into the administration, and even the repressive measures which had been in force for so many years ceased to be applied as rigidly as heretofore. It must not be thought that the censorship of the press and the supervision of university teaching were relaxed on account of any sympathy with Liberal ideas; such slight degree of freedom as prevailed after 1840 was due to the laziness and inactivity of the officials and to their unwillingness to work together for the thorough maintenance of the Metternich system. Nor was there any general relaxation; it happened that newspapers occasionally succeeded in publishing articles which called for reforms and for constitutional progress, that Liberal speeches were occasionally made, that lectures with a Liberal tendency were delivered now and then to university students.

Between 1840 and 1848 a distinct development of the spirit of unrest was to be observed in various parts of the Austrian Empire. If the dominions of the Emperor had been inhabited by peoples of one race and language this movement might have taken the form of a demand for constitutional monarchy on the English pattern, with a Parliament representative of every part of the state and with ministers responsible to it. Or it might have gone farther and aimed at the establishment of an Austrian republic. But the Austrian Empire contained many peoples, and the desire of most of them was for independence, partial or complete, of the Austrian yoke. Had the revolutionary movements of 1848 and 1849 been completely successful the ramshackle Empire would have split up into a number of separate states, either fully independent or owing no more than a nominal allegiance to Vienna, in much the same way as the Turkish Empire fell to pieces during the nineteenth century and as the Austrian Empire itself did in 1918. To no small extent the success of the Austrian Government in averting such a catastrophe in 1848–9 was due to its ability to make the most of dissensions among the different groups of its rebellious subjects—to play off one group against another.

In Lombardy and Venetia, the Austrian provinces in Italy, the rebels aimed at complete separation from the Austrian Empire, and this outbreak was hailed by Italian patriots with delight as being directed against one of the chief obstacles to Italian unity. The revolt, and the firm stand made against it by Radetzky, together with its collapse, are described elsewhere. It contributed, however, in a material degree to the temporary successes gained in Hungary, since a large part of the Austrian army was necessarily detained in Italy.

Apart from Italy, the most serious disturbances occurred in Hungary, Bohemia, and Vienna. Hungary, though it had, long possessed the form of a constitution, was one of the most backward countries in Europe. Its social life was medieval rather than modern. A division of the populace into privileged nobles and peasants subject to serfdom, such as had prevailed in many countries before the French Revolution but had disappeared before the advance of the French armies, still existed in Hungary. Peasants paid most of the taxation, but they were not represented in the Diet. This Assembly consisted of two Chambers—an Upper House of great nobles, and a Chamber of Deputies, who were elected by local assemblies which themselves were composed of representatives of the lesser nobility. Controlled as it was by the Hungarian nobility, the Diet, which met only every third year, was not a body in which social reforms might be demanded with any hope of success. But it was willing to ask for changes of another character and to claim for Hungary concessions which would place it in a position of equality with Austria. For some years the point about which discussion was carried on was that of language. The Diet wished the Magyar language, instead of Latin, to be the official language of Hungary, and its demand was conceded in 1844. This would have been entirely reasonable if Hungary had been inhabited only by Magyars, but the country included Croats and Serbs and people of other races, and the Diet was not prepared to extend to these minorities the same freedom of language as it had just won for itself.

Although the Hungarian Diet as a whole was opposed to reform, a small party which advocated the most extensive changes came into existence under the leadership of Louis Kossuth. By profession a lawyer, Kossuth turned to journalism and edited a newspaper by means of which he spread his views. He demanded the abolition of serfdom and of noble privileges, so that all the people should be of equal status, with equal rights and equal liability to taxation; he claimed full freedom for the press and full right of public meeting, and he contended that the Diet should be really representative of the whole nation, with full control over taxation and legislation, and that Hungary should be no longer subject to but on an equal footing with Austria. Francis Deák, another of the Liberal leaders, was more moderate in his demands and hoped for reform on less extreme lines. But in revolutionary times moderate men are left behind, and extremists are apt to seize the leadership of the movement.

The news of the fall of Louis Philippe and the establishment of the second French Republic in February, 1848, inspired Kossuth, on 3rd March, to make in the Hungarian Diet a speech at once violent and eloquent, denouncing the Vienna Government, and the Diet resolved to demand of the Emperor a constitution for Hungary. Kossuth's speech had an unexpected result in Vienna itself. Revolt, headed by workmen and university students, broke out in the city, and the rioters demanded the dismissal of Metternich. The Government, taken by surprise, was helpless. Metternich fled in disguise to England, his house was burned down, and his whole system of repression collapsed at once. The Emperor not only promised a constitution in Austria, but sanctioned the abolition of the press censorship and the establishment of a National Guard.

The Hungarian petition being granted, the Diet at Pressburg at once set to work and passed a series of constitutional laws, known as the March Laws. It was not to be expected that the reactionary nobles in the Diet would change their views completely and at once, but public meetings in various parts of Hungary testified to the strength of popular feeling, and the deputies, either acting from fear or carried away by the general enthusiasm, agreed to the proposals of Kossuth and his friends. Serfdom was abolished. The Diet was henceforth to be a really representative Parliament meeting at Budapest. The press was to be free. And, above all, Hungary was to be independent of, and on an equality with, Austria. It was to have its own ministry responsible to the Diet, and the Emperor, as King of Hungary, was to be the sole remaining link with Austria. By the end of the month the helpless Ferdinand had assented to the March Laws, and steps were taken to make them effective. A national army was raised, a national flag was adopted, and Hungarian ambassadors were appointed to foreign countries.

Meanwhile, unrest had developed in Bohemia. In this province the majority of the people were Czechs, but the dominant minority was German. In the first half of the nineteenth century a determined and successful effort had been made to revive the language and the sense of nationality of the Czechs, and, encouraged by the boldness and success of the Magyars in Hungary, the Bohemians sent a number of demands to Vienna. They asked for and were granted a constitutional government in which German and Czech would be of equal status.

Thus, within the single month of March, 1848, the Metternich system of repression entirely collapsed, and its author passed into exile. Hungary and Bohemia obtained constitutions which left them subject to the Emperor but independent in all other respects; Austria proper was promised a similar grant; the Italian provinces were in revolt, even against the Emperor. The Empire seemed to be on the verge of dissolution.

A Diet representative of all parts of the Empire was summoned to meet in Vienna to consider the promised constitution, but a new scheme of government was proclaimed in April, 1848, before the Diet had even met. The new constitution was to apply to the whole Austrian Empire with the exception of Hungary, Croatia, and Transylvania. It failed to please the Vienna mob, and in May rioting was renewed in the city, which the Government was unable to suppress.

The Emperor had lost all authority in Vienna, and he decided to leave the city. He withdrew to Innsbruck, in the Tyrol, where he was joined by the aristocrats and reactionaries. From Innsbruck began the work of the counter-revolution. The court was able again to communicate with its partisans in various parts of the Empire and to direct their activities. It encouraged the divisions which developed among the revolutionaries, and it made use of the racial hatreds which soon appeared. The next few months were to witness an astonishing revival of the power of the central Government and the reversal of nearly all that had taken place.

The first victory for reaction was in Bohemia. The two races in that country, Czech and German, had combined in March to demand a constitution, but disagreements soon appeared. The Germans wished Bohemia to be represented in the Parliament which was meeting at Frankfort and to be included in a united Germany; the Czechs wanted Bohemia to recover her ancient status as an independent kingdom. Feeling ran high, and fighting occurred between Czechs and Germans in the streets of Prague. Windischgratz, the commander of the Imperial troops in Bohemia, decided to restore order by force. On 17th June, 1848, he bombarded Prague for twelve hours and reduced it to submission. The Bohemian revolution was at an end.

A few weeks later, on 25th July, Rabetzky defeated the Piedmontese forces at Custozza. Austrian authority was restored in Lombardy, and Milan, which had been lost for a time, was recovered at the beginning of August.

The most stubborn resistance to the re-establishment of absolute power was maintained by Hungary, where the diversity of races was turned to good account by the Imperial Government. Croats, Serbs, and Roumanians demanded of the Hungarian Diet privileges similar to those which the Magyars had won from the Austrians. The Magyars refused these demands and aroused the hostility of the Slav races. In so doing they committed a fatal blunder. The support of the minor races would have been invaluable to them when they had to fight against the Austrians to retain the privileges they had won.

War broke out between Hungary and Austria in the autumn of 1848 and continued till the middle of the following year. The Croats under Jellachich supported the Imperial cause, but the Magyars fought stubbornly and even drove the Austrians out of the country. Instead of coming to terms with the Austrians at the moment of their exhaustion, the Magyars proclaimed a republic. This angered the Tsar, who offered his assistance to Francis Joseph (who had succeeded Ferdinand as Emperor of Austria in December, 1848). It was accepted, and Austrian authority was re-established in Hungary, to no small extent by Russian bayonets.

When the news of the fall of Louis Philippe in Paris was followed by that of Metternich in Vienna, the effect throughout the German Confederation was electrical. The flight of Metternich was regarded as the most important event in European affairs since the Battle of Waterloo. It was more than the retirement of a statesman; it was the collapse of the system which he had maintained for a generation.

Revolutionary movements spread from state to state throughout the German Confederation. There was a general demand for constitutional liberty within the states, while a strong body of advanced opinion thought the time was ripe for the achievement of German unity. The Governments were not prepared to resist, and constitutions were granted in many states.

As already stated in an earlier chapter, there had for some time been in Prussia an agitation for the establishment of a really representative Parliament. Berlin was the scene of popular disturbances. The streets were crowded with an excited mob, public meetings were held, and collisions occurred between the people and the troops. Frederick William IV yielded to popular clamour by abolishing the censorship of the press and by calling together again the Prussian United Diet to frame a constitution. Disorder continued, however; barricades were raised in the streets, and fighting broke out. The King, at first undecided whether to make further concessions or to restore order by force, resolved upon the former course. He called upon the people to disperse, and withdrew his troops from Berlin. He permitted the formation of a National Guard and rode in procession through the streets, wearing the colours (red, black, and gold) of the Holy Roman Empire. He promised to co-operate in the movement which was proceeding elsewhere for the promotion of German unity, and he went so far as to pronounce Prussia to be "absorbed in Germany."

Men of Liberal views in Germany had always been dissatisfied with the loose Confederation established by the Congress of Vienna, and the opportunity seemed to have come for the formation of a strong and united German state. An informal reform meeting was held at Heidelberg early in March, 1848, and it took steps for the summoning of a *Vorparlament*, popularly elected, to consider the best means of establishing a united Germany. This body met at the beginning of April and arranged for the election of a National Assembly to draw up a constitution. This National Assembly, often referred to as the Constituent Parliament, met in the middle of May at Frankfort. The princes were powerless to prevent the elections, and the Diet of the Confederation, faced by firm expressions of opinion in every part of Germany, sanctioned the proceedings.

The Frankfort Parliament failed to fulfil expectations. Its members were inexperienced in the practical work of government; yet they ought to have understood the necessity for the immediate establishment of a German constitution while Austria was still too much absorbed by internal disorders to interfere and Prussia was still dominated by the democrats. Neither of the two great monarchies could be expected to view the proceedings at Frankfort with favour, but if a constitution for Germany had been drawn up and put into working order before they had settled their internal troubles they might have hesitated to attack it. The Parliament, unfortunately, wasted much time in debates on abstract rights, and during this period the two most powerful states in the Confederation were recovering their authority over their turbulent subjects.

After some months the Frankfort Parliament set to work seriously to draft a constitution. The real difficulties in the work lay in two points—the boundaries of the new state and its headship. Austrian dominions were partly within and partly outside the old German Confederation. If the whole of the Austrian Empire were included in united Germany the new state would not be wholly, perhaps not even predominantly, German, and German questions might be decided by the votes of Italians, Roumanians, and Magyars. A proposal to admit only the distinctively German provinces, so that the boundaries of the new Germany would coincide with those of the German Confederation, was refused by Austria, who was determined to maintain the unity of her dominions. The Frankfort Assembly thereupon excluded Austria altogether from the proposed state, and, as it was not in the least likely that she would assent to her exclusion from a country in which hitherto she had been predominant, the Assembly turned to Prussia for support. It decided, in March, 1849, to offer the headship of a hereditary German Empire to the King of Prussia.

Exactly a year earlier, Frederick William IV had declared his sympathy with the idea of German unity, but he had had time to change his mind, and he now declined the offer of the Imperial Crown. Many motives probably influenced him. The position of a German Emperor, as contemplated at Frankfort, would have been one of greater dignity than power, for the authority of the head of the new German state was to be strictly limited. Perhaps Frederick William did not relish occupying a position which would be full of difficulties. A more potent reason lay in his respect for Austria. The Holy Roman Empire had been extinct for nearly half a century, but the traditional veneration for the Hapsburgs remained, and Frederick William felt instinctively that the headship of united Germany ought to be offered to the living representative of the most exalted family in Europe. It was probable, moreover, that if Frederick William accepted an Imperial Crown he would find himself at war with Austria. But, most of all, he disliked the idea of receiving the Imperial Crown as a gift from the representatives of the people. The monarch who was raised to the throne in that way would be merely the chief official of the state, and the power which had conferred the crown upon him would have the right to take it away. The King of Prussia considered that he and the other German rulers held their authority from God; if his fellow-princes cared to surrender the whole or part of their power to an Emperor they might properly do so, but Imperial authority could never be conferred by the people.

The constitution drawn up by the Frankfort Parliament thus failed to win the approval of Austria and Prussia, and the other four German kingdoms, Hanover, Saxony, Bavaria, and Würtemberg, also declined to sanction it. The acceptance of the constitution by twenty-eight smaller states was of little importance in view of the withdrawal of the kingdoms, and the Frankfort Parliament, after having removed to Stuttgart, dispersed in June, 1849, without having achieved its object.

The movement for a united Germany was not yet at an end. Frederick William in 1849 made an attempt to establish a German Union under Prussian leadership. Saxony and Hanover at first supported the proposal, but before long they withdrew. By this time order was restored in the Austrian dominions, and when, soon after, a dispute arose between Prussia and Austria with regard to the course to be followed in dealing with affairs in the state of Hesse-Cassel, Prussia shrank from conflict. By the Convention of Olmütz the German Confederation, as established in 1815, was restored, and the German Union under Prussian leadership was dissolved. Prussian humiliation was complete; Austria was as triumphant in the Confederation as in her own dominions.

The revolutionary movements in Italy, Hungary, Bohemia, Austria, and Germany ended in failure. For this result several causes may be assigned. Many of the revolutionaries were not practical people; while they were discussing abstract principles their opponents were reorganising their forces. In most countries in which disturbances occurred there was no unity of aim among men of Liberal views, and they failed to recognise the necessity of subordinating individual opinions in order to ensure the success of a great cause. The reactionaries, on the other hand, were united in aim, and, in addition, they were able to take advantage of dissensions among their opponents and so to reduce them to impotence. Moreover, autocracy had organised military force at its disposal, while revolution could look for support only to levies hastily improvised and ill-equipped.

Yet the general failure of the movements should not lead the reader to suppose that nothing was gained by them. In the Austrian dominions serfdom became a thing of the past, and this was the prelude to its abolition in Russia a few years later, so that the extension of personal freedom to all the inhabitants of Europe was not unconnected with the events of 1848. And, though Liberalism lay crushed, it was not dead. Aspirations for political freedom and for national independence and unity remained. From failure lessons were learned, and the history of Europe in the second half of the nineteenth century showed to how great an extent the hopes of 1848 were realised in later years.

SUMMARIES OF THE CHAPTERS

INTRODUCTION: THE RELIGIOUS WARS AND THE PEACE OF WESTPHALIA

THE RELIGIOUS WARS:

Wars which arose out of the religious controversies of the sixteenth century. Other motives associated with the religious.

1587–1604. Anglo-Spanish War.
1572–1609. Revolt of the Netherlands.
1562–98. Civil Wars in France.

THE THIRTY YEARS' WAR:

Two aspects:

(1) Religious. Catholic effort to overcome Protestantism and restore unity of western Christendom.
(2) Political. Attempt to make Imperial power a reality and to reduce princes to subjection.

Periods of the war:

1618–23. Bohemian.
1624–9. Danish.
1630–5. Swedish.
1635–48. French.

THE FRENCH PERIOD OF THE WAR:

French policy of hostility towards Hapsburgs.

1638. Capture of Breisach.
1639. French occupation of Alsace.
1643. Battle of Rocroy. Condé defeated Spanish.
Further victories by Condé and Turenne in subsequent years.

1648. PEACE OF WESTPHALIA:

Religious:

(1) *Cuius regio eius religio.*
(2) Inclusion of Calvinists.
(3) Mixed tribunals.
(4) Ecclesiastical lands secularised before 1624 to remain Protestant.

Territorial:

(1) Maximilian of Bavaria retained electorate as a hereditary dignity, with Upper Palatinate.
(2) Charles Lewis (son of Frederick) to receive Lower Palatinate, with an eighth electorate.

(3) Sweden a member of the Empire; to receive Western Pomerania, Bremen, and Verden.
(4) Brandenburg to receive Eastern Pomerania, with Halberstadt, Camin, Minden, and reversion of most of Magdeburg; right to Cleves, Mark, and Ravensburg recognised.
(5) Saxony to receive Lusatia and remainder of Magdeburg.
(6) France to receive Alsace (except Strassburg), with Breisach and Philippsburg; to retain Pinerolo; right to Metz, Toul, and Verdun recognised.
(7) Independence of United Provinces and Switzerland.

Constitutional :
    Princely independence:
        (1) War and peace.
        (2) Ambassadors.
        (3) Treaties (not against Emperor or Empire).
        (4) Laws.
        (5) Coining.

RESULTS:
(1) Imperial constitution in final form.
(2) End of German religious controversy. Religious toleration not formally conceded, but persecution became rare.
(3) Future Hapsburg policy directed towards south-east and south-west. Aimed at dominance of Balkan peninsula and Italy. Led to antagonism between Austria and Russia.
(4) Zenith of Swedish power. Greatness transitory.
(5) France enjoyed enhanced prestige, extension of territory, and more secure frontiers.
(6) Exhaustion of Spain.
(7) Weakness of Empire. Foreign influences in Diet.
(8) Destruction of German prosperity for many years.

1. MAZARIN

CONTRASTED WITH RICHELIEU:
Inferior. Merely completed Richelieu's work. No new policy. Different means. Persuasion, bribery, intrigue, instead of ruthlessness.

ACCESSION TO POWER:
Served under Richelieu. Recommended by him to Louis XIII as chief minister.
1643. Anne of Austria Regent.
Close friendship of Mazarin and Anne.
Mazarin's unpopularity:
    (1) Foreigner.
    (2) Low birth.
    (3) Cruel and selfish.
    (4) Avaricious.
Continued Richelieu's policy of suppression of nobles. Duke of Beaufort imprisoned.

THE FRONDE:

Aspects:

  (1) Constitutional struggle against absolutism.

  (2) Popular rising against oppression.

  (3) Disturbance fomented by agitators.

  (4) Attempt of factious nobles to recover lost power and privileges.

Common element: Hatred of Mazarin.

Constitutional movement:

1648.   Edict imposing octroi in Paris. Parlement refused to register it. *Lit de justice.* Parlement declared registration invalid.

Chamber of St. Louis, a committee of Parlement, made twenty-seven demands, including:

  (1) Abolition of office of Intendant.

  (2) Reduction of *taille.*

  (3) Right of speedy trial of arrested persons.

  (4) Control of taxation by Parlement.

The last two were important constitutional principles which would be a check upon absolutism, but the Parlement itself was not a constitutional body.

The court:

  (1) Abolished some Intendancies.

  (2) Reduced *taille.*

  (3) Promised inquiry into abuses.

Victory of Condé at Lens. Te Deum at Notre Dame. Mazarin resolved to take advantage of popular enthusiasm to crush Parlement.

Arrest of Broussel. Popular indignation. Release of Broussel.

Court retired to Rueil. Returned to capital. Conceded demands of Chamber of St. Louis.

Later stages:

Nobles joined movement, taking advantage of restlessness of mob.

Ambition of Gondi (de Retz).

Court at St. Germain. Siege of Paris. Neither side quite ready for civil war.

1649.   Peace of Rueil. Temporary settlement.

Arrest of Condé and other princes. Some revolts. Suppressed.

Mazarin retired to Brühl. Nobles released. General rejoicing.

Condé quarrelled with Gondi. Gondi allied with Queen. Condé left Paris. Raised rebellion in south of France.

Mazarin returned.

Turenne defeated Condé, who retired into Paris.

1652.   Mazarin withdrew to Sedan. Paris admitted King. Condé fled to Spain.

1653.   Mazarin returned.

Results of Fronde:

  (1) Affected character of Louis XIV. Became determined opponent of democracy.

(2) Power of Parlement reduced.
(3) End of political power of nobles.

WAR WITH SPAIN:
    (Continuation of Thirty Years' War.)

Before the Fronde:
    French captured Mardyck and Dunkirk.
    French occupied Roussillon and Cerdagne.
    French occupied Catalonia.

1648.   Battle of Lens. Condé defeated Spanish.

Fronde:
    Respite for Spain. Catalonia recovered. French abandoned Mardyck and Dunkirk.
1652–9.   Condé in service of Spain.

After Fronde:
    War in favour of France.
1656.   Failure of negotiations for peace.
1657.   Anglo-French alliance.
1658.   Battle of the Dunes. Turenne, with assistance of New Model Army, defeated Spanish. Capture of Dunkirk and Mardyck, which were given to English.

1659.   *Treaty of the Pyrenees:*
    (1) France surrendered part of conquests in north-east.
    (2) France retained Artois, Gravelines, Landrecies, Avesnes.
    (3) France acquired Thionville in Luxemburg.
    (4) Spain recognised French possession of Alsace.
    (5) France retained Roussillon.
    (6) Condé pardoned; estates restored.
    (7) Louis XIV to marry Maria Theresa. Dowry. (Not paid.)

Results:
    (1) France secured defensible frontiers:
    Pyrenees in south-west.
    Alps and Vosges in south-east and east.
    Passes in mountains provided means of future attack.
    Frontier in north-east still unsatisfactory.
    (2) Exhaustion of Spain.

2. LOUIS XIV

THE REIGN:
1643–61. Minority. Anne of Austria and Mazarin.
1661–1715. Effective rule.

THE KING:
    Supreme representative of absolute monarchy.
    His court a pattern of elegance, culture, dignity, splendour.
    Nobles no longer independent of Crown. Lived at court.

The Crown the centre of every aspect of French life. No place in France for independence of thought and action. Therefore, the reign produced few great men, and these were already prominent at the beginning of the reign.

Patronage of art, letters, music, poetry, science, philosophy.

Dignity and refinement of King.

His close personal attention to work of government.

Mastery of diplomacy. Few mistakes.

COLBERT:

Controller-General of Finances after fall of Fouquet.

Finance:

  Existing abuses:

    (1) Heavy debt. Excessive rates of interest.

    (2) Farming of taxes.

    (3) Arrears in collection.

    (4) Sale of official appointments.

    (5) Absence of accounting.

  Reforms:

    (1) Some loans repudiated.

    (2) Reduction of rate of interest.

    (3) Punishment of dishonest tax-farmers, who were compelled to refund.

    (4) New assessment of *taille.* Exemptions scrutinised.

    (5) Accounts kept.

    (6) Collection of revenue supervised by Intendants.

    (7) Economy in public expenditure, except that of court.

  Results:

    (1) No increase of taxation.

    (2) Annual deficit eliminated.

    (3) Surplus in treasury.

    (4) Debt reduced.

Colbertism:

Regulation of national economic activity in order to achieve self-sufficiency and prosperity.

  (1) Abolition of many provincial customs duties and octrois.

  (2) Protection of foreign trade.

  (3) Colonisation, and trading companies. Little success, on account of excess of state control.

  (4) Prohibition of export of corn. Unwise.

  (5) Industries strengthened. Royal patronage.

  (6) Immigration of foreign artisans encouraged; emigration of French artisans forbidden.

  (7) Communications improved. Roads. Canals. (Languedoc.)

Forces:

  (1) Navy increased. Galleys in Mediterranean.

  (2) Arsenals.

  (3) Army enlarged. (Louvois.)

(4) Status of infantry improved.
(5) Bayonets.
(6) Hôtel des Invalides.

Results of Colbert's work:

(1) Order in the finances.
(2) Increase of trade.
(3) Fighting forces augmented.
(4) Corn policy tended to famine.
(5) No permanent advantage from policy of protection. Based on mistaken notion that prosperity of France must be built on the impoverishment of other countries.

LITERARY ACTIVITY OF THE REIGN:

Corneille } reputations already established.
Molière }
Racine.
Boileau.
La Fontaine. Fables.
Bossuet. Theologian and philosopher. Divine Right.
Fénelon. *Télémaque.*
New academies (science and music) established.
Royal patronage made literature fashionable.

COURT:

Atmosphere of flattery. Licentiousness.
Maintenance of religious observances. Culture, elegance.
King associated with a succession of mistresses.

1684. King married Madame de Maintenon. Became deeply religious. Her influence over him.

RELIGIOUS QUESTIONS:

Gallicanism:

Gallican independence of Rome:

1516. Concordat.
Crown opposed extension of papal authority.
Jesuits permitted in France only on certain conditions.
Tridentine decrees accepted with reservations.

The régale:
Louis extended it to all parts of France.
Bishops of Alet and Pamiers appealed to Pope (Innocent XI).
Conflict of Crown and papacy.

1681. *Assembly of clergy:*
Asserted royal right to *régale* in all parts of France.

1682. *The Four Resolutions:*
(1) Papal authority limited to spiritual matters. Kings could not be deposed by Pope.
(2) General Council superior to Pope.
(3) Denied right of Pope to override customs and constitutions of the Gallican Church.

(4) Papal decisions on faith were not irrevocable until they had received assent of Church.

Pope condemned resolutions. Refused nominations to bishoprics. Many sees became vacant. Struggle conducted with moderation.

1691. Innocent XII, Pope.
1693. Compromise:
    (1) Resolutions withdrawn.
    (2) Royal nominees to bishoprics accepted.

Huguenots:

Reasons for persecution:
    (1) Louis resented divergence from his ideal of uniformity.
    (2) Louis devout in later life.
    (3) In view of quarrel with Pope, Louis wanted to avoid all suspicion of compromise with heresy.
    (4) Influence of Madame de Maintenon (?)
    (5) Influence of Bossuet.

1666. Edict limiting application of Edict of Nantes.
    General Synods of Huguenots forbidden.
    Newly conquered territories outside scope of Edict of Nantes.
1669. Edict of 1666 modified. Some clauses withdrawn.
    Penalties for conversion to Protestantism.
1677. Treasury for Conversions to Catholicism. Rewards offered.
    Bishops active.
1681. Huguenots excluded from official or professional careers.
    Children of seven permitted to turn Catholic.
    Bribery used in effecting conversions.
    Closing of many Huguenot churches and schools.
1682. Emigration of Huguenots forbidden. Galleys.
1683. Cévennes rising. The Dragonnades.
1685. Revocation of the Edict of Nantes:
    Protestant worship forbidden.
    All Protestant churches closed.
    Protestant ministers exiled.
    Other Protestants forbidden to migrate.

Results of the Revocation:
    (1) Much migration.
    (2) Continuance of Dragonnades.
    (3) Disturbances in Cévennes for many years.
    (4) Military and economic weakening of France; strengthening of her enemies.

Jansenists:
    "Puritans of the Roman Catholic Church." Attached more importance to spiritual life than to ecclesiastical ceremonies. Opposed ultramontanism of Jesuits.

    Jansen. Professor at Louvain. Wrote *Augustinus.* Taught the importance of conversion. Brought about by God alone. Led to belief in predestination.

    Jansenism unacceptable:
    To Church—as it cast doubts upon the efficacy of normal way of salvation.

To Louis XIV—as representing independence of thought and a deviation from orthodoxy.

The Arnaulds:

Angélique, Abbess of Port Royal, which became head-quarters of Jansenism.

Antoine, member of the Sorbonne.

1649.   Sorbonne condemned as heretical five propositions from the *Augustinus*.

1653.   Pope (Innocent X) approved action of Sorbonne.

Jansenists accepted papal decision, but declared that Jansen did not hold the propositions in the sense condemned.

1656.   Pope (Alexander VII) declared that Innocent X had condemned propositions in the sense intended by Jansen.

All French priests and religious required to take oath accepting condemnation of *Augustinus*.

Later years of Louis's reign:

Arnauld left France.

Quesnel published *Moral Reflections.* Approval of Noailles. Jansenist practice of "respectful silence."

1705.   Pope condemned "respectful silence."

1711.   Port Royal destroyed.

1713.   Bull *Unigenitus.* Complete condemnation of Jansenism. Strong protests.

1715.   Louis died.

3. THE FOREIGN POLICY OF LOUIS XIV

I. TO THE PEACE OF RYSWICK

1661. STATE OF EUROPE:

(1) Supremacy of Crown in France.

(2) France the strongest power in Europe.

(3) Spain exhausted.

(4) Empire a loose confederation.

(5) Emperor faced with Turkish menace.

(6) England less powerful than France, and Charles II usually allied with France.

(7) United Provinces unequal to strain of ranking as a great power.

AIMS OF LOUIS XIV:

(1) Natural frontiers, especially Rhine.

(2) Acquisition of territories west of Rhine, in Empire, Spanish Netherlands, and United Provinces.

(3) Spanish succession.

(4) Predominance in Italy.

(5) England a subject-ally.

(6) Imperial Crown.

The Ideal:

Louis supreme in western and central Europe:

King of France.

Holy Roman Empire.
Vassal-rulers in Spain, Italy, and England.
United Provinces a dependency.

EARLY INCIDENTS:
(1) The London incident.   Precedence of ambassadors.
(2) The Rome incident.   Insult to French ambassador.   Papal
apology.

1664–7. (3) Unimportant war with England.

1667–8. WAR OF DEVOLUTION:

Cause:
Application by Louis of the principle of Devolution to the whole
of the Spanish Netherlands.

State of affairs:
England and Holland at war.
Emperor menaced by Turks.
Spain could not offer effective resistance.
Europe not yet apprehensive of Louis's aggressions.

Events:
French overran Spanish Netherlands without difficulty.
French conquered Franche Comté.

1668.   *Triple Alliance:*
England ⎫
Holland ⎬ To resist French aggression.
Sweden ⎭

1668.   *Treaty of Aix-la-Chapelle:*
(1) Louis restored Franche Comté and a part of Netherlands.
(2) Louis retained some border fortresses and part of Flanders.

Results:
(1) Strengthened north-east frontier.
(2) Louis determined to punish Dutch.

LOUIS'S PREPARATIONS FOR DUTCH WAR:
1670.   (1) Detached England from Triple Alliance by Treaty of Dover.
(2) Detached Sweden from Triple Alliance by bribery of Swedish
politicians.
(3) Treaties of alliance with Rhineland princes.

DUTCH ATTITUDE:
De Witt failed to realise danger.   Made inadequate preparations.
Reduced garrisons.   Feared revival of Orange power.

1672–8. DUTCH WAR:
1672.   England and Sweden in alliance with France against Dutch.
Invasion of United Provinces by Louis, with Turenne, Condé,
and Luxemburg, via Rhine.   Little resistance.   Amsterdam
might have fallen.
Overthrow of De Witt.   William of Orange Stadtholder.
Estates offered cession of certain territories.

Louis demanded:
(1) Greater territorial concessions.
(2) Toleration for Roman Catholics.
(3) Abrogation of tariffs hostile to France.
(4) Heavy indemnity.
(5) Annual public acknowledgment of dependence on France.
Estates refused.   Amsterdam saved by cutting the dykes.
Alarm of other powers.

1673. Alliance:
Emperor
Spain v. France. Louis now on the defensive
Brandenburg   against European coalition.
United Provinces

1674. England made peace with Dutch.
French occupied Franche Comté and captured Besançon.
Dutch and Spanish attack on north-east France. William defeated
    Condé at Le Fay.
Allied attack on France via Alsace.   Checked by Turenne.
Spanish attack on south-west France.   Failed.

1675. Turenne killed.
Condé retired.
Battle of Fehrbellin. Frederick William of Brandenburg
    defeated Swedes.

1676–7. Fighting in north-east.   French captured Valenciennes, Cambray,
    and St. Omer.

1677. William of Orange married Mary of York. Probable English
    intervention in the war.

1678. *Treaty of Nijmegen:*

(1) France gained Franche Comté and certain north-east
    frontier fortresses at expense of Spain.
(2) Holland lost nothing.

Results:

(1) Louis had gained territory.
(2) Louis had failed to punish Dutch.
(3) Louis exposed as an aggressor.
(4) Future French aggression would be met by a combination
    of powers.

CHAMBRES DE RÉUNION:

Louis seized various territories, including Luxemburg, Casale,
    and Strassburg.
Emperor unable to act.   (Turks at Vienna.)

1684. Spain made war. Beaten. Truce of Regensburg.

1686. LEAGUE OF AUGSBURG:

Princes of the Empire:

Emperor.
King of Sweden.
King of Spain.
Elector of Bavaria.
Others.

Supported by :
Pope.
United Provinces.
Duke of Savoy.
Allied with Emperor, but not a member of League:
Brandenburg.

EVENTS PRECEDING THE WAR:

(1) *Palatinate:*

1685. Dispute after death of Elector Palatine. Louis supported claims of Duchess of Orleans to part of electorate. Arbitration of Pope.

(2) *Cologne :*

1688. Elector died.
Two candidates:
(a) Cardinal von Fürstenberg. Supported by Louis.
(b) Joseph Clement of Bavaria. Supported by Emperor.
Neither obtained sufficient votes.
Pope decided for Joseph Clement.

(3) Louis complained to Emperor:
(a) Delay in settling Palatinate question. (Delay due to Pope.)
(b) Refusal to concede Cologne to Fürstenberg. (Pope.)
(c) That he had hastened on peace with Turks in order to be free to fight in the west.
(d) Demanded that Truce of Regensburg should be recognised as a definite peace.

1688-9. (4) The English Revolution:
William of Orange and James II. Louis misjudged the situation. William became King. England adhered to the League of Augsburg.

1688-97. WAR OF THE LEAGUE OF AUGSBURG:

Palatinate :

1688. Louis besieged Philippsburg. Captured. Part of Palatinate occupied.
After news of William's success French withdrew from the Palatinate. Ravaged.

Ireland :

1689. James landed in Ireland. Sieges of Londonderry and Enniskillen. Unsuccessful.
1690. Battle of the Boyne.
1691. Fall of Limerick and end of Irish campaign.

Naval :

1690. Battle of Beachy Head. Tourville defeated English and Dutch French. Teignmouth burnt.
1692. Battle of La Hogue. Russell defeated Tourville.

South-east :

1690. Battle of Staffarda. Catinat defeated Duke of Savoy and occupied duchy.
1691. French took Nice.

Netherlands:

1691.	French captured Mons.
1692.	French captured Namur.
	Battle of Steinkirk. Luxemburg defeated William.
1693.	French failed to take Liége.
	Battle of Landen. Luxemburg defeated William.
	French suffered heavy losses.
	French captured Charleroi.
1695.	William recovered Namur.

1697.   *Treaty of Ryswick:*

(1) Independence of Savoy recognised. Duke recovered Pinerolo, Casale, and Nice.
(2) French conquests in south-west and north-east at expense of Spain were surrendered.   (France thus gave up all gains since 1678, except Strassburg.)
(3) William III recognised as King of Great Britain.
(4) Louis promised to give no help to the Stuarts.
(5) Dutch given certain barrier fortresses.
(6) Louis recognised Joseph Clement as Elector of Cologne.
(7) Money payment to Duchess of Orleans.

N.B. (*a*) Louis humiliated and checked, but not crushed. Armies remained intact.   Resources vast.

(*b*) Louis agreed to Treaty of Ryswick in order to be ready for War of Spanish Succession.

4. THE FOREIGN POLICY OF LOUIS XIV

II. THE SPANISH SUCCESSION

CONDITION OF SPAIN:

(1) Decline of power:

1572–1659.	(*a*) Continuous wars.
1667–97.	(*b*) Four wars with Louis XIV.
	(*c*) Every treaty (except Ryswick) involved loss of territory.

(2) Treasure from New World.   No development of Spanish internal resources.
(3) Maritime powers resented Spanish monopoly of New World trade.
(4) Medievalism:
(*a*) Noble privileges.   Oppression of peasantry.
(*b*) Inquisition stifled freedom of thought.
(*c*) Influence and wealth of Church.
(5) Declining population.
(6) Finances in disorder.

1665–1700. CHARLES II:

Feeble in body and mind.   Twice married.   No children. Succession uncertain.

SPANISH DOMINIONS:

Europe :
Spain.
Netherlands.
Kingdom of Naples.
Duchy of Milan.
Tuscan ports.
Sicily, Sardinia, Balearic Islands.

Africa :
Towns on north coast.

America :
West Indies.
Mexico.
Central America.
South America (except Brazil and Guiana).

Asia :
Philippine Islands.

CLAIMANTS TO THE SPANISH CROWN:

Philip, Duke of Anjou :
Grandson of Louis XIV. Best genealogical claim, but it was invalidated by the renunciations of his grandmother, Maria Theresa, and his great-grandmother, Anne of Austria. His succession to Spain would endanger the Balance of Power by making France too powerful.

Archduke Charles :
Second son of Leopold I, Holy Roman Emperor and Archduke of Austria. Strongest legal claim, as others were affected by renunciations. His succession to Spain would endanger the Balance of Power by making Austria too powerful.

Joseph Ferdinand :
Electoral Prince of Bavaria. Claim affected by renunciation made by his mother, Maria Antonia. His succession to Spain would not affect the Balance of Power, and as he was a child he might be brought up in Spain as a Spaniard.

OTHER FACTORS IN THE PROBLEM:

(1) Maritime powers wanted share of trade in New World.
(2) English need for a naval base in the Mediterranean to protect Levantine trade from the Spanish and the Corsairs.
(3) Austrian aspirations in Italy.

PARTITION TREATIES:

1668.   *Early Partition Treaty* (between Leopold I and Louis XIV):
(1) Leopold to have crown of Spain with Milan and colonies.
(2) Louis to receive Netherlands, Franche Comté, Navarre, Naples, and Sicily.

By 1698. Louis now possessed Franche Comté and part of Spanish Netherlands.

England friendly in 1668; unfriendly in 1698.

New partition treaty arranged between Louis XIV and William III, in order to settle the succession question without war, if possible.

1698.   *First Partition Treaty:*

Joseph Ferdinand: King of Spain, with Spanish Netherlands and New World possessions.

Philip: Naples, Sicily, Tuscan ports, Guipuscoa.

Charles: Milan.

King and people of Spain angry.   Charles II made a will leaving all Spanish dominions to Joseph Ferdinand.

1699.   Joseph Ferdinand died.

1700.   *Second Partition Treaty:*

Charles: King of Spain, with Spanish Netherlands and New World possessions.

Philip: Napies, Sicily, Tuscan ports, Guipuscoa, and Lorraine.

Duke of Lorraine: To receive Milan in exchange for Lorraine.

Advantages of Treaty to France:

(1) Strong position in Italy.
(2) Duke of Lorraine would be subservient to France.
(3) Control of Milan would enable France to sever communications between Spain and Austria.
(4) Guipuscoa would offer a French gateway into Spain.

CHARLES II:

Indignant at partition.   Rival influences at Spanish court. Charles made a will leaving all Spanish dominions to Philip. If he did not accept, the whole was to be offered to Charles.

WILL *v.* TREATY:

Offer of Spanish crown to Philip.   Real decision rested with Louis.

(1) If Louis accepted the will he might secure the whole inheritance for Philip.
    (*a*) England unwilling to fight.
    (*b*) Dutch republican party disliked William.
    (*c*) Enthusiastic approval of France and Spain.
(2) If Louis adhered to treaty:
    (*a*) He might lose everything, as offer would be transferred to Charles.
    (*b*) Charles could accept without hesitation, as Emperor was not a party to the Partition Treaty.
    (*c*) He would have to fight for his grandson's share, since Emperor would fight for whole inheritance.
    (*d*) France would fight for the treaty with reluctance.
Louis disregarded treaty, and recognised Philip as King of Spain.

PROVOCATIVE ACTIONS BY LOUIS:

(1) Expulsion of Dutch from barrier fortresses.
(2) Refusal of territorial compensation to Emperor.
(3) Edicts giving French ships commercial privileges in Spanish colonial ports.

1701.   (4) Recognition of Pretender as King of England. Violation of Treaty of Ryswick. Roused England to war.

1701. GRAND ALLIANCE:

> *Original members:*
> Emperor.
> England.
> United Provinces.

> *Five Electors joined alliance:*
> Brandenburg.
> Hanover.
> Palatine.
> Trier.
> Mainz.

> *Joined later:*

1703.   Savoy.
1703.   Portugal.

OPPOSED TO GRAND ALLIANCE:

> Spain.
> France. (Technically, an ally of Spain in the war.)
> Cologne ⎱ brother Electors.
> Bavaria ⎰

ADVANTAGES:

> *France:*
> (1) Large undefeated army.
> (2) Experienced marshals.
> (3) Interior lines of communication.
> (4) Undivided control.
> (5) No longer without allies.

> *Allies:*
> (1) Large military forces, including those of the greater electorates.
> (2) Naval strength of maritime powers.
> (3) Marlborough and Eugene.

EVENTS IN NETHERLANDS AND CENTRAL EUROPE:

1702.   Marlborough on Dutch frontier as Captain-General of English and Dutch. Faced French in Spanish Netherlands. Yet Vienna the critical point. Marlborough not free to march to Vienna. Marlborough firmly established on lower Meuse and Rhine.

1703.   Marlborough captured Bonn. Elector of Cologne withdrew from war.
      French (Tallard and Villars) moved towards Bavaria. Elector of Bavaria hesitated to attack Vienna.

1704.   French (Tallard and Marsin) and Bavarians marched on Vienna. Opposed by Eugene.

Villeroi detailed to hold Marlborough in check. Marlborough evaded Villeroi. Marched up Rhine. Joined by force from Brandenburg at Mainz. Junction with Eugene.

Battle of Blenheim. French defeated. Tallard captured. Emperor saved. Bavaria withdrew from war. Enhanced English prestige. Marlborough's great reputation.

1705. Marlborough drove Villars back in Netherlands.

1706. Battle of Ramillies. Marlborough defeated Villeroi. French driven back to frontier. Marlborough occupied Spanish Netherlands.

1707–8. French recovered some lost ground.

1708. Battle of Oudenarde. Marlborough defeated Vendôme. Captured Lille.

1709. Battle of Malplaquet. Marlborough defeated Villars. Captured Mons.

1710. Villars established strong entrenchments.
Marlborough captured Douai.

1711. Marlborough dismissed. Ormond, Captain-General.

1712. Battle of Denain. Villars defeated Eugene.

1713. Fighting on Rhine between Villars and Eugene. Loss of Freiburg.

EVENTS IN ITALY:

1701. Catinat captured Milan. Advanced eastward to meet Eugene. Retreated.
Villeroi replaced Catinat. Battle of Chiari. Eugene defeated Villeroi; captured him at Cremona.

1702. Eugene maintained position.

1703. Eugene driven back to Tyrol by Vendôme.
Savoy changed sides. French communications imperilled.

1704. Duke of Savoy hard pressed.

1705. Eugene reinforced Duke of Savoy.

1706. Vendôme again drove Austrians back to Tyrol. Eugene returned with reinforcements.
Battle of Turin. Eugene defeated Marsin. Captured Milan.

1707. French abandoned Italy.
Austrians conquered Naples.
Eugene failed in attack on Toulon.

EVENTS IN SPAIN:

1702. Naval operations by Rooke.

1703. Capture of Plate fleet.
Portugal joined alliance.

1704. Charles landed at Lisbon.
Rooke captured Gibraltar.

1705. Peterborough and English army landed in Portugal.
Charles taken round to Barcelona. Catalonia and Valencia supported Charles.
English army in Portugal, under Galway, advanced into Spain.

1706. Galway captured Madrid. Spanish opposition. Galway retired towards Aragon and joined Peterborough.

1707. Battle of Almanza. Berwick defeated Galway. Aragon and Valencia lost. Catalonia still held by Charles.

1708. Galway returned to Portugal.
Stanhope captured Minorca.
1710. Battles of Almenara and Saragossa. Starhemberg defeated Spanish. Entered Madrid. Withdrew.
Battle of Brihuega. Stanhope defeated.
Battle of Villa Viciosa. Starhemberg defeated.
Archduke retained only Barcelona.

NEGOTIATIONS FOR PEACE:

1706. *After Ramillies:*
Louis offered:
  (1) To recognise Charles as King of Spain.
  (2) Philip to retain Milan, Naples, and Sicily.
  (3) Dutch to have barrier fortresses.
I.e. he proposed the terms of the Second Partition Treaty.
Rejected. Whig determination. "No peace without Spain."
1707–8. *Proposals by Louis to Dutch:*
Rejected through British influence.
1709. *After Oudenarde* (at The Hague):
Louis offered:
  (1) Withdrawal of recognition of Philip.
  (2) Recognition of Protestant succession in Great Britain.
  (3) To cede Newfoundland to Great Britain.
Allies demanded:
  (1) Barrier fortresses for Dutch.
  (2) Alsace and Franche Comté.
  (3) Dismantling of Dunkirk.
  (4) Expulsion of the Pretender.
  (5) Louis to join alliance against Philip.
Louis rejected last demand.
1710. *After Malplaquet* (at Gertruydenberg):
Hague terms treated as a basis for discussion.
Louis offered to subsidise allies against Philip, but not to fight against him.
Terms rejected by Dutch.

POLITICAL CHANGES:

1710. (1) Fall of the Whigs in Great Britain.
(2) Archduke Charles became Emperor as Charles VI.

1713. PEACE OF UTRECHT:
  (1) Philip V recognised as King of Spain on condition of renouncing French succession.
  (2) Crowns of France and Spain never to be united.
  (3) Charles VI to receive Naples, Milan, Sardinia, Tuscan ports, and Spanish Netherlands.
  (4) Dutch to receive barrier fortresses.
  (5) Great Britain to guarantee Dutch safety.
  (6) Duke of Savoy to receive Sicily and be King.
  (7) Elector of Brandenburg recognised as King of Prussia.

(8) Great Britain to retain Gibraltar, Minorca, Nova Scotia, Newfoundland, the Hudson Bay territory, and the island of St. Christopher's.

(9) Louis to recognise Anne as Queen of Great Britain and to recognise all persons ascending British throne by virtue of Act of Settlement.

(10) Pretender to leave France.

(11) Fortifications of Dunkirk to be dismantled.

(12) Great Britain to receive the Asiento—the monopoly of supply of negro slaves to Spanish colonies—for thirty years.

(13) Great Britain authorised to send one ship per annum to Porto Bello for general trade.

N.B. The peace was incomplete:
   (a) Emperor did not recognise Philip as King of Spain.
   (b) Philip gave no formal consent to partition of Spanish dominions.

CRITICISM OF THE PEACE:

(1) Allies fought for Charles, and, after winning victories, conceded recognition to Philip.
   But, the position was changed after Charles became Emperor. The Utrecht arrangement maintained Balance of Power.

(2) The Whigs in Great Britain supported the war; peace was made by the Tories.
   But, British interests were adequately considered in the peace.

(3) Abandonment of the Catalans.
   Serious blemish.

GENERAL COMMENT:

(1) Basis of European settlement for many years. Balance of Power maintained.

(2) Spain received the king she desired.

(3) Territorial arrangements on the basis of existing facts.

(4) British aims realised:
   (a) Protestant succession.
   (b) Naval bases in Mediterrane.
   (c) South American trade.

(5) End of an epoch. Wars of religion replaced by wars for trade and colonial empire.

(6) Failure of the schemes of Louis XIV.

5. THE UNITED PROVINCES

1647–50. WILLIAM II:
   Married Mary, daughter of Charles I.
   Aimed at monarchy.

1650. *Coup d'état* against Amsterdam. Failed. Death of William II.

REPUBLICAN ASCENDANCY:
   William of Orange an infant. Stadtholderate in abeyance.

John de Witt, Grand Pensionary of Holland. Aimed at strengthening republican ascendancy and preventing revival of
Orange power.

War with England:

    Causes:

        (1) Commercial rivalry:

1623.   Massacre of Amboyna.

1651.   Navigation Act.

        (2) Political differences:

          Support of Stuarts by Dutch.

          Murder of Dorislaus.

    Events:

        Defeat of Tromp by Blake.

1654.   *Treaty of Westminster:*

        (1) Dutch recognised Navigation Act.

        (2) Dutch to salute English flag.

        (3) Dutch to pay compensation for massacre of Amboyna.

        (4) Dutch to exclude House of Orange from stadtholderate.

AFTER 1660:

    Louis XIV:

        Viewed republican institutions with disfavour.

1664–7. *War with England:*

        Treaty of Breda. Loss of Dutch settlements in North America.

1668.   *Perpetual Edict:*

        Passed at suggestion of De Witt:

          (1) Stadtholderate and supreme command to be kept separate.

          (2) William of Orange to be Captain-General and Admiral-
             General.

    War of Devolution:

        Aggression of Louis XIV alarmed Dutch.

1668.   Triple Alliance of England, Sweden, and United Provinces.

    Louis XIV:

        Determined to punish Dutch.

1670.   England won over by Treaty of Dover.

        Sweden won over by bribes.

        Alliance with German princes.

1672.   *Invasion.* Fall of De Witt. William became Stadtholder.

1672–8. WAR:

1672.   Invasion. Peril of Amsterdam. Dykes cut.

1672–3. Formation of European coalition saved Dutch.

1673–8. War fought on Rhine and in Spanish Netherlands.

1678.   Treaty of Nijmegen. No loss of territory.

    WILLIAM OF ORANGE:

        The hero of the struggle against Louis XIV.

1677.   Marriage with Mary of York.

Hoped for crown of England in order to secure English alliance against France.

1686. League of Augsburg.

1688–97. WAR OF THE LEAGUE OF AUGSBURG:

1697. *Treaty of Ryswick:*

 (1) Louis lost his acquisitions (except Strassburg) since 1678.
 (2) Recognition of William as King of Great Britain.

SPANISH SUCCESSION:

Partition Treaties:

William's efforts to settle the question and secure the safety of the United Provinces without war.

Failure, when Philip of Anjou became King of Spain.

1702–13. *War:*

1713. *Treaty of Utrecht:*

Safety of United Provinces secured by:

 (1) Cession of Spanish Netherlands to Emperor.
 (2) Barrier fortresses.
 (3) British guarantee.

18th C. DECLINE OF DUTCH POWER:

 (1) Republic controlled by lesser men.
 (2) Political dependence upon England.
 (3) Resources impaired.
 (4) Navy declined in importance.
 (5) Trade ceased to expand.

6. BRANDENBURG-PRUSSIA, 1640-1740

1640–88. FREDERICK WILLIAM, THE GREAT ELECTOR:

Able and unscrupulous.

Aims:

 (1) Strong centralised government.
 (2) Strong military forces.
 (3) Territorial aggression.

Dominions:

Frederick William succeeded to claims rather than territories:

 (1) Brandenburg and Pomerania. Occupied by Swedes.
 (2) Rhenish duchies. Occupied by Dutch.
 (3) East Prussia. Under Polish suzerainty.

1641. Swedes left Brandenburg.

1640–8. Frederick William organised forces. Strong position by 1648.

Peace of Westphalia:

 (1) Frederick William to receive:

  (a) Eastern Pomerania. (Swedes left it in 1653.)
  (b) Minden, Halberstadt, Camin.
  (c) Reversion of greater part of Magdeburg. (Secured in 1680.)

 (2) Right to Rhenish duchies confirmed.

Sweden and Poland:

1655. War between Sweden and Poland.

Charles X landed in Eastern Pomerania. Defeated John Casimir. Besieged Danzig.

Frederick William formed triple alliance of Brandenburg, Poland, and Denmark against Sweden.

1656. Charles abandoned Danzig. Invaded East Prussia. By Treaty of Königsberg Frederick William was forced to acknowledge Swedish suzerainty over East Prussia.

Charles again invaded Poland, with assistance of Elector. Defeated John Casimir at Battle of Warsaw.

Danes prepared to invade Sweden. Russians invaded East Prussia.

Frederick William demanded Swedish help in repelling Russian attack. Charles released him from vassalage by Treaty

1656. of Labiau.

1657. By Treaty of Wehlau Frederick William was freed from Polish suzerainty.

1660. Peace of Oliva. General recognition of Frederick William's independence in East Prussia.

Electoral absolutism:

(1) Diet of Brandenburg ceased to meet.

(2) Diet of Cleves overawed by Brandenburg troops.

(3) Diet of Prussia:

Nobles led by Kalkstein.

Burghers led by Rhode.

1662. Rhode arrested. Burghers overawed.

1663. Charter of Liberties. Narrowly interpreted.

Kalkstein fled into Poland. Arrested by Frederick William. Beheaded.

Administrative organisation:

All territories of Elector made subject to Brandenburg Council of State.

Separation of military and civil finance.

Local authorities made directly subject to Elector.

Increase of bureaucracy.

Religious policy:

Genuine toleration. Included all Protestants, Roman Catholics, Jews, etc.

Economic policy:

Settlement of religious refugees. Grants of land and exemption from taxation.

Revival of agriculture. Horticulture.

Woollen manufacture.

Encouragement of science and art.

Trading companies. West Africa Co.

Forces:

Army of 30,000.

Beginning of navy.

Foreign policy:

1667. Alliance with France. Elector aloof from Triple Alliance.

1672–8.   Alarmed by French aggression. Alliance with Dutch. Battle
            of Fehrbellin. Frederick William defeated Swedes. Occu-
1675.   pied Pomerania.
1679.   Treaty of St. Germain-en-Laye:
                (1) Western Pomerania restored to Sweden.
                (2) Elector received 300,000 crowns.
1679.   Reversion to French alliance.
1684.   Again alarmed by French aggression, as shown by Truce of
            Regensburg. Further alienated by Revocation of Edict of
            Nantes.
1685.   Alliance with Dutch and Emperor.
1688.   Prepared to defend United Provinces during William's absence
            in England.
1688.   Death of Frederick William.

1688–1713. FREDERICK III:
            Royal title:
                Elector's ambition to become a king.
                Supported allies in Augsburg war. Disappointment at
                Ryswick.
                Emperor wanted Elector's support in Spanish Succession War.
                Frederick demanded title first. Emperor granted title of
                King of Prussia.
1701.   Coronation at Königsberg, as Frederick I.
            Court modelled on that of Versailles.
            Learning:
1694.   University of Halle.
            Berlin Academies of Arts and Sciences.
            Independence:
                Discontinuance of appeals from electoral courts to Imperial
                Chamber.
                Supreme Court of Appeal at Berlin.

1713–40. FREDERICK WILLIAM I:
            Administrative system:
                Council of State overshadowed by inner Council of Ministers.
                Local officials appointed by Crown.
            Army:
                Strength of 80,000. Conscription.
                Heavy cost. Economy at court and in administration.
                No serious war.
            Economic progress:
                Immigration still encouraged.
                Manufactures developed. State control.

7. THE EARLIER PART OF LOUIS XV'S REIGN

THE REGENCY:
    Duke of Orleans. Recognition by Parlement.
    Contrast with Louis XIV:
        Reversal of home and foreign policy.
        Profligacy.

Patronage of Jansenists and Huguenots.
Nobles employed in administration.

Administrative system:

Seven councils of nobles. System did not work well.

1718. Abolition of councils. Reversion to system of single minister responsible for each department.

Religion:

Regent inclined to favour Jansenism. Jesuits in disfavour.
Noailles president of Council of Religion. Some Jansenists released from prison.
Revival of controversy.
Bull *Unigenitus* modified. Accepted by Noailles and the Parlement of Paris.
Jansenism lingered on. Parlement favoured it. Sorbonne supported Jesuits. Jansenism became debased and squalid.

Finances:

Heavy debt. Expenditure exceeded income.
Some loans repudiated; interest on others reduced. Public credit lowered.

Law's schemes:

(1) A national bank which would issue paper money on security, which need not be gold.
(2) A monopolistic trading company. All foreign trade of France. Profits would pay off national debt and reduce taxation.

1716. Private bank. Successful.
1718. Became State Bank.
1717. Company of the West:
Monopoly of Louisiana trade.
Acquired tobacco monopoly.
Absorbed Senegal Company, East India Company, and China Company.
Acquired mint.
Acquired right of farming indirect taxes.
Lent Government 1,500 million livres at 3 per cent to pay off national debt. Sole creditor of state.

1720. Bank and Company amalgamated:
Bank issued paper money.
Company issued new shares.
Speculation, followed by crash.
Government reassumed responsibility for debt.
Bank abolished. Company became private trading company.

Foreign policy:

Controlled by Dubois.
Succession question. Conflicting interests of Philip V and Philip of Orleans.

1717. *Triple Alliance:*

Great Britain, United Provinces, France.
(1) Fortifications of Mardyck to be abolished.

*M 1643-1848

        (2) Expulsion of Pretender from Avignon.

        (3) Great Britain to maintain Peace of Utrecht in whatever concerned crown of France.

        (4) France to uphold Protestant succession in Great Britain.

        N.B. (a) Ended diplomatic isolation of France.

            (b) Alliance unpopular in France.

1718.   Emperor joined alliance.   Quadruple.

War:

1717.	Spanish conquered Sardinia.
1718.	Spanish overran Sicily.
	Battle of Cape Passaro. Byng defeated Spanish.
	Alberoni intrigued for Swedish attack on Great Britain.
1718.	Great Britain declared war on Spain.
	France declared war on Spain.
1719.	French invasion of Spain.
	British fleet attacked Spanish ports.
1720.	Alberoni dismissed.
1720.	Treaty of London. Philip joined Quadruple Alliance.

Dubois:

1721.	Cardinal.
1722.	First Minister of France.
	Succession question less pressing. Dubois considered revival of Franco-Spanish friendship.
1721.	Louis XV betrothed to Spanish Infanta.
1723.	Louis of age. Regency at an end.
1723.	Dubois died. Orleans First Minister. Died.

1723-6. BOURBON:

        First Minister.   Practically Regent.

        Bourbon disliked Orleans, heir to throne.   Anxious for King to marry at once.   Cancelled Spanish betrothal.

1725.	King married Maria Leszczynska.
1729.	(Birth of Dauphin.)
	Bourbon jealous of Fleury. Tried to procure his exile from court.
1726.	Fall of Bourbon.

FLEURY:

        Policy comparable with that of Walpole.   Aimed at peace, and the prosperity of France.

        Financial reforms.   Strict economy.

        Neglect of army and navy.

        Influence at court challenged by war party under Villars which hoped for abandonment of Anglo-French entente and the establishment of Franco-Spanish alliance against the Emperor.

        True interests of France demanded co-operation of France and Spain against the colonial ambitions of Great Britain.

8. PHILIP V AND ELIZABETH FARNESE

AIMS OF PHILIP V:

> (1) French succession.
> (2) Recovery of lost Spanish possessions.

AIM OF ELIZABETH:

> Principalities in Italy for Don Carlos and Don Philip. (Parma, Tuscany, Naples.)

1715–20. ALBERONI:

> Chief minister of Spain. Desired ten years (five at least) of peace in order to establish reforms.
>
> *Reforms:*
>> (1) Finances put in order.
>> (2) Development of agriculture, industry, and commerce.
>> (3) Strengthening of the forces.
>> (4) Improvement of communications.
>
> *Foreign policy:*
>> Approved of Italian aims of King and Queen, but not French aim.
>> Hoped for agreement with Great Britain. After Triple Alliance, sought alliance of Sweden.
>
> *War:*

1717.
> Arrest of Spanish Inquisitor-General in Milan.
> Spanish conquered Sardinia.

1718.
> Spanish conquered Sicily.
> N.B. (a) A breach of the Utrecht settlement was already being contemplated by Emperor and Duke of Savoy.
>   (b) Pro-Spanish sentiment in Sardinia and Sicily.
> Arrangements for Swedish attack on Bremen and Verden and on British coast.
> British fleets in Baltic and Mediterranean.
> Battle of Cape Passaro. Byng defeated Spanish.

1718–19.
> Great Britain and France declared war on Spain:
> French invasion of Spain.
> British attack on Spanish ports.
> Austrian conquest of Sicily.

1720.
> Dismissal of Alberoni.
>
> *Treaty of London:*
>> (1) Philip adhered to Quadruple Alliance.
>> (2) Emperor to retain Sicily.
>> (3) Duke of Savoy to receive Sardinia. (King.)

FRANCO-SPANISH ENTENTE:

1721.
> Betrothal of Louis XV to Infanta.
> Bourbon broke off the match.

1725.
> Louis XV married Maria Leszczynska.

AUSTRO-SPANISH ALLIANCE:

1725.   *First Treaty of Vienna:*

     (1) Emperor renounced claim to Spain, and recognised Philip V.

     (2) Emperor recognised right of Don Carlos to Parmesan succession.

     (3) Emperor to use good offices for recovery of Gibraltar.

     (4) Philip guaranteed Pragmatic Sanction.

     (5) Philip granted privileges to Ostend East India Company.

     (6) Certain marriages arranged.

1726.   *Treaty of Hanover:*

     Great Britain, France, and Prussia. Then, United Provinces, Denmark, and Sweden.

     To oppose Vienna alliance.

1726.   Prussia changed sides and guaranteed Pragmatic Sanction.

     War:

     British attack on Porto Bello.

     Spanish attack on Gibraltar.

1728.   Peace negotiations:

     (1) Gibraltar to remain British.

     (2) Privileges of Ostend Company suspended.

FRANCO-SPANISH ALLIANCE:

1729.   Birth of Dauphin. Extinction of Philip's French ambitions, and removal of obstacle to reconciliation of Bourbon powers.

1729.   *Treaty of Seville:*

     Great Britain, France, and Spain.

     (1) Spanish claim to Minorca and Gibraltar tacitly dropped.

     (2) Privileges of Ostend Company discontinued.

     (3) Parmesan succession to Don Carlos.

1731.   Duke of Parma died. Emperor occupied duchies. Walpole's action to avert war.

     Second Treaty of Vienna:

     (1) Emperor recognised Don Carlos as Duke of Parma.

     (2) Emperor withdrew support from Ostend Company.

     (3) Great Britain and United Provinces guaranteed Pragmatic Sanction.

1732. THE EUROPEAN POSITION:

     (1) Friendship of France, Spain, and Great Britain.

     (2) Spain had gained a foothold in Italy; Don Carlos in Parma.

     (3) Spanish resources and prestige augmented.

     (4) Apprehensions of maritime powers with regard to the Ostend Company removed.

     (5) Growing hostility of Emperor and Spain.

     (6) Likelihood of friction between Great Britain and Spain (South American trade).

POLISH SUCCESSION:

1733.　Augustus II died.
　　　Candidates:
　　　Augustus III.　Supported by Austria and Russia.
　　　Stanislaus Leszczynski.　Supported by France, Spain, and
　　　　Sardinia.
　　　Great Britain neutral.

1733.　*First Family Compact* (France and Spain):
　　　(1) To establish Stanislaus as King of Poland.
　　　(2) Mutual guarantee against attack by Great Britain or
　　　　Emperor.
　　　(3) To support Don Carlos in Parma and Piacenza and to
　　　　recognise his right to the Tuscan succession.
　　　(4) Commercial privileges exchanged.
　　　(5) Not to negotiate separately about the Pragmatic Sanction.

　　　War:
　　　　Poland:
1733.　　　Stanislaus elected.
　　　　　Russian and Saxon armies invaded Poland and established
　　　　　　Augustus.
　　　　　Stanislaus at Danzig.　French help.　Fall of Danzig.
　　　　　Stanislaus fled into Prussia.

　　　　Italy:
　　　　　Sardinians overran Milanese.
　　　　　Don Carlos conquered kingdom of Naples and Sicily.

1735.　*Third Treaty of Vienna:*
1738.　Ratified.
1739.　Accepted by Spain and Naples.
　　　(1) Augustus III recognised as King of Poland.
　　　(2) Stanislaus to receive Bar at once.
　　　(3) Stanislaus to receive Lorraine when Francis Stephen, Duke
　　　　of Lorraine, became Grand Duke of Tuscany.
　　　(4) Bar and Lorraine to be annexed to France on death of
　　　　Stanislaus.
　　　(5) Parma and Piacenza to Emperor.
　　　(6) Milanese to be restored to Emperor.
　　　(7) Don Carlos to be King of Naples and Sicily.
　　　(8) France guaranteed the Pragmatic Sanction.

9. THE AUSTRIAN SUCCESSION

THE YEAR 1740:

　　　(1) Change of persons and problems in Europe at this time:
　　　Philip V and Elizabeth.　Declining influence.
1742.　Walpole.　Retired.
1743.　Fleury.　Died.
1740.　Charles VI, Emperor.　Died.
1740.　Frederick William I of Prussia.　Died.
1740.　Anne of Russia.　Died.

(2) Period of war began.
Great Britain and Spain.   American trade.
Great Britain and France.   Colonial, commercial, and naval
supremacy.
Austria and Prussia.   Supremacy in central Europe.

THE PRAGMATIC SANCTION:

Charles VI. No son. Daughter, Maria Theresa. The Pragmatic Sanction recognised Maria Theresa as heiress of all Hapsburg dominions.
Recognised by Diets of:

1720.	Austria.
1722.	Hungary.
1724.	Austrian Netherlands.
1732.	Empire.

Guaranteed by:

1725.	Spain. First Treaty of Vienna.
1726.	Russia.
1726.	Prussia. Treaty of Wusterhausen.
1731.	Great Britain } Second Treaty of Vienna.
1731.	United Provinces
1733.	Saxony.
1738.	France.
1739.	Spain. } Third Treaty of Vienna.
1739.	Sardinia.

IMPERIAL CROWN:

Charles hoped that Electors would choose Maria Theresa's husband, Francis Stephen, Grand Duke of Tuscany.

1740. ACCESSION OF MARIA THERESA:

Proclaimed in Austria, Hungary, Bohemia. Francis Stephen co-regent.
Recognised by Great Britain, United Provinces, Russia, Prussia, Venice, Saxony, Pope.
France, Spain, and Sardinia delayed recognition.
Elector of Bavaria asserted claim. His wife a daughter of Joseph I. (No claim to Milan or Netherlands.)
Austrian army ill-organised.
Austrian finances exhausted by recent wars.
Archduchess inexperienced.
Danger from France and Prussia.

FRANCE:

Fleury acted with caution. Might support attack, but would not initiate it.

PRUSSIA:

Frederick the Great, of outstanding ability.
Large well-trained army.

Finances in good order.
Frederick resolved to seize Silesia.

THE WAR IN CENTRAL EUROPE:

1740. Frederick invaded and overran Silesia.
1741. Battle of Mollwitz. Austrians defeated.

Spain
Sardinia
Saxony } joined in the attack on Austrian dominions.
Bavaria
France

Franco-Prussian alliance:

(1) France to recognise Prussian possession of Lower Silesia.
(2) France to support candidature of Charles Albert to the Empire.
(3) France to induce Sweden to declare war on Russia.

French invaded Empire as allies of Prussia and Bavaria.
  No formal declaration of war against Austria at this time.
Spanish in Italy. Ready to attack Milan.
Maria Theresa obtained Hungarian support.
French and Bavarians captured Linz. Invaded Bohemia and captured Prague.
Frederick made secret compact with Maria Theresa. To receive Neisse.
Frederick captured Glatz. Invaded Moravia.

1742. Austrians recovered Linz and invaded Bavaria.
Charles Albert Emperor, as Charles VII.
Austrians captured Munich.
Carteret prepared to support Maria Theresa.
King of Sardinia changed sides and agreed to defend Milan.
Don Carlos, King of Naples, forced to withdraw.

Treaty of Breslau (Prussia and Austria):

Frederick to withdraw from war and to retain Silesia and Glatz.

Saxony made peace.
Emperor recovered Munich.
Austrians recovered Bohemia.

1743. Austrians overran Bavaria. Emperor at Frankfort.
Battle of Dettingen. English and Hanoverians (George II) defeated French.
Treaty of Worms. Maria Theresa and King of Sardinia allied to expel Spanish from Italy.
Second Family Compact. France and Spain.

1744. France declared war on Great Britain.

Aims of Maria Theresa (at this time):

(1) To recover Silesia and former Austrian possessions in Italy.
(2) To conquer Lorraine from France.
(3) To conquer Bavaria from Emperor.
(4) To depose Charles VII.

Frederick alarmed. Formed Union of Frankfort, to support Emperor.
New Franco-Prussian treaty.

Second Silesian War:

> Frederick invaded Bohemia and took Prague. Retired into Silesia.

1745. Death of Charles VII. New Elector not a candidate for Imperial throne.

> *Treaty of Füssen* (Austria and Bavaria):
>
> (1) Peace between Austria and Bavaria.
> (2) Bavaria restored to Elector.
> (3) Elector to vote for Francis Stephen.
> (4) Elector to recognise Pragmatic Sanction.
>
> *Treaty of Warsaw* (Austria and Saxony):
>
> (1) Saxon vote for Francis Stephen.
> (2) Joint action against Prussia.

> Battle of Fontenoy. French defeated British and Hanoverians (Cumberland). British forces withdrawn.
> Frederick isolated in Germany. Austro-Saxon invasion of Silesia. Defeated by Frederick at Hohenfriedberg. Frederick invaded Bohemia.
> Francis Stephen, Emperor.
> Battle of Sohr. Frederick defeated Austrians. Then withdrew from Bohemia.
> Frederick invaded Saxony and occupied Dresden.

> *Treaty of Dresden:*
>
> (1) Frederick retained Silesia.
> (2) Frederick recognised Francis Stephen as Emperor.

THE WAR IN ITALY:

1747. Spanish captured Milan. Austrian reinforcements in Italy. Milan recovered.

THE WAR IN THE AUSTRIAN NETHERLANDS:

1746. Marshal Saxe captured Brussels, and overran Netherlands.
1747. Saxe invaded United Provinces. Great Britain prepared to act with vigour.

RUSSIA:

1747. *Treaty of St. Petersburg:*

> Russian assistance promised to Maria Theresa.

TREATY OF AIX-LA-CHAPELLE (Aachen):

> (1) Pragmatic Sanction confirmed, except:
>   (a) Silesia and Glatz to Prussia.
>   (b) Parma and Piacenza to Don Philip.
>   (c) Part of Milanese to Sardinia.
> (2) Conquests restored:
>   (a) French withdrew from Austrian Netherlands.
>   (b) Barrier fortresses to Dutch.
>   (c) Madras to English.
>   (d) Louisburg to French.

(3) Renewal of Asiento by Spain.
(4) Expulsion of Pretender from France.
(5) Fortifications of Dunkirk to be dismantled.
(6) Recognition of Francis Stephen as Emperor.

RESULTS:

(1) No real settlement of main points at issue:
  (a) Between Austria and Prussia.
  (b) Between Great Britain and France.
  Renewal of war likely.
(2) Permanent achievements:
  (a) Pragmatic Sanction vindicated.
  (b) Italian settlement.
  (c) Prussian hold on Silesia.
(3) Importance of Russia and Sardinia.
(4) Austria stronger than at beginning of war.
(5) Aims of Elizabeth Farnese achieved.
(6) Exhaustion of France.

10. THE DIPLOMATIC REVOLUTION AND THE SEVEN YEARS' WAR

AUSTRIAN INTERNAL REFORMS:

(1) Administrative reorganisation:
  Noble power diminished.
  Central government strengthened.
(2) Courts of justice reformed.
(3) Finance:
  Income tax.
  Poll tax.
  Exemptions scrutinised.
  Corruption checked.
(4) Trade:
  Internal customs abolished.
  Communications improved.
  Port of Trieste enlarged.
  Merchant fleet increased.
(5) Army:
  Enlarged.
  Conditions of living improved.
  Training schools for officers.
  Artillery strengthened.

DIPLOMATIC REVOLUTION:

Maria Theresa wanted new alliance. Ministers advised continuance of existing alliance with Great Britain. Kaunitz suggested alliance with France.
Frederick feared Austro-Russian designs.
George II feared for safety of Hanover.

1755.   Great Britain proposed renewal of Austrian alliance. Kaunitz refused.
        Great Britain allied with Russia.
1756.   Treaty of Westminster. Frederick allied with Great Britain.
        Elizabeth hated Frederick. Withdrew from British alliance.
1757.   Came to terms with Austria.
1756.   Treaty of Versailles. France and Austria. (Pompadour influence.)
1757.   Second Treaty of Versailles. France and Austria. Sweden joined alliance. Spain neutral.

ALLIANCES IN THE WAR:

France
Austria
Russia
Sweden   *v.*   { Great Britain.
Saxony   { Prussia.
1761.   Spain

QUESTIONS AT ISSUE:

(1) Silesia. Supremacy in central Europe.
(2) Maritime supremacy and colonial empire.

THE WAR:

1756.   Frederick invaded Saxony. Battle of Lobositz. Frederick defeated Austrians. Saxons capitulated at Pirna. Frederick entered Dresden.
1757.   Frederick invaded Bohemia. Besieged Prague. Battle of Kolin. Austrians (Daun) defeated Frederick; raised siege of Prague; drove Frederick out of Bohemia. Failed to follow up victory.
        Battle of Hastenbeck. French defeated Cumberland. Convention of Klosterseven. French occupied Hanover.
        Battle of Gross-Jägerndorf. Russians (Apraksin) defeated Prussians. Failed to follow up victory.
        Swedes invaded Pomerania.
        Austrians invaded Silesia and Brandenburg. Entered Berlin.
        Pitt repudiated Convention of Klosterseven. Appointed Ferdinand of Brunswick to command of British and Hanoverian armies.
        Battle of Rossbach. Frederick defeated French; drove them west of Rhine.
        Battle of Leuthen. Frederick defeated Austrians; drove them out of Silesia.
        French left Hanover.
        British subsidy to Frederick.
1758.   Frederick invaded Moravia. Besieged Olmütz, which was saved by Loudon. Frederick retired into Silesia.
        Battle of Zorndorf. Frederick defeated Russians (Fermor).
        Austrians invaded Saxony and Silesia. Battle of Hochkirch. Frederick defeated, but Austrians compelled to withdraw.
        Battle of Krefeld. Ferdinand defeated French (Clermont).

1759. Choiseul in power in France. New plans, not realised.
(Naval and colonial activity—see below.)
Battle of Minden. Ferdinand defeated French.
Battle of Kunersdorf. Frederick defeated by Russians (Solti-
koff) and Austrians (Loudon). Daun captured Dresden. Solti-
koff remained inactive.

1760. Battle of Liegnitz. Frederick defeated Austrians (Loudon).
Russians entered Berlin. Retired.
Battle of Torgau. Frederick defeated Daun and recovered
Saxony, except Dresden.
Battle of Warburg. Ferdinand defeated French.

1761. Less strenuous fighting.
Third Family Compact. France and Spain.
  (1) Spain to declare war on Great Britain on 1st May, 1762,
  unless peace had previously been concluded between Great
  Britain and France.
  (2) France to cede Minorca to Spain.
  (3) Intervening year for preparation.
Pitt suspected existence of compact. Proposed immediate war
with Spain. George III dissented. Fall of Pitt.
Bute declared war on Spain.

1762. End of Anglo-Prussian alliance. Subsidy discontinued.
Death of Elizabeth of Russia.
Peter III allied with Frederick.
Sweden made peace.
Battle of Burkersdorf. Frederick defeated Austrians and re-
covered Silesia.

NAVAL AND COLONIAL ACTIVITY:

1756. French captured Minorca.
1757. Battle of Plassey. Clive's victory in India.
1758. British captured Fort Duquesne.
1759. Choiseul's plan for invasion of England.
Battle of Lagos. Boscawen defeated Toulon fleet.
Battle of Quiberon. Hawke defeated Brest fleet.
Havre. Rodney destroyed transports.
Wolfe captured Quebec.
1760. Amherst captured Montreal.
1760. Battle of Wandewash. Coote defeated French in India.
1761-2. Capture of French islands in West Indies.
1762. Havana and Manila captured from Spanish.

1763. TREATY OF PARIS (Great Britain, France, Spain):
  (1) French possessions in India, except three trading posts,
  ceded to Great Britain.
  (2) French possessions east of Mississippi, except New Orleans,
  ceded to Great Britain.
  (3) Certain West Indian islands retained by Great Britain; others
  restored to France.
  (4) Great Britain retained the Senegal settlement in West Africa
  (5) Great Britain recovered Minorca; France recovered Belle Isle.
  (6) Fortifications of Dunkirk to be destroyed.

    (7) Havana and Manila restored to Spain.
    (8) Spain ceded Florida to Great Britain.

1763. TREATY OF HUBERTSBURG (Austria and Prussia):

    (1) Frederick retained Silesia and Glatz.
    (2) Frederick to vote for Archduke Joseph at Imperial Election.
    (3) Saxony restored to Augustus III.

CAUSES OF FREDERICK'S SUCCESS:

    (1) His genius and perseverance.
    (2) Interior lines of communication.
    (3) Single control.
    (4) Failure of his enemies to co-operate.
    (5) Inactivity of Russian generals in view of position at Russian court.
    (6) British assistance.

RESULTS OF THE STRUGGLE:

    (1) Great Britain's naval and colonial supremacy.
    (2) Failure of Austria to crush Prussia.
    (3) Growing importance of Russia in European affairs.
    (4) Continuance of Franco-Austrian alliance.
    (5) Exhaustion of France.
    (6) Hostility of Frederick to Great Britain.

11. BENEVOLENT DESPOTISM

BENEVOLENT DESPOTISM:

Absolute monarchy.
Government for the good of the governed.
Not democratic.   Reforms to spring from will of ruler, not from people.
Benevolent statesmen as well as benevolent despots.
Eighteenth-century philosophy not democratic.

Defects:

    (1) Reforms had no roots.
    (2) Reforms could be maintained only by constant watchfulness.
    (3) No guarantee of permanence; reforms might be reversed by successor.
    (4) Lack of administrative machinery.
    (5) Officials often interested in maintenance of privileges and abuses.
    (6) Reforms not always well thought out.

1740–80. MARIA THERESA:

Many reforms. Intention of strengthening Austria against Prussia rather than a genuine desire to improve condition of people.

1759–88. CHARLES III, KING OF SPAIN:

> Cheerful and capable.
> Restrictions on ecclesiastical privilege.
> Development of national resources.
> Encouragement of trade.
> *But*, evils too deeply rooted.   Reforms unsuccessful.

1750–77. POMBAL (Portugal):

> Trading companies.
> Agriculture.
> Finances set in order.   Expenditure reduced.   Corruption checked.
> Noble privileges reduced.
> Expulsion of Jesuits.
> *But*, little ultimate result.

1759–76. TANUCCI (Naples):

> Ecclesiastical privileges and exemptions restricted.
> Judicial system reformed.
> Education encouraged.
> Finances set in order.
> Industry and commerce.
> Brigandage checked.
> *But*, no permanent result.   Naples relapsed into former condition after Tanucci's fall.

FRANCE:

> Government not intentionally oppressive.   People suffered from aristocratic privilege rather than from state tyranny.

1765–90. JOSEPH II, EMPEROR:

> Active in the period 1780–90
> Work based on reason.
> Well-meaning.   Able.   Hard-working.

> *Condition of his dominions:*

>> (1) Varied.   Peoples of many races.   No common interests. Lands not geographically contiguous.
>> (2) The only common factors were:
>>> (a) Common allegiance.
>>> (b) Catholic religion.

> *Joseph's aims:*

>> (1) To unify his dominions in every possible way.
>> (2) Religious toleration.
>> (3) To consolidate dominions by exchanging Austrian Netherlands for Bavaria.

> *His reforms:*

>> (1) Unification:
>>> (a) Dominions to form a single state, with thirteen provinces.
>>> (b) No Diets without Emperor's express command.

    (c) Municipal privileges abolished.

    (d) German to be the official language everywhere.

(2) Serfdom:

    Abolition attempted.   Could not be carried out.

(3) Law:

    (a) Codes of Civil and Criminal Law.

    (b) Legal costs reduced and procedure simplified.

    (c) Torture abolished.   Death penalty rare.

    (d) Marriage a civil contract.

    (e) System of courts revised.

(4) Religion:

1781.
    (a) Privileges of Church of Rome curtailed.

    (b) Payments to Rome ceased.

    (c) Monasteries not to pay tribute to foreign superiors.

    (d) Some monasteries abolished; others to undertake charitable work.

    (e) Education of candidates for priesthood.

    (f) Toleration.

(5) Social and economic:

    (a) Exemptions from taxation annulled.

    (b) Harbour works at Trieste and Fiume.

    (c) Commercial treaties with Russia and Turkey.

Opposition:

From all classes.   Regarded by Joseph as unreasonable, since his proposals were based on reason.   Determined to suppress opposition.

Austrian Netherlands:

Resented:

    (a) Annulment of charters.

    (b) Abolition of Estates.

    (c) Ecclesiastical reform.

    (d) Judicial reform.

Revolt.   Not comparable with French Revolution.   A movement to maintain *ancien régime*.   Joseph was the revolutionary.

1790.   *Revocation of the reforms:*

Many reforms revoked by Joseph before his death.

Reasons for failure:

    (1) Attempts to abolish racial and linguistic distinctions were futile.

    (2) Ecclesiastical policy unwise.   The Catholic religion was the only factor common to all his people.   Joseph should have maintained friendship with Church.

    (3) Attempted too much in too short a time.

    (4) Internal reforms and ambitious foreign schemes were attempted at the same time.

Permanent results of Joseph's work:

    (1) Toleration.

    (2) Alleviation of lot of serfs.

    (3) Economic reforms of lasting value.

    (4) Work a failure only in the sense that it was premature.

LEOPOLD II:

1765–90. *Grand Duke of Tuscany:*

(1) Administrative:
   Local government remodelled.
(2) Judicial:
   (*a*) Abolition of torture.
   (*b*) Death penalty rare.
   (*c*) Corruption checked.
   (*d*) Procedure simplified.
(3) Social and economic:
   (*a*) Alleviation of serfdom.
   (*b*) Agricultural improvements.
   (*c*) Abolition of monopolies.
   (*d*) New industries.
(4) Financial:
   (*a*) Order established.
   (*b*) Taxation reduced.
(5) Ecclesiastical:
   (*a*) Some religious houses suppressed.
   (*b*) Others reformed.
   (*c*) Inquisition abolished.
   (*d*) Limitation of authority of ecclesiastical courts.

Failure:

(1) Resistance of nobles and clergy.
(2) Common people ignorant and apprehensive.

1790–2. *Emperor:*

Brought about collapse of Netherlands revolt by making judicious concessions.

12. THE CHURCH AND THE JESUITS IN THE EIGHTEENTH CENTURY

SOURCES OF ATTACK ON THE CHURCH:

(1) Autocratic monarchs resented ecclesiastical claims.
(2) Jansenism. Theological and moral grounds of attack.
(3) Philosophy. The appeal to reason.

REASONS FOR HOSTILITY TO JESUITS:

(1) Wealth and power of Order.
(2) Their support of papacy and the ecclesiastical system.
(3) Casuistry.
(4) Commercial activity.

THE ATTACK ON THE JESUITS:

Portugal:

1751.   Jesuit control of Paraguay.   Opposed cession of Paraguay to Spain.

Pombal complained to Pope of Jesuit commercial activity.
Saldanha's inquiry. Hostile report.
Assassination plot. Charges of Jesuit complicity. Clement
XIII forbade trial in Portuguese courts.

1759. Pombal imprisoned 200 Jesuits and deported 6,000 to Papal
States. Property confiscated.

France:

Jesuits opposed by Jansenists.
Parlements.
Philosophers.
Madame de Pompadour.
Choiseul.

Bankruptcy of Lavalette. Legal proceedings. Investigation
of constitution of Society by Parlement.
Proposal to appoint French Vicar-General. Ricci (General)
refused.
Measures against Jesuits:
(1) Property confiscated.
(2) French subjects forbidden to join the Order.
(3) Schools closed.
1764. (4) Order suppressed.

Spain:

Charles III at first friendly towards Jesuits. Aranda hostile.
Suspicion of complicity in assassination plot.
Expulsion of Jesuits. Temporary refuge in Corsica. Then
in Papal States.

Naples:

Jesuits expelled by Tanucci.

Parma:

Quarrel of Duke with Pope. Clement XIII threatened ex-
communication and deposition of Duke.
Duke expelled Jesuits.
Bourbon powers united to demand withdrawal of papal threat.
Pope refused.
War of Bourbons with Pope.
French seized Avignon.
King of Naples seized Beneventum.
King of Spain demanded suppression of Jesuits.
1769. Clement XIII died.

FALL OF JESUITS:

1769. Clement XIV became Pope.
1773. Bull *Dominus ac Redemptor.*
Order suppressed.
Property confiscated.
Ricci imprisoned and died.
Pensions to individual Jesuits.

RESULT OF SUPPRESSION:

Loss to Church of a body of able defenders.

REVIVAL OF THE ORDER:

Early | Continued to exist, in Prussia and Russia, under Vicars.
19th c. | Papal sanction to revival of Order in Russia and Sicily.
1814. | Order formally reconstituted.
19th c. | Varying fortunes of Order. Great influence at Rome.

13. POLAND

1648–66. JOHN CASIMIR:

1649–51. Cossack revolt. Crushed.
1655–60. Swedish War. Loss of suzerainty over East Prussia.
1654–67. Russian War. Carried on with some vigour.
Treaty of Andrussowa. Poland lost territory.

WEAKNESS OF POLAND:
(1) Religious revival long spent.
(2) Foreign corrupt influence. Bribes from France and Russia.
(3) Selfishness of nobles.
(4) *Liberum veto.*

1674–96. JOHN SOBIESKI:
Failure of attempts at constitutional reform.

1683–99. *War with Turks:*
1683. Relief of Vienna.
1699. Peace of Carlowitz.

1697–1733. AUGUSTUS II:
War with Sweden:
Augustus deposed by Charles XII in favour of Stanislaus Leszczynski. After defeat of Charles at Pultava Stanislaus fled and Augustus was restored.

1733–63. AUGUSTUS III:
1733–5. *War of the Polish Succession:*
Stanislaus again failed to secure throne.

Czartoryskis:
Noble family in favour of reform. Attempted to abolish *liberum veto.*
Hostility of Austria, Prussia, and Russia to the proposal. King inactive.
Czartoryskis sent Stanislaus Poniatowski to St. Petersburg.
Seven Years' War:
Disregard of Polish neutrality.

1764–95. STANISLAUS PONIATOWSKI:
Enthronement:
By help of Russia and Prussia. Disorder continued. *Liberum veto* to be maintained. No hereditary monarchy to be established.

Czartoryskis pressed for reform. Opposed by Potockis, who were supported by Russia and Prussia.

Religious questions:

Afforded pretexts for Russian and Prussian intervention in support of Dissidents.

1766.   Diet refused to grant full political rights to Dissidents.

Confederation of Radom. Dissident nobles. Russian support.

1768.   Treaty between Russia and Prussia:

(1) To maintain *liberum veto.*
(2) To maintain elective monarchy.
(3) To maintain Dissident rights.

Confederation of Bar. Catholic nobles. Appealed to France for support.

France brought about Russo-Turkish War. Russian successes. Alarm of Austria.

Frederick proposed Partition of Poland. Russia to give up Turkish conquests in return for a share of Poland.

1772.   *First Partition:*

Russia: White Russia.

Austria: Red Russia and Galicia.

Prussia: West Prussia, Ermeland, Kulmerland (except Danzig and Thorn).

N.B. (1) Not a new principle in European politics.
(2) West Prussia was German in race and language.
(3) White Russia contained Russian people, Orthodox in religion.
(4) No popular resentment. Only a change of masters.
(5) West Prussia linked up East Prussia with Brandenburg.
(6) Catherine unwise. Might have secured the whole country in course of time.

1788–91. *Reform movement:*

New constitution proposed by Stanislaus to Diet.

(1) Hereditary monarchy.
(2) Noble privileges curtailed. End of *liberum veto.*
(3) Legislature of two chambers.
(4) Catholicism to be state religion. Toleration.
(5) Some alleviation of serfdom.

Disliked by Russia and Prussia.

Supported by Leopold II as being likely to establish a power which would be a check upon Prussia.

1793.   *Second Partition:*

Prussia: Thorn, Posen, Danzig.

Russia: Volhynia, Podolia.

No share to Austria.

1794.   *Kosciuszko's rising:*

Seized Cracow and Warsaw.

No support from nobles or townsmen.

Russians defeated Kosciuszko and recovered Warsaw.

1795. *Third Partition:*

Russia: Between Lower Dwina and Galicia.
Prussia: Between Bug and Niemen, with Warsaw.
Austria: South of Warsaw.

CAUSES OF THE FALL OF POLAND:

(1) Geographical.
(2) Constitutional.
    (a) Elective monarchy.
    (b) *Liberum veto.*
(3) Lack of patriotism of nobles.
(4) Religious. Grievances of Dissidents offered opportunities of foreign intervention.
(5) Foreign. Powerful neighbours.
(6) Social. Serfdom. No feeling of national pride among peasantry.

14. SWEDEN

1632–54. CHRISTINA:

1632–44. *Regency:*

Oxenstjerna. Oligarchy of nobles profited from continuance of war. Heavy taxation.

1648. *Peace of Westphalia:*

Zenith of greatness of Sweden. Could not maintain her position. Insufficient resources. Baltic territories a source of weakness.

1642–5. *Danish War:*

1645.   *Treaty of Brömsebro:*

(1) Swedish shipping freed from tolls.
(2) Sweden recovered Halland.

1654. *Abdication* of Christina.

1654–60. CHARLES X (CHARLES GUSTAVUS):

War with Poland. John Casimir refused recognition of Charles X.
Charles invaded Poland. Defeated John Casimir. Besieged Danzig.
Frederick William of Brandenburg formed triple alliance of Brandenburg, Poland, and Denmark against Sweden.

1656.   Charles abandoned Danzig and marched against Frederick William. Treaty of Königsberg. Frederick William acknowledged Swedish suzerainty over East Prussia.
Charles again attacked Poland. Defeated John Casimir at Warsaw. Russian invasion of East Prussia. Danes prepared to attack Sweden.

1656.   Charles released Frederick William from vassalage by Treaty of Labiau. Sailed for Denmark. Defeated Danes.
1660.   Charles X died.

Peace :
> Treaty of Oliva. Sweden and Poland.
> Treaty of Copenhagen. Sweden and Denmark.
> Treaty of Kardis. Sweden and Russia.

1660–97. CHARLES XI:
> *Minority :*
>> Power of nobles, who enriched themselves by:
>>> (1) Seizing Crown lands.
>>> (2) Taking French bribes.

1668.   *Triple Alliance :*
> England, United Provinces, and Sweden against France.
> Sweden soon reverted to French alliance.

1672–8. *Dutch War :*
> Sweden in alliance with France.
1675.   Battle of Fehrbellin. Swedes defeated by Frederick William
> of Brandenburg, who overran Western Pomerania.
1679.   Treaty of St. Germain-en-Laye. Western Pomerania restored
> to Sweden.

1679–97. *Peace :*
> Power of nobles reduced.
> Recovery of Crown lands.
> Prosperity.

1697–1718. CHARLES XII:
> Fifteen years old at accession. Exceptional military skill.

1700–21. *War :*
> Alliance of Denmark, Poland, and Russia against Sweden.
1700.   Charles forced Denmark to make peace.
1700.   Battle of Narva. Charles defeated Peter the Great.
1702.   Charles captured Warsaw.
1703.   Charles captured Thorn and Danzig.
1704.   Augustus II of Poland deposed. Stanislaus Leszczynsk
> chosen.
1707.   Treaty of Altranstadt. Augustus compelled to recognise
> Stanislaus.
> Louis XIV negotiated for Swedish alliance in Spanish Suc-
> cession War. Failed, because:
>> (1) Louis was persecuting Huguenots.
>> (2) Marlborough flattered Charles into neutrality.
>> (3) Charles's interests lay farther east.
1709.   Battle of Pultava. Peter defeated Charles.
> Charles fled into Turkey.
> Augustus recovered crown of Poland.
> Peter conquered Esthonia and Livonia.
1710–11. Russo-Turkish War.
1713.   Charles returned to Sweden.
> Swedes lost Finland.
1718.   Charles killed at Fredrikssten.

PEACE:

1719-20. *Treaties of Stockholm* (Sweden and Hanover):

    (1) Bremen and Verden to Hanover.

    (2) Stettin to Brandenburg.

1720.   *Treaty of Frederiksborg* (Sweden and Denmark):

    (1) Schleswig to Denmark.

    (2) Sweden lost exemption from tolls in Sound.

    Treaty of Nystad (Sweden and Russia):

    (1) Esthonia, Livonia, Ingria, Carelia, and part of Finland including Viborg, to Russia.

    (2) Finland west of Viborg, to Sweden.

1720. CONSTITUTION:

    (1) Diet of four estates.

    (2) Legislation by any three estates.

    (3) When Diet was in session, administration controlled by secret committee of three estates. (Nominated ministers.)

    (4) When Diet was not in session, administration controlled by Senate.

    (5) Power of Crown insignificant.

PARTIES:

    Caps:

    Under Horn. Peace. Friendly with Great Britain. Bribery from Russia.

    Hats:

    Under Gyllenborg and Tessin. Policy of alliance with France. Bribery from France.

1720-38. CAPS IN POWER:

    Horn's rule was peaceful. Country prosperous. French bribes in Diet.

1738.   Caps defeated in Diet.

1738-65. HATS IN POWER:

1741-3. *War with Russia:*

    Undertaken upon French persuasion. Losses in Finland.

1743.   *Treaty of Abo:*

    (1) Most of Swedish Finland restored.

    (2) Adolphus Frederick of Holstein accepted as Crown Prince of Sweden.

1751-71. *Adolphus Frederick, King:*

    Little power.

    Corruption of Swedish politics.

    Swedish intervention in Seven Years' War. Disastrous.

1765-9. CAPS IN POWER:

    Economy in public expenditure.

    Alliance with Russia. Unpopular, and not in Swedish interests.

1769.   Defeated.

1769. HATS IN POWER.

1771–92. GUSTAVUS III:

    State of Sweden:

        Approaching anarchy.

        Possibility of partition by Frederick the Great and Catherine II.

        King attempted, without success, to reconcile parties.

        Coup d'état.

    New Constitution:

        (1) Crown recovered right of appointing ministers and senators and summoning Diet.

        (2) Crown recovered command of forces.

        (3) Diet retained right of legislation and taxation.

        (4) Consent of Diet necessary for declaration of war.

        (5) Independence of judges.

    Reforms:

        (1) Finances in order.

        (2) Administration of justice reformed.

        (3) Army and navy increased.

1788–9. *War with Russia:*

        Mutiny of Swedish army.

        Denmark joined in war.   Invaded Sweden.

1789.   Gustavus obtained support of peasantry.   Danes defeated.

1790.   Vigorous and successful action against Russia.   Peace.

1791.   Alliance of Gustavus and Catherine.

1789.   *Act of Union and Security:*

        Revision of constitution.   Increase of royal power.

    French Revolution:

        Gustavus hostile.   Tried to arrange European alliance for its suppression.

1792.   Assassination of Gustavus.

1792–1809. GUSTAVUS IV:

1792–6. *Minority:*

        Duke of Sudermania, Regent.   Friendly with Jacobins.

    Gustavus:

        Hostile to France.

1805.   Joined Third Coalition.   Swedish intervention too slow to be effective.   French occupied Swedish Pomerania.

1808.   War with Russia.   Final loss of Finland.

1809.   Deposition of Gustavus.

1809–18. CHARLES XIII:

        The former Duke-Regent.   Feeble.   Childless.

1810.   *Bernadotte:*

        Selected as Crown Prince.

        (1) Devoted himself to interests of Sweden, to the disregard of those of Napoleon.

(2) Treated Finland as lost.
(3) Aimed at securing Norway as compensation.
(4) Friendly with Russia.
(5) Joined Fourth Coalition. Battle of Leipzig.
(6) Congress of Vienna assigned Norway to Sweden.

1818–44. CHARLES XIV (Bernadotte):

Peace and internal reform.

15. THE ANCIEN RÉGIME IN FRANCE

SOCIAL GRADES IN FRANCE:

Clergy. }
Nobles. } Privileged.
Third estate. Unprivileged.
Also, Middle class of officials, professional men, etc. Technically, belonged to third estate.

NOBLES:

Hereditary caste. Estimated at 140,000.

Great nobles:

Lived at court. Large incomes. Absentee landlords.

Lesser nobles:

Country gentlemen.

Poor nobles:

Of peasant circumstances, but retentive of privileges.

Origin of privileges:

In Middle Ages, powerful lords defended their inferiors from oppression. Early Bourbons destroyed political power of nobles. Privileges of nobles outlived their usefulness.

Privileges included:

(1) Right of hunting, fishing, shooting.
(2) Provision of mill, winepress, oven, slaughterhouse, for use of peasantry.
(3) Levying of dues on produce of peasant's land.
(4) Exemption from:
　　(a) Service in ranks of army.
　　(b) Forced labour on roads.
　　(c) Payment of *taille.*

CLERGY:

Also privileged.

Origin of privileges:

In Middle Ages, Church was guardian of morality and learning; it protected the weak; it relieved the poor, sick, homeless.
By eighteenth century, Church was corrupt.

Privileges included:

(1) Exemption from ordinary taxation.
(2) Collection of tithes.
(3) Control of education.
(4) Censorship of the press.

MIDDLE CLASS:

Lawyers, officials, merchants, gildsmen, financiers, etc.
Equal to nobles in wealth and intelligence; inferior in social position.

PEASANTS:

General condition:

(1) No serfdom (except in east and north-east France).
(2) Accompaniments of serfdom survived.
(3) Peasants were usually landed proprietors; tenancy system in north and north-west.
(4) Condition improved in eighteenth century. Purchase of land.
(5) Hard toil under primitive conditions. Agriculture backward.

Disadvantages:

(1) Lord's pigeons on crops.
(2) Lord might ride across growing crops.
(3) Forced labour on roads.
(4) Military service (for the unmarried).
(5) Burden of taxation.

TOWNS:

(1) Industry controlled by gilds.
(2) Internal customs barriers hindered trade.
(3) Paris:
    (a) Many officials.
    (b) Important manufacturing centre.
    (c) Industrial population.
    (d) City attracted the discontented from other parts of France.

GOVERNMENT:

Centralised despotism. Inefficient.
Ministers appointed by King.
Taxation and legislation by royal edict. Registration by Parlements. *Lits de justice.*
Justice administered by Parlements.
Local administration by Intendants.

FINANCE:

Revenue:

(1) *Taille,* on non-noble lands.
(2) Poll-tax.
(3) *Vingtième.*

(4) Customs and excise, and inter-provincial customs.

(5) *Gabelle.*

Defects of system:

(1) Exemptions.

(2) Inequalities of assessment.

(3) Tax farming.

(4) Corruption.

(5) No proper accounting.

Financial difficulties of France:

(1) Eighteenth-century wars.

(2) Extravagance of court.

Debt:

Heavy. Increasing.

PHILOSOPHICAL MOVEMENT:

Abuses in eighteenth-century France invited attack. The appeal to reason. The Church the special object of attack.

Defects of the movement:

(1) Destructive, not constructive.

(2) Superficial and imaginative. No basis of historical fact.

(3) Little knowledge of the past.

(4) Admiration, but no real understanding, of British institutions.

(5) Failure to realise difficulty of transferring British institutions to France.

Montesquieu:

1721.   *Lettres Persanes.*

1749.   *L'Esprit des Lois.* Admiration for British constitution. "Separation of powers."

Voltaire:

No system of philosophy.

Appeal to reason.

Criticised Church.

Taught the perfectibility of man.

Advocated many specific reforms.

Not a democrat.

Encyclopaedists:

In form, respectful of existing institutions.

In fact, conclusions based on reason. Critical of Church and state.

Physiocrats:

Criticised the existing economic system.

Advocated the abolition of restrictions upon, and regulation of, economic activity; i.e. *laissez-faire.*

Emphasized the importance of agriculture. Net increase.

Considered industry and commerce to be sterile.

Their views had some influence on Adam Smith.

Rousseau :

A romantic rather than a philosopher.

1762.   *Contrat Social :*

Primitive man lived in a state of nature.

Civil society originated in contract, drawn up at the instance of the wealthy for the protection of property.

Advocated:

Termination of existing contract.

Back to state of nature.

Establishment of new contract on fairer terms.

Ultimate sovereignty rested with people, and was inalienable.

Great influence of Rousseau before and during the Revolution.

COMPARISON OF FRANCE WITH OTHER COUNTRIES:

A. *Other continental countries :*

Serfdom existed, with many oppressive accompaniments.

Extensive noble privileges, including jurisdiction over peasants.

B. *Great Britain :*

Universal rule of law.

No special privileges of nobles.

Serfdom extinct for centuries.

Taxation heaviest on landed gentry.

Advanced agriculture.

No absentee landlordism.

National finances in order.

WHY THE REVOLUTION CAME FIRST IN FRANCE:

(1) France more advanced than other countries, except Great Britain.

(2) French peasantry capable of aspiring to a better state of things.   Not, as in some countries, so utterly crushed as to be without hope of improvement.

(3) French people were conscious of currents of revolutionary thought.

(4) Admiration for British institutions.

(5) Example of American revolt.

FRANCE UNDER LOUIS XV:

Decay of monarchy :

Indolence of King.

His suspicion of ministers.

Extravagance of court.

Immorality of King.   Mistresses influenced policy.

Opposition :

Parlement.   *Lits de justice.*   Exile in 1771.

Remnants of Jansenist controversy.

Riots.   Bloodshed.

National prestige :

Low after Seven Years' War.

1758–70. *Choiseul:*

    Remodelled army. Prussian system of drill.
    Navy rebuilt.
    Maintained alliance of Bourbon powers.
    Maintained Austrian alliance. Dauphin married Marie Antoinette.

    Acquisitions of territory:

1767.   Lorraine and Bar, at death of Stanislaus Leszczynski.
1768.   Corsica purchased from Genoa.

1771–4. *Triumvirate:*

    D'Aiguillon, Terray, Maupeou.

LOUIS XVI:

    Better man than Louis XV. Sincere Christian. Good intentions. Yet unfit for kingship. Lacked qualities of leadership. Hesitant. Failed to realise gravity of condition of France.

MARIE ANTOINETTE:

    Capable. Strong personality. Exercised influence over King in the direction of maintenance of privilege. Extravagance and love of display.

1774–81. MAUREPAS:

    First Minister. Recalled the Parlement.

1774–6. TURGOT, CONTROLLER-GENERAL:

    Measures:

      (1) Reduced expenditure—of court, on pension list, etc.
      (2) Abolished *corvée.*
      (3) Abolished gilds.
      (4) Internal free trade in corn and wine.
      (5) Cancelled illegal exemptions from *taille.*
      (6) Payment of capitation without exemption.
      (7) Proposed:
        (a) System of education independent of the Church.
        (b) System of councils.
        (c) Religious toleration.

    Opposition:

    From nobles and clergy—attack on privileges.
    From Parlements. *Lits de justice.*
    From the Queen.
    Dismissal of Turgot.

1776–7. CLUGNY, CONTROLLER-GENERAL:

    Reversed Turgot's work.
    Revived *corvée.*
          gilds.
          internal customs.
    State lottery.

1777–81. NECKER:

> In charge of the finances. Not formally appointed Controller-General.
> Honest, but irresolute.
> Devised expedients, but failed to recast financial system.
> War of American Independence. Further financial embarrassment.

1781. *Compte Rendu.* Aroused hostility of privileged classes.
Dismissal of Necker.

1783–7. CALONNE, CONTROLLER-GENERAL:

> Policy of extravagance, in order to inspire confidence.

1786. No further loans possible.
1787. Assembly of Notables.
Dismissal of Calonne.

1787–8. BRIENNE, CONTROLLER-GENERAL:

> *Corvée* abolished.
> Provincial assemblies established. ⎫ Accepted by Parlement.
> Inter-provincial free trade in corn. ⎭
> New land tax, with no exemptions. *Lit de justice.*
> Struggle between court and Parlement. New series of edicts.
> Further resistance.
> Louis resolved to summon States-General.

1788–9. NECKER:

> His appointment restored credit of Government. Raised loans for immediate needs.
> Arrangements made for meeting of States-General.

16. THE FRENCH REVOLUTION

1789–91. STATES-GENERAL (NATIONAL ASSEMBLY):

> Met at Versailles. No programme of reform proposed by the Government. Deputies without political experience. Uncertain how to proceed.
> Question of estates sitting together or separately. Struggle of third estate with nobles and clergy. Tennis Court oath.
> Decision of the estates to sit together as the National Assembly. King sanctioned joint meeting.
> Court policy reversed. Troops in Paris and at Versailles to overawe Assembly.
> Activity of Paris mob (swollen with provincial refugees):
> (1) Demonstrations in the streets.
> (2) Capture of the Bastille.
> (3) March of the women to Versailles. Court and Assembly returned to Paris.
> Formation of National Guard, to protect property.
> Provincial rioting. Burning of the châteaux. Volunteer forces in provincial towns.

Proceedings of the Assembly:

(1) Declaration of the Rights of Man.
(2) Abolition of noble privileges.
(3) New system of local government.
(4) New judicial system.
(5) Confiscation of Church property.
(6) Civil Constitution of the Clergy—reorganisation of the Church in France as a department of state.
(7) New system of taxation.
(8) Issue of paper money.
(9) New constitution. Strictly limited monarchy. Regular meetings of the Assembly.

1791.   King and royal family attempted flight. Overtaken at Varennes. Returned to Paris.

1791.   King accepted constitution.

Leading personalities in the Assembly:

Lafayette:

Brave, popular, and incorruptible. Not sufficiently statesmanlike to direct Revolution.

Mirabeau:

Attacked abuses and privileges.
Realised need for strong government.
Tried to secure co-operation between King and Assembly.

1791.   His death ended all possibility of reconciliation.

1791.   Assembly dissolved, after passing self-denying ordinance.

1791–2. LEGISLATIVE ASSEMBLY:

Parties:

(1) Feuillants. Constitutional party. Majority.
(2) Girondins. Revolutionary. High ideals. Support from certain provinces.
(3) Jacobins. Revolutionary. Relied on brute force. Well-organised. System of affiliated clubs. Support of Paris mob.

Friction with King:

1791.   King vetoed decrees against *émigrés* and non-juring clergy.
King and Assembly unlikely to agree, since their points of view were irreconcilable.

1792.   *War with Austria and Prussia:*

Invasion of France. Brunswick's declaration. King suspended. Panic in Paris. Massacre of royalist prisoners in September. Assembly dissolved.

1792–5. CONVENTION:

1792.   *Republic:*
King deposed. France a republic.

Struggle of Jacobins and Girondins:

1793.   Occurred over trial of King. Louis put to death. Victory for Jacobins.
Fall of Girondins. Arrest of Girondin deputies.

1793–4. *The Terror:*

To punish treachery and to inspire people to desperate courage in national emergency. Committee of Public Safety and Revolutionary Tribunal. Terror spread to provinces by Deputies on Mission. Execution of large

1793 (Oct.) numbers of nobles, priests, and wealthy men. Execution of Marie Antoinette. Danton and Robespierre, leaders of Terror, ultimately overthrown and put to death.

Abolition of Christian worship. Worship of Reason established. Republican Calendar drawn up.

1795.   Terror ended. Revolutionary Tribunal and Committee of Public Safety reorganised. Jacobin Club closed. Convention recovered authority.

Other work of Convention (during Terror):

(a) System of education planned.
(b) Codification of law begun.
(c) Metric system.
(d) Relief of poor.
(e) Improvement of agriculture.

1795.   (f) New constitution. Law of Two-Thirds.
1795.   Paris rising. Unpopularity of Law of Two-Thirds. Rising quelled by Bonaparte. Mob dispersed. End of violent Revolution. Restoration of constitutional government.

1795–9. DIRECTORY:

(a) Five members to hold office for five years, one retiring each year.
(b) Two Councils:
(i) Five Hundred. To propose legislation.
(ii) Ancients. To accept or reject legislation.
Unpopular and inefficient. Real power in hands of generals.

1799–1804. CONSULATE:

Bonaparte First Consul. Return to the rule of a single person, i.e. monarchy.

GAINS FROM THE REVOLUTION:

(1) Feudal privileges not revived.
(2) Pre-Revolution power and wealth of the Church not restored.
(3) Efficiency of administration.
(4) Justice open to all.
(5) Taxation on a fair basis.

EFFECT OF FRENCH REVOLUTION IN OTHER COUNTRIES:

Alarm of absolute rulers lest Revolution should spread. Repression of revolutionary tendencies wherever they appeared.

17. THE FRENCH REVOLUTIONARY WAR

IMMEDIATE EFFECT OF FRENCH REVOLUTION:

To diminish French influence in Europe.   No likelihood of war.

1791. AUSTRO-PRUSSIAN ACTION:

Meeting of Leopold II and Frederick William II at Pillnitz. Activity of French émigré nobles and princes.

Declaration of Pillnitz:

(a) Authority of French King ought to be restored.
(b) Hope that other states would co-operate.
(c) *If other powers would co-operate,* Austria and Prussia would employ adequate forces for the purpose.

But it was known that Great Britain was averse to intervention.   Therefore, Declaration meant little.   After Louis XVI accepted constitution of 1791 the Declaration was withdrawn.

CAUSES OF WAR:

Immediate:

(1) *Émigré* princes and nobles in states of the Empire.   Army at Coblentz.
(2) Rights of princes of Empire who held lands in France were affected by decrees of Assembly.

Real and ultimate:

French resented foreign interference.   Austria and Prussia feared spread of Revolution.   Incompatibility of revolutionary principles with absolute monarchy.

1792. DECLARATION OF WAR:

(April). By France against Austria.   Prussia assumed it to apply to her also.

CONDITION OF THE WARRING POWERS:

French:

Army badly organised and ill-equipped.   Discipline lax. Recruiting poor.

Allies:

Distrusted each other.   Feared Catherine II.

1792. OPENING CAMPAIGN:

Prussians invaded France from the east.   Brunswick's manifesto to Paris.   Prussians captured Longwy and Verdun.   Kellermann and Dumouriez defeated Prussians at Cannonade of Valmy.   Prussians abandoned Longwy and Verdun and left France.   French invaded Empire and captured Worms, Mainz, and Frankfort.

Austrians invaded France from north-east. Besieged Lille. Relieved by Dumouriez, who invaded Austrian Netherlands and defeated Austrians at Jemappes. Netherlands overrun. Sardinians entered war against France. French captured Savoy and Nice.

AGGRESSIVE ATTITUDE OF FRENCH REPUBLIC:

1792 (Nov.). Edict of Fraternity. Invited oppressed peoples to rise against their rulers.

1792 (Dec.). Edict ordering that republican institutions should be established and feudal rights abolished in all territories occupied by French armies.

CAUSES OF BRITISH ENTRY INTO WAR:

(1) British obligation, under the Treaty of Utrecht, to defend Holland.

(2) Opening of the Scheldt. Antwerp a menace to Great Britain.

(3) Edict of Fraternity.

(4) Execution of Louis XVI moved British opinion.

1793. **FIRST COALITION:**

Fifteen countries, including:

Austria
Prussia
Holland   *v.* France.
Spain
Sardinia
Great Britain

Events of 1793–5:

1793. (1) Dumouriez invaded Holland. Retired. Defeated by Austrians at Neerwinden. Dumouriez feared arrest and fled to enemy. British army under Duke of York joined Austrians. Netherlands recovered. France invaded. Dunkirk besieged.

Spanish invaded Roussillon.

British naval force occupied Toulon.

Royalist revolt in La Vendée.

Prussians and Austrians recovered Mainz. Threatened invasion of France from east.

(2) French enthusiasm to meet emergency. *Levée en masse.* Conscription.

(3) York driven from Dunkirk.

Vendéan revolt checked.

English driven from Toulon.

Austrians and Prussians driven back.

1794. Spanish driven out. Catalonia invaded.

Austrian Netherlands invaded. Jourdan defeated Austrians at Battle of Fleurus. York driven into Holland and recalled to England.

Battle of First of June; naval battle off Ushant; French fleet defeated, but a convoy of corn ships reached port.

1795. Holland conquered. Peace.
    (a) Indemnity.
    (b) Territory to be ceded.
    (c) Alliance with France, offensive and defensive.
    (d) Dutch to equip and maintain body of French troops.
    Stadtholder fled to England. British captured Cape of Good Hope.
    French sugar islands in West Indies captured by British.

(5 Apr.). Treaty of Basel. Peace with Prussia. Rhenish territories ceded to France.

(22 July). Treaty of Basel. Peace with Spain.

1796. Treaty of San Ildefonso. Alliance of France and Spain.

1796–7. *Bonaparte's Italian Campaign:*

The only enemies of importance remaining against France were Austria, Sardinia, and Great Britain.

Carnot's plan against Austria:

Jourdan ⎰
Moreau ⎱ to invade Austria by the Rhine.

Bonaparte to attack Austrian power in Italy.

1796. Bonaparte invaded Italy. Separated Sardinians from Austrians. Defeated Sardinians and drove them towards Turin. Treaty of Cherasco; peace. Savoy and Nice left in French hands.

Bonaparte marched south-east of Milan. Austrians abandoned Milan and retreated towards Mantua. Battle of Lodi; Bonaparte defeated Austrians and conquered Lombardy. Occupied Milan. Indemnity. Pictures. Rising of Lombard peasants crushed.

Bonaparte defeated Austrians at Peschiera. Besieged Mantua. Expedition against Pope, who agreed to armistice, gave up pictures, and paid indemnity.

Austrian reinforcements in Italy. Bonaparte abandoned siege of Mantua. Defeated Austrians. Renewed siege of Mantua. Captured Mantua.

Cispadane Republic formed (Modena and some papal territory). Alliance with France.

1797. Bonaparte again invaded Papal States. Peace of Tolentino; Pope made peace.

Bonaparte advanced against Archduke Charles, who had defeated Jourdan and compelled Moreau to retire from Bavaria. Battle of the Tagliamento; Bonaparte defeated Charles and invaded Carinthia.

1797. *Treaty of Campo Formio:*

(1) Lombardy and Austrian Netherlands to France. (Lombardy added to Cispadane Republic to form Cisalpine Republic, recognised by Austria.)

(2) Venetia east of the Adige, with Istria and Dalmatia, to Austria. (Venetian Republic ended.)

(3) Congress to be held at Rastadt to settle terms of peace with Holy Roman Empire. Emperor to use influence to secure Rhine boundary for France.

Results of the War—to 1797:
(1) Rhine boundary for France.
(2) Substantial French gains in Italy—vassal republics.
(3) Austrian dominions consolidated—Venetia instead of Lombardy and Netherlands.
(4) Neither Austria nor Prussia ready to defend Germany. Concerned with their own interests.
(5) Only Great Britain left at war with France.

1797. THE CRITICAL YEAR:

France
Spain } *v.* Great Britain.
Holland

Aim of allies:
To effect a junction of fleets, in order that the British fleet might be overpowered and an invasion of England effected.

British aim:
To prevent junction.

Events of 1797:
Battle of St. Vincent; Jervis and Nelson defeated Spanish fleet.
Mutiny at Spithead. Easily suppressed.
Mutiny at the Nore. Crushed.
Battle of Camperdown; Duncan defeated Dutch.

1798–9. EGYPTIAN CAMPAIGN:

1798. Bonaparte sailed from Toulon. Captured Malta from the Knights of St. John.
Bonaparte reached Egypt. On the way to India. Its conquest would deal a great blow to British trade. Possibility of conquering Turkey and attacking Austria from south-east.
Bonaparte defeated Mamelukes at Battle of the Pyramids.
Nelson searched for French fleet. Destroyed French fleet at the Battle of the Nile.

1799. Bonaparte marched into Syria to re-establish his communications with France. Defeated at Acre. Returned to Egypt.

1799. Bonaparte returned alone to France.

VASSAL REPUBLICS:

Established by the French:

1795.	Batavian Republic.	Holland.
1797.	Cisalpine Republic.	North Italy.
1798.	Helvetic Republic.	Switzerland.
	Roman Republic.	Rome. (Pope a prisoner at Valence.)
	Ligurian Republic.	Genoa.
1799.	Parthenopean Republic.	Naples.

1798. SECOND COALITION:

Russia
Austria
Turkey } *v.* France.
Great Britain

1799. Russians and Austrians reconquered northern Italy. French abandoned Naples and Rome. Defeated at Battle of Novi. Cisalpine Republic overthrown. French remnant at Genoa. Jealousies of allies. Masséna defeated Russians at Zürich. Russians withdrew from the war.

1800. Bonaparte, First Consul, invaded Italy. Recovered Milan. Masséna compelled to surrender at Genoa. Battle of Marengo; Bonaparte defeated Austrians, who retreated east of the Mincio. French occupied Piedmont. Cisalpine Republic restored.

1800. British captured Malta.

1801. *Treaty of Lunéville:*
  (1) Austria reaffirmed settlement at Campo Formio.
  (2) Austria agreed to Rhine boundary for France.
  (3) Princes who lost lands west of Rhine to be compensated with other German lands with sanction of Consulate. (German settlement would be in accordance with French ideas.)
  (4) Emperor to recognise Batavian and Helvetic Republics.
Great Britain again alone against France.

1800. NORTHERN LEAGUE (ARMED NEUTRALITY):

  Causes:
  (1) Tsar Paul became Grand Master of Knights of St. John. Resented British capture of Malta.
  (2) Resentment of neutral powers at search of their ships by British.

  The League
  Russia ⎫
  Sweden ⎪
  Denmark ⎬ *v.* Great Britain.
  Prussia ⎭

  Events:
  Denmark possessed fleet. Parker and Nelson demanded its surrender. Battle of Copenhagen; Danish ships captured or destroyed.
  Tsar Paul died. Tsar Alexander I reached agreement with Great Britain. Armed Neutrality ended.

1802. TREATY OF AMIENS:

  Between Great Britain and France:
  (1) Great Britain to restore French West Indian islands.
  (2) Great Britain to restore Cape of Good Hope to Dutch.
  (3) Great Britain to retain Ceylon and Trinidad, captured during the war.
  (4) Great Britain to restore Malta to Knights of St. John.
  (5) French to withdraw from Papal States and Naples.
  (6) British and French to withdraw from Egypt.
  N.B. (*a*) Treaty settled nothing. A mere truce.
        (*b*) Peace made because of war-weariness.

(c) Neither side victorious. French victories had been gained on land. British victories at sea.

(d) Treaty less satisfactory to Great Britain than to France. Great Britain returned important conquests. Bonaparte gave back only Egypt, which he could not retain, and central and southern Italy, which he could recover at any time.

(e) Great Britain had not achieved her object in the war.

REASONS FOR FRENCH SUCCESS:

(In spite of bankruptcy, lack of discipline, and lack of supplies.)
(1) Enthusiasm of a people fighting for liberty.
(2) Eighteenth-century despotisms played out.
N.B. Great Britain escaped defeat only through her geographical position and her navy.

18. NAPOLEON'S RULE IN FRANCE

THE CONSULATE:

The Consuls:

Three in number. First Consul possessed all power, including military command. Second and Third Consuls were mere assistants. Despotic monarchy under constitutional forms. Vigorous and ruthless.

Constitutional forms:

Council of State. Appointed by First Consul. Dealt with administrative matters. Proposed legislation.
Senate. Appointed tribunes and legislators.
Tribunes. Criticised legislation. (Abolished soon after establishment of Empire.)
Legislative Corps. Accepted or rejected legislation.

POLICY:

(1) *Centralisation:*

Over-centralisation of Bourbon rule had been followed by decentralisation under Revolution. Now corrected. Local government divisions retained, but departments were made subject to prefects and communes to mayors, appointed by First Consul. Paris in twelve divisions, each under a mayor. Whole city under prefect of police.

(2) *Sound finance:*

Revenue collected promptly. Arrears collected. Bank of France established.

(3) *Conciliation:*

(i) *Émigrés.* Invited to return. Political prisoners released.
(ii) Church. Hitherto supported Bourbons. Bonaparte entered into an agreement (the Concordat) with the Pope.

1801. THE CONCORDAT:

(a) Roman Catholic religion to be recognised.
(b) Bishops to be appointed by First Consul and instituted by Pope.
(c) Parish priests to be appointed by bishops.
(d) Church property not to be given back, but cathedrals and churches to be restored.
(e) Salaries of clergy to be paid by state.
(f) Prayers for Republic and Consuls.

N.B. Existing bishops resigned or were deposed. New appointments.

BONAPARTE'S ADVANCE IN POWER:

1799.   First Consul.   Ten years.
1802.   First Consul.   Life.   "Napoleon."
1804.   Emperor of the French.   Plebiscite in France.   Recognition by other powers.   Coronation.   Pope present.

THE FRENCH EMPIRE AND THE ROMAN EMPIRE:

(a) Both developed from republics.
(b) Vast territories conquered.   Subject peoples and kings.
(c) Pope at coronation.
(d) Heir to Holy Roman Emperor was "King of the Romans." Heir to Napoleon was "King of Rome."
(e) Eastern and Western Empires.
(f) Marriage-alliance of Napoleon with Hapsburgs.

GRANDEUR OF THE EMPIRE:

(a) Court and etiquette.
(b) New nobility.
(c) Body of marshals.
(d) Legion of Honour.

THE CODES:

(a) Civil Code (Code Napoléon).   Begun by Convention.   French civil law.
(b) Code of Civil Procedure.
(c) Criminal Code.
(d) Code of Criminal Procedure.
(e) Code of Commercial Law.

CONFLICT WITH THE PAPACY:

Causes:

(1) Treatment of the Pope at Napoleon's coronation.
(2) Matters arising out of the Concordat.
(3) Papal claim to overlordship of kingdom of Naples, of which Joseph Bonaparte was King.

Quarrel:

Napoleon demanded that one-third of the cardinals should be French.   Pope refused to institute French bishops.   Napoleon annexed Papal States. Pope excommunicated invaders (not Napoleon by name). Napoleon arrested Pope. Prisoner at Fontainebleau.

FINANCE UNDER THE EMPIRE:

(a) Land reassessed for taxation.
(b) Indirect taxes on tobacco and salt.
(c) Extraordinary Domain. Received indemnities and tributes. Paid expenses of new expeditions.

PRESS:

Censorship. Few papers. Official journal, *Le Moniteur*.

MATERIAL PROSPERITY:

No invasion. Machine industry. Improvement in agriculture. Declining prosperity when blockade was rigidly enforced.

19. THE NAPOLEONIC WARS—TO THE TREATY OF TILSIT

CAUSES OF RENEWAL OF WAR:

(1) Treaty of Amiens was a mere truce. Ill-feeling remained.
(2) Refusal of Great Britain to evacuate Malta.
(3) British alarm at growth of Napoleon's influence.
    (a) Napoleon annexed Piedmont.
    (b) Napoleon became President of the Cisalpine Republic (Italian Republic).
    (c) Swiss Confederation formed, in alliance with France.
    (d) Western part of Holy Roman Empire reorganised under French direction.
    (e) French troops in Batavian Republic.
(4) Napoleon's refusal to revive Anglo-French commercial treaty.
(5) Insulting references to Napoleon in the British press.
(6) British suspicion of Napoleon's designs upon Egypt.

THE WAR:

1803. Great Britain *v.* France.
1804. Great Britain *v.* Spain.

CHARACTER OF THE WAR:

In the French Revolutionary War Great Britain was on the side of despotic monarchies against a nation fighting for liberty.
In the Napoleonic Wars Great Britain was on the side of nations fighting for freedom and independence against the despotism of Napoleon.

EARLY MEASURES:

French occupied Hanover. Frederick William III, King of Prussia, protested. Great Britain blockaded Elbe and Weser, to the detriment of Prussian trade.

French troops in Neapolitan ports. Subsidies demanded by
France from Spain and Portugal. Troops from Dutch and
Swiss.

FRENCH PLAN OF INVASION:

Napoleon:

1804.   Army at Boulogne.

     British defence measures:
     Volunteer force raised.
     Martello towers built.
     Militia strengthened.
     Signalling system installed.
     Possible transfer of Government to Midlands.
     Preparation to evacuate invaded regions.

     French naval plan:
     Toulon fleet under Villeneuve to join Spanish fleet at Cadiz.
     To go to West Indies and join squadron escaped from
     Rochefort. Nelson to pursue, to defend West Indian colonies.
     Villeneuve to return to European waters, leaving Nelson in
     the West Indies. Villeneuve to join Brest fleet, to overpower
     British Channel fleet, and to convoy troops to England.

     Events (as differing from plan):

1805.   Villeneuve did not meet Rochefort squadron. Nelson did not
     wait in the West Indies. Warned Admiralty. Returned to
     the Channel. Villeneuve checked by Calder at the Battle
     of Cape Finisterre. Retreated towards Ferrol and Vigo.
     Thence to Cadiz. Brest fleet unable to escape blockade.
     French naval plan foiled.

1805.   Battle of Trafalgar; French and Spanish fleets destroyed.
     Nelson killed.

1805. THIRD COALITION:

     Austria
     Russia   }   *v.* France.
     Great Britain

     Events:

1805.   Austrian general, Mack, in Bavaria, awaited Russians. Napoleon
     attacked Mack at Ulm. Mack surrendered. Napoleon
     entered Vienna.
     Archduke Charles attacked the kingdom of Italy. Withdrew
     after Mack's defeat.
     Junction of Austrians with Russians. Bernadotte, from
     Hanover, joined Napoleon.
     Battle of Austerlitz; Napoleon defeated Austrians and Russians.

1805.   *Treaty of Pressburg:*
         (1) Austria to cede Venetia, Istria, and Dalmatia to France.
         (Austria retained Trieste.)
         (2) Austria to cede Tyrol to Bavaria.
         (3) Other lands ceded to Baden and Würtemberg.

VASSAL STATES:

Naples. Joseph Bonaparte, King. (Ferdinand continued to rule in Sicily.)
Lucca. Élise Bonaparte, Princess.
Holland. Louis Bonaparte, King.
Berg. Joachim Murat, Grand Duke.
Italy. Eugène de Beauharnais, Viceroy.

1806. CONFEDERATION OF THE RHINE:

Founded by Napoleon as a counterpoise to the power of Austria and Prussia.
Consisted of sixteen large states. Army of 63,000 to support Napoleon. Trained by French officers.
Confederation withdrew from Holy Roman Empire. Francis II dropped title of Holy Roman Emperor. Known henceforth as Francis I, Emperor of Austria.

1806. WAR WITH PRUSSIA:

Frederick William allied with Tsar. Required Napoleon to withdraw west of Rhine.
Napoleon marched against Prussia. Defeated Prussians at Battle of Jena. Davoust defeated Prussians at Battle of Auerstadt.
Fortresses surrendered. Napoleon entered Berlin.

1807. WAR WITH RUSSIA:

(Continuation of War of Third Coalition.)
Battle of Eylau; indecisive.
Battle of Friedland; Russians defeated.

1807. TREATY OF TILSIT:

(1) Prussia to lose lands west of the Elbe. These were to form a new kingdom of Westphalia, under Jerome Bonaparte.
(2) Prussia to lose Polish lands, except part of West Prussia. These were to form Grand Duchy of Warsaw.
(3) Prussia to pay war indemnity.
(4) Prussian army to be limited to 42,000 men.
(5) Alliance of France and Russia.
(6) Tsar agreed to support Continental System.

ZENITH OF NAPOLEON'S POWER:

Great Britain alone against France for the fourth time in ten years.

20. THE DECLINE OF NAPOLEON'S POWER

ECONOMIC WARFARE:

1806–7. *Continental System:*

Established by Napoleon as a means of overcoming Great Britain. Aimed at destroying British trade and making it impossible for Great Britain to maintain her navy.

(1) Blockade of British Isles.
(2) European ports closed to British trade.
(3) France and her allies forbidden to trade with Great Britain.
(4) Neutrals not to touch at a British port before reaching Continent.
(5) British merchandise to be destroyed.

1806–7. *Orders in Council:*

The British reply to the Continental System.
(1) Blockade of France and her allies.
(2) Neutrals forbidden to enter continental ports, and those on the way there were to be diverted to British ports.

Effects:

(1) Damage to British trade by the closing of European markets.
(2) Damage to British merchant shipping by privateers.

1807.
(3) British seizure of Danish fleet.
(4) Hardship on the Continent through the blockade.
(5) Smuggling into Europe.
(6) Growing unpopularity of Napoleon on the Continent.
(7) Napoleon issued licences permitting the import of certain classes of British goods.
(8) Irritation of neutrals, especially against Great Britain.

1808–14. PENINSULAR WAR:

Causes:

(1) Portugal refused to accept Continental System. French invasion.

1808.
(2) Spain. Napoleon deposed Charles IV and appointed Joseph Bonaparte to be King of Spain.

Events:

1808.
French under Dupont defeated at Baylen; 18,000 men captured.

1808.
Wellesley in command of British forces in Portugal. Battle of Vimiero; French under Junot defeated. Wellesley superseded on eve of battle by Burrard and Dalrymple. Convention of Cintra; Junot retired with spoils of war. Court-martial on the British generals. Wellesley acquitted and restored to his command.

1808.
Joseph Bonaparte in Madrid. Retreated north of the Ebro. Napoleon entered Spain and reached Madrid. Moore (commanding British in absence of Wellesley) retreated to Corunna.

1809.
Moore pursued by Soult. Battle of Corunna; French defeated, but Moore was slain.

1809.
French captured Saragossa. Soult captured Oporto. Wellesley recovered Oporto. Threatened Soult's communications. Soult retreated into Spain with loss of fifty-eight guns. Wellesley invaded Spain. Battle of Talavera; Wellesley defeated Victor and King Joseph. Wellesley retired into Portugal.

1810.
Lines of Torres Vedras constructed. Masséna marched towards Lisbon. Checked by the lines.

1811.   Wellesley (now Viscount Wellington) defeated Masséna at
             Fuentes d'Onoro. Beresford besieged Badajos. Beresford
             defeated Soult at Albuera. Retreated into Portugal for the
             winter.
1812.   British captured Ciudad Rodrigo and Badajos. French
             weakened by withdrawal of troops for Russian campaign.
             Wellington in Spain. Battle of Salamanca; Wellington
             defeated Marmont and entered Madrid. Retired to Ciudad
             Rodrigo for the winter.
1813.   Joseph retired behind the Ebro. Battle of Vittoria; Wellington
             defeated Joseph and Marshal Jourdan, who lost 150 guns.
             Soult replaced Jourdan. Wellington captured San Sebastian
             and Pampeluna.
1814.   Wellington (a duke) invaded France. Defeated Soult at
             Orthez and Toulouse.

1809. AUSTRIAN WAR:

   Cause :

   Austrian hope that Napoleon could not spare large forces for
   another war.

   Events :

   Napoleon occupied Vienna. Austrian army under Archduke
   Charles north of the Danube.

   Battle of Aspern; Napoleon's attempt to cross the Danube
   checked.

   Battle of Wagram; Napoleon defeated Charles, who retired in
   good order.

1809.   *Treaty of Vienna :*

   (a) Austria to pay indemnity.
   (b) Austrian army limited to 150,000 men.
   (c) Austria to cede Galicia to Grand Duchy of Warsaw.
   (d) Austria to cede Illyrian provinces (Carniola, Trieste, and
       Fiume, and parts of Carinthia and Croatia) to France.

1810.   Napoleon married Marie Louise, daughter of Francis I, Emperor
        of Austria.

1812. RUSSIAN WAR:

   Causes :

   (1) Friction between Alexander and Napoleon.
       (a) Addition of Galicia to Grand Duchy of Warsaw.
       (b) French annexation of Oldenburg.
   (2) Alexander's refusal to enforce the Continental System.

   Preparations :

   Russia:
       (a) Made peace with Turkey.
       (b) Made agreement with Sweden (Bernadotte).

   Napoleon:
       (a) Treaty with Prussia; 20,000 men to serve under French
           orders.

(b) Treaty with Austria; 30,000 men to serve under Austrian command; promise that Illyrian provinces should be restored.

(c) Concentration of army of 600,000 men (100,000 cavalry) in eastern Germany.

(d) Depots of food.

Events:

Invasion of Russia.

Difficulties:

Commissariat broke down.

Desertion and sickness.

Horses affected by Russian pasture.

Russian army under Barclay de Tolly retreated. Napoleon hoped to overtake Barclay before he could be joined by Bagration. Barclay and Bagration met at Smolensk. Barclay continued to retreat. Napoleon reached Smolensk.

Kutusoff replaced Barclay. Resolved to fight. Battle of Borodino. Heavy losses. Napoleon continued his march.

Napoleon reached Moscow. City deserted. Fires.

Kutusoff opened negotiations, really in order to detain Napoleon till winter.

French retreated. Southerly route barred. Return by same route as was followed in the invasion. Russian attacks. Ney and the rearguard. Battle of the Beresina. Napoleon left army and hastened to France. Remnant of army under Murat recrossed Niemen. Loss of over half a million men.

1813. FOURTH COALITION:

Great Britain ⎫
Russia ⎪
Prussia ⎬ *v.* France.
Austria (after Bautzen) ⎭

1813. WAR OF LIBERATION:

The position:

Napoleon still powerful.

Confederation of the Rhine ⎫
Italy ⎬ faithful to him.

Austria had not yet broken with him.

Events:

Battle of Lützen. Napoleon defeated Russians and Prussians.

Battle of Bautzen. Napoleon defeated Russians and Prussians. Austria offered mediation and, upon its rejection, joined Coalition.

Battle of Dresden. Napoleon defeated allies. Allied armies concentrated upon Leipzig.

Battle of Leipzig. Napoleon defeated by the allies. Fled into France.

Losses in 1813 as heavy as those in 1812.

1814.   *The position:*

Austria recovered Illyrian provinces.

Holland in revolt.

Collapse of Confederation of the Rhine and of kingdom of Westphalia.

Eugène de Beauharnais driven from Italy.

Allies offered terms of peace:

(a) Rhine boundary for France.

(b) Napoleon to recognise independence of Germany, Italy, Spain, and Holland.

Napoleon refused terms.

1814.   *Invasion of France:*

(1) Wellington, from Spain.

(2) Schwarzenberg (Austrians), from Switzerland.

(3) Blücher (Prussians), from the Rhine.

Allies did not co-operate well. Napoleon fought several battles. Defeated Blücher on the Marne. Allies pressed on to Paris.

1814.   FALL OF NAPOLEON:

Deposed by Senate. Abdicated a few days later. Permitted to retire to Elba as "Emperor." Louis XVIII restored.

1814.   FIRST TREATY OF PARIS:

Terms:

(1) French boundaries of 1st January, 1792. (Avignon retained.)

(2) Great Britain restored French colonies, except Mauritius, Seychelles, Tobago, and St. Lucia.

(3) Balance of Prussian indemnity under the Treaty of Tilsit was cancelled.

(4) No indemnity from France; no army of occupation; no demand for restoration of works of art.

Criticism:

(a) France, though defeated, was larger than before the war.

(b) France had enforced payment of indemnities and tributes; yet no indemnity was demanded.

(c) France had tried to destroy British commerce; yet French colonies were restored.

1814-15. CONGRESS OF VIENNA:

To settle the affairs of Europe.

1815.   THE HUNDRED DAYS:

Napoleon's return:

Napoleon landed in south of France. Welcomed. Reached Paris. Louis XVIII fled. Napoleon again Emperor. Asked for peace. Stated that he would honour the Treaty of Paris.

Allies refused to agree. Alliance renewed. Each power to contribute 150,000 men. Double attack arranged:

British and Prussians from north-east.

Austrians and Russians from east.

The Campaign:

Napoleon with 120,000 men. Marched towards Netherlands. Aimed at preventing junction of British and Prussians. Ney attacked Wellington at Quatre Bras, while Napoleon defeated Blücher at Ligny and compelled him to retreat.

Wellington defeated Ney, but, on account of Blücher's retirement, was compelled to fall back to Waterloo.

Blücher's retreat was parallel to Wellington's. Grouchy pursued Blücher, but could not prevent junction at Waterloo.

Battle of Waterloo; Napoleon hoped to break British left before junction could be made with Prussians. Prussians arrived. General British advance. French ranks broke. Pursuit by Prussian cavalry.

Napoleon fled to Paris. Thence to Rochefort. Surrendered to the *Bellerophon.* St. Helena.

1815. SECOND TREATY OF PARIS:

(1) French boundaries of 1790, but including Avignon.
(2) France to pay indemnity of £28,000,000.
(3) France to receive army of occupation of 150,000 men.
(4) Works of art to be restored.

CAUSES OF NAPOLEON'S FALL:

(1) Possible decline in his military capacity.
(2) Exhaustion of France. Enormous losses in the Peninsula, in Russia, and in the War of Liberation.
(3) National enthusiasm and determination aroused in conquered countries.
(4) British naval strength:
  (a) Blockade of Continent.
  (b) Development of British industry and trade. Increase of wealth.
  (c) Enemy colonies captured.
  (d) Communications with Peninsula.

SOME RESULTS OF NAPOLEON'S RULE:

(1) Encouraged growth of military strength among European powers in the nineteenth century.
(2) Disappearance of feudalism in many parts of Europe.
(3) Widespread adoption of the *Code Napoléon.*
(4) Sound government.
(5) Spirit of nationality aroused.

21. PRUSSIA, 1740-1815

1740–86. FREDERICK II, THE GREAT:

Typical eighteenth-century monarch.
(1) Disregard of rights of weaker neighbours.
(2) Benevolent despotism. No democracy.
(3) Agnosticism. Philosophy. Decay of religious belief.

1740–63. FIRST HALF OF REIGN:
>Wars of the Austrian Succession and Seven Years.

1763–86. SECOND HALF OF REIGN:
>*Foreign affairs:*
>>Mainly peaceful. No alliance with Great Britain.
>>*Russia:*
>>>Alliance continued till 1781.
>>*Poland:*

1772.
>>>First Partition. Frederick gained West Prussia, Ermeland, and Kulmerland.
>>>Important to Frederick, because:
>>>>(1) Stretch of Baltic coast.
>>>>(2) Increase of population.
>>>>(3) Linking up of Brandenburg and East Prussia.
>>*Bavaria:*
>>>Joseph II wanted:
>>>>(1) To annex Bavaria. Frederick opposed.
>>>>(2) To exchange Bavaria for Netherlands. Frederick again opposed. Emperor gave way by Treaty of Teschen, and Charles Theodore, Elector Palatine, became Elector of Bavaria.
>>>>(3) To offer the exchange to Charles Theodore, with title of King of Burgundy. Frederick sent protests to the powers and the project was dropped.

1785.
>>*Fürstenbund:*
>>>League of German princes to defend Imperial constitution.
>*Internal Reforms:*
>>*Restoration after war:*
>>>Towns and villages rebuilt.
>>>Farms restocked.
>>>War horses for agriculture.
>>>Coinage restored.
>>*New development:*
>>>Waste lands cultivated.
>>>Land drainage.
>>>Communications.
>>*Finance:*
>>>Heavy taxation.
>>>Treasure in reserve.
>>>Remissions of taxation in certain districts.
>>*Law:*
>>>Codification.
>>>Courts reorganised.
>>*Immigration.*
>*Defects of Frederick's rule:*
>>(1) No attempt to diminish social distinctions.
>>(2) Excessive personal supervision in administration—no room for initiative of officials. System bound to collapse after his death.

1786–97. FREDERICK WILLIAM II:

Nephew of Frederick the Great. Less capable ruler. Less attention to business of state. Growing weakness of the state

Foreign affairs:

Holland:

1787. Frederick William intervened to restore Stadtholder.
1788. Triple Alliance of Great Britain, Prussia, Holland to support Stadtholder.

French Revolution:

1791. Declaration of Pillnitz.
1792–5. War with France. Little co-operation with Austrians. Treaty of Basel.

Poland:

1793. Second Partition. Prussia gained Danzig, Posen, Thorn.
1795. Third Partition. Warsaw, and region south and west of Niemen.

1797–1840. FREDERICK WILLIAM III:

At peace with France for some years. Took no part in the War of the Second Coalition.

Internal reforms:

(*a*) Improved condition of serfs.
(*b*) Reforms in government of provinces.
(*c*) Tariffs rearranged.
(*d*) Some internal customs abolished.

Third Coalition:

1805. French troops crossed Anspach without permission. Frederick William negotiated with the Tsar, but after French victory at Austerlitz he allied with France and occupied Hanover.
Napoleon negotiated with Great Britain and offered to restore Hanover. Insult to Frederick William, who required Napoleon to withdraw west of the Rhine.

1806. *War with France:*

Battle of Jena; Napoleon defeated Prussians.
Battle of Auerstadt; Davoust defeated Prussians.
Fortresses surrendered. Napoleon entered Berlin.
Frederick William retired to East Prussia.

1807. *Treaty of Tilsit:*

(1) Prussia lost lands west of the Elbe.
(2) Prussia lost gains from Partitions of Poland (except West Prussia).
(3) Indemnity.
(4) Army of occupation.
(5) Prussian army limited to 42,000 men.

REORGANISATION OF PRUSSIA:

By Stein:

(*a*) Serfdom abolished.

(b) Class distinctions relaxed. Citizens could hold commissions and could purchase lands of nobles. Nobles could engage in trade.

(c) Town councils elected. Controlled some features of local government.

(d) State Council of Ministers established.

(e) Civil Service improved.

By Hardenberg:

(a) Peasants fully freed from control of lords. One-third of lands of peasants surrendered to lords as compensation.

(b) Reform of finance.

(c) Industry freed from gild control.

By Humboldt:

(a) Reform of public schools.

(b) Established University of Berlin.

By Scharnhorst and Gneisenau:

(a) Incompetent officers removed from the army.

(b) Conditions of army service improved. Citizens enlisted. Discipline maintained by imprisonment instead of flogging.

(c) Short service system. Large reserve army built up.

WAR OF 1812:

Prussia forced to assist Napoleon with 20,000 men. Prussians under Yorck served under Marshal Macdonald at siege of Riga. After French retreat Yorck came to terms with Russians. Frederick William endorsed Yorck's action.

1813-15. WARS OF LIBERATION AND HUNDRED DAYS:

Prussia took part in the battles in Saxony and at Leipzig. Invaded France and assisted in the first overthrow of Napoleon. Blücher at Waterloo.

1815. CONGRESS OF VIENNA:

Prussia recovered much of her lost territory, though most of the Polish lands remained Russian, and Prussia received other lands as compensation.
Prussia once more a great power.

22. THE CONGRESS OF VIENNA

THE CONGRESS:

All great powers and most smaller powers represented by sovereigns or statesmen. Metternich was President. Great influence over the Congress. Work of Congress done through Committees. Some powers already committed to secret agreements.

ITS AIMS:

(1) To settle the affairs of Europe. Impossibility of returning to pre-war conditions.

(2) To establish a ring of strong states round France.

(3) To reward the opponents of France and to punish her allies.

(4) To base its decisions on the principle of "legitimacy," i.e., the restoration of "rightful" rulers.

But: (a) Holy Roman Empire could not be restored.

(b) Congress disliked republics and would not restore Genoa and Venice.

(5) To secure permanent peace by discouraging revolutionary movements.

TERRITORIAL ARRANGEMENTS:

(1) German Confederation formed, under leadership of Austria. Metternich opposed suggestions for closer union.

(2) Austria recovered Lombardy and Venetia. (She had already recovered Illyrian provinces.)

(3) Ex-Empress Marie Louise received Parma.

(4) Prussia recovered her Rhenish lands and received Cologne and Trier, Swedish Pomerania, and part of Saxony. Most of the Prussian share of Polish territory was left in the hands of Russia.

(5) Russia retained her Polish lands and Finland.

(6) Sweden received Norway.

(7) Holland received Belgium (Austrian Netherlands).

(8) Swiss Confederation restored, with three cantons added to it.

(9) Sardinia recovered Piedmont, Nice, and Savoy, and received Genoa.

(10) Kings of Naples and Spain restored.

(11) Pope recovered States of the Church.

(12) Great Britain retained some of her colonial conquests, including Malta, Mauritius, and Cape of Good Hope. Great Britain paid £6,000,000 to Holland as compensation.

(13) Hanover recognised as a kingdom.

N.B. (a) Prussia became natural protector of Germany against France.

(b) France hemmed in on the east by four powers, Dutch, Prussian, Swiss, and Piedmontese.

CRITICISM OF THE ARRANGEMENTS:

Con:

Made in the interests of sovereigns and not of nations.

Belgium resented connection with Holland.

Norway resented connection with Sweden.

Poles wanted independence.

Germans wanted unity.

Italians wanted unity.

Much of the work of the Congress was undone during the nineteenth century.

Pro:

Peace was maintained in Europe for forty years.

SLAVE TRADE:

1807.   France, Spain, and Holland agreed to its abolition. (Great Britain had already abolished it.)

THE BARBARY CORSAIRS:

1816.   The Congress approved of measures against them. British fleet under Lord Exmouth bombarded Algiers. Released a large number of Christian slaves.

1815. THE HOLY ALLIANCE:

Proposed by the Tsar. Supported by Metternich. Consisted of Russia, Prussia, and Austria. Great Britain refused to join.

Aim:

Nominal:

To direct European affairs on Christian principles.

Real:

To suppress revolutionary movements and maintain absolute monarchy everywhere in Europe. It was thought that revolutionary movements were likely to lead to war and that they were unchristian. (But the Alliance was not intended by the Tsar as an instrument of repression.)

BRITISH FOREIGN POLICY:

To oppose the absolutism favoured by the Holy Alliance. Policy of non-intervention. Each state to settle its internal affairs without interference.

Castlereagh protested against intervention by the Holy Alliance.

Canning was ready to intervene in order to neutralise the intervention of the Holy Alliance.

THE QUADRUPLE ALLIANCE:

Consisted of Great Britain and the three eastern powers.

Aims:

(1) To maintain the Treaty of Paris.

(2) To meet from time to time in congresses to settle matters of importance in Europe.

Great Britain was not committed to the support of a definite line of policy at these congresses.

23. THE BREAK-UP OF THE CONCERT OF EUROPE

1818. CONGRESS OF AACHEN:

No serious dissension.

Army of occupation withdrawn from France.

France invited to join the Quadruple Alliance. The inclusion of France changed the original aim of the Alliance (which was, substantially, to limit French power).

Tsar proposed:
  (1) That the Quadruple Alliance should undertake general supervision of European affairs.
  (2) That periodic congresses should be held.
Great Britain:
  (1) Opposed interference in internal affairs of other states.
  (2) Agreed to send representatives to congresses summoned for specific purposes. Opposed periodic meetings.

SPAIN:

Constitution of 1812 annulled by Ferdinand VII.
1820. Revolt of Riego at Cadiz. Spread to north of Spain. Demand for restoration of constitution. Granted by Ferdinand VII.

NAPLES:

Discontent:
  Administration corrupt.
  Peasants oppressed.
  Army administration unsatisfactory.
Carbonari. Secret society with revolutionary aims.
1820. Revolt. Encouraged by example of Spain. Demanded Spanish constitution of 1812. Granted by Ferdinand I.

1820. CONGRESS OF TROPPAU:

Summoned by Metternich, who was more alarmed at Neapolitan than at Spanish rising.
Issue of the Protocol of Troppau. The powers claimed the right to intervene in countries where revolts had broken out. Castlereagh protested.

1821. CONGRESS OF LAIBACH:

Ferdinand I of Naples present. Disregarded oath to maintain constitution. Congress authorised Austria to suppress constitutional movement in Naples. Ferdinand again absolute.

PIEDMONT:

Victor Emmanuel I absolute.
1821. Constitutional movement. Demanded Spanish constitution of 1812. Victor Emmanuel abdicated. Charles Felix became King. In his absence Charles Albert acted as regent. Granted constitution. Charles Felix returned and annulled it. Austrians invaded Piedmont and defeated revolutionists at Battle of Novara.

1822. CONGRESS OF VERONA:

Authorised French intervention to restore absolutism in Spain.

SPAIN:

1823. French invaded Spain. Defeated Constitutional party. Ferdinand VII again absolute. Reprisals.

SPANISH COLONIES:

1823.
In revolt since 1809. Holy Alliance intervention threatened. Canning recognised independence of South American republics. President James Monroe, of the United States, issued the Monroe Doctrine—that the United States did not admit that there was any further field in America for colonial extension by European powers. Holy Alliance protested, but took no further action.

PORTUGAL:

1820. Constitutional movement.
John VI in Brazil.

1821. John returned to Portugal. Granted constitution. Miguel, the King's second son, supported by the French, opposed the constitution. Revolted. Canning sent fleet to the Tagus. Miguel's revolt collapsed.

1822. Brazil became independent of Portugal, with Pedro, John's eldest son, as Emperor.

1825. John VI died. Pedro granted new constitution to Portugal and then resigned Portuguese crown to his daughter Maria.
Miguel attempted to secure throne. British assistance to the party of Maria, which was victorious.

24. METTERNICH AND THE GERMAN CONFEDERATION

GERMAN CONFEDERATION:

Thirty-eight states.

Diet:
To meet at Frankfort under Austrian presidency. Represented state rulers. More votes to large states than to smaller.
Minor matters settled by majority vote.
Important matters settled by two-thirds vote.
Constitutional matters settled by unanimous vote.

States:
Independent in most respects. But:
(a) Might not wage war against other members of Confederation.
(b) Might not make treaties with foreign powers against other members.
(c) Bound to support Confederation when it was at war.

Policy of smaller states:
To maintain independence, and to guard against encroachments by Austria and Prussia. They opposed suggestions for strengthening the Confederation.

Non-German interests of rulers:
Austria: Large part of dominions outside Confederation.
Hanover: Great Britain.
Holstein: Denmark.

Luxemburg: Holland.
Prussia: East Prussia.
Questions affecting Germany might be settled in accordance
with the non-German interests of members of the Diet.

GERMAN NATIONAL FEELING:

Many German patriots hoped for the formation of a single state,
based on nationality and language.
But: (1) Rulers of lesser states were certain to oppose.
      (2) Prussia not yet strong enough to achieve German unity.
      (3) Austria had extensive non-German interests.

METTERNICH:

Austrian Chancellor. Maintained despotic government and
opposed all change.

In Austria:
Diversity of races. Could be ruled only by the prevention
of reforms.
(a) Censorship of the press.
(b) Exclusion of foreigners of Liberal opinions.
(c) Control of university teaching.
(d) Suppressing revolutionary movements.

In the German Confederation:
Similar system.

1817.	Wartburg Festival.
1819.	Murder of Kotzebue.
	Metternich alarmed. Called meeting of state representatives at Carlsbad.
1819.	*Carlsbad Decrees:*

    Drawn up at Carlsbad. Sanctioned by Diet at Frankfort.
Enforced rigidly.
(a) University teaching under close inspection.
(b) Professors and students to be expelled if they showed
dangerous tendencies.
(c) Student associations forbidden without permission.
(d) Strict control of press.
(e) Special commissions to seek out traces of conspiracy.

LIBERAL ACTIVITY IN GERMANY AFTER 1830:

Constitutions in a few states, e.g. Hanover and Saxony.
(a) Press restrictions reduced.
(b) Trial by jury.
(c) Rulers retained much personal power.

STRENGTHENING OF METTERNICH'S SYSTEM AFTER 1830:

(a) Political societies and meetings forbidden.
(b) Press restrictions renewed throughout the Confederation.
(c) Control of universities strengthened.

1818. ZOLLVEREIN:

Customs Union under Prussian leadership. Internal customs abolished. Revenue divided in proportion to population of states in Union. Many North German states joined.

Other customs unions formed under Saxony and Bavaria, but these merged into Zollverein. Austria not a member.

PRUSSIA:

Little agitation for constitution in lifetime of Frederick William III.

1840. Frederick William III died. Frederick William IV became King. Released political prisoners. Relaxed censorship. Growing demand for Prussian Parliament.

1847. Provincial Assemblies summoned to meet together as a United Diet. Limited power. Liberals disappointed. Petitioned King to establish a really representative Parliament.

25. THE RESTORED MONARCHY IN FRANCE

CHARACTER OF THE RESTORATION:

Restoration of the Bourbon monarchy. Not a restoration of the *ancien régime*.

1814. THE CHARTER:

The constitution of France till 1848.

(1) Government in hands of King. Powers exercised by ministers. (King not a nonentity.)

(a) Command of army and navy.

(b) War and treaties.

(c) Appointments to public service and to Chamber of Peers.

(d) The proposing of legislation.

(2) Legislature:

(a) Chamber of Peers. Some hereditary nobles and some members appointed by King.

(b) Chamber of Deputies. Elected for five years.

Members had to be forty years old and to pay 1,000 francs per annum in direct taxes.

Electors had to be thirty years old and to pay 300 francs per annum in direct taxes.

Laws to be proposed by Crown.

No tax to be levied without consent of Legislature.

(3) Other provisions:

(i) Trial by jury.

(ii) Freedom of press.

(iii) Titles to property confirmed.

(iv) Religious toleration.

(v) Napoleonic nobility recognised.

Importance of the Charter:
    (1) Accepted much of the work of the Revolution and the Empire.
    (2) Not inconsistent with Divine Right. Granted by Crown; not forced upon Crown.

PARTIES:

Ultra-Royalists:
    Returned *émigrés*. More royalist than the King. Not conspicuously loyal. Led by Count of Artois.
    Aims:
        (1) Recovery of ancient noble privileges.
        (2) Acquisition of political power by nobles.
    Methods:
        (1) Charter a starting point. Violations and strained interpretations.
        (2) Revival of power of Church.
        (3) Suppression of freedom of the press.
Moderates:
    Loyal to Crown. Aimed at maintaining Charter. Several groups. Ineffective, on account of divisions.
Left:
    Republicans, Bonapartists, etc. Small representation in Chamber.

THE KINGS:

1814–24. *Louis XVIII:*
    Moderate. Little sympathy with Ultras.
1824–30. *Charles X:*
    Extreme.
1830–48. *Louis Philippe:*
    The Bourgeois King.

MINISTERS:

1815–18. *Richelieu:*
    Moderate. Ultra majority in first Chamber of Deputies but not in Chamber of Peers. King and Richelieu tried to restrain Ultras. Amnesty Bill passed (though Ney was shot). New electoral law, which would have strengthened Ultras, was rejected by Peers. Ultras proposed partial repudiation of Napoleonic debt. Chamber dissolved.
1818.   New Chamber. Moderate majority. War indemnity paid off. Army of occupation withdrawn.
    New electoral law passed, advantageous to Moderates. Growing strength of Left. Richelieu resigned.
1818–20. *Decazes:*
1819.   Press law. Censorship abolished. Trial by jury instituted for press cases. Moderates alarmed. Some veered round to Ultras.
1820.   Murder of Duke of Berry. Advantage to Ultras. Decazes resigned.

1820–1. *Richelieu:*

Electoral law revised, to advantage of Ultras. Press censorship restored.

1821–7. *Villèle:*

Reactionary, but cautious and able.

Vigorous foreign policy, to distract popular attention from restrictions on liberty. Expedition into Spain.

Press censorship strengthened.

New tariff.

Public education under control of university.

After accession of Charles X, compensation in the form of pensions was given to *émigrés* for the loss of their lands by reducing rate of interest on National Debt and using the money thus saved for this purpose.

Jesuits permitted to return.

Villèle lost confidence of extremists on both sides. Resigned.

1828–9. *Martignac:*

Hostile majority in Chamber of Deputies. Policy of conciliation. Press law modified. Jesuit activity limited.

Failed to win confidence of extremists. Fell.

1829–30. *Polignac:*

Policy of reaction. Chamber of Deputies petitioned King to dismiss Polignac. King dissolved Chamber. New Chamber had larger majority against Polignac.

1830. REVOLUTION:

(July). *Ordinances:*

Issued by the King.

(a) No newspapers without assent of Government.

(b) Recent elections annulled.

(c) Electoral law altered.

(d) Date of new elections fixed.

Revolt:

By deputies, journalists, and workmen. Barricades in Paris. Fighting. Troops withdrawn.

Provisional Government:

Louis Philippe, Duke of Orleans, appointed Lieutenant-General of the Kingdom.

Charles X withdrew ordinances. Too late. Abdicated. Louis Philippe became King.

Results:

(1) No more Divine Right.

(2) Very slight changes in the constitution.

(3) Ultras no longer powerful.

(4) Reversal of one feature of Vienna settlement.

EARLY LIFE OF LOUIS PHILIPPE:

Fought for France at Valmy and Jemappes. Travelled in many countries. Returned to France at Bourbon restoration. Recovered estates. Entered Chamber of Peers. Liberal opinions. Association with bourgeois and even with workmen.

CONSTITUTIONAL CHANGES AT ACCESSION:

(1) Royal power to make ordinances restricted.
(2) Chambers could propose legislation.
(3) Press censorship abolished.
(4) Slight extension of franchise.

Monarchy depended on support of bourgeois (wealthy traders and manufacturers). Opposed by working classes.

PARTIES:

Progressive:
(1) Aimed at democratic and social reform at home.
(2) Vigorous foreign policy on behalf of oppressed peoples.

Conservative:
Opposed to changes in direction of democracy.

Legitimists:
Schemed for accession of Count of Chambord.

Bonapartists:
Cultivated the " Napoleonic legend."

Republicans:
Wanted a republic.

DISTURBANCES:

Legitimist attempt in La Vendée.
Republican outbreaks in Paris and at Lyons.
Strikes.
Attempts to assassinate the King.

REPRESSION:

(a) Government sanction required for associations.
(b) Censorship of press.
(c) Prosecution of journalists.
(d) New courts and new offences.

NAPOLEONIC LEGEND:

Glorification of Napoleon. A hero, and a regenerator of society. Contrast of Orleanist with Napoleonic régime.
Yet Louis Philippe patronised the movement.
Arc de Triomphe completed.
Streets named after Napoleon's battles.
1840.   Reburial of Napoleon's body in Paris.

FOREIGN POLICY:

Not consistent. Vigorous foreign policy necessary to conciliate people. Yet it would arouse the apprehensions of the powers.

Thiers:
Advocated strong policy. Louis Philippe supported Mehemet Ali in his quarrel with the Sultan. Quadruple Alliance supported Sultan. France isolated. Thiers wanted war, 1840.   but Louis Philippe drew back. Thiers fell.

O 1643–1848

Guizot:

1846.
Favoured peace. Friendly relations with Great Britain. Louis Philippe's double-dealing in the question of the Spanish marriages. Lost friendship of Great Britain. Gained no prestige at home or abroad.

GROWTH OF ABSOLUTISM:

Control of Chamber of Deputies by corrupt means. Limited franchise. Many deputies and electors held official posts.

INDUSTRIAL REVOLUTION:

Extension of factory system. Working classes suffered from long hours, low wages, unsatisfactory conditions, labour of children.

Socialism propounded by Proudhon, Leroux, and Louis Blanc. Workers discontented because of their exclusion from political power.

1848. REVOLUTION:

(Feb.). "Reform banquets" forbidden by the Government.

Rioting in Paris. Barricades. Troops refused to fire. Louis Philippe alarmed. Concessions. Guizot retired. Street fighting. Demand for a republic. Louis Philippe abdicated.

CAUSES OF FALL OF LOUIS PHILIPPE:

(1) Reliance for support upon one class, the bourgeois, which had no right or fitness to control state. More interested in acquisition of wealth than of political power.

(2) No programme of political and social reform; this was left to the Republicans.

(3) No vigorous foreign policy. Bonapartists profited by French desire for glory.

26. BELGIAN INDEPENDENCE

EARLIER HISTORY OF THE NETHERLANDS:

In Middle Ages:

Seventeen provinces under Burgundy and, later, under Spain.

1572–   *Revolt:*

1609.
Southern provinces recovered by Spain. Became Spanish Netherlands (Belgium).

Northern provinces became independent. Became United Provinces (Holland).

Spanish Netherlands:

Became Austrian Netherlands after 1713.

United Provinces:

Aristocratic republic under Prince of Orange as Stadtholder.

French conquest:

During the French Revolutionary War. Austrian Netherlands added to France. United Provinces became Batavian Republic. Afterwards, Kingdom of Holland under Louis Bonaparte.

1814. KINGDOM OF HOLLAND:

Under Prince of Orange as King, with extensive powers. States-General possessed certain rights.

1815. CONGRESS OF VIENNA:

Added Belgium to Holland, to form a strong state north-east of France.

DIFFERENCES BETWEEN BELGIUM AND HOLLAND:

(1) Language.
(2) Religion. Belgians Catholic; Dutch Protestant.
(3) Dutch were a colonising and commercial race; Belgians were mining and manufacturing.
(4) Belgians outnumbered Dutch.
(5) Dutch inclined to despise Belgians.

CONSTITUTION OF UNITED KINGDOM:

States-General established. Fifty-five members from each part of the kingdom, despite difference of population.

BELGIAN GRIEVANCES:

(1) Exclusion from most official posts.
(2) States-General met regularly at The Hague—never in Belgium.
(3) Government able to control States-General. Belgians unable to exert effective influence.
(4) The official language was Dutch.
(5) Debt burden of the two countries very unequal; taxation spread uniformly over the kingdom.
(6) New taxes on flour and meat.
(7) Determination of the Government to control education; Catholic bishops wanted to direct it.

ADVANTAGES OF UNION TO THE BELGIANS:

Dutch colonies provided markets for Belgian manufactured goods.

1830. THE REVOLT:

Exhibition at Brussels. News of the July Revolution in Paris caused outbreak. Prince of Orange (King's eldest son) unable to conciliate rebels.
Army of 10,000 men sent to Brussels. Driven out. Retired to Antwerp.
National Congress met. Declared Belgium to be independent.

ATTITUDE OF THE POWERS:

Holy Alliance interested at this time in Polish affairs and could not intervene.

Great Britain and France well-disposed to Belgium.

Conference at London. Powers recognised Belgian independence.

Crown offered to Duke of Nemours; unacceptable to Great Britain. Then to Leopold of Saxe-Coburg; accepted.

STRUGGLE:

1831. Dutch invaded Belgium. French sent army against Dutch. French and Dutch at length withdrew from Belgium, but Dutch retained Antwerp for some years.

1839. Antwerp taken from the Dutch.

1839. TREATY OF LONDON:

Belgian independence and neutrality recognised by all the powers, including Holland.

27. ITALY IN THE FIRST HALF OF THE NINETEENTH CENTURY

ITALY:

Apparently well situated for the attainment of unity and independence. Good natural boundaries.

Under the rule of other powers for many centuries.

Italian nationality persisted:
  (a) Common language and religion.
  (b) Recollection of greatness of ancient Rome.

Effects of Napoleon's conquests:
  (a) Swept away petty despotisms.
  (b) Efficient government.
  (c) Italy under only three Governments, all directed by Napoleon. Approximation to unity.

1815. VIENNA SETTLEMENT:

Restoration of old divisions. Disappointment of Italian patriots.

The Two Sicilies:
  Society feudal. Government corrupt. People lazy and ignorant.

Papal States:
  Included Romagna, Ancona, Umbria, and the Patrimony of St. Peter. Government corrupt, oppressive, and incompetent.

Tuscany:
  Grand Duchy. Under a Hapsburg prince. Ruled well.

Lucca:
  Small duchy.

Parma:

Ruled by the ex-Empress Marie Louise. French system of government retained.

Modena:

Reactionary rule. Under a Hapsburg prince.

Lombardy and Venetia:

Austrian rule. Efficient, but autocratic.

Piedmont and Savoy:

Part of the kingdom of Sardinia.

N.B. Republican institutions were not restored in Genoa, Lucca, and Venice.

THE PROBLEM:

To secure unity and constitutional government.

DIFFICULTIES:

(1) Opposition of all state rulers.

(2) People ignorant and superstitious.

(3) Opposition of Austria. Strong. Claimed right to control the peninsula.

(4) Opposition of the Pope. Military power slight. Spiritual penalties. Catholic opinion elsewhere.

REPRESSION:

(1) Newspapers censored (but newspapers had little influence, as people were illiterate).

(2) Public meetings suppressed.

STAGES IN THE MOVEMENT:

(1) *The Carbonari:*

Secret society in kingdom of Naples. Spread throughout Italy. All classes of people included. Not well organised, but kept the revolutionary spirit alive.

(2) *Naples and Piedmont:*

1820.   Risings. Lack of support and of sound leadership. Movements crushed by Austria. More thorough preparation needed.

(3) *Central Italy:*

1831.   Rulers of Parma and Modena expelled. Rising in Papal States. Suppressed by Austria. The failure of these efforts proved that merely local risings were useless.

(4) *Literary men:*

Mazzini. Inspired the movement for Italian unity and independence. Founded the society of Young Italy, which aimed at expelling the Austrians from Italy and establishing an Italian Republic.

Gioberti. *The Moral and Civil Primacy of the Italians.*
Advocated the expulsion of the Austrians and the establishment of a federation of Italian states under the Pope. (But the Papal States were badly governed.)

Other writers. Advocated the annexation of other states by Piedmont.

1846.   (5) *Pius IX:*

At first inclined towards Liberalism. Released political prisoners. Permitted establishment of a civil guard in Rome.

1847.   His example followed in other states. In Piedmont, press
1848.   censorship abolished. Constitutions granted in Piedmont and Naples.

Pope withdrew concessions. Retired to Gaeta. Republics in Rome and Tuscany.

Republics overthrown. Pope restored by the French, who left a garrison in Rome.

1848.   (6) *Lombardo-Venetian rising:*
Tobacco riots in Milan. Order restored.

Venetia, under Manin, proclaimed itself a republic.

Lombardy invaded by Piedmontese, who received assistance from Liberals in Tuscany, Papal States, and Naples. Radetzky, the Austrian governor, abandoned Milan and retired to the Quadrilateral. Waited for dissensions to develop among the Italians. Troops from central and southern Italy soon withdrawn.

1848.   Radetzky defeated Charles Albert at Custozza. Austrians recovered Lombardy. Armistice.

1849.   Renewed fighting between Austria and Piedmont. Battle of Novara; Austrians defeated Charles Albert, who abdicated. Piedmontese constitution remained.

28. RUSSIA

IN MIDDLE AGES:

Russia under Mongol and Tartar control.

14th c.   House of Rurik overthrew Tartar domination.
1533–84. Ivan the Terrible. Assumed title of Tsar.
1598.   House of Rurik ended.

1613–45. MICHAEL ROMANOFF:

Russia Asiatic rather than European. No access to Baltic or Black Sea.

1645–76. ALEXIUS:

1655–67. *War with Poland:*
Russian successes.

1667.   *Treaty of Andrussowa:*
Russian boundary extended to Dnieper.

The Patriarch Nikon:
  Maintained equality with civil power. Contest with Tsar.
  Tsar successful. Patriarch deposed.

1676–82. THEODORE III:

1682–1725. PETER THE GREAT:
  Foreign:
    Aim:
      Outlet to the west.
    Black Sea:
1696.   Capture of Azov.
    Baltic Sea:
      Peter's visit to the west. Learned of projected attack on
        Sweden by Poland and Denmark. Joined alliance.
1700–21. War with Sweden:
1700.   Battle of Narva. Peter defeated by Charles XII.
          Conquest of Ingria. St. Petersburg founded.
1709.   Battle of Pultava. Peter defeated Charles.
1711.   Loss of Azov.
1721.   Treaty of Nystad:
            Peter gained Ingria, Carelia, Livonia, Esthonia, and part
              of Finland.

  Internal:
    Aim:
      The westernising of Russia.
    Reforms:
      Industries.
      Education.
      Administrative system.
      Calendar reform.
      Abolition of patriarchate. Holy Synod.
  Character of Peter:
      Violent. Opposed slothfulness and indolence of people.
        Achieved little, but established the "westernising" ideal.
      Cruel. Death of son Alexius.
      Great alike in virtues and vices.
      Idealist and barbarian.

1725–7. CATHERINE I.

1727–30. PETER II.

1730–40. ANNE:
  Administration carried on by Biren, with German officials.

1740–1. IVAN VI.

1741–62. ELIZABETH:
  Daughter of Peter and Catherine I.
  Disliked German methods. Appointed Russian officials.
  Hostility to Frederick the Great. Russian participation in Seven
    Years' War.

1762. PETER III.

1762–96. CATHERINE II:

> *Internal:*
>> Carried on the work of westernising Russia.
>> Western culture. Patronised the philosophers.
>> Founded Russian Academy.
>> Administrative and judicial reforms.

> *Foreign:*
>> *Aims:*
>>> (1) Extension of Russian power to Black Sea.
>>> (2) Crimea.
>>> (3) Poland.
>>> (4) Revived Byzantine Empire.

>> *Achievements:*
>>> (1) Annexation of Courland.
>>> (2) Shares of Poland. (Three Partitions.)
>>> (3) Right of intervention in Turkish Empire. (Treaty of Kutchuk Kainardji.)
>>> (4) Annexation of Crimea.

1796–1801. PAUL:

> Capricious and incapable.
> Reversed some of Catherine's measures. Disorganisation of administrative system.
> Joined Second Coalition against France. Soon made peace.
> The reign had no lasting effect upon Russia.

Early RUSSIAN EMPIRE:

19th c. Great extent. Peoples of many races, religions, and languages.
> People mainly Slav and Orthodox, but included also Finns (Lutheran) and Poles (Roman Catholic).
> Medieval and Asiatic rather than modern and European.

> CLASSES OF PEOPLE:

>> *Serfs:*
>>> Worked on lords' estates. Held their lands from lords. No rights. Ill-treatment. Burden of taxation. Ignorant and superstitious. Serfs on Imperial domain were better off than others. Agriculture was backward.

>> *Nobles:*
>>> Privileged. Exempt from most of taxation. Commissions in army. Wealthy, through labour of serfs.

1801–25. ALEXANDER I:

> Religious. Inclined to reform. Constitution granted to Poland, which for a time was as free as Great Britain.
> Tsar tried to check corruption and to improve condition of serfs. Accomplished little.
> Tsar afterwards veered round to views of Metternich and ruled as an absolute monarch.

1825–55. NICHOLAS I:

> Decembrist revolt crushed.
> Policy of repression:
>> (a) Censorship of press.   Forbidden books might be neither printed nor imported.
>> (b) Secret police (the Third Section) to seek out disaffection.
>> (c) Foreign travel forbidden except under strict conditions.
>> (d) Education discouraged.
>> (e) Abolition of Polish constitution (following Polish revolt).
>
> Two wars with Turkey on account of Turkish oppression of Balkan peoples, who were Orthodox in religion and looked to Tsar for protection.
> Loss of Russian prestige in Crimean War.   Unsuspected weakness of Russian army.

LATER HISTORY OF RUSSIA:

1855–81. *Alexander II:*
> Freed serfs.
> Suppressed Polish rising.

1877–8. Russo-Turkish War.

1881–94. *Alexander III:*
> Economic progress.
> Political repression.

1894–1917. *Nicholas II:*
> Dual Alliance.
> Constitutional experiments.
> Russian disasters in European war.

1917. Bolshevik revolution.   End of the Tsardom.

29. THE TURKS

THE KIUPRILI REVIVAL:

1644–69. *War with Venice:*
> Mocenigo sailed through Dardanelles.   Threatened Constantinople.

1656–61. *Mohammed Kiuprili, Grand Vizier:*
> Revived administration.
> Restored discipline in army.
> Drove off Mocenigo.
> Recovered lost islands in Aegean.

1661–76. *Ahmed Kiuprili, Grand Vizier:*
> *War with Emperor:*

1664.
>> Turks defeated at St. Gothard.
>> Treaty of Vasvar.   Turks to evacuate Transylvania but to receive tribute.

> *War with Venice:*

1669.
>> Ended with Turkish conquest of Crete.

1672-6.   *War with Poland:*
           Podolia conquered by Turks.   Tribute promised.
           John Sobieski became King of Poland.   Disavowed treaty.
              Renewed war.
1676.   Peace on similar terms, but no tribute.
1676-89. *Kara Mustafa, Grand Vizier:*
           Less capable.
           War with Emperor:
1683.   Siege of Vienna.   Relieved by John Sobieski.
           Alliance:
              Pope
              Emperor
              Venice   } *v.* Turks.
              Poland
           Venice (Morosini) successful in Morea.
           Russian advance in Crimea.
1688.   Austrians overran Hungary and captured Belgrade.
1689-91. *Mustafa Kiuprili, Grand Vizier:*
           Revival of discipline and vigour.
           War (continued):
1690.   Recovery of Belgrade by Turks.
1691.   Battle of Szalankemen.   Turks defeated.   Grand Vizier
              killed.
1697.   Battle of Zenta.   Eugene defeated Sultan.
1697-9. *Hussein Kiuprili, Grand Vizier:*
           Peace of Carlowitz (Austria, Venice, Poland, Turks):
              (1) Emperor recovered Hungary (except Temesvar) and
                 most of Croatia and Slavonia.
              (2) Emperor overlord of Transylvania.
              (3) Poland recovered Podolia and Ukraine.
              (4) Poland restored conquests in Moldavia.
              (5) Venice retained conquests in Morea and Dalmatia.
1700.   *Peace of Constantinople* (Russia and Turks):
              Russia retained Azov.

1710-11. WAR WITH RUSSIA:
           Peter in difficulties on the Pruť
1711.   *Treaty of the Pruth:*
           Peter yielded Azov, and renounced claim on Crimea or Poland.

1715-18. WAR WITH VENICE.

1716-18. WAR WITH AUSTRIA:
           Turks overran Morea.
           Battle of Peterwardein.   Austrians defeated Turks.   Conquered
              Temesvar and captured Belgrade.
1718.   *Treaty of Passarowitz:*
              (1) Austria retained Temesvar and Belgrade.
              (2) Turks retained Morea.

WAR WITH PERSIA:

1724. Treaty of Constantinople between Turks and Russia. To partition Persia.
Russia took little part in the war.
Turks fought till 1736.
Persian revival under Nadir Shah. Turks defeated.

1736. *Treaty of Erzerum:*
Turks renounced claims on Georgia and Azarbijan.

1736-9. WAR WITH RUSSIA AND AUSTRIA:

1726. Secret Austro-Russian treaty of mutual assistance against Turks.
1736. Russians captured Azov. Overran Crimea. Withdrew. Little Turkish resistance.
Turks appealed in vain to Austria for help.
1737. Renewal of Austro-Russian agreement of 1726.
Austrians attacked Serbia, Wallachia, and Bosnia. Driven back.
Russians invaded Crimea again. Again withdrew.
1738. Third Russian invasion of Crimea. Unsuccessful.
Austrians held in check.
1739. Russians attacked Moldavia. Battle of Chocsim. Russians defeated Turks.
Turks besieged Belgrade.

1739. *Treaty of Belgrade* (Austria and Turks):
(1) Turks recovered Belgrade.
(2) Austrians withdrew from Wallachia, but retained Temesvar.

1739. *Treaty of Constantinople* (Russia and Turks):
(1) Russia retained Azov, but agreed to devastate a stretch of territory in order to hinder future invasion of Crimea.
(2) Russians to withdraw from Crimea.
(3) Russia not to maintain warships in Black Sea.

1768-74. WAR WITH RUSSIA:

Russian victories in Crimea, Moldavia, and Wallachia.
Battle of Tchesmé. Russian naval victory.
Risings in Syria, Egypt, Morea.
No help for Turks from France.
Austria and Prussia alarmed. Possible assistance to Turks against Russia. Partition of Poland arranged as an alternative to a European war.

1772.

1774. *Treaty of Kutchuk Kainardji:*
(1) Russian conquests restored, except Azov.
(2) Crimea independent, under Tartar Khan
(3) Black Sea open to both nations.
(4) Russia secured an indefinite right of intervention on behalf of Christian subjects of Sultan.

CATHERINE II:
Her aims:
(1) Expulsion of Turks from Europe.
(2) Liberation of Christian races.

(3) Access to Mediterranean.
(4) Revived Greek Empire at Constantinople.
(5) (Immediate.) Acquisition of Crimea.

Crimea :

1781.	Alliance of Catherine and Joseph II. Difficulty of joint action.
1784.	Crimea annexed by Russia.
1787.	Crimea visited by Catherine and Joseph II.

1787-92. WAR WITH RUSSIA AND AUSTRIA:

1787.	Emperor attacked Belgrade. Failed.
	Turks invaded Hungary (Temesvar).
1788.	Russians defeated Turkish fleet.
	Russians captured Ochakov.
1789.	Turks defeated by Austrians. Driven from Temesvar.
	Russians overran Moldavia and Bessarabia.
	Austrians captured Belgrade and Bucharest. Invaded Wallachia.
	Austrian attention distracted by revolt in Netherlands and by Prussian intrigues.
1790.	Leopold ready to make peace.
1791.	*Treaty of Sistova* (Austria and Turks):
	Austrian conquests, including Belgrade, restored.
1792.	*Treaty of Jassy* (Russia and Turks):
	(1) Russia retained Crimea and Ochakov.
	(2) In other respects the Treaty of Kutchuk Kainardji restored.

1789-1807. SELIM III, SULTAN:

	Military and naval reforms.
1798– 1802.	War of Second Coalition. Turks involved through Bonaparte's invasion of Egypt. Peace with France by Treaty of Constantinople.
	Friction with Russia over the government of Moldavia and Wallachia. Developed into war.
1807.	Sultan deposed.

1806-12. WAR WITH RUSSIA:

1812.	*Treaty of Bucharest :*
	Russia retained Bessarabia.

1815. CONGRESS OF VIENNA:

Did not attempt a settlement of the Eastern Question.

19th c. THE EASTERN QUESTION:

Turkish Empire in decline.
Balkan Peninsula contained several Christian races.   Occasional barbaric outbursts by Turks against Christian peoples in the Empire.   Russian right of protection.   European sympathy with oppressed.   Fear of Russian aggression in the Balkans. Jealousies of the powers.

The problem :

To obtain relief for the Christian peoples of the Turkish Empire without sanctioning increase of Russian power.

SERBS:

1804.   Rising under Karageorge. Supported by Russia till 1812.
         Turks recovered Serbia.
         Rising renewed under Milosh Obrenovitch.
1820.   Milosh recognised as "Prince of the Serbians."
1830.   Serbia practically independent under princes of the Obrenovitch
         line.

GREEKS:

         Oppressed by Turks. Heavy taxation. Brutal treatment.
         Religion tolerated. Revival of Greek national spirit. Greek
         literature and language.
1814.   *Hetairia Philike:*
         Society of Greeks at Odessa. To secure Greek independence
         and, ultimately, to expel Turks from Europe.
1821-9. *War in the Morea:*
         Greeks led by Ypsilanti. Great cruelty on both sides. Greeks
1821.   massacred Turkish peasants. Turks hanged Greek Patri-
         arch at Constantinople. European sympathy with Greeks.
         Assisted them with money and volunteers.
         Difficulties of the powers:
           (1) Holy Alliance could not, on Christian principles, inter-
               vene to put down the revolt.
           (2) Great Britain and Austria reluctant to weaken Turkey
               lest Russia be strengthened.
           (3) Greek success would encourage other discontented
               peoples in Europe.
1825.   Egyptian help for Turkey. Ibrahim Pasha in the Morea.
1825.   Nicholas I, Tsar, determined to intervene. Canning proposed
         united action.
1826.   Sultan refused mediation of Great Britain and Russia.
1827.   Great Britain, France, and Russia agreed to compel Sultan to
         accept mediation. British and French fleets in Turkish waters.
         Battle of Navarino. Turkish and Egyptian fleets destroyed.
         Decisive of Greek independence.
1829.   Wellington withdrew from participation in the settlement.
         Russians invaded Turkey. Treaty of Adrianople. Offered
         Greek freedom under Turkish overlordship. Greeks refused.
1832.   Greece fully independent. Otto of Bavaria King. Moldavia
         and Wallachia partly freed from Turkish control.
         The first step towards the dissolution of the Turkish Empire in
         Europe. Diplomatic victory for Russia.

SYRIAN QUESTION:

         Mehemet Ali:
         Viceroy of Egypt. Overran Syria. Sultan sought Russian
         assistance.
1833.   *Treaty of Unkiar Skelessi:*
         The Dardanelles to be closed to the warships of all nations
         except Russia. Great Britain, France, and Austria pro-
         tested.

1839.   *Mehemet Ali:*
Invaded Syria again. French supported Mehemet Ali. Russia
supported Turkey. Palmerston intervened to prevent an
accession of strength to either France or Russia.

1840.   *Quadruple Alliance:*
Great Britain, Russia, Prussia, and Austria. To settle the
question by offering terms to Mehemet Ali and compelling
him to accept them.

1841.   *Treaty of London:*
(1) Mehemet Ali to renounce his claim on Syria.
(2) Mehemet Ali placed under joint guarantee of the powers
of the Alliance with regard to his position as hereditary Pasha
of Egypt.

1841.   *Convention of the Straits:*
The Dardanelles to be closed to the warships of all nations.
Russia thus renounced the Treaty of Unkiar Skelessi.

Palmerston's action:
Revived British prestige. Sultan less inclined to rely solely
on Russia.

REASONS FOR ULTIMATE TURKISH FAILURE:

(1) Turks overwhelmed, but did not destroy, Christian nations.
(2) Turks strong only while advancing. Decline began when
conquest ceased. National life reappeared.
(3) Administration left in hands of conquered peoples.
(4) Turks slothful, corrupt, and inefficient in time of peace.

30. THE YEAR OF REVOLUTIONS

FRANCE:

February Revolution:
Deposition of Louis Philippe. Overthrow of bourgeois
dominance. Establishment of Second Republic.

Provisional Government:
Republicans. Concerned only with abolition of monarchy and
establishment of republic.
Socialists. Led by Louis Blanc. Aimed at social changes in
the interests of working classes. Blanc advocated establishment of co-operative workshops, to be managed by workmen.
State to provide capital.
Friction between the two groups. Government opened
National Workshops. Work unsuitable. Scheme unpopular. Differed from that of Louis Blanc, but Socialists
were blamed for its failure.

National Constituent Assembly:
Majority of moderate Republicans. Decided to close National
Workshops.
Revolt in Paris. Fighting. Much loss of life.

Constitution:

President to be elected for four years. Disqualified for immediate re-election.

Louis Napoleon elected President. Used his position for the purpose of re-establishing Empire.

Empire:

1852. Louis Napoleon proclaimed Emperor as Napoleon III.

AUSTRIA:

The Empire before 1848:

1835. *Ferdinand I:*

Succeeded Francis I. Little capacity. Government carried on by Metternich and other ministers. Lack of co-ordination among ministers. System of repression not fully maintained.

Unrest after 1840:

Many races in the Empire. Desire for independence, partial or total, of Austrian rule. Tendency for Empire to split up into a number of states owing only nominal allegiance to Emperor. Government able to play off one group against another.

Revolution:

Lombardy and Venetia:

Revolt. Aimed at expulsion of Austrians from Italy. Austrians retired from Milan to the Quadrilateral.

Hungary:

Backward. Medieval rather than modern.

Nobles privileged.

Peasants were serfs. Peasants paid taxation. Not represented in the Diet.

Diet of two Chambers. Great nobles, and representative of lesser nobles. Aimed at securing for Hungary equality with Austria.

1844. Secured recognition of Magyar language as official. Refused to recognise Serb and Croat languages.

Party of advanced reform. Led by Kossuth. Aimed at:

(1) Abolition of serfdom and noble privileges.

(2) Equality of rights and liabilities for all.

(3) Freedom of public meeting and of the press.

(4) Diet representative of whole nation, and to control taxation and legislation.

(5) Equality of Hungary with Austria.

Kossuth induced Hungarian Diet to demand constitution for Hungary. Emperor granted demand.

March Laws (passed by Hungarian Diet at Pressburg):

(1) Abolition of serfdom.

(2) Diet to be a representative Parliament, meeting at Budapest.

(3) Freedom of the press.

(4) Equality of Hungary with Austria.

(5) Responsible ministry.

Ferdinand I assented. Hungarian army, flag, ambassadors.

Vienna:

March   Revolt of workmen and students. Flight of Metternich.
             Collapse of his system.
             Ferdinand promised:
             (1) Constitution in Austria.
             (2) Abolition of press censorship.
             (3) National Guard.
             Diet summoned to frame constitution for Empire.

April.   Constitution proclaimed before meeting of Diet.

May.   Second revolt in Vienna. Flight of Emperor to Innsbruck.

Bohemia:

             Population Czech and German. National feeling among
             Czechs. Germans wanted Bohemian representation in
             German Parliament at Frankfort and inclusion of Bohemia
             in united Germany.

Reaction:

             Emperor at Innsbruck. Rallying point for reactionaries and
             all supporters of the court. Divisions among rebels en-
             couraged.

Bohemia:

             Fighting at Prague between Czechs and Germans.
             Windischgrätz bombarded Prague and restored order.
             Bohemian movement collapsed.

Italy:

             Radetzky held the Quadrilateral. Defeated Piedmontese at
             Custozza and recovered Milan.

Hungary:

             Short-sighted Magyar policy in refusing concessions to minor
             races. No support from Croats, Serbs, or Roumanians in
             the Austro-Hungarian struggle.
             Jellachich, Croat leader, supported Austria against Hungary.
             Vigorous Hungarian resistance to Austrian attempt at
             suppression. Austrians driven out of Hungary.
             Hungarian republic proclaimed. Alarm of Tsar, who
             offered assistance to Austria. Hungarians crushed.

GERMANY:

Aims of German Liberals:

             (1) Constitutional liberty.
             (2) German unity.

Constitutional movement:

             Constitutions granted in many states.

Prussia:

             Disturbances in Berlin. Frederick William IV abolished cen-
             sorship of the press. Called together the Prussian United
             Diet. Diet followed by a Constituent Assembly.
             Continued disturbances. Further concessions. Troops with-
             drawn from Berlin. National Guard formed. King asso-
             ciated himself with Liberals. Promised to support move-
             ment for German unity.

Movement for German unity :

National Assembly at Frankfort, to draw up a constitution. Princes powerless. Diet sanctioned Assembly.

Assembly wasted time in debating abstract principles, instead of acting while Austria and Prussia were in difficulties.

Difficulties:

(1) Boundaries } of a united Germany.
(2) Headship }

Austrian dominions were partly within and partly outside the German Confederation.

(1) If the whole Austrian Empire were included, the new state would not be wholly German.
(2) If only the distinctively German provinces were included, the Austrian Empire would be split up. Austria would not agree.

Assembly excluded Austria, and offered headship of united Germany to Frederick William IV of Prussia. Refused, because:

(1) Position was one of limited power.
(2) Respect for House of Hapsburg.
(3) Fear of war with Austria.
(4) The offer came from representatives of the people.

Constitution drawn up at Frankfort accepted by twenty-eight states, but rejected by the large states.

Frankfort Parliament dispersed.

1849.   Prussian movement for German Union. Supported at first by Saxony and Hanover. Austrian opposition. Saxony and Hanover withdrew. Prussia submitted.

German Confederation restored.

CAUSES OF FAILURE OF MOVEMENT:

(1) Revolutionaries wasted time in discussion while reactionaries prepared to act.
(2) No unity of aim among revolutionaries.
(3) Dissensions among revolutionaries.
(4) Military forces available for support of autocracy.

RESULTS OF MOVEMENT:

(1) Serfdom abolished in Austrian dominions, and, soon after in Russia.
(2) Liberal ideals remained. Lessons from the failure of the movements of 1848 were not forgotten.

GENEALOGICAL TABLES

THE HAPSBURGS

(Austria)

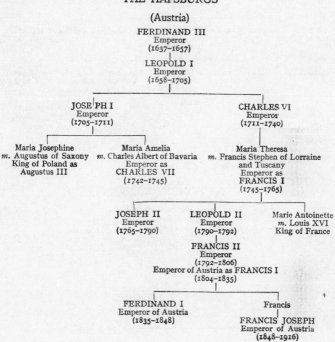

FERDINAND III
Emperor
(1637–1657)

LEOPOLD I
Emperor
(1658–1705)

JOSEPH I
Emperor
(1705–1711)

CHARLES VI
Emperor
(1711–1740)

Maria Josephine
m. Augustus of Saxony
King of Poland as
Augustus III

Maria Amelia
m. Charles Albert of Bavaria
Emperor as
CHARLES VII
(1742–1745)

Maria Theresa
m. Francis Stephen of Lorraine
and Tuscany
Emperor as
FRANCIS I
(1745–1765)

JOSEPH II
Emperor
(1765–1790)

LEOPOLD II
Emperor
(1790–1792)

Marie Antoinette
m. Louis XVI
King of France

FRANCIS II
Emperor
(1792–1806)
Emperor of Austria as FRANCIS I
(1804–1835)

FERDINAND I
Emperor of Austria
(1835–1848)

Francis

FRANCIS JOSEPH
Emperor of Austria
(1848–1916)

THE HAPSBURGS

(Spain)

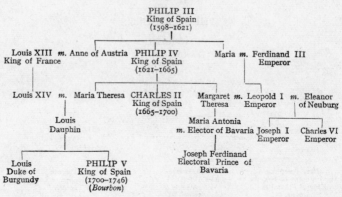

THE HOHENZOLLERNS

FREDERICK WILLIAM
Elector of Brandenburg
(1640–1688)

FREDERICK III
Elector of Brandenburg
(1688–1713)
FREDERICK I
King of Prussia
(1701–1713)

FREDERICK WILLIAM I
King of Prussia
(1713–1740)

FREDERICK II
King of Prussia
(1740–1786)

Augustus

FREDERICK WILLIAM II
King of Prussia
(1786–1797)

FREDERICK WILLIAM III
King of Prussia
(1797–1840)

FREDERICK WILLIAM IV
King of Prussia
(1840–1861)

THE BOURBONS
In France, Spain, and Naples

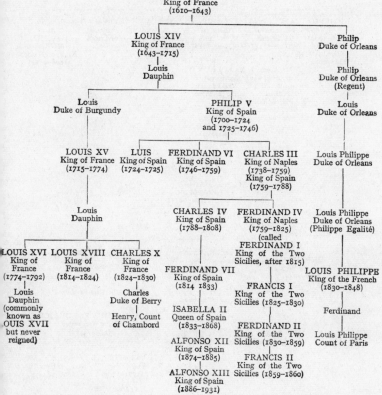

LOUIS XIII
King of France
(1610–1643)

LOUIS XIV
King of France
(1643–1715)

Philip
Duke of Orleans

Louis
Dauphin

Philip
Duke of Orleans
(Regent)

Louis
Duke of Burgundy

PHILIP V
King of Spain
(1700–1724
and 1725–1746)

Louis
Duke of Orleans

LOUIS XV
King of France
(1715–1774)

LUIS
King of Spain
(1724–1725)

FERDINAND VI
King of Spain
(1746–1759)

CHARLES III
King of Naples
(1738–1759)
King of Spain
(1759–1788)

Louis Philippe
Duke of Orleans

Louis
Dauphin

CHARLES IV
King of Spain
(1788–1808)

FERDINAND IV
King of Naples
(1759–1825)
(called
FERDINAND I
King of the Two
Sicilies, after 1815)

Louis Philippe
Duke of Orleans
(Philippe Egalité)

LOUIS XVI
King of
France
(1774–1792)

LOUIS XVIII
King of
France
(1814–1824)

CHARLES X
King of
France
(1824–1830)

FERDINAND VII
King of Spain
(1814 1833)

LOUIS PHILIPPE
King of the French
(1830–1848)

Louis
Dauphin
(commonly
known as
LOUIS XVII
but never
reigned)

Charles
Duke of Berry

Henry, Count
of Chambord

FRANCIS I
King of the Two
Sicilies (1825–1830)

Ferdinand

ISABELLA II
Queen of Spain
(1833–1868)

FERDINAND II
King of the Two
Sicilies (1830–1859)

Louis Philippe
Count of Paris

ALFONSO XII
King of Spain
(1874–1885)

FRANCIS II
King of the Two
Sicilies (1859–1860)

ALFONSO XIII
King of Spain
(1886–1931)

THE BONAPARTES

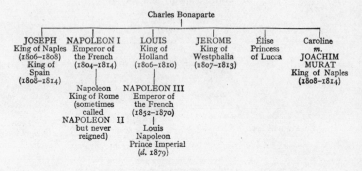

Charles Bonaparte

JOSEPH
King of Naples
(1806–1808)
King of
Spain
(1808–1814)

NAPOLEON I
Emperor of
the French
(1804–1814)

Napoleon
King of Rome
(sometimes
called
NAPOLEON II
but never
reigned)

LOUIS
King of
Holland
(1806–1810)

NAPOLEON III
Emperor of
the French
(1852–1870)

Louis
Napoleon
Prince Imperial
(d. 1879)

JEROME
King of
Westphalia
(1807–1813)

Élise
Princess
of Lucca

Caroline
m.
JOACHIM
MURAT
King of Naples
(1808–1814)

THE VASAS

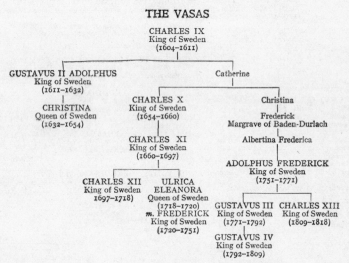

CHARLES IX
King of Sweden
(1604–1611)

GUSTAVUS II ADOLPHUS
King of Sweden
(1611–1632)

CHRISTINA
Queen of Sweden
(1632–1654)

Catherine

CHARLES X
King of Sweden
(1654–1660)

CHARLES XI
King of Sweden
(1660–1697)

CHARLES XII
King of Sweden
1697–1718)

ULRICA
ELEANORA
Queen of Sweden
(1718–1720)
m. FREDERICK
King of Sweden
(1720–1751)

Christina

Frederick
Margrave of Baden-Durlach

Albertina Frederica

ADOLPHUS FREDERICK
King of Sweden
(1751–1771)

GUSTAVUS III
King of Sweden
(1771–1792)

GUSTAVUS IV
King of Sweden
(1792–1809)

CHARLES XIII
King of Sweden
(1809–1818)

THE ROMANOFFS

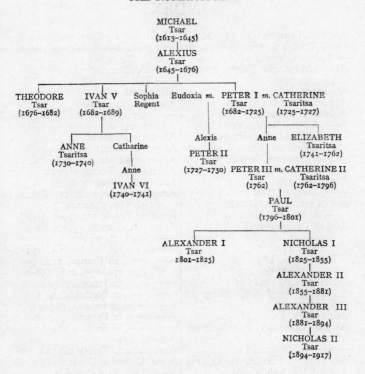

MICHAEL
Tsar
(1613–1645)

ALEXIUS
Tsar
(1645–1676)

THEODORE
Tsar
(1676–1682)

IVAN V
Tsar
(1682–1689)

Sophia
Regent

Eudoxia *m.* PETER I *m.* CATHERINE
Tsar   Tsaritsa
(1682–1725)   (1725–1727)

ANNE
Tsaritsa
(1730–1740)

Catharine

Anne

IVAN VI
(1740–1741)

Alexis

PETER II
Tsar
(1727–1730)

Anne

PETER III *m.* CATHERINE II
Tsar   Tsaritsa
(1762)   (1762–1796)

ELIZABETH
Tsaritsa
(1741–1762)

PAUL
Tsar
(1796–1801)

ALEXANDER I
Tsar
1801–1825)

NICHOLAS I
Tsar
(1825–1855)

ALEXANDER II
Tsar
(1855–1881)

ALEXANDER III
Tsar
(1881–1894)

NICHOLAS II
Tsar
(1894–1917)

INDEX

418

Popes (*continued*)
  Pius VI, 124
  —— VII, 133, 194–5, 197, 240
  —— IX, 275–7
Port Mahon, 51
  —— Royal, 21–2
Porto Bello, 55, 89
  —— Carrero, Cardinal, 43–4
Portugal, 46, 51, 116, 121, 129–30, 200, 208–11, 241, 248–9
Posen, 140, 232
Potockis, 137
Potsdam, Edict of, 70
Pragmatic Sanction, 88–90, 93, 96, 98, 105–6, 293
Prague, 100, 103, 311
  ——, Battle of, 110
  ——, Siege of, 110
Pressburg, Treaty of, 204
Pretender, James Stuart, 45, 53, 55–6, 64, 80–1, 105
Privateers, 208
Progressive party, in France, 262
Protocol of Troppau, 247
Proudhon, French Socialist, 264
Pruth, Battle of the, 291
  ——, Treaty of the, 280, 291
Pultava, Battle of, 135, 144, 280, 291
Pyramids, Battle of the, 188
Pyrenees, Treaty of the, xxi, 6–7, 29, 39

Quadrilateral, 275–6
Quadruple Alliance, 1718; 82, 86, 88
  ——, 1815; 243–5
  ——, 1840; 263, 303
Quatre Bras, Battle of, 220
Quebec, capture of, 113
Quesnay, 157
Quesnel, 21
Quiberon Bay, Battle of, 113
Quietism, 15

Racine, 14
Radetzky, Austrian field-marshal, 275–6, 308, 312
Radom, Confederation of, 137

Ramillies, Battle of, 48, 52
Rastadt, Congress of, 186, 189, 199
  ——, Treaty of, 54
Ravensburg, xix, 66–7
Reason, worship of, 176
Rebellions:
  American, 1776–83; 161–2, 165, 170, 224
  Cossack, 1648–51; 134
  Decembrist, 1825; 287
  Greek, 1821–30; 287, 300–2
  Hungarian, 1848–9; 287
  Italy, 1830–1; 273–4
  Jacobite, 1715; 80
  ——, 1745; 103
  La Vendée, 1793; 183
  Naples, 1820; 246–7, 273
  Netherlands, 1572–1609; 125, 266
  ——, 1789–90; 125, 127, 297
  Papal States, 1831; 274
  Paris, 1848; 265, 306–7
  Piedmont, 1820; 247, 273
  Poland, 1830–1; 262, 268, 287
  ——, 1863–4; 288
  Serbia, 1804–30; 299
  Spain, 1820; 246–8
  Spanish colonies, 1809–23; 246, 248
  Vienna, 1848; 310–11
Reformation, the, xvii, 128, 132
Reform banquets in France, 264
Régale, the, 16–17
Regencies:
  Anne of Austria, 1–2, 76
  Marie de Medici, 76
  Orleans, Philip, Duke of, 76–82
  Oxenstjerna, 141
  Sophia Romanoff, 279
  Sudermania, Duke of, 148
Regensburg, Truce of, 30, 32, 37, 72
Reign of Terror, 152, 176–7
Republican calendar, 176
  —— party, in France, 258, 262, 265, 306–7
Republics:
  Batavian, 189–90, 199, 266